Monsters, Law, Crime

The Fairleigh Dickinson University Press Series in Law, Culture, and the Humanities

Series Editor:
Caroline Joan "Kay" S. Picart, M.Phil. (Cantab), Ph.D., J.D., Esquire; Attorney at Law; Adjunct Professor, FAMU College of Law; former English & HUM professor, FSU

The Fairleigh Dickinson University Press Series in Law, Culture, and the Humanities publishes scholarly works in which the field of Law intersects with, among others, Film, Criminology, Sociology, Communication, Critical/Cultural Studies, Literature, History, Philosophy, and the Humanities.

On the Web at http://www.fdu.edu/fdupress

Publications

Caroline Joan "Kay" S. Picart, *Monsters, Law, Crime: Explorations in Gothic Criminology* (2020)

Elaine Wood, *Gender Justice and the Law: Theoretical Practices of Intersectional Identity* (2020)

Orit Kamir, *Betraying Dignity: The Toxic Seduction of Social Media, Shaming, and Radicalization* (2019)

Marouf A. Hasian, Jr., *Lawfare and the Ovaherero and Nama Pursuit of Restorative Justice, 1918–2018* (2019)

George Pate, *Enter the Undead Author: Intellectual Property, the Ideology of Authorship, and Performance Practices since the 1960s* (2019)

Victor Li, *Nixon in New York: How Wall Street Helped Richard Nixon Win the White House* (2017)

Marouf A. Hasian, Jr., *Kafkaesque Laws, Nisour Square, and the Trials of the Former Blackwater Guards* (2017)

Michaela Stockey-Bridge, *The Lure of Hope: On the Transnational Surrogacy Trail from Australia to India* (2017)

Ted Laros, *Literature and the Law in South Africa, 1910–2010: The Long Walk to Artistic Freedom* (2017)

Peter Robson and Johnny Rodger, *The Spaces of Justice: The Architecture of the Scottish Court* (2017)

Doran Larson, *Witness in the Era of Mass Incarceration: Discovering the Ethical Prison* (2017)

Raymond J. McKoski, *Judges in Street Clothes: Acting Ethically Off-the-Bench* (2017)

H. Lowell Brown, *The American Constitutional Tradition: Colonial Charters, Covenants, and Revolutionary State Constitutions 1578–1786* (2017)

Arua Oko Omaka, *The Biafran Humanitarian Crisis, 1967–1970: International Human Rights and Joint Church Aid* (2016)

Marouf A. Hasian, Jr., *Representing Ebola: Culture, Law, and Public Discourse about the 2013–2015 West Africa Ebola Outbreak* (2016)

Jacqueline O'Connor, *Law and Sexuality in Tennessee Williams's America* (2016)

Caroline Joan "Kay" S. Picart, Michael Hviid Jacobsen, and Cecil E. Greek, *Framing Law and Crime: An Interdisciplinary Anthology* (2016)

Caroline Joan "Kay" S. Picart, *Law In and As Culture: Intellectual Property, Minority Rights, and the Rights of Indigenous Peoples* (2016)

Monsters, Law, Crime

Explorations in Gothic Criminology

Edited by Caroline Joan "Kay" S. Picart

FAIRLEIGH DICKINSON UNIVERSITY PRESS
Vancouver • Madison • Teaneck • Wroxton

Published by Fairleigh Dickinson University Press
Copublished by The Rowman & Littlefield Publishing Group, Inc.
4501 Forbes Boulevard, Suite 200, Lanham, Maryland 20706
www.rowman.com

6 Tinworth Street, London SE11 5AL, United Kingdom

Fairleigh Dickinson University Press gratefully acknowledges the support received for scholarly publishing from the Friends of FDU Press.

British Library Cataloguing in Publication Information Available

Library of Congress Cataloging-in-Publication Data Available

Library of Congress Control Number: 2020948713

ISBN 978-1-68393-079-2 (cloth)
ISBN 978-1-68393-080-0 (electronic)

For my husband and love of my life, Jerry Rivera, whose love and loyalty are powerfully enduring, and the Picart, Terrell, and Rivera families, whose devotion and support help ease many of life's storms and contingencies. Without all of you, my life would be less filled with lightness, balance, peace, and joy. I also wish to acknowledge a debt to my mother, Anarose Santos Picart, and my father, Robert Miranda Picart, whose exemplary commitment to a life of scholarship, teaching, and service inspired me to forge my own path. I am always grateful to my Tallahassean parents, Jim and Carolyn Terrell, whose groundedness and humor have always helped me adapt during difficult times.

Contents

Acknowledgments

I dedicate this book to both my loving husband, Jerry Rivera, and the Picart, Terrell, and Rivera families. A part of my chapter, "Monstrous Discourses, Jihadi Cool, and Emergent Counter-Terrorist Narratives: The Case of Ahmad Khan Rahami (a.k.a. Ahmad Rahimi) and the 2016 New York/New Jersey Bombings," was adapted and updated from a peer-reviewed scholarly article previously published as: Caroline Joan S. Picart, "'Jihad Cool/Jihad Chic': The Roles of the Internet and Imagined Relations in the Self-Radicalization of Colleen LaRose (Jihad Jane)," *Societies*, 5 (April 2015): 354–383, to which I retained copyright. I thank Jon Frauley, the editor of that special issue of *Societies*, and the staff of *Societies*, for their kind and thorough assistance with publishing the article. I am also thankful to Adam Rummens, Hannah Kent, and the administrative staff of Cambridge Scholars Publishing for permission to print an adaptation of the description of "Jihadi Cool" from a prior published book, Caroline Joan "Kay" S. Picart, *American Self-Radicalizing Terrorists and the Allure of "Jihadi Cool/Chic"* (Newcastle Upon Tyne: Cambridge Scholars Publishing 2017). I am also grateful for the enduring support and encouragement of Berta Hernandez-Truyol, Danaya Wright, John Stinneford, and Randy Abate, among many others. Additionally, I wish to thank all the contributors to this edited collection, whose cooperative spirit, integrity, and scholarly genius have greatly enriched this edited collection, which has taken over three years to bring together, and has weathered the obstacles presented by the Covid-19 pandemic. I also wish to thank an anonymous reader for the reader's meticulous, astute, and insightful comments on an earlier draft. Finally, I owe a huge debt of gratitude to Margaret Petty for her conscientious, cheerful, and thorough assistance with preparing this edited collection in its final form; to Margaret Petty, Amany Garcia, Jerry Rivera, and all contributors for the saving grace of their help with preparing the index, and to Harry Keyishian, James Gifford, and

Zach Nycum, whose collegiality and kindness are without peer, and the editorial staff of Rowman & Littlefield, especially Ashleigh Cooke and Kris Patenaude, for their professionalism and attentiveness to detail.

Explorations in Gothic Criminology

Ruminating on Monsters, Law and Crime

Caroline Joan "Kay" S. Picart[1]

Gothic Criminology refers to a theoretical framework initially developed by Caroline Joan "Kay" S. Picart, a Philosophy and Film professor turned Attorney and Law professor, and Cecil Greek, a Sociologist (Picart and Greek 2008). Noting the proliferation of Gothic modes of narration and visualization in American popular culture, academia and even public policy, Picart and Greek proposed a framework, which they described as a "Gothic Criminology," to attempt to analyze the fertile synapses connecting the "real" and the "reel" in the flow of Gothic metaphors and narratives that abound around criminological phenomena that populate not only popular culture but also academic and public policy discourses. Although there are intersections in the way Picart and Greek deploy the tools of Gothic Criminology, which was adapted from Stanford M. Lyman's "Gothic sociology" (Lyman 1990), there are also differences. Picart has used Gothic Criminology generally in a more limited way; that is, Picart tracks the "social construction of crime and the nature of criminality, focusing specifically on the proliferation of Gothic tropes and mise-en-scene in the media's accounts, often fluctuating between fact and fiction and teratological rhetorics (i.e., 'monster talk')." Picart's past work focused principally on tracking evolving representations of a particular type of "monster"—serial killers—along the registers of race, class, gender and sexuality, although her most recent work, as illustrated in the last chapter of this edited collection, extends this analysis to American self-radicalizing terrorists.[2] In comparison, Greek's use of a Gothic Criminology is more expansive, and seems more focused on overtly theological or religious themes that intersect with Criminology and Sociology, such as "blood lust, compulsion, fear, godlike vengeance, power and domination" (Picart and Greek 2008, 17).[3] Notwithstanding these differences (which stem from disciplinary orientations and boundaries), a Gothic Criminological framework potentially offers a fertile ground from which various studies on monsters, law and crime may emerge, as this edited collection illustrates.

Any attempt to grapple with the "monstrous" will find one locked in combat with a many-limbed, multi-headed beast, resembling a hydra, capable of eternal adaptation and regeneration. As Jeffrey Andrew Weinstock noted: "Like the monsters it theorizes, monster theory transgresses categorical boundaries, spreading out into different disciplines. . . . Because all cultures have their own monsters, monster theory is by necessity an international endeavor" (2020, 1). This edited collection, composed of chapters written by US and international experts in Law, Criminology, Sociology, Anthropology, Communication and Film, constitutes a rigorous attempt to explore fertile interdisciplinary inquiries into "monsters" and "monster-talk," in relation to law and crime. "Monsters" may refer to allegorical or symbolic fantastic beings (as in literature, film, legends, myths etc.), or actual or real-life monsters, as well as the interplay/ambiguity between the two general types of "monsters." The sense in which this collection of chapters wrestles with the issue of the "monstrous" is classical in that, both etymologically and functionally, the term "monster" may be traced to "monere" ("to warn [against]") and "monstrare" ("to point to" or "to show") (Kyff 2016); (Picart and Greek 2007a, 12).[4] Indeed, the ancient Greeks believed that only a god or a monster could survive beyond the civilized walls of the city state—an insight that converges with the first chapter in this edited collection by Australian anthropologist John Morton. "Monster-talk," generally construed, serves to delimit the spheres of the "monstrous," "uncivilized" or "criminal" from the realms of the "normal," "wild" or the "good citizen" (Ingebretsen 2003), though it may also serve a variety of other functions, for different communities (Cohen 1997). An additional area of discussion, using an example from film, is the interplay between the realms of the "real" and the "reel," though such a discussion can be extended to other media or fields of study. For example, for an anthropologist, the "monsters" of the communities they study are "real" (Musharbash and Presterudstuen 2014, 2)—but often, in a very complex sense, and there is a murkiness about the relationship between real human "monsters" (e.g., humans who kill out of a "compunction") and monsters of legend. For a legal scholar, sociologist or criminologist, the plethora of media-mediated representations of various "real life" or fantastic monsters, in different genres, could be instructive about how representations of crime and the law, and the "monstrous" operate (Picart 2014b). For a scholar of literature and/or film, the modes of narration regarding "real" or other-than-real monsters often resist a simple binary (Jancovich 2012). This edited collection thus explores and updates contemporary discussions of the emergent and evolving fronts of monster theory in relation to cutting-edge research on law and crime, and may be seen as extensions of a

Gothic Criminology, generally construed. What distinguishes this collection, as edited by Picart, is a more sustained focus on law and the social sciences in relation to crime and the monstrous.

Edited collections, by their nature, are hybrid creatures insofar as they derive their genesis from different authors, and are conceived within variant contexts, often initially in isolation from each other; one could even pun, as many authors have done, on the "Frankensteinian" nature of the endeavor, as creating an edited collection involves, analogically, the stitching together of disparate body parts, aspirationally to give life to an integrated corpus, which one hopes to bid, as Mary Wollstonecraft Shelley did, to go forth and prosper.[5] Punning aside, one feature of a coherently edited collection of chapters is the effectiveness of its introduction in setting forth a general map of the trajectory of the chapters, and in its persuasive force in showing how and why this particular volume is significant for its intended audiences. Another hallmark is whether fertile thematic intersections spontaneously emerge from these chapters. This introduction thus aims to serve these two objectives.

The first section of the collection focusing on the theme "Of Myths and Monsters," is comprised of three chapters. The first, entitled "'Deeds of Treachery and Violence and Lust and Cruelty': Revisiting Freud's Primal Crimes in Aboriginal Central Australia," is written from the perspective of an experienced Australian anthropologist. In this chapter, John Morton continues an ongoing research trajectory of inquiring more deeply into the relationship/s between monsters and gods. The chapter builds from themes initially explored in a previously published essay (2014) that partly illustrates the relationship between monsters and gods in the context of a totemic religion in central Australia: that of the Aboriginal people variously known in ethnographic literature as "Arunta," "Aranda" or "Arrernte." The chapter takes as its starting point Freud's claim in *Totem and Taboo* that, in totemic religion, we can detect how the origins of human society lie in reactions to originary criminal acts of parricide and cannibalism; such reactions allegedly led to archaic forms of society, morality and religion. In this chapter, Morton subjects Freud's propositions about the so-called "primal horde" to an ethnographic test. He demonstrates that, in certain respects, Freud's account of human origins is loudly echoed in central Australia ethnography, where myths explain society as the outcome of ancestral strife and rituals that stage acts of intergenerational aggression and symbolic cannibalism. However, the ethnography as a whole, when psychoanalytically framed in terms of the life-cycle, also serves to reveal biases and misconstruals in Freud's account of human origins; Morton contends that Freud's psychoanalytic framework overestimates the importance of the paternal order and misconstrues the meaning of primal violence and incestuous desire, as well as the nature and character of totems. Morton proposes that the totem is not "the father"; rather, it is "the self as other"—the self as either monster or god, depending on the morality and ethics appropriate to one's situation in the cycle of life and death. Morton's chapter argues that while monsters and totemic ancestors share characteristic tendencies towards animality, intemperance and excess, such a commonality makes them less-than-human as monsters, but more-than-human as gods. Hence, this chapter speaks not only to the strange identity between monsters and gods, but also to a corresponding uncanny resemblance between criminal actions and the means by which those actions are policed.

Carrying on the theme of "Myths and Monsters," the second chapter is titled "Criminal Anthropology, Fabulism, and Criminology's Unacknowledged Teratological Lineage." Jon Frauley, a Canadian criminologist, unflinchingly argues that the monster is central to crime narratives. Furthermore, as his chapter illustrates, the concept of the monstrous was central to nineteenth century criminal anthropology, which according to the "standard view" of criminology's origins is the precursor of modern "scientific" criminology. The "standard view" traces "scientific" criminology to the originator of criminal anthropology, Italian physician Cesare Lombroso. Frauley argues that what is neglected by the standard view, however, is Lombroso's positioning within the subfields of medical jurisprudence and teratology and his belief that the "atavist" (i.e., the born criminal) was a medical monster. Thus the standard view neglects criminology's teratological lineage. Frauley's chapter demonstrates that Lombroso's criminal anthropology was concerned with the clinical monsters of medicine and that criminology emerged from the nineteenth century as a science of monster detection. Frauley argues that contemporary neuro-criminology, although in a more sophisticated way, continues to promote a version of Lombroso's "wrong way brain" theory of criminality. Ultimately, the chapter analyzes how bio-criminological discourses promote the study of human defects and the myth of the born criminal to substantiate the existence of monstrous others amenable to scientific detection.

The third chapter, "Vampire Fictions and the Conflation of Violent Criminality with Real Vampirism: A Practical Overview," is a collaboration between John Edgar Browning, a literature professor, and DJ Williams, a social and behavioral scientist. Browning and Williams's chapter overtly draws from Picart and Greek's Gothic Criminology framework and adds auto-ethnographic elements. Their chapter builds upon their recent scholarly work by examining the common conflation, by both media and various professionals, of fictional vampire narratives with real vampirism to characterize certain violent criminals and the subsequent effect this has had on the real vampire community. The chapter introduces some notable historical cases of extreme violence associated with vampirism to highlight what they interpret as a fusion of fact and fiction, and how this merging has long been crucial in shaping cultural interpretation. From there, Browning and Williams summarize the recent history and general characteristics of the real vampire community, based on largely auto-ethnographic scholarship, before focusing on two recent forensic cases that illustrate that common (but faulty) real/reel conflations by media and law enforcement professionals can negatively impact the administration of justice in profound ways. In the sense that Browning and Williams's principal focus is the demythologization of popular myths about the vampire community in relation to violent crime, their use of Gothic Criminology ultimately returns to a more standard criminological focus.

The second section in this edited collection focuses on synapses connecting the themes of "Contagion, Monstrosity, Ethics" and is comprised of three chapters. The first chapter, titled "A Double-Tap 'Lilith Moral Panic' in Israel, 2014: How Labeling Others as 'Monsters' Conceals Their Victimization," is written by Israeli law professor Orit Kamir. In this chapter, Kamir examines an evolving Israeli case which, she argues, demonstrates the dynamics of monstrous moral panics. Kamir recounts how in the summer of 2014, Israeli media was fixated on reports that in the southern town of Kiryat Gat, a forty-year-old woman was raping hundreds of boys, perhaps infecting them with HIV. The woman was portrayed as a child-endangering, deviant monster on the loose, with the story of such a monster attracting public fascination and outcry. Media preoccupation with the sensational monstrous child molestation disguised the reality that, in fact, dozens of adolescent youngsters were systematically taking advantage of a mentally and socially challenged woman. Kamir then points out that immediately following the fading of this titillating media event, Israel was once again seized with righteous indignation directed at another "monstrous other": the Israeli-Palestinian female MP, Hanin Zuabi. As the Israeli public was holding its breath, following the kidnapping of three teenage youngsters from Israeli settlements in the West Bank, Zuabi refused to refer to the anonymous kidnappers as "terrorists." Zuabi's instant portrayal, in Israeli media, as a child-endangering, deviant monster, silenced her claim that Israeli crimes against Palestinians drove the kidnappers to commit this hurtful deed. By juxtaposing these two instances of contagious "monster-talk," and drawing attention to the centrality of the Lilith myth—an archetypal female monster of Jewish folklore, which intersects with the themes of the first section, Kamir aims to make sense of the complex "monster and crime" dynamics these two instances illustrate.

The second chapter in this section, "Evil-By-Proxy and Everyday Monsters—Toward a Moral Sociology for Overcoming the Passive Observation of Evil," is written by Danish sociologist Michael Hviid Jacobsen. This chapter, continuing the theme of "Contagion, Monstrosity, Ethics," is concerned with delineating and discussing the rise and the consequences of "spectator society." The chapter first seeks to develop an understanding of the notions of "monsters by-proxy" and "contributory evil." From there, the chapter argues that passivity vis-à-vis harm-doing and suffering is socially contagious and that such passivity creates, at both the micro-level as well as at the macro-level, the conditions for the perpetuation of evil. The chapter then examines two cases to illustrate this point. At the micro-sociological level, the chapter reviews and discusses the notion of a "spectator mentality" based on the classic study of the murder of Kitty Genovese. At the macro-sociological level, the chapter examines how the media contributes to "compassion fatigue" and the passive observation of "distant suffering." Ultimately, the chapter argues that the "monster" is not only the perpetrator of evil, but that we (i.e., everyday citizens) are all potentially "monsters by-proxy" by passively witnessing and accepting acts of evil—an insight very much resonant with Hannah Arendt's observations on the banality of evil in relation to Eichmann's defense at the infamous trial, in relation to Holocaust atrocities, in Jerusalem (Arendt and Elon 2006). Jacobsen's chapter thus arrives at a "modern," rather than a "classic," sensibility of monstrosity (which it treats interchangeably with "evil") in that the monstrous resides in the ordinary and banal, rather than as a separate ontological category (Pinedo 2004; Picart 2014a).

The third chapter in this section is titled "Monstering Madness: Criminal Lunatics in Broadmoor 1863–1913," and is the result of collaborative criminological and sociological research by Lucy Williams, Sandra Walklate and Barry Godfrey of the University of Liverpool in England. Spontaneously intersecting with Kamir's focus on "monster-talk" and media transmogrification and panics, this chapter explores the ways in which inmates at Britain's first (and, until the twentieth century, only) criminal lunatic asylum, Broadmoor Hospital in Berkshire, were interpreted and represented in the popular press. Taking a small sample of inmates across the institutions first half-century, the chapter uses biographical and offending data taken from patient case files at Broadmoor, and contemporary newspapers sourced from online digital archives, in order to assess which facets of each patient's case and crime were highlighted by the press, and for what purpose. The chapter argues that Broadmoor patients, suffering from mental illness, were quickly subject to processes of monstering by Victorian newspapers, who seized upon the opportunity to portray them as subjects of both moral and mental degeneration. Ultimately, the chapter investigates the construction of Broadmoor "monsters" in the popular press, and illustrate their divergence from the real, and often tragic, lives of the Broadmoor patients.

The third section examines the theme of "Monsters in Reel/Real Life" viewed from the analytic lenses of Film and Media Studies; Criminology; and Law and Film. In the first chapter, "The Purge, or the Law of Universal Monstrous," which studies monsters in "reel life," US Film and Media Studies scholar Matthew Sorrento argues that the three films in *The Purge* series (2013–2015) depict humanity in the United States as universally monstrous (or potentially so). This chapter analyzes how the *Purge* series moves beyond the figure of the outsider human monster of the realistic killer tradition—this human monster typically invading an insular community positioned to defeat the threat. By reading the three films as a progression—part one as a siege film (a take on the home invasion film), part two as a hunt in the urban jungle (a revision of *The Warriors*, 1979, and *Predator 2*, 1990) and the third as an attempted political assassination (with echoes of *The Manchurian Candidate*, 1962)—Sorrento aims to illustrate how the series uses an extremist take on horror (ironically in its threat/terror instead of gore) to present capitalism-cum-fascism as the ultimate source of terror for the genre. The chapter details both the evolution of horror and the influence of the "new French extremity," which the film hybridizes with the horror tradition, to build Sorrento's analysis of this important development (and commentary) on the genre.

The third chapter in this section, "Contrasting Depictions of Medical Serial Killers: Doctors Pétiot and Shipman from the Manic to the Mundane," now turns to the complex interrelation between the real and the reel—a nexus initially explored by Picart and Greek in their explication of a Gothic Criminology (Picart and Greek 2007a; 2007b; 2003). In this chapter, Steve Greenfield, a law professor whose collaborative pioneering work on law and film is well known (Greenfield, Osborn and Robson 2010), begins with the observation that the portrayal of serial killers, on film, television and via streaming services, has expanded to encompass fiction, docudrama and documentary. He also notes that new dramatic works have been produced, and old cases retold, to fuel a seemingly insatiable audience desire and construct a blurring of more traditional genre boundaries. Greenfield attributes the observation of this changing dynamic to Picart and Greek's work, which applied a framework of Gothic Criminology to the "monstrous" and explored this altered relationship between fact and fiction. Citing from Picart's more recent work, Greenfield states: "That is not to say there is no such thing as 'fact,' or that 'fact' and 'fiction' are the same thing: rather, it is to point out that fact and fiction do not form a simple binary, especially in media depictions" (Picart, 2016, 319). Greenfield, drawing from the "compunction" theory of the serial killer,[6] states that due to the extent of the crimes committed almost automatically, for the viewer, the serial killer appears with a cloak of "monstrosity." Within this trope, Greenfield aims to identify characteristics of medical practitioners who are also serial killers. Greenfield adds that these stories and the portrayals (of serial killer doctors) are highly troubling as someone sworn into a profession to save lives moves to a polar opposite—a serial murderer. For Greenfield, it is this leap, from savior to slaughterer, which renders the behavior even more inexplicable and disturbing to the audience. Motive thus becomes an imperative to provide some semblance of reassurance that this deviancy can be explained, if not completely understood. This chapter thus focuses on the depiction of two such figures: Dr. Marcel Pétiot and Dr. Harold Shipman, who were both medical practitioners and contemporaneously notorious serial killers.

Greenfield's chapter considers two specific films: the French film *Docteur Pétiot* (1990) and the British television film *Harold Shipman: Doctor Death* (2002). The former is set during the Second World War in Paris and covers the killings, by Dr. Pétiot, of those seeking to escape the German occupation. The latter film dramatizes the case of the English general practitioner Dr. Harold Shipman, who murdered at least 215 of his patients in the north of England over a long period. For Greenfield, the two films offer contrasting perspectives on motive and behavior but contain similarities in terms of the method of killing and personality traits, even as both were, ironically, revered and respected medical professionals within their communities. Greenfield concludes that Pétiot seems to fit squarely into the characterization of a dramatic cold-blooded killer, motivated purely by greed. He argues that in contrast, Shipman, Britain's most prolific serial killer, is a very different breed because Shipman defies traditional classification, and his motivations are unknown and unsubstantiated and his killings mundane. For Greenfield, Shipman is neither an angel of mercy nor motivated by greed and so is set apart from the usual categorization of medical professionals who kill. Greenfield's chapter explores the extent to which a prolific but undramatic serial killer fits into the serial killer portrayal and the concept of the "monstrous." For Greenfield, the sheer "ordinariness" of killing, by a doctor, constructs a more frightening and disturbing vision that his correlate, Dr. Pétiot, whose motivation is clear and his killing visually dramatic. In so doing, Greenfield arrives at a similar conclusion as Hannah Arendt does in relation to the infamous Eichmann trial (Arendt 2006): that "evil"/the "monstrous" resides in the banal, mundane and commonplace—an insight that converges, to some extent, with Jacobsen's earlier chapter, although Jacobsen's ultimate emphasis is on the ethical in response to the monstrous.[7]

In the third (and last) book chapter in this third section, "The Redactasaurus Chronicles: Fear, Consumption and Graffiti Regulation in Capital City," Canadian independent scholar Deborah Landry drew from observations she had made in her ethnographic work on unsanctioned graffiti in the City of

Ottawa—an example of the "monstrous"/criminal in real life. The chapter uses Kenneth Burke's Dramaturgical approach to critique this quest for fantastic urban aesthetics of security in this capital city. Informed by Cultural Criminology[8] in terms of its methodology, the chapter offers an ironic reading of the remains of conspicuous consumption in order to problematize the absences created in the Wars on Graffiti. Ultimately, the chapter concludes that in a double-edged turn, "The Redactasaurus," created to rid the city of viral threat of graffiti imagined in municipal regulation of urban performance, has scarred the city in ways that are harmful to civic life.

The fourth (and final) section focuses on themes of Law, War, and Monstrous Discourses. The first chapter, "Human Trafficking, Empathy for Victims, the Tool of Eradication," written by Attorney DW Duke, examines in particular the ongoing war against human trafficking, which Duke views as a contemporary extension of slavery. This chapter begins by discussing the historical roots of European slavery in order to track some of the factors that allowed slavery to flourish, and what are some of the events that catalyzed a change in perception of victims of slavery, ultimately resulting in slavery's abolition. Duke hypothesizes that one or more threshold events that changed society's perception of slavery in Britain and the United States occurred in the eighteenth and nineteenth centuries. The chapter attempts to assess what conditions existed prior to this "threshold" event that prevented empathy so that the victims of slavery were viewed as proverbial "monsters behind the curtain" who deserved their fate—an insight that converges with Williams, Walklate and Godfrey's earlier chapter on the public perception of the inmates of the Broadmoor asylum. For Duke, one of most significant events that led to the development of empathy for victims of human trafficking was an occurrence in the personal life of Lord Justice Mansfield who wrote two important legal opinions that laid the foundation for the eventual abolition of slavery in Britain. Conversely, Duke gestures to various social institutions in different societies that normalize human trafficking, such as the family or the state, often in the name of economic stability, revealing these to be more monstrous in function, seen from a perspective of empathy for the victims of human trafficking. To close, drawing from an auto-ethnographic perspective, in a manner resembling the way Browning and DJ Williams do in their chapter, Duke's chapter examines the conditions of human trafficking today to analyze if there is a persistent "monster image" (and a moral panic, in a manner that echoes Kamir's earlier chapter) that prevents society from empathizing with victims of human trafficking. Much as Jacobsen's earlier chapter eventually arrives at an ethical imperative, Duke's chapter aims to replace this "monster image" of victims of human trafficking as unwanted people who remain in their place as a result of their own immoral behavior and choices with a more empathic portrait. Duke's chapter concludes with concrete and pragmatic suggestions on how to more effectively combat this persistently prejudicial "monster image" of human trafficking victims.

The second chapter in this section, continuing the theme of "Law, War, Monstrous Discourses," is titled "Visualizing Monsters and Just Wars in Legal, and Public Analyses of Eastwood's *American Sniper*." In this chapter, US Communication Professor, Marouf Hasian, Jr., extends the work of critical security studies scholars in order to analyze how various mediated conversations about Clint Eastwood's movie *American Sniper* are used in legal, military and public debates about the legality of long-distance killings of enemies during just wars. Hasian argues that by visualizing the acts of particular terrorist or counterterrorist "monsters," diverse US communities are provided with vernacular ways of understanding *jus in bello* (justifications for going to war in the first place) and *jus ad bellum* (the methods that we use during war) issues. The chapter further argues that, more specifically, these communities are invited to debate about the legitimacy of the Coalition rules of engagement that are associated with sniping during the global war on terrorism (GWOT). Hasian notes that heated polemic debates about the politicization of the personal life of a famed American hero have quickly morphed into more complex discussions about the legality and morality of the strategies, tactics and operational decisions that are made by superiors who send out snipers to fight terrorist monsters. Thus, for some critics seeing the acts of Chris Kyle (the real person upon whom *American Sniper*'s cinematic narrative hinges) through select ocular lens raises the question of whether some types of warfighting —including sniping—risks turning some counter-terrorists into the very "monsters" they are supposed to be fighting. To some extent, this observation intersects with an insight common to profilers of serial killers—that to be effective at catching serial killers, one must learn to think as they do and, thus, blur the line separating the hunted from the hunter.

The third chapter in this section is titled "Monstrous Discourses, Jihadi Cool, and Emergent Counter-Terrorist Narratives: The Case of Ahmad Khan Rahami (a.k.a. Ahmad Rahimi) and the 2016 New York/New Jersey Bombings." Written by Law Professor and Attorney Caroline Joan "Kay" S. Picart, this chapter continues an ongoing research program that analyzes the genesis and mutations of discourses and images interrelating the monstrous with terrorism in law and media (Picart and Greek 2007c, 256–88), and the study of the emergence of US self-radicalizing terrorists as linked to mainly emotional (or at least non-rational) catalyzing (though non-determinative) factors (Picart 2019, 43–59). Both of these (monstrous discourses and self-radicalization) are often catalyzed and intensified by imagined relations facilitated by virtual relations made possible by the Internet (Picart 2015a,

354–83; Picart 2015b, 58–74). Nevertheless, this chapter develops these prior lines of inquiry by evaluating how the concept of the monstrous functions in counter-terrorist rhetorical mechanisms that are placed in relief against the allure of "jihadi cool" culture. Using analytic tools derived from studies of terrorism, this study limits, for pragmatic purposes, its principal focus to the study of a recent and particular instance of an American self-radicalizing terrorist: Ahmad Khan Rahami (a.k.a. Ahmad Rahimi), the 2016 New York/New Jersey Bomber. The chapter's argument regarding an emergent counter-narrative against the master narrative of jihadi cool hinges on an analysis of the counter-terrorist rhetorical tactics that were deployed, both in various media and in the courtroom, to reframe Rahami's self-proclaimed attempt to declare himself a "Soldier of the Caliphate." Hence, the chapter argues that Rahami's case is instructive because it enables us critically to weigh whether or to what extent a culture of "jihadi cool" (Picart 2017, 41–62) was a significant factor in Rahami's self-radicalization. For Picart, a key factor in the formation of this template of a counter-narrative lies in a review of the evidence and rhetorical arguments used in prosecuting Jahar Tsarnaev, the younger of the two Boston Marathon bombers, which the Rahami trial seemed to reference. Finally, in closing, the chapter notes a significant difference between the monstrous rhetoric generated by "jihadi cool's" master-narrative, and the monstrous discourses generated by the evolving jurisprudence in relation to sentencing US self-radicalizing individuals. While the "jihadi cool" narrative stresses *ontological* differences as the basis for propagating a morality of conquest, its emergent counter-narrative/s emphasizes differences based on *delusion* or *action* that results in *violence that harms innocents*, as the moral imperative for countering "jihadi cool."[9]

Rounding out the edited collection, Cecil Greek, a sociologist with whom Picart collaborated in creating the original framework of Gothic Criminology, reflects on how this new edited collection adds to contemporary scholarly discussions on monsters, law and crime in three ways: (1) the incorporation of major theorists whose work includes Gothic elements crucial to thinking through law and crime, such as Michel Foucault; (2) the expansion of Gothic character types and figures from history that can be used to analyze contemporary persons, events and processes (such as the Lilith myth); and (3) the deepening of the Gothic fixation with place. For Greek, some environments and situations seem inherently imbued with the Gothic while other mundane everyday spaces can be transformed quite dramatically into places where the monstrously evil appear. Greek then moves on to some suggestions for how a Gothic Criminological lens might be useful to analyze America under Donald Trump's presidency, building upon an earlier essay on behemoth and dystopia (Greek 2016). He closes on the optimistic and open-ended aspiration that the use of a Gothic criminological lens may illuminate possible ways to work towards a better future, while recognizing the diligence required to avoid giving in to the "evil" and "monstrous," and the ensuing chaos they can bring.

This edited collection does not claim to provide an exhaustive master narrative regarding discourses binding the themes of monsters, law and crime that make up the subject matter of an evolving Gothic Criminological approach. It aspires to be a useful tool or catalyst for further scholarly analysis (and possible policy application) for audiences interested in understanding and even revaluating how the Monstrous (and its discourses or modes of visualization) stand in relation to the proverbial gates of the City State—gates that delineate the jungle of the criminal from the civilized sphere of the law. As the various chapters illustrate, the relations binding the monstrous, law and crime resist a simple binary (while not collapsing the spheres of the Monstrous and the law into a confusing morass). As such, this volume locates itself squarely within the parameters of Contemporary Monster Theory in that it focuses, not on the "what"-ness of a "monster" but on the "how"-and "why"-nesses of how "monsters," not monsters, come to be, rooted in specific cultural contexts, often deployed in multifarious forms of "monster-talk," which are narratives wielded to achieve particular socio-political objectives (Weinstock, 2020). The edited collection does draw from, to some extent, Michel Foucault's deconstructive critique of the social construction of the "natural" and "unnatural" by analyzing how these categories intersect with the often invisible reinforcement of power hierarchies and regulation of social behaviors (Foucault, 1988). Nevertheless, it is important to note that several of the chapters aim to discern some kind of basis (whether that be a reliance on an appeal to an ethical imperative or a notion of social justice or what is actually "real" based on experience) upon which a more refined plotting of narratives may be achieved. As such, the volume resists a simple relativism—a revolving door of warring fictions—in relation to the process through which the "monsterized" are constructed. Finally, a Gothic criminological approach acknowledges the complex flows and ambivalences of the interrelations between the "real" and the "reel," especially in today's hyper-saturated and multiple-mediated universe of global discourses (see also Jewkes and Linnemann, eds., 2017). As such, it continues to generate new questions and methods in relation to how "monsters" and "monster-talk" are useful analytic tools to understand what law and crime are, and their relationships with each other.

NOTES

1. Picart owes a debt of gratitude to Harry Keyishian, for his insightful comments and meticulous, carefully articulated suggestions on an earlier draft; to an anonymous

reader, for helpful and encouraging commentaries that have helped reshape the introduction; and to James Gifford, for his principled guidance of the scholarly review of the edited collection and, more generally, his support. Picart is also extremely grateful to Margaret Petty for her infinite diligence with weaving an Ariadne-an thread through a labyrinth of formatting requirements, and to Zach Nycum, Ashleigh Cooke, and Kris Patenaude whose patience and attentiveness to detail were unflagging in relation to copyediting and preparation for production.

2. See also: "'Jihad Cool/Jihad Chic': The Roles of the Internet and Imagined Relations in the Self-Radicalization of Colleen LaRose (Jihad Jane)" (Picart 2015a); "The Radicalization of American Lone Wolves in Real/Reel Worlds: Strategically Mapping the Roles of the Internet, and Beyond, in the Cases of Colleen LaRose (Jihad Jane) and the Tsarnaev Brothers (the Boston Marathon Bombers)" (Picart 2015b); *American Self-Radicalizing Terrorists and the Allure of "Jihadi Cool/Chic"* (Picart, 2017).

3. For recent examples illustrating these differences, see: "Race and Serial Killing in the Media: The Case of Wayne Williams" (Picart 2016); "Globalization and the Rise of the Behemoth: A Study in Gothic Criminology" (Greek 2016, 343–370); "A Depiction of Evil, Order and Chaos: The Symbiotic Relationship of Law and the Supernatural in Film and Television" (Britto and Greek 2016, 371–397).

4. Similarly, Timothy Beal traces the derivation of the term "monster" to the Latin *monstrum*, which is connected to the verbs *monstrare* (to "show" or "reveal") and monere (to "warn" or "portend") (Beal 2002, 6–7).

5. *Shelley's Ghost: Reshaping The Image of a Literary Family*, A Bodleian Libraries Exhibition in Partnership with the New York Public Library, http://shelleysghost.bodleian.ox.ac.uk/frankenstein, downloaded 01/29/2020.

6. A detailed analysis of the compunction theory in relation to a Gothic Criminology first appeared in Caroline Joan S. Picart and Cecil Greek, "The Compulsions of Serial Killers as Vampires: Toward a Gothic Criminology," *Journal of Criminal Justice and Popular Culture*, 10 (1) (2003) 39–68, available at: http://www.albany.edu/scj/jcjpc/vol10is1/picart.html, downloaded 11/08/2019.

7. Arguably, one could view Greenfield's emphasis on the "ordinariness" of the monstrous as in opposition to Picart and Greek's earlier explication of a Gothic Criminology. However, on a parallel observation, it is important to note that Picart and Greek's earliest published essay on this topic also analyzed the dynamics of documentary or docu-dramatic modes of narration (which are, oxymoronically, "remarkable" for the "ordinariness" of their depiction of "senseless" killings), as depicted specifically in *Henry: Portrait of a Serial Killer*, who is characterized as a Gothic cypher, resisting rational explanation (Picart and Greek 2003). Nevertheless, Greenfield's painstakingly thorough analysis of doctors who are also serial killers opens the field to further discussion and critical study.

8. As characterized by Thaddeus Müller, "[c]ultural criminology is a branch of criminology with a strong emphasis on meaning (culture) and structural conditions, such as marginali[z]ation and late modernity" (Müller 2019, 211).

9. The most recent development, the overturning of Jahar Tsarnaev's death sentence, illustrates how the emerging jurisprudence regarding the younger Tsarnaev wrestles with balancing the strictures of due process with the punitive dimensions of

criminal law in relation to US self-radicalizing individuals. See, for example, Masha Gessen, "Why the Court Overturned the Death Sentence for Dzhokhar Tsarnaev, The Boston Marathon Bomber," *The New Yorker*, August 5, 2020, downloaded August 16, 2020, https://www.newyorker.com/news/our-columnists/why-a-court-overturned-the-death-sentence-for-dzhokhar-tsarnaev-the-boston-marathon-bomber.

REFERENCES

Arendt, Hannah. 2006. *Eichmann in Jerusalem*. New York, NY: Penguin Books.

Arendt, Hannah and Amos Elon. 2006. *Eichmann in Jerusalem: A Report on the Banality of Evil*. London, England: Penguin Books.

Beal, Timothy. 2002. *Religion and Its Monsters*. New York: Routledge.

Britto, Farah and Cecil Greek. 2016. "A Depiction of Evil, Order and Chaos: The Symbiotic Relationship of Law and the Supernatural in Film and Television." *Framing Law and Crime: An Interdisciplinary Anthology*, edited by Caroline Joan "Kay" S. Picart, Michael Hviid Jacobsen, and Cecil Greek, 371–397. Madison, WI and Teaneck, NJ: Fairleigh Dickinson University Press.

Cohen, Jeffrey Jerome (Ed.). 1997. *Monster Theory: Reading Culture*. Minneapolis, MN: University of Minnesota Press.

Foucault, Michel. 1988. *Madness and Civilization: A History of Insanity in the Age of Reason*. New York: Vintage Books.

Gessen, Masha. 2020. "Why the Court Overturned the Death Sentence for Dzhokhar Tsarnaev, The Boston Marathon Bomber." *The New Yorker*, August 5. https://www.newyorker.com/news/our-columnists/why-a-court-overturned-the-death-sentence-for-dzhokhar-tsarnaev-the-boston-marathon-bomber.

Greek, Cecil. 2016. "Globalization and the Rise of the Behemoth: A Study in Gothic Criminology." *Framing Law and Crime: An Anthology*, edited by Caroline Joan "Kay" S. Picart, Michael Hviid Jacobsen, and Cecil Greek, 343–370. Madison, NJ: Farleigh Dickinson University Press.

Greenfield, Steve, Guy Osborn and Peter Robson. 2010. *Film and the Law: The Cinema of Justice*, 2nd edition. London, U.K.: Hart Publishing.

Ingebretsen, Edward J. 2003. *At Stake: Monsters and the Rhetoric of Fear in Public Culture*. Chicago, IL: University of Chicago Press.

Jancovich, Mark. 2012. "'Psychological Thriller': Dead of the Night (1945), British Film Culture, and the 1940s Horror Cycle." *Speaking of Monsters: A Teratological Anthology*, edited by Caroline Joan S. Picart and John Edgar Browning, 39–49. New York: Palgrave MacMillan.

Jewkes, Yvonne and Linnemann, Travis. (Eds.) 2017. *Media and Crime in the U.S.* Thousand Oaks, California: Sage Publications, Inc.

Kyff, Rob. 2016. "Latin verb is the monster behind many words." *Trib Live: Tribune-Review*, March 18. https://archive.triblive.com/lifestyles/more-lifestyles/latin-verb-is-the-monster-behind-many-words/.

Lyman, Stanford. 1990. "Rereading Robert E. Park: Toward a Gothic Perspective on Capitalism and Imperialism." *Explorations: The Age of Enlightenment* (Volume

IV), edited by M.W. duQuesnay, 29–108. Lafayette, LA: University of Southwestern Louisiana Foundation.

Morton, John. 2014. "A Murder of Monsters: Terror and Morality in an Aboriginal Religion." *Monster Anthropology in Australasia and Beyond*, edited by Yasmine Musharbash and Geir Presterudstuen, 75–92. New York: Palgrave Macmillan.

Müller, Thaddeus. 2019. "Cultural Criminology and Its Incitement for Symbolic Interactionism: Transgression, Marginali[z]ation, Resistance and Media in the Wider Context of Power and Culture of Late Modernity." *Critical and Cultural Interactionism: Insights from Sociology and Criminology*, edited by Michael Hviid Jacobsen, 210–227. London and New York: Routledge.

Musharbash, Yasmine and Geir Henning Presterudstuen (Eds.). 2014. *Monster Anthropology: In Australasia and Beyond.* New York: Palgrave Macmillan.

Picart, Caroline Joan "Kay" S. 2017. *American Self-Radicalizing Terrorists and the Allure of "Jihadi Cool/Chic."* Newcastle Upon Tyne: Cambridge Scholars Publishing.

———. 2019. "American Self-Radicalizing Terrorists and Conversions to Radical Action: Emotional Factors and the Allure of 'Jihadi Cool/Chic.'" In *Emotions and Crime: Towards a Criminology of Emotions*, edited by Michael Hviid Jacobsen and Sandra Walklate, 43–59. London: Routledge.

———. 2014a. "The Documentary Impulse and Reel/Real Horror." *A Companion to the Horror Film*, edited by Harry M. Benshoff, 536–553. Sussex, U.K.: Wiley Blackwell.

———. 2015a. "'Jihad Cool/Jihad Chic': The Roles of the Internet and Imagined Relations in the Self-Radicalization of Colleen LaRose (Jihad Jane)." *Societies* 5, no. 2 (April): 354–83.

———. 2014b. "Media Myths Regarding Serial Killers: A Gothic Criminology" in *The Poetics of Crime—Excursions into Creative Criminologies*, edited by Michael Hviid Jacobsen, Chapter 8. Surrey, UK: Ashgate; republished London and New York: Routledge (2016).

———. 2016. "Race and Serial Killing in the Media: The Case of Wayne Williams." *Framing Law and Crime: An Interdisciplinary Anthology*, edited by Caroline Joan "Kay" S. Picart, Michael Hviid Jacobsen, and Cecil Greek. Lanham, Maryland: Fairleigh Dickinson University Press.

———. 2015b. "The Radicalization of American Lone Wolves in Real/Reel Worlds: Strategically Mapping the Role of the Internet, and Beyond, in the Cases of Colleen LaRose (Jihad Jane) and the Tsarnaev Brothers (the Boston Marathon Bombers)." *Lone Actors—An Emerging Security Threat*, edited by Aaron Richman and Yair Sharan, 58–74. NATO Science for Peace and Security Studies. Amsterdam, Netherlands: IOS Press.

Picart, Caroline Joan "Kay" S. and Cecil Greek. 2003. "The Compulsions of Serial Killers as Vampires: Toward a Gothic Criminology." *Journal of Criminal Justice and Popular Culture* 10 (1): 39–68.

———. 2007a. "Introduction: Toward a Gothic Criminology." *Monsters In and Among Us: Toward a Gothic Criminology,* edited by Caroline Joan "Kay" S. Picart and Cecil Greek, 11–43. Madison, NJ: Fairleigh Dickinson University Press.

———. (Eds.). 2007b. *Monsters In and Among Us: Toward a Gothic Criminology*. Madison and Teaneck: Fairleigh Dickinson University Press.

———. 2007c. "Profiling the Terrorist as a Mass Murderer." *Monsters In and Among Us: Toward a Gothic Criminology*, edited by Caroline Joan "Kay" Picart and Cecil Greek, 256–88. Madison, NJ: Fairleigh Dickinson University Press/Associated University Presses.

Pinedo, Isabel Christina. 2004. "Postmodern Elements of the Contemporary Horror Film." *The Horror Film*, edited by Steven Prince, 85–117. New Brunswick, NJ: Rutgers University Press.

Weinstock, Jeffrey Andrew. 2020. "Introduction: A Genealogy of Monster Theory." *The Monster Theory Reader*, edited by Jeffrey Andrew Weinstock, 25. Minneapolis: University of Minnesota Press.

Part I

OF MYTHS AND MONSTERS

Chapter One

"Deeds of Treachery and Violence and Lust and Cruelty"

Revisiting Freud's Primal Crimes in Aboriginal Central Australia

John Morton

According to W. H. Auden (1948, 407), all crimes are offenses against both God and oneself, but murder alone is also an offense against society at large—this, because it forestalls the possibility of restitution and absolution from the victim. For this reason, murder epitomizes "breaking the law," a formula partially in line with Freud's suggestion, in *Totem and Taboo*, that murder was one of "only two crimes which troubled primitive society" (2001, 143) after the primordial inauguration of "social organization, moral restrictions and religion" (2001, 142). Freud's other crime was incest, a transgression which also surely qualifies as an offense against society. Indeed, for Freud, the desire for incest was originally murder's twin.

As is well known, Freud suggested in *Totem and Taboo* that proto-humans once dwelt in small bands, each dominated by a single polygynous patriarch who disallowed mating between his sons and all the females in the group. But one day, the sons banded together, killed their father and consumed him, although they were soon overcome by remorse and a sense of guilt. As a result, they renounced sexual access to their female kin and, associating their father with a totemic species, apotheosized him as the originator of Law. They then commemorated him through periodic ceremonies which re-enacted the primordial events as a kind of holy communion—the "totem meal" (Freud 2001, 141–142).

Totem and Taboo has only occasionally received sympathetic attention in anthropology (e.g., Fox 1967; 1980; Freeman 1969; Paul 1976; 2010), but, whether dealt with sympathetically or not, Freud's critics have by and large been interested in what the story has to say about the primordial nature of society and how it was ineradicably altered by the alleged primal crime. However, in this chapter, I am only indirectly interested in Freud's story as an account of the passage from "nature" to "culture," although I do have things to say about that problematic. Rather, I am chiefly concerned with the *ethnographic* value of his story for understanding a particular totemic religion—that of the Arrernte of central Australia (also widely known in the literature as "Arunta" or "Aranda"). According to its most methodical recorder, T.G.H Strehlow, Arrernte religion—the religion of a hunter-gatherer people[1]—sometimes strikingly evokes "the primitive horde as pictured by psychoanalysis" (1933, 199). It therefore represents an interesting test case against which to measure not only Freud's views, but also Auden's assertions about the relationship between crime, society, divinity and the self.

My account here builds upon a previously published paper exploring the relationship between monsters and gods in this religion (Morton 2014) and further engages arguments from a series of papers that interprets Arrernte ontology largely from a psychoanalytic perspective (Morton 1987a; 1987b; 1989a; 1989b; 1997; 2011). The chapter comprises two main parts. In the first, I give a broad description of Arrernte notions of selfhood, concentrating on the ideal development of subjectivity within the cosmological framework of what has come to be known as "The Dreaming"—a mode of ethical existence encompassing both human beings and other beings who are either less than human (monsters) or more than human (totemic gods). In the second part, I link this description to key aspects of traditional Arrernte social life—to kinship, marriage and the regulatory domain that Arrernte people call "The Law," particularly as it relates to the control of the potential for intergenerational violence.

It is my contention that this overall discussion not only implies a number of criticisms of Freud's primal scenario, which is only partially reflected in Arrernte ethnography, but also entails a clarification of Auden's statement that crimes in general are at once offenses against both oneself and divinity. As will become clear, Arrernte monsters, known collectively as *arrentye*, are violently ranged against the very idea of a human "self," yet they share those aggressive qualities with the totemic gods to whom people owe allegiance in the manner outlined by Freud. As will also become clear, given the superhuman powers of the gods, that situation is less paradoxical than it might first seem, since violence is intrinsic to the re-creation of Arrernte Law.

THE DREAMING

Arrernte people describe the order of the world in terms of the metaphysical concept of *altyerre*, which has come to be known in English as The Dreaming (Green 2012). Although unitary, The Dreaming also has a fundamentally dualistic design. In particular, it is highly gendered and has esoteric and exoteric domains occupied independently by both men and women, although the male cult tends to be most weightily identified with The Law. Both male and female domains are grounded in narratives that account for the origin of the world and which refer to totemic beings who remain omnipresent in that world. These beings, while superhuman, are typically also intimately identified with animal and plant species or other non-human phenomena. They are totemic (Strehlow 1964).

Correlated with gendered dualism is the idea that there are two forms of human corporeality: bodies of flesh and blood, and *tywerrenge* bodies, which are sacred objects of stone or wood regarded as the "other bodies" of the living (Strehlow 1908, 66–67). There are also two forms of human spirit, or two souls—the *kwerrene*, which is associated with fleshly bodies, life and the visible world, and is obliterated at death, and the *artwe nyaltye*, which is permanently associated with *tywerrenge* bodies, death and the hidden world (Strehlow 1964, 731–732; 1971, 594–601). Although the term *tywerrenge* is commonly used to designate sacred objects, it translates etymologically as "one's own secret" (Strehlow 1908, 75), and it has wide application with reference to sacred knowledge and ritual paraphernalia—mainly that used in the esoteric male cult. While women are aware of this knowledge, depend on it and participate in it in specific ways, it is largely hidden from them. Women's concern is more with the reproduction of bodies "in the flesh," not those of stone and wood, which are always made by men (Strehlow 1908, 78).

Tywerrenge might be translated simply as "Law" in certain contexts, but also as "much loved" or "precious" (Henderson and Dobson 1994, 332). The objects are not only the second bodies of the living; they embody, in their entirety, all of the many totemic ancestors associated with Arrernte country. They are The Dreaming itself and often carry symbolic designs depicting the originary journeys and activities—the "work"—of the ancestors with which they are identified. Mythic narratives explain this identification with a stylized ending that indicates that the ancestors "became exhausted" and "became *tywerrenge*" (Strehlow 1964, 729)—a point of significant agreement with Freud's association of totems with death. People say that they "follow" The Dreaming in the sense of "coming behind" the totemic ancestors, inheriting and reproducing the world they created (Strehlow 1947, 35). The totemic beings are thus ancestral in a strict sense—the people who came before, deceased and transmuted, and left behind as *tywerrenge*. Again, this is a point of partial agreement with Freud's totemic apotheosis of the deceased patriarch as the author of Law.

COMING INTO BEING

The religious field as a whole is best understood in terms of the life cycle—the creation and destruction of an Arrernte "subject." All people begin life as reincarnations of an ancestor, with the entry of an ancestral "fragment" or "cell" into a pregnant woman, who thus fully conceives. These cells reside in sacred objects or sites in the landscape associated with ancestral activity and travel. As an infant grows and mobilizes under care (both *in-* and *ex-utero*), it is said to leave its *tywerrenge* behind, with its ancestral identity becoming foreclosed (Strehlow 1947, 86–96). A distressed infant is said to cry for its *tywerrenge*, wishing to return to a state of calm that will foster healthy maturation, indicating that the stable growth of its *kwerrene*, its active "life force," depends on sufficient rest. A dedicated form of *tywerrenge* may be wrapped and placed in a cradle in order to pacify a troubled child (Strehlow 1908, 80). Even a child in the womb is said to be preoccupied and quietened by its *tywerrenge* (Róheim 1933, 251–252).

As a healthy child grows beyond infancy, it internalizes the totemic spirit of its mother, which is specifically named as the child's own *altyerre* ("dreaming"). The maternal totem is said to look after and protect a child in the same way as the mother protected it in infancy, when growing away from its sacred object; and it can be seen in dreams, where it warns the dreamer or his relatives of danger (Strehlow 1908, 57–58). The relationship between one's original totemic identity, embodied by one's personal *tywerrenge,* and one's mother's totem is one of displacement, with the latter coming to take the place of the former. The process is identical to what psychoanalysis construes as the formation of an ideal ego—a "good self" created through parental nurturance, or "the agency whose gaze I try to impress," the one "who watches over me and propels me to give my best, the ideal I try to follow and actualize" (Žižek 2009). It is the *kwerrene* that witnesses the *altyerre* (and all else) in dreams and this aspect of the person is explicitly regarded as a watching agency (Strehlow 1964, 732).

Coming into being (being conceived or born) is referred to as *alkngirreme* —literally "to become eyes"—but *alkngerrentye*, which may refer to a newborn or in-utero baby (Henderson and Dobson 1994, 97), is also the term for female totemic ancestors noted for their beauty and power, and for their independence. The name derives from the fact that these ancestresses resist the sexual attentions of men by averting their eyes (Róheim 1974, 122). Hence, a child's alienation from its *tywerrenge* body is understood as a coming out of darkness into light—"coming to see" or "discover" the world. Given the theory of conception, where the child fathers itself by entering its mother, the process begins as "virgin birth" and continues as a mutually exclusive relationship where mother and child alone return each other's gaze—a relationship which is later reflexively internalized within the self. In psychoanalytic terms, this is a passage from ideal ego to ego ideal, from watching "the other" and coordinating one's feelings with its image—a mirroring relationship that Lacan describes as a state of "normal transitivism" (1977, 19) and which is depicted in Arrernte myth as helpless, immobile pre-subjective proto-humans joined together as formless masses awaiting individuation (Strehlow 1907, 2–3, 6–8)—to watching oneself *as* other (as "me"). The archetypal mother (*alkngerrentye*) in this situation implicitly refers to women's exclusive ceremonial life, and the association of this ritual with early child development and motor coordination is made quite explicit in Arrernte mythology (Róheim 1945, 206–208).

The form of the ego ideal is well illustrated by Arrernte discourse pertaining to the idea of monstrosity, which is specific to the egoic domain and functions precisely as negative self-image. Monsters (*arrentye*) come in many guises, the best known being gigantic, hairy, cannibalistic ogres (*pangkelangke*) that occupy caves and are used to scare children away from restricted areas (Morton 2014, 78–81). Other monsters may take a dazzling variety of forms, with wildly distorted human features typically mixed with exaggerated animal characteristics. These humanoid creatures cause serious illness by occupying the *kwerrene* and dismembering or devouring it (Strehlow 1907, 11–15), and typically appear in fatiguing nightmares (Strehlow 1964, 732). Monsters, especially ogres, also appear in exoteric dreaming narratives, where they likewise commit or threaten murder and cannibalism, largely of children. In these stories, *arrentye* are ranged against people described as *intwerte*—"good" or "beautiful." Always in the prime of life, these glamorous, reassuring protectors are the antithesis of the monsters they typically kill and incinerate (Róheim 1988, 95–198). They are the good adults that children wish to emulate.

The idealization is both physical and ethical. In everyday life, a person may be labeled a monster if he or she is quick to anger and subject to uncontrolled outbursts of selfishness and greed (Morton 2014, 78). Inasmuch as a person's *kwerrene* is his or her life, it is a relational concept implying action on the world that is generally life affirming within the universe of kin. To deny another is also to deny one's better self; hence monsters torment the self, appearing *as* the self if one has not lived up to standards. Compassion and generosity are primary virtues basic to family life and the proper order of things, so monsters represent, to oneself and to others, the obnoxious denial of positive ideals. One well-known Arrernte narrative tells of a group of people called *arrentyepernentye*—"a family of monsters." Its members live in a perverse world, conducting all their affairs in deviant form—for example, eating feces and urine, dressing in live animals, and so on (Strehlow 1907, 104). But what monsters are best known for is murder and cannibalism—the specific form of the denial of kinship in Freud's primal horde.

At this point, a specific observation can be made about Freud's primal scenario and its narrow emphasis on conflict and reparation in the father-son relationship. It is critical to Freud's account that the patriarch's sons loved and admired their father, and this allegedly formed the basis for their eventual respect for him as a totemic god. Freud even speaks emphatically of "the *affectionate* current of feeling towards the father" (2001, 145), but he says nothing about the origins of this feeling, presumably assuming it to be "natural" and not an aspect of either "social organization" or "religion," as if it were a pre-social fact free of "moral restriction." Arrernte ethnography suggests otherwise, showing that love and sympathy find their genesis within the scope of The Dreaming and, in that sense, The Law is not simply "men's business;" it is also "women's business." This is not to say that Freud's account is entirely wide of the mark; it is only that, in Arrernte terms, his origin story presupposes forms of identification specific to the maternal order that he failed properly to consider. That said, *Totem and Taboo* does carry a section in which Freud (2001, 127–132) states that totemism likely had its genesis in children's "animal phobias"; and the extent to which Arrernte monsters are a "beastly" feature of The Dreaming suggests that he was perhaps on the right track (cf. Róheim 1934, 157).

The aspirational idea of "growing up" is totemically metaphorized in Arrernte life by a family that dwells in the farthest reaches of the sky. Children, although they know nothing of totemic *tywerrenge* as they approach adolescence, are told about this family and its immortal constitution (Strehlow 1997, 17). All the members of the family are, like the good people of monster stories, beautiful and in the prime of life. The father and his sons are absolutely identical, but have the feet of emus, while his wives and their daughters are also of equivalent age, but with the feet of dingoes. As emus and dingoes are known to be enemies (fights between emus and dogs are a strong feature of Arrernte mythology), this ideal world of narcissistic self-containment is explicitly one without strife, without difference between the generations and without conjunction between the sexes (Strehlow 1971, 613–620). In reality, what adolescents must come to know is that this world is out of reach—hence, the sky beings play no role in ritual observances. A man or woman cannot become a full adult without gaining and relying on a wife or husband; nor can a man be absolutely like his father, or a woman be absolutely like her mother. Adults must instead become themselves. As the animal feet of the sky dwellers metonymically indicate, they must become grounded, brought "down to earth"—the place where their totemic *tywerrenge* lie. This is initially enacted as a prelude to initiation, when the immature aspirations of a youth are ritually mocked by a group of men holding him by his limbs and tossing him towards the sky, ensuring that he will be hurt on his descent (Spencer and Gillen 1927, 176–178).

SUBMISSION TO THE LAW

Gender separation begins as Arrernte children approach adolescence, this in preparation for their mature participation in the maternal and paternal orders. Young women are prepared for marriage and are eventually introduced to those aspects of The Dreaming appropriate to their status—exoteric aspects of mythology, as well as eventual participation in restricted female ceremonies, which are heavily weighted towards reproduction (Róheim 1933). As the description above implies, a woman's standing is in the main measured by her ability to successfully produce living bodies—life in the flesh—those same bodies counterpointed by *tywerrenge* bodies, whose reproduction is allied to the male cult, but which are nonetheless responsible for women's conception. Young men develop along a different trajectory.

Of particular note is the fact that young men are said to be initiated into the male cult because, were they not subject to the ordeals and disciplines of initiation—circumcision, subincision and other ritual attacks on the body, as well as periods of arduous labor—they would become monsters and consume their elders (Róheim 1932, 72). In exoteric knowledge, circumcision, as the most critical entrée into the world of men, is understood as the killing and reviving of a youth by a particular type of monster (Strehlow 1997, 17); but it is secretly clarified to a youth that this creature is really a *tywerrenge* associated with his mother's dreaming, which he receives and is said to enter his *kwerrene* to act as his protector (Strehlow 1908, 80–81). The circumcision operation itself is dramatized as a violent rush of fury (Strehlow 1971, 398–403), but the operation is desired as keenly as it is feared, since the esoterica that senior men hold are the mark of male status. Circumcision is also dramatized as an exit from the maternal fold and marriage cannot be realized until all trials are completed over a long term. The initial revelation of the mother's dreaming appears to be a substitutive maneuver, replacing her "life in the flesh" with knowledge of her deeper, hidden "self"; but later, after subincision, when a youth's status is changed to that of "young man," he will receive a second *tywerrenge* representing his *own* dreaming, thus indicating that he has begun to know *himself* (Strehlow 1908, 81).

The ceremonial climax of initiation, as a series of events traversing up to a decade, is highly reminiscent of Freud's parricidal deed. The ceremony is a grand, protracted event in which male elders divulge an array of esoteric ceremonial acts, knowledge of which is paid for by young men's hunting labors and gifts of meat. When all acts are complete, a cohort of the most mature young men stages a dramatic reversal of fortunes by ritually attacking senior men's emblems of power. They dance aggressively and, in so doing, break open the ceremonial ground which, together with a tall ceremonial pole, has been the centerpiece of the ceremonial arena. The pole is decorated with various small *tywerrenge* objects which the young men strip after bringing the pole to ground (Strehlow 1947, 110–111). Subsequent to this, the young men bring in hunted game, which they are told is *artwe kere*, ("man meat"), in exchange for which they are "made open mouthed" by having a sacred object pressed to the mouth (Spencer and Gillen 1927, 298–303)—that is, they are given the freedom to speak as fully made men.

Although accessible to him, Freud strangely paid this ritual no attention in *Totem and Taboo*. Freud thought that parricide and cannibalism were repeated in the so called "totem meal" (2001, 142)—the killing and consumption of one's own totem by men otherwise forbidden to kill or eat it (which I describe in more detail below). However, the ceremonial killing of "the father" in Arrernte ritual appears as the long-term outcome of a series of dramatic events that in fact begins with the symbolic murder of "the sons" (circumcision). While Freud could be taken to allude to such potential murder in his remarks about the tyrannical side of the primal patriarch, whom he depicts as a "violent, jealous father" (2001, 141), he finds no room for filicide in his account. The action of the sons remains his primary focus, which reflects his generally skewed understanding of Oedipus, where parricide and incest become so central as to occlude the fact that Oedipus's father, Laius, set the relevant happenings in motion through the abandonment of his baby son, for fear of being succeeded. In Arrernte ritual, juniors are brought to initiation to *encourage* them to succeed their elders, with the vitally necessary aggressivity being ceremonially released.

In Aboriginal English, initiation is sometimes called "going through the rules," a formula that invokes the idea of the super-ego, which Žižek summarizes as equivalent to the ego-ideal, but in its "revengeful, sadistic, punishing, aspect" (2009)—a formula that evokes the "monstrous" side of initiation and the duties attendant upon it. The super-ego limits the ego ideal and makes the subject responsive to different demands—obedience to "the rules." Women similarly submit, but it is in the male cult that one clearly witnesses submission to The Law—not only in regard to young men's submission to elders' authority, but also in regard to the elders' duty to surrender their valued esoteric knowledge, and eventually their ruling status. While the ceremonial deeds of initiation might validly be seen as "monstrous," they are not performed by tyrants and usurpers. They are, however, an essential preliminary to the ceremonial performance that Freud characterized as the "totem meal"—a performance in which men become not monsters, but totemic gods.

Before describing this ceremonial consumption, I need to clarify how Arrernte understand the agency that corresponds to the super-ego. A person's own *tywerrenge* body corresponds to his or her "other soul," called *artwe nyaltye*, which Strehlow suggests carries the meaning of "self-father" (1964, 731–732). The *artwe nyaltye* is a kind of doppelgänger and, while it can occasionally be seen by others beside the person, it is never visible to its living counterpart. It can, however, be heard and will call to the living person when in danger (Strehlow 1971, 598–599). Hence it parallels the mother's dreaming, but outside of the visual field. Its agency and its demands are heard and "understood" rather than seen. As an aspect of one's own *tywerrenge* body, it is also identified with the spiritual cell that enters a woman to make her conceive—itself an act of "self-fathering," the meaning of which becomes clearer when we look further at the male cult and those ceremonies that involve the "totem meal."

Freud's appreciation of totemism was partly inspired by his understanding of Arrernte "increase rituals," so called because of their purpose in reinvigorating totemic species. Terms for these rites often include the word *iweme*, which has the basic meaning of "to throw" or "discard"; this, because totemic actors in the ceremonies are said to "scatter" themselves into their world, amongst other things leaving behind the fertile cells that stir in-utero children into life, as well as their equivalent totemic species (Strehlow 1971, 329). The movement parallels myths in which the totemic ancestors bring the world into being by naming its features and making them consubstantial with their being (Morton 1987b, 107–109). The rites can only be conducted by fully initiated men and generally involve the consumption of a portion of the relevant totem, which in other circumstances must either be respectfully avoided as food or otherwise marked as sacred (Spencer and Gillen 1927, 147–148). In everyday terms, one's own totem is regarded as a sibling; but in myth, the totemic ancestors invariably feed on their own species (Strehlow 1908, 58–60)—their "kin."

While Freud understood this to be a recapitulation of parricidal cannibalism, this is in fact not the case. The "scattering" action is related to the stylized ending of the sacred myths, where a totemic ancestor's travails culminate in him or her "becoming *tywerrenge*." In increase rites, which dramatically commemorate ancestral labor, the *tywerrenge* require oblations drawn from men's veins and are described as "bloodthirsty" (Strehlow 1971, 447), indicating how a man in his ancestral guise empties himself into the world, ultimately leaving only his *tywerrenge* behind. The use of blood is reminiscent of the way Arrernte people inflict deep mourning cuts on themselves to show sorrow or remorse (Strehlow 1971, 602–603) and an exhibition of sacred objects similarly arouses such sorrow, because the objects, and the ancestral places where they belong, remind the living of the departed (cf. Strehlow 1947, 30–31; and see Myers 1986, 117–118). Hence, in ritual, cannibalism has to be understood as *auto*-cannibalism—an "eating away" of the self—and this same practice of self-consumption is sometimes highly elaborated in myth (Strehlow 1947, 7–9). In exchange for their "man meat," mature initiates see this consumption for the first time, giving them the "gift of speech" and the right to be heard as authors of The Law.

In Freud's primal scenario, remorse follows the consumption of the father, but the ingested totem here is not the father *per se*; it is oneself *as* father, identified with the *tywerrenge* which a child abandons when growing into life—and in fact, a person's totem is not called "father," but "elder brother" (Strehlow 1908, 58). Psychoanalytically, the totem corresponds to the demands of the id, celebrating as it does a kind of obligatory but joyful suffering through normally forbidden action; or to what Lacan refers to as "the law of desire"—"the agency which tells you to act in conformity with your desire" (Žižek 2009). Arrernte myth typifies this in ancestral striving, the work that Strehlow describes as "beyond good and evil"—as replete with "deeds of treachery and violence and lust and cruelty," and with "[t]heft and robbery and murder" and "treacherous deceit" in a world free of "love or courtesy or honour or kindness" (Strehlow 1947, 38). This world is truly monstrous, and it is so precisely to the extent that totemic ancestors behave like *arrentye* in demolishing the self. Yet to live this world as The Dreaming is required as an ethical demand to "take power" and become god-like within the terms of The Law. Mythology depicts this explicitly as violent mortality, in line with the position of the father in Freud's primal situation and with Lacan's dictum that "the symbolic Father is, in so far as he signifies [The] Law, the dead Father" (1977, 199).

In contrast to the life of the family of sky-dwellers, sons cannot be like their fathers, nor daughters be like their mothers, without the necessary detour of struggling to find their place within The Law, which first involves being prepared for exogamous marriage and then requires the carriage of arduous duties associated with raising a family—the social situation correlative to "being-for-death." But Arrernte religion depicts the transition from "incest" (identification with the nuclear family) to exogamy in terms somewhat different to Freud's. While there are profound echoes of the primal horde in Arrernte religion, they are distorted. In particular, a life-cycle view of Arrernte subjectivity illustrates how the commemorative "totem meal," differently construed, is allied to a series of other aspects of The Dreaming already consistent with "social organization, moral restrictions and religion." In the first place, The Dreaming includes a women's domain which one cannot envisage as external to The Law—and it is indeed said that, in the final analysis, men and women "follow one Law" (Bell 1983, 182-228), albeit largely in segregated domains. Secondly, in his consideration of murder, Freud fails to pay due attention to initiation as a form of ritual killing of "the sons"—a murder that necessarily precedes that of "the father," which in any case is not actually depicted in the autophagous totemic sacrament, but is rather a prelude to it. Certain sociological dimensions of The Law shed further light on these matters and raise important questions about murder and incest as primordial crimes.

KINSHIP, MARRIAGE AND CRIME

Arrernte society is entirely organized by kinship, but, like Arrernte religion, the system is dualistic, articulated by two basic distinctions: one between the generations, the other between those who are kin and others who are affines ("in-laws")—the very distinctions that are absent in the mythical vision of the perfectly contained family living beyond the sky. The kinship system, known as *anpernirrentye* (Dobson and Henderson 2013), is a system of address, with all known people called directly by kinship terms, as well as by class names ("skins") that describe the system in the abstract. The kin/affine distinction is reciprocal, in the sense that one marries into one's "opposite side" to avoid incestuous relationships of various degrees, but always within one's own generational level. Hence the system conjugates similarity and difference as a negation of the "perfect" family that dwells, out of reach, beyond the sky. All kin relationships carry behavioral expectations. Relative to age, people are expected to treat particular relatives in certain ways, which broadly range from familiarity to reserve. It is here that one grasps the fundamentals of Arrernte morality.

Since Freud makes intergenerational conflict and incest critical to his understanding of the primal situation, I now briefly describe some of the relational dynamics accompanying initiation as a rite preliminary to marriage. A man's first marriage is typically by promise and is arranged through negotiations between a number of relatives, both kin and affines (Strehlow 1913, 89–91). A promised bride is normally given to a young man when his initiatory ordeals are complete, but the promise is made much earlier, when he is readied for initiation. The father and other close relatives are responsible for bringing a boy to initiation, but not alone, since they must negotiate with the prospective in-laws who are actually responsible for initiating the boy.

The role of the father-in-law is especially critical. The father-in-law/son-in-law relationship is the most respectful and formal of all in Arrernte society and it is the father-in-law, together with other "in laws," who acts out the ferocity of circumcision on his son-in-law (Spencer and Gillen 1927, 189). For a son-in-law to insult or physically abuse his father-in-law would be a mightily serious crime, although suspicion of aggressive feeling against the father-in-law is intense (Róheim 1988, 91). A son-in-law must not only submit to the father-in-law's ritual killing, he must also work hard for his prospective wife's father for many years prior to the realization of the bridal promise, including on the ceremonial ground. A son-in-law must also inflict the most exaggerated bloody mourning cuts on himself when his father-in-law dies, thereby showing not only his sorrow, but also his innocence of evil intent. Any insufficient display of mourning by a son-in-law arouses suspicion that would likely lead to execution (Strehlow 1997, 41).

Hence, it is fair to say that it is not the criminal murder of the father that most deeply troubles Arrernte society, but the killing of the father "in Law." There is no evidence that the possibility of parricide *per se* troubles Arrernte society in this way. Moreover, it is the father-in-law, not the father, who at the climax of initiation receives "man meat" from a young man and reveals to his son-in-law the esoteric meaning of "auto-cannibalism" as a mature state of manhood attended by the authority to speak (Spencer and Gillen 1927, 302). It appears, therefore, that the ritual killing of the ceremonial leader of the final initiation ceremony is less the "murder" of the father and more the disposal of the father "in Law," who acts as the "symbolic Father" in "making a man" of his son-in-law, who may now procure a wife, which he will later do by way of dramatized seizure (Róheim 1974, 228–233).

Correlative to this situation is the further formal relationship between a man and his mother-in-law—a woman likely to be much younger than her husband. Sexual relationships with mothers-in-law (or potential mothers-in-law, to whom the term for "mother-in-law" applies) are as strictly forbidden as are sexual liaisons with mothers, sisters and daughters, but they alone are accompanied by a strong undercurrent of desire (Strehlow 1913, 91). A man may not so much as set eyes on his mother-in-law, nor she on him; they may not speak to each other and all communication is generally mediated through the father-in-law or his daughter. Physical distance must be obtained at all times, for fear of intense shame. It is said that "sexual relations by totemic ancestors with their potential mother-in-law" is one of the few occasions when Arrernte storytellers emphasize "strong moral censure" (Strehlow 1997, 26). A well-known Arrernte myth concerns an ugly, brute-tempered, murderous ancestor who avoids appropriate women and has sexual relations only with women in the mother-in-law class. Strehlow refers to him as the Arrernte "monster of immorality" (1997, 26) and adds that, while elopements of this kind might sometimes occur, they have always been "punishable by death" (1997, 27).

On a broader canvas, older married men in Arrernte society are generally anxious of losing their younger wives to younger men (Strehlow 1997, 14), but liaison with the mother-in-law is seen to be the most heinous form of adultery and flouting of "the rules." While incestuous relations between people classified as close kin are very much "against The Law," it appears that the most strongly forbidden, yet desired, sexual relations in Arrernte society are between sons and mothers "in Law," which are nonetheless defined as incestuous in the universal system of kin-relatedness, with a mother-in-law being regarded as a kind of aunt. The taboo is clearly correlative with the protection of the father-in-law's interests, which, while sexual, are also economic because of the gendered division of labor within the family. The prohibition appears to gain its formality from the fact that, during initiation, a man acquires "another father" whom he must learn to love and respect, in the process making this father's wife "another mother." In short, a man becomes part of another family, but one to which he is sexually connected by way of Law.

In *Totem and Taboo* Freud discounted explanations of incest avoidance that rely on the idea of instinctual aversion within the family, suggesting, after James Frazer, that "law only forbids men to do what their instincts incline them to do; what nature itself prohibits and punishes it would be superfluous for the law to prohibit and punish" (2001, 123). In Arrernte society, mother-in-law avoidance most clearly conforms to the first dictum because of its highly contractual nature and its grounding in formal respect relationships. No such contracted formality is found within the familiar, affectionate universe of immediate kin. However, there is increasing gender separation between brothers and sisters as they approach adolescence, as well as respectful changes in attitudes between same-sex siblings, who are graded by age, and between parents and children. But sexual relationships within the family are out of the question, with this attitude being generalized within the larger universe of classificatory kin. They correspond to what Freud called "the horror of incest" (2001, 1–17) and, while possible, appear to be less "thought" than affinal incest—or more perverse than criminal.

It is noteworthy that, in *Totem and Taboo*, Freud himself restricts the desire for incest only to "the earliest sexual excitations of youthful human beings," which are eventually "repressed" (2001, 124). He does not extend this desire to maturing adults, but nevertheless assumes that this was once the case under primordial conditions, giving rise to the primal murder—guided as he was by the idea that proto-humans lived in "cyclopean" families, each led by an aggressive male who would drive out up-and-coming competitors for sexual access to females. We now know that this was not the case and that humanity's "pre-cultural" heritage was more likely characterized by groups of cooperative, pair-bonded families organized into hierarchies and possessing mechanisms for reducing in-group conflict (Paul 2010, 233). These mechanisms likely included incest avoidance by preference rather than by coercion, with pair bonds often being forged across groups (Pusey 1990)—a situation that is actually more in line with Freud's own view that infantile incestuous desire is, in the nature of things, "repressed."

Arrernte child rearing accords with this process (Strehlow 1997, 17–18). After prolonged dependence on the mother, active young children are never subject to punishment and parents rarely take a moralistic approach to education, although fear of monsters is instilled to restrict far-ranging movement and to promote safety. Children learn by example, particularly by accompanying groups of women foragers, and by listening in to adult exchanges and experiencing direct care and protection. When young, they also accompany women in their ceremonies. The ego ideal is forged in this informal environment and, beyond the latency period, there is no indication that mature kin become sexually charged love objects. While, cross-sibling relationships are restrained after initiation, this is less like formal avoidance and more like the prevention of embarrassment. Given the difference between this kind of sexual avoidance—a kind of "shyness" one sees symbolically depicted in the Arrernte family living beyond the sky—and that which pertains to relations with in-laws, it is clear that incest prohibition is of two kinds, only one of which is in place because incest is actually desired.

The main candidate for primal murder motivated by incest is thus to be found in the affinal register. Anthropologists speak of marriage in this context as "alliance" and, in the Arrernte case, marriage contracts invariably forge common interests across territorial divisions or totemic clan estates, such that these adjoining areas are integrated across a much larger domain (Strehlow 1965, 136–141). Estates are generally formed around fraternities of senior men, one of whom is likely to have risen to most senior status due to superior ritual standing. Youths leave these territories at initiation and take up residence in their prospective wives' areas, working for their promised bride's parents, but generally return to their fathers' areas upon acquisition of their female partners. This territorial aspect of alliance is intimately related to the formality and legal restriction that governs a man's relations with his in-laws.

If there is jealousy that motivates such restriction, then it is not that of "the father," although that is not to say that sons are not keen to be like their fathers in the sense of succeeding to their place. As the articulation of alliance indicates, with newly married men returning home to their paternal estates, the father's desire is not to vanquish his sons, but to guarantee his own lineage and continuity of landed property—a guarantee that can only be put in place by his sons' ability to acquire wives from other groups by peaceful means. Hence, one sees more plainly the logic of the statement that, without initiation, young men would become violent monsters who would murder their elders—if not their fathers, then certainly their fathers-in-law and other men in their groups. The primary focus of monstrous aggression is thus centrifugal, not centripetal as suggested by Freud, representing war rather than civil strife.

Successful marital alliance, and the commerce attendant upon it, ideally neutralizes aggression and brings peace, in line with Tylor's (1889, 267) well-known dictum that early humans were constantly faced with the choice between marrying out and being killed out. It is consistent with this view to say that Freud's primal father, as a man with envied access to women, was not *the* father at all, but rather *a* father with the potential to become a father *in Law*. This father protects his own interests by surrendering a daughter and keeping his wife, on the understanding that others will do the same. Correlatively, his sons surrender their sisters, expecting to receive wives in return. At the same time, fathers and sons ensure safe succession to the estates of their allies, as do their allies for them, thereby extending the scope of civil society (cf. Lévi-Strauss 1969). The generalized system of kinship and affinity maps the requisite relationships across the board as the family writ large, with the murder of the father-in-law and the taking of his wife regarded as its most heinous violation, epitomizing crime itself.

Law cannot of course be reduced to the policing of this crime alone, since the entire "machinery" of relationships within the kinship system is related to it and must be broadly upheld according to the norms and expectations attendant on all of the specific relationships, which Strehlow (1997) has described in some detail. Strehlow's summary account suggests that, by and large, punishment for most delicts is appropriately carried out within an estate group and under the direction of its senior men, one of whom will have most to say because of his standing as "ceremonial chief" (1997, 19–34). What he calls "civil" offenses are generally dealt with by retaliatory action by or on behalf of injured parties—interpersonal or small group confrontations normally limited in intensity by public scrutiny so as to not cause dangerous injury or death (1997, 22). He distinguishes these offenses from "criminal" or "public" matters more directly under the control of male elders often acting in closed council—the same men responsible for controlling totemic ceremonies appropriate to the dreamings of the estate.

"The [criminal] offences might range from incest to murder," but they also include "the betrayal of the sacred ritual of the totemic clan to strangers or to women" (Strehlow 1997, 24)—a definition fairly in line with Freud's appreciation of murder and incest as archetypal criminality, but with the addition of direct offenses against *tywerrenge*. Offenders, depending on the precise nature of the crime, generally have to withstand formally inflicted injury by weapons such as boomerangs or spears, or they are placed under a death sentence, with executions carried out by spearing and knifing (Strehlow 1997, 14–25). Sacrilegious crimes, such as unauthorized or careless handling of sacred objects and knowledge, always carry the death penalty (Strehlow 1997, 27), which is aligned with the meaning of *tywerrenge* as supremely treasured possessions. It is also consistent with the way these totemic paraphernalia are both the "other bodies" of the living and the remaining bodies of the dead, since that measures the strong sentimental attachments that people have towards Law as a cultural inheritance. For although *tywerrenge* as a whole are the embodiment of ancestors in the abstract (The Dreaming), they are ancestral in a strict sense, with any number at any given time known to be recently deceased relatives. The men who hold these objects are greatly feared for their ability to authorize violent retribution (Strehlow 1970, 110–128) and they are by no means beyond ruthlessness in the pursuit of what they see to be their just interests (Strehlow 1969, 35–49).

Of particular note in relation to Freud's view of paternal deification is the fact that a man's *tywerrenge* "will pass after his death into the possession of his son" (Strehlow 1947, 133); or, if there is no heir, into the collective hands of a patrigroup—the "totemic clan"—associated with the father's estate (Strehlow 1947, 142–143). So close is the identification between father and son that, even when they have different totemic identities through conception, the son will regard his own *tywerrenge* and his father's *tywerrenge* as "the same thing" (Strehlow 1947, 133). Both are regarded as personal property and a man will also claim proprietorial interests in his mother's *tywerrenge*, for which he acts as guardian. *Tywerrenge* are also exchanged more widely amongst allied groups as a sign of friendship (Strehlow 1947, 150–153), reflecting the interdependence that is forged through marriage ties between estates. But the sacred relationship between men and their fathers is central to the system and is ideally realized as patrilineal succession to estates in perpetuity. In this sense, *tywerrenge* function as deeds of title—deeds guaranteed by the "law of the father."

Possession of *tywerrenge* is subject to intense politicking and competition, resulting in a highly unequal distribution of authority and power among older men (Strehlow 1947, 84–172). It is certainly the case that a man seeks to take his father's place, but no man is able to achieve that without suffering the discipline and costs associated with initiation and marital alliance. The degree to which a man proves his worthiness through obedience to The Law, discharging his obligations to his living elders and to his deceased ancestors, measures not only his worldly reputation, but also his ultimate status as an ancestor himself—his standing not *in relation to* sacred objects, but his eventual position *as* a sacred object, his "other body" from which "fragments" or "cells" emerge to father themselves in the bodies of women. Incest is thus equivalent to a state of death; it remains "unconscious." One can only achieve this state via the detour of The Law, following the mortal path taken by one's father and one's father before him.

The kinship system maps the pattern by its basic distinctions between the generations and between "us" (kin) and "them" (affines), and by the forbidden degrees of incestuous relationship embedded in that grid. Law requires that every family marries into its opposite side in order to receive back husbands and wives in the following generation, which has the effect of reconstituting the family in its "original" form in every other generation. Alternate generations are "the same" in Arrernte understanding, and men are ideally identified with their paternal grandfathers by being conceived into the same dreaming. As one Arrernte man put it, a grandfather dies, but he retains his "feeling" to give to his grandson (Morton 1987a, 464)—if not from the grave, then from the *tywerrenge* that are his objective remains. The ideal implies that, in every generation, men must submit to new fathers and mothers to prevent them becoming monsters. But this submission also gives them the opportunity to become gods—"fathers themselves," whose mythical deeds, while certainly monstrous, take place in a world that is neither good nor evil, yet fundamentally necessary to human existence.

CONCLUSION

There is evidence that the type of kinship system of which the Arrernte system is a variant is of great antiquity, and that it was heavily implicated in greatly increased reproductive success, leading to the early rapid movement of *Homo sapiens* across the globe (Hamilton 2006). Freud may have been correct to assume that the ancestors of *Homo sapiens* once lived in "cyclopean" families, but he was wrong to believe that this form of the family was immediately prior to the type of family that characterizes "modern man." Freud was not unaware of the problem, referring to the "uncertainties of [his] premises" and "the difficulties involved in [his] conclusions" (2001, 157). Nevertheless, the inquiry I have undertaken here suggests that he was correct to suppose that "the beginnings of religion, morals [and] society" revolve, at least in part, around the problem of "a man's relationship to his father" (2001, 156–157).

Framed in the present tense, the problem would be that men cannot succeed directly to their fathers' estates, as the sons of "primal hordes" allegedly wished to do, but must instead search afar for the means of reproduction—not because young men are violently cast out of the family, but because their own desire demands that they leave. This suggests that Law, as an originary "social contract," likely arose as the result of negotiating friendship and putting in place "elementary structures of kinship" (Lévi-Strauss 1969) covering relationships between erstwhile rival families. It further suggests that the primordial "step forward" to alliance was not based on the ethical renunciation of aggression towards the father, but on submission to the authority of the father-in-law, who, at the father's behest, guaranteed young men's passage to responsible adulthood and reproductive success. Hence, primordial criminality must have originally been defined in terms of external aggression—the violation of "society" and its archetypal representative, the man who is a father "by Law" rather than natural sentiment.

I have been at pains to show that, when society is understood this way, it presupposes a particular psychological structure—a specific kind of "spirit" articulated as dialectical tension between the ego and the id, between the "subject of life" and the "object of death." One may suppose this structure to also be of great antiquity, articulating humanity's earliest relationships with both monsters and gods—those uncanny "others" who intrude upon the subject by making themselves seen or heard in moments of moral crisis and ethical dilemma. But monsters and gods are not all of a piece. The monster shows itself when the self is prone to violently come undone—when life, love, sympathy, kinship and one's "better self" are denied. Gods, however, demand sacrifice and obedience to The Law, whose violation is the undoing of the general principles, rules and contractual bonds that give effect to "society" at large. Such submission holds the promise of status and power, but those who violate the inviolable must bring violence upon themselves—not from monsters, but from those who hold, and will become, The Law.

NOTE

1. Context demands that I write in the ethnographic present for this chapter, but the writing largely pertains to "classical" (pre-colonial) Arrernte culture as reconstructed through postcolonial ethnography dating back to the late nineteenth century. Arrernte people, together with several dialects of the language and much of the original way of life, remain a strong presence in central Australia, but much has also been modified, sometimes greatly, as a result of colonization. While contemporary Arrernte people often do hunt or gather, they do not possess a "hunter-gatherer economy" in any strict sense, having long been mostly reliant on a welfare or market economy. See Morton (1999) for a summary account of the recent situation of Arrernte people in central Australia.

REFERENCES

Auden, W. H. 1948. "The Guilty Vicarage: Notes on the Detective Story, by an Addict." *Harper's Magazine*, May Issue, 406–412.

Bell, Diane. 1983. *Daughters of the Dreaming*. Melbourne: McPhee Gribble.

Dobson, Veronica and John Henderson. 2013. *Anpernirrentye: Kin and Skin*. Alice Springs: IAD Press.

Fox, Robin. 1967. "*Totem and Taboo* Reconsidered." *The Structural Study of Myth and Totemism*, edited by Edmund Leach, 161–178. London: Tavistock.

———. 1980. *The Red Lamp of Incest: A Study in the Origins of Mind and Society*. London: Hutchinson.

Freeman, Derek. 1969. "Totem and Taboo: A Reappraisal." In *Man and his Culture: Psychoanalytic Anthropology after "Totem and Taboo,"* edited by Warner Muensterberger, 53–78. New York: Taplinger.

Freud, Sigmund. 2001 [1913]. *Totem and Taboo.* In *The Standard Edition of the Complete Works of Sigmund Freud, Volume 13*, 1–161. London: Vintage.

Green, Jenny. 2012. "The Altyerre Story—'Suffering Badly by Translation.'" *Australian Journal of Anthropology* 23 (2): 158–178.

Hamilton, Annette. 2006. "Kinship and Ontology: The Success of Homo Sapiens." In *Human Evolution: Facts and Factors*, edited by É. B. Bodzsár and C. Susanne, 57–85. Budapest: Eötvös University Press.

Henderson, John and Veronica Dobson. 1994. *Eastern and Central Arrernte to English Dictionary*. Alice Springs: IAD Press.

Lacan, Jacques. 1977. *Écrits: A Selection*. London: Tavistock.

Lévi-Strauss, Claude. 1969. *The Elementary Structures of Kinship*. London: Eyre and Spottiswoode.

Morton, John. 1987a. "The Effectiveness of Totemism: 'Increase Ritual' and Resource Control in Central Australia." *Man* 22 (3): 453–474.

———. 1987b. "Singing Subjects and Sacred Objects: More on Munn's 'Transformation of Subjects into Objects' in Central Australian Myth." *Oceania* 58 (2): 100–18.

———. 1989a. "Singing Subjects and Sacred Objects: A Psychological Interpretation of the 'Transformation of Subjects into Objects' in Central Australian Myth." *Oceania* 59 (4): 280–98.

———. 1989b. "Mama, *Papa*, and the Space Between: Children, Sacred Objects, and Transitional Phenomena in Aboriginal Central Australia." *The Psychoanalytic Study of Society* 14: 191–225.

———. 1997. "Totemism Now and Then: A Natural Science of Society?" In *Scholar and Sceptic: Australian Aboriginal Studies in Honour of L.R. Hiatt*, edited by Francesca Merlan, John Morton and Alan Rumsey, 151–70. Canberra: Aboriginal Studies Press.

———. 1999. "The Arrernte of Central Australia." In *The Cambridge Encyclopedia of Hunters and Gatherers*, edited by Richard Lee and Richard Daly, 329–334. Cambridge: Cambridge University Press.

———. 2011. "'Less was hidden with these children': Géza Róheim, Anthropology and the Politics of Aboriginal Childhood." In *Growing Up in Central Australia: New Anthropological Studies of Aboriginal Childhood and Adolescence*, edited by Ute Eickelkamp, 15–48. New York: Berghahn Books.

———. 2014. "A Murder of Monsters: Terror and Morality in an Aboriginal Religion." In *Monster Anthropology in Australasia and Beyond*, edited by Yasmine Musharbash and Geir Presterudstuen, 75–92. New York: Palgrave Macmillan.

Myers, Fred. 1986. *Pintupi Country, Pintupi Self: Sentiment, Place, and Politics among Western Desert Aborigines*. Washington: Smithsonian Institution Press.

Paul, Robert. 1976. "Did the Primal Crime Take Place?" *Ethos* 4 (3): 311–352.

———. 2010. "Yes, the Primal Crime did Take Place: a Further Defense of Freud's *Totem and Taboo*." *Ethos* 38 (2): 230–249.

Pusey, Anne. 1990. "Mechanisms of Inbreeding Avoidance in Nonhuman Primates." In *Pedophilia*, edited by J. R. Feierman, 201–220. New York: Springer Verlag.

Róheim, Géza. 1932. "Psycho-Analysis of Primitive Cultural Types." *International Journal of Psycho-Analysis* 13 (1–2): 1–224.

———. 1933. "Women and their Life in Central Australia." *Journal of the Anthropological Institute of Great Britain and Ireland* 63 (1): 207–265.

———. 1934. *The Riddle of the Sphinx, or Human Origins*. London: Hogarth Press.

———. 1945. *The Eternal Ones of the Dream: A Psychoanalytic Interpretation of Australian Myth and Ritual*. New York: International Universities Press.

———. 1974. *Children of the Desert: The Western Tribes of Central Australia*. New York: Basic Books.

———. 1988. *Children of the Desert II: Myths and Dreams of the Aborigines of Central Australia*. Sydney: Oceania Ethnographies.

Spencer, Baldwin and F. J. Gillen. 1927. *The Arunta: A Study of a Stone Age People, Vol. 1*. London: Macmillan.

Strehlow, Carl. 1907. *Die Aranda- und Loritja-Stämme in Zentral-Australien, I Teil: Mythen, Sagen und Märchen des Aranda-Stammes*. Frankfurt am Main: Joseph Baer.

———. 1908. *Die Aranda- und Loritja-Stämme in Zentral-Australien, II Teil: Mythen, Sagen und Märchen des Loritja-Stammes, die Totemistischen Vorstellungen und die Tjurunga der Aranda und Loritja*. Frankfurt am Main: Joseph Baer.

———. 1913. *Die Aranda- und Loritja-Stämme in Zentral-Australien, IV Teil, I Abteilung: Das Soziale Leben der Aranda und Loritja*. Frankfurt am Main: Joseph Baer.

Strehlow, T. G. H. 1933. "Ankotarinja, an Aranda Myth." *Oceania* 4 (2): 187–200.

———. 1947. *Aranda Traditions*. Melbourne: Melbourne University Press.

———. 1964. "Personal Monototemism in a Polytotemic Community." In *Festschrift für Ad. E. Jensen*, edited by Eike Haberland, Meinhard Schüster and Helmut Straube, 723–754. München: Klaus Renner.

———. 1965. "Culture, Social Structure and Environment in Aboriginal Central Australia." In *Aboriginal Man in Australia: Essays in Honour of Emeritus Professor A. P. Elkin*, edited by Ronald Berndt and Catherine Berndt, 121–145. Sydney: Angus and Robertson.

———. 1969. *Journey to Horseshoe Bend*. Sydney: Angus and Robertson.

———. 1970. “Geography and the Totemic Landscape in Central Australia: A Functional Study.” In *Australian Aboriginal Anthropology*, edited by Ronald Berndt, 92–140. Perth: University of Western Australia Press.

———. 1971. *Songs of Central Australia*. Sydney: Angus and Robertson.

———. 1997. “Agencies of Social Control in Central Australian Aboriginal Societies.” In *Strehlow Research Centre Occasional Paper Number One*, edited by David Hugo, 1–50. Alice Springs: Strehlow Research Centre.

Tylor, Edward. 1889. “On a Method of Investigating the Development of Institutions: Applied to Laws of Marriage and Descent.” *Journal of the Anthropological Institute of Great Britain and Ireland* 18 (3): 245–272.

Žižek, Slavoj. 2009. “Ego Ideal and the Superego: Lacan as a Viewer of Casablanca.” http://www.lacan.com/essays/?p=182.

Chapter Two

Criminal Anthropology, Fabulism, and Criminology's Unacknowledged Teratological Lineage

Jon Frauley

CRIMINAL ANTHROPOLOGY AND CRIMINOLOGY'S UNACKNOWLEDGED TERATOLOGICAL LINEAGE

> Our fascination with the monstrous and freakish is not new. Victorian literature—medical, literary, popular, historical—already had discovered the monstrous as a topic which would fascinate every audience. And this Victorian tradition built on earlier scholarly books on teratology (the study of the monstrous) in medicine and mass culture going back to the beginning of the printed book and beyond. In the past two decades the monstrous has re-emerged as a means of examining the margins that each age employs to define the normal . . . recent work has sketched the contours of the western fascination with the monstrous as part of the universal history of Otherness
>
> (Gilman 1997, 119).

The popular press and true crime writing trade on a widespread public fascination with monstrosity. The monster has become a central motif of crime narratives and, as I argue, was central to nineteenth century criminal anthropology, which according to the "standard view" of criminology's origins is the precursor of modern "scientific" criminology. The "standard view" traces "scientific" criminology to the originator of criminal anthropology, Italian physician Cesare Lombroso.[1] What is neglected by the standard view, however, is Lombroso's own positioning within the subfields of medical jurisprudence and teratology and his belief that the "atavist" (i.e., the born criminal) was a medical monster.[2] Thus the standard view neglects criminology's teratological lineage. I show here that Lombroso's criminal anthropology was concerned with the clinical monsters of medicine and that criminology emerged from the nineteenth century as a science of monster detection.

A TALE OF CONTRASTS

Criminology's origin story is a tale of contrasts.[3] On the one hand we have the utilitarian "Classical School of Criminology" and its deductive and (what is characterized as) its metaphysical view of crime. Thinkers such as Jeremy Bentham and Cesare Beccaria are considered representatives of this position. This rationalist approach to crime is juxtaposed to what, on the other hand, is held to be the materialist, inductive, and scientific view of criminality promulgated by the "Positivist School of Criminal Anthropology." This caricature sets up the latter's empiricism as scientific in contrast to rationalism and deduction which are situated as part of a speculative philosophical metaphysics.[4] The scientific status of Lombroso's work trades on his locus within medicine as well as a presumed relationship between his "positivist" criminal anthropology and the nineteenth century "positivist" movement in science. This positivist philosophy of science was first promulgated in the early nineteenth century by philosopher Auguste Comte[5] and later championed by sociologist and philosopher Herbert Spencer, who coined the term "survival of the fittest" and invented "Social Darwinism." The growth of the positivist movement and the work of Charles Darwin had a profound impact on medicine and studies of crime and criminality. This impact did not escape Lombroso who fetishized anthropometric measurement and proffered that criminality was a manifestation of heritable degeneracy.[6]

Medicine was slowly transitioning away from "speculation" and rationalism to "scientific empiricism" (Shyrock 1969). By the end of the nineteenth century medicine had all but abandoned metaphysical explanations to materialist ones. As Nicole Rafter, Chad Posick, and Michael Rocque (2016), and others, have outlined with respect to criminology, there was a similar move away from religious and metaphysical understandings of deviance to a "scientific" medical model whereby explanations of crime underwent a change from spiritual and metaphysical explanations that situated demonic possession as cause to a more Enlightened explanation that eventually led to scientific empiricist explanations. Working in medicine and medical jurisprudence as he did, trained as a physician as he was, and influenced by the positivism and evolutionary theory of Herbert Spencer, the phrenology of Franz Joseph Gall and Johann Spurzheim, Darwin's work, and the degeneracy theory of Ernst Haeckel, Lombroso's work reflected his times and was "consistent with his medical training" (Gibson and Rafter 2006, 5, 7).

The standard view sets in place the bedrock for modern criminology's claim to (social) scientific status as the standard view forges a direct connection between modern criminology and scientific empiricism (via Lombroso, the "first scientific criminologist"). This origin tale of contrasts I think has done much to secure the supreme reign of empiricist epistemology within the field of criminology for most of its history and it has obscured the fact that Lombroso was working in both the fields of medical jurisprudence and teratology. Moreover, it implicitly holds that criminology is a science of difference. We are told that the Classical thinkers held to the same ontology for both criminals and the law-abiding (we shall call this the "representative view" following Schmid [2010], below) but that this view of criminals as like us was displaced by a "scientific empiricist" view of transgressors as possessing innate biological differences, making them inherently dangerous:

> Over the course of the eighteenth century, it became common to hear the criminal's point of view in crime narratives, first in reports of the criminal's dying words, and then later in the form of full-fledged biographies. The rhetoric of monstrosity, which aimed to place the criminal definitively outside the boundaries of community, also began to assume an important role in these new forms of crime narrative. The criminal was now viewed as a distinctly asocial creature and consequently, by the early decades of the nineteenth century, we have traveled a long way from the Puritan notion of the criminal as a representative member of the community (Schmid 2010, 199).

Long before anything called "criminology" was established, crime and criminality were the subject of much contemplation and extensively written about by the pious, philosophers, novelists, journalists, jurists, and magistrates. As David Schmid (2010, 199) observes, one of the earliest views of crime as sin (which reigned supreme until the nineteenth century) framed the criminal as a "representative member of their community" and not as a dangerous or threatening outsider. This served in part as a cautionary tale emphasizing the "dangerously thin line" separating sinners from the morally righteous and how the slide toward evil was always a possibility for the morally weak. Once we leave the "crime as sin" paradigm, criminality becomes less about moral fortitude and free will and more about determinants that produced a type of subject different to the point that similarities of human being were no longer easily recognized if at all.[7] Indeed animalization and dehumanization are significant consequences of Lombroso's criminal anthropology (see Beirne 1995; Cassata 2011; Gould 1996; Harrowitz 1994a and b; Horn 2003; Olson 2013; Pick 1989; Roberts 2008). A legacy of this is hidden in popular culture today. "From the point of view of the modern true crime writer," Schmid (2010, 207) states, "stressing the monstrosity of murderers is also a practical necessity, solving as it does the problem of how to build a compelling narrative around such a dull and ordinary individual as the average killer."

SCIENTIFIC EMPIRICISM, TRUE CRIME, AND SCIENTIFIC FICTION

The success of empiricism and the "monster paradigm" was in excluding and casting as suspicious other ways of conceptualizing crime and criminality such as the rationalist view as well as aesthetic and poetic forms of understanding (Sagarin 1980; Wilson 2015). As Edward Sagarin (1980, 74) argues, alongside these more literary images of crime, criminals, and criminality "grew up a body of thought, philosophic and later social scientific, concerned with the same themes." Drawing on C.P. Snow's idea of "two cultures"—one of science and one of the arts—Sagarin (1980, 75) argues the history of criminology is a tale of two groups both examining the same object but "going their separate ways":

> The interest in social science as science, given its great impetus in France and England during the first half of the nineteenth century, spurred the development of criminology. Then Darwin published *The Origin of the Species*, and the era of evolution, anthropology and biology was reflected in the growth and refinement of criminological thought, particularly in Italy (Sagarin 1980, 75).

The most prominent Italian to engage in what is today considered to be criminology, the first "scientific criminologist" according to the standard view, is Cesare Lombroso. His "criminal anthropology" became renown, garnering admirers and detractors worldwide. An 1898 article in *Popular Science* encapsulated Lombroso's doctrine:

> The delinquent, they argue, acts abnormally. Acts being the visible results of functions performed by the brain and reflective nervous system, it follows that these functions are abnormal. . . . The founders of this new school, therefore, dedicate themselves first of all to the study of the skull, brain, and nervous system of the criminals. . . . The brain itself, say the investigators, shows unmistakable signs of a degraded form, in the number and distribution of the cerebral convolutions, in the entire atrophy of some parts, in the extraordinary development of others. The shape and structure of the skull and brain, says Lombroso, connects criminals very closely with primitive man, and even with his animal ancestors. Criminals . . . form a distinct species, in need of scientific investigation. . . . For the facts collected by Lombroso place beyond all doubt the intimate connection between crime and mental derangements which has so long been suspected to exist. Madmen and criminals belong to the same family . . . both classes are in a similar pathological state, which manifests on the one hand in lunacy, on the other in crime (Zimmern 1898, 744–45, 746–47).

Lombroso's hunches about the innate nature of criminality were speculative musings not unlike those of novelists. It was the autopsy in 1870 of Giuseppe Villella, Lombroso tells us, that led to his flash of insight that criminality was an outcome of "atavism," a heritable degenerative disorder. Lombroso describes his epiphany thusly:

> A brigand from Calabria, Villella, had a median occipital fossetta of extraordinary dimensions. . . . Such a brain suggests not the sublimity of the primate, but the lower level of the rodent or lemur, or the brain of a human fetus of three or four months (Lombroso in Olson 2013, 279; see also Gibson 2006; Lombroso 2006, 47–48, Rafter, Posick, and Rocque 2016, 72).

According to Rafter, Posick, and Rocque (2016, 72), this is the moment criminal anthropology's foundational myth was installed. With Lambroso's supposition of atavism, "The criminal was biologically linked to inferior animals. His deviance was thus the consequence of his constitution (of which the median occipital depression was nothing other than a morphological trait), which in turn amounted to an evolutionary throwback" (Mazzarello 2011, 98; see also Beirne 1995; Olson 2013; Rafter, Posick and Rocque 2016). The "atavist" was conceptualized as a defective and lower order humanoid, even animal. As Courtney Kenny (1910, 222; see also Horn 2003; Olson 2013; Rafter 1997) states, the "criminal's anatomical and physiological abnormalities . . . involved so much which was suggestive of the ape that it was an easy inference to regard them as returns to an ancestral animalism." As Paul Mazzarello (2011, 98) puts it, criminal anthropology was shaped by and also fed into a convergence of the "*mythological ethology* of the wild animal" and that of "primitive man."

> Lombroso had a disquieting habit of making sweeping generalizations about criminal offenders with little to no data in the way of empirical justification and support. Several of the chapters in the various editions of *Criminal Man* are a mere one to two pages in length and amount to little more than rambling thoughts or musings on disparate topics. . . . Lombroso studied an array of causes and correlates of crime that suggest an impressive generalist's interest in and scientific curiosity about the etiology of criminal behavior . . . despite all of his rhetoric, there is a surprising level of nuanced understanding and insight in Lombroso's work (DeLisi 2012, 7).

The "monstrous other" of criminal anthropology was at this time also becoming a central focus of a burgeoning true crime genre of fiction (Ross 1996; Schmid 2010; Wilson 2015), and it is interesting that Lombroso's "scientific" portrait of the criminal parallels this development (congruent with Sagarin's [1980] observations, described above).

Lombroso's discovery is the stuff of true crime but since his accounts of human animals are scientistic whereas someone such as author Daniel Dafoe's account of criminality is categorized as fiction, he is accorded a place in the standard view of criminology's history whereas the latter is excluded. Dafoe's, *Moll Flanders,* is arguably a proto-sociology, "a forerunner of such later works as descriptions of criminals by [journalist] Hutchins Hapgood, of a professional thief by Edwin Sutherland, of a safebreaker by Bill Chambliss, or of a professional fence by Carl Klockars" (Sagarin 1980, 79). Jeffrey Wilson (2015) has persuasively illustrated, in a fascinating account of the history of the term, "criminology," the modern field can be traced back to the nineteenth century English "Newgate tradition" of crime fiction which offered "systematic, rigorous, organized, and methodical" argument yet wasn't scientistic in its presentation. This lack of scientism accounts for the exclusion of true crime writing from the "standard view." The most significant difference between the scientist's narrative and that of fiction writers, according to Sagarin (1980, 78, 80), is the respective methods used to produce their understanding and the devices used to craft and present these. Novelists would tend to create compositional characters and utilize metaphor to explore whereas scientific accounts offer a composite drawn from a sufficient sample in which information is condensed and assembled into an ideal type as the result of inductive inference.

The nineteenth century was an era of great cultural and scientific advances. In this era we have the birth of the "three great modern prototypes of monstrosity" in Mary Shelley's *Frankenstein*, Robert Louis Stevenson's *Dr. Jekyll and Mr. Hyde*, and Bram Stoker's *Dracula* (Claeys 2017). We also see the rise of criminal anthropology and that specific type of monstrosity Lombroso named "atavism." As Nicole Rafter and Per Ystehede (2010) and others (e.g., Twine 2002, 72–73; Vrettos 1995; Yea 2016) have argued, much scientific thinking in the nineteenth century was influenced by fiction just as some fiction was driven by new scientific discoveries. Given Lombroso included "folklore, pictures of freaks, popular maxims, Shakespeare's characters, and improbable anecdotes as evidence for his theories" (Rafter, Posick and Rocque 2016, 85), it is not inconceivable that the atavist as monster is just as much a true crime fiction device as it is the result of scientific empiricism.

Many (such as Jacobsen and Peterson 2016; Piamonte 2015; Ruggiero 2003, 2015; Sagarin 1980; Schmid 2010; Wilson 2015; and others) have argued for the criminological utility of literature, as great novelists explore and debate the human condition through their constructed fictional realities, but no one argues that Dostoevsky, Shakespeare, Balzac, or many other insightful writers, are criminologists (see Ruggiero 2003; Sagarin 1980). In this same vein, however, no one has argued Lombroso be regarded as a novelist, but perhaps such an argument is overdue. As Rafter and Ystehede (2010) note, Lombroso's ideas were infused with the tropes of the gothic prominent in literature at the time and as has already been suggested his basic idea of the atavist as monster paralleled that of the burgeoning true crime genre of fiction.[8] As Uberto Gatti and Alfredo Verdi (2012, 22) argue, Lombroso's thinking was muddled as he failed properly to engage in verification of this hypothesis about atavism and this led to his work gradually taking on a literary tone, "so much so that this text [*Criminal Woman*] has been compared to the serialized novels that were in vogue at the time." Criminal anthropology is replete with engaging characters, the most famous being the "atavist." These are threatening others so different from "us" as to be seen as monsters. The protagonist is the criminal anthropologist who seeks to detect and then sequester the monster for the safety, security, political unity, and stability of the society.

Despite any advances he might have made for criminology and medicine, Lombroso's work contains within it an element of magical realism or fabulism. It is well-documented that Bram Stoker utilized the biological notion of criminality promulgated by Lombroso to construct the physiognomy of Dracula as an atavistic, degenerative monster. Stoker clearly references Lombroso in his novel (see Arata 1990; Dager 2014; Marshall 2000; Rafter and Ystehede 2010; Vrettos 1995, 171–73). This element of Lombroso's work—its focus on the gothic and its monsters—is drawn out and concretized in explicit fashion by Stoker. In a 1975 annotated version of the novel, the scholar Leonard Wolf juxtaposed the character Harker's full description of Dracula with Lombroso's portrait of criminal man (see also Harrowitz 1994b, 53–54; Vrettos 1995):

> Harker: His face was . . . aquiline, with a high bridge of the thin nose and peculiarly arched nostrils.
>
> Lombroso: [The criminal's] nose on the contrary . . . is often aquiline like the beak of a bird of prey.
>
> Harker: His eyebrows were very massive, almost meeting over the nose.
>
> Lombroso: The eyebrows are bushy and tend to meet across the nose.
>
> Harker: . . . his ears were pale and at the tops extremely pointed . . .
>
> Lombroso: . . . with a protuberance on the upper part of the posterior margin . . . a relic of the pointed ear.

Turning to Rafter and Ystehede (2010, 282):

> criminal anthropology turned the criminal into a creature utterly different from normal man: a vampire, an atavism, a degenerate, closer to apes and savages

> and rodents than to law-abiding citizens. Lombroso's science demonstrates how completely a science can absorb coloration from its social context. It shows that, to a degree not usually recognized, a science can be shaped by the artistic sensibilities and traditions of the times in which it develops.

Additionally, arguments have been made to see Stoker's Count Dracula as a metaphor for fear of the other and of internal colonialism in the Victoria era (Arata 1990; Dager 2014; Pick 1988). Although Lombroso's work and that of Stoker have been compared, much more should be made of the themes of internal colonialism and animalism that subtend Lombroso's work and how the atavistic character type plays out in this. Influenced as Lombroso was by both theories of heredity and evolutionary theory, he posited that criminals were a distinct species. The popularity of criminal anthropology's teratology at a time when there were widespread and pressing political concerns about southern Italians as too different to be assimilated into the new unified Italy (see Horn 2003; Pick 1986, 1989; Rafter, Posick and Rocque 2016) helped to cement processes of othering and differentiation as foundational for modern criminology with the other as abject object and effect.

THE POLITICS OF MONSTER DETECTION

Lombroso, according to Kenny (1910, 221), at least early in his career, was known as the "scales-and-weights surgeon." He was working at a time when medicine, science, and the social science were undergoing great epistemological and methodological change, and Western societies, Italy especially, major social and political upheaval.[9] He was among the first to apply a type of positivistic methodology to the study of criminals (Mazzarello 2011,100). He utilized physiognomy and employed the anthropological technique of anthropometry to classify, catalogue, and compare the bodies of criminals and, later, all manner of non-conformists (see Twine 2002).[10] He interpreted what he observed through an eclectic amalgam of phrenology, Spencerian social Darwinism, and Haeckel's degeneration theory (Gatti and Verde 2012; Gould 1996, 142-75; Mazarello 2011). For Lombroso the backwardness of Italy's south, the perceived threat this posed to the strength of the new state, and the need to forge a post-unification national Italian identity were pressing problems (Pick 1986).

The newly formed modern Italian state presented pressing political and economic problems to which Lombroso and others responded. It was believed that criminal anthropology could and should inform social policy and play an important role in a newly unified Italy, particularly in the drafting of a new criminal code (Pick 1986). "Through science," Gatti and Verde (2012, 24) state, "he strove to modernize Italy, which at that time was somewhat backward, by acting as a conduit for the most important scientific currents in Europe and by adopting a rational approach to the problems of poverty, mental illness, and diseases caused by deprivation and poverty, particularly in the southern regions of Italy." Lombroso did this in an attempt to advance Italian interests in the scientific community abroad and to produce politically useful knowledge that could be immediately employed in policy to deal with the "Southern question" that cast Southern Italians with their darker skin and pauperism as "other" (Gatti and Verde 2012, 24; Gibson 2002; Gibson and Rafter 2006, 13–15; Horn 2003; Nye 1976; Pick 1989). This was the problem of what constituted an "Italian" as a moral and political subject. The political designation of the criminal is bound up, in complex ways, with the opposing but reciprocal process of defining the good citizen, or the good subject and the need to defend a newly unified state against the potential political and moral danger posed by "somatic deviance" (Mazzarello 2011: 99; see also Garland 1985; Gatti and Verde 2012, 24; Nye 1976; Pick 1986, 61; Rafter, Posick and Rocque 2016).

The populations diseased with cretinism and pellagra that Lombroso studied in the late 1850s (Wolfgang 1961, 362) were formative for his eventual interest in criminality. His next study was of ethnic diversity, and he took 3,000 Italian army soldiers as his sample (Pick 1986, 62; Wolfgang 1961, 362). It is with this work that he began to employ photography and physiognomy as he would do, famously, with his study of criminals. In these early studies we see the impact of not only Darwin's work but also pre-Darwinian theories of heredity as well as the use of "weights and scales" typical of physical anthropology and the study of morbidity. Lombroso held a tepid commitment to biological determinism at this time (Pick 1986, 62), but with the autopsy of Villella some years later Lombroso was moved to fully embrace this aetiology. The latter studies on criminality are simply an extension of his earlier work. Key in all of this, as David Pick (1986) is at pains to stress, is the political context of this writing. Criminal anthropology's mission was prevention: prevention of crime and of, importantly, the destabilization of Italian society. As Pick (1986, 76) characterizes it, criminal anthropology had to do with the "containment of disorder" and, in order to do this, it helped to elaborate "criteria for political exclusion" and, concomitantly, construction of the "Italian Subject" based on his biomedical aetiology.[11]

LOMBROSO'S TERATOLOGICAL PARADIGM

Lombroso died in 1909 yet his work continued to influence criminology in a paradigmatic way into the twentieth century and beyond (Gibson 2002, 129; Rafter 1997, Rafter, Posick, and Roque 2016, 73; Simon 2006).[12] Of Lombroso's *Criminal Man* De Quiros (1912, 234) states:

> His book has been thought by some almost as a revelation, by others as the most baneful the Code has ever known, and by others, more kindly inclined, as an attempt to solve certain questions already known and discussed by a small professional circle, affirming the existence of a man fully destined to crime by nature, absolutely incorrigible and ostensibly revealed in a monstrous type, with its list of unheard-of theories, like atavism, epilepsy, infantilism, etc.

In Thomas Kuhn's (1962/1996, 19–20, 136–40) monumentally influential text, *The Structure of Scientific Revolutions*, he argues that the "textbook" is the hallmark of a mature and established field of inquiry as it offers a specification of that field's governing paradigm. The textbook does not seek to convey arguments for a theoretical model or explanation but simply conveys this information as the intellectual foundation of a field of study, a foundation that is largely taken for granted in order to alleviate researchers from having to expound first principles to get on with the business of "normal science." Such texts in criminology begin to appear after Lombroso's 1876 text, *Criminal Man*. Lombroso's text is an example of a "pre-paradigmatic" text that seeks to establish a governing framework and new field of enquiry.

In England, Havelock Ellis's (1890), *The Criminal*, offers an overview of criminal anthropology as if it is an already established field. As Arthur MacDonald's (1890) review in the *American Journal of Psychology* indicates, there is nothing original in this book, but this is what one would expect from a textbook. As Kuhn (1996, 137) has argued, textbooks "record the stable outcome of past revolutions and thus display the bases of the current normal-scientific tradition." In doing so they are often misleading in that they portray a field as internally coherent and as emerging slowly, piece by piece over time, but as this is "not the way a science develops" what textbooks do best is provide a reconstruction of a field's history (Kuhn 1996, 137–140). As Havelock Ellis (1890) states in his Preface, the aim of the text is simply to "present to the English reader a critical summary of the results of the science now commonly called criminal anthropology," not to engage in debate or defense of the doctrine. It presents the precepts from within which one can understand and investigate the puzzles of criminal anthropology and, in so doing, further refine, extend, and entrench criminal anthropology as a science. In 1892 in the United States Arthur MacDonald published his textbook, *Criminology,* which is dedicated to "Cesare Lombroso the founder of criminology." This text also reiterated the basic tenets of criminal anthropology but also goes beyond this to outline the science of "criminology."[13] With this work the foundation of "criminology" as a distinct science is laid, incorporating not only Lombroso but also the more sociological work of Enrico Ferri and others.

Importantly, Lombroso's paradigmatic impact was not a result of a concern with "criminogenesis" but rather with "teratogenesis" or the production of human malformations. Teratology is

> a branch of medicine, schemes for classifying congenital malformations, like those for disease, fall mostly into the categories of causation, pathogenesis, and outcome. Systems founded on causation—etiology—are ultimately oriented toward prevention, in distinction to those based on pathogenesis and outcome, which are directed as much toward theoretical considerations (Kalter 2010, 6).

Lombroso's teratological orientation comes through in several interpretations of his writings. Of her father's work, Gina Lombroso states:

> This fact, that the germs of moral insanity and criminality are found normally in mankind in the first stages of his existence, in the same way as forms considered monstrous when exhibited by adults, frequently exist in the foetus, is such a simple and common phenomenon that it eluded notice until it was demonstrated clearly by observers like Moreau, Perez, and Bain. The child, like certain adults, whose abnormality consists in a lack of moral sense, represents what is known to alienists as a morally insane being and to criminologists as a born criminal, and it certainly resembles these types in its impetuous violence (G. Lombroso 1911, 130).[14]

And as C. Bernaldo De Quiros writes:

> As for the method, we can easily perceive that in the beginning it consisted in the mere accumulation of all that appeared abnormal and teratologic, namely, the criminalization of every unusual trait, which, as a result, gives us a type of the most abstract nature (De Quiros 1912, 18).

MacDonald (1892, 53, 55) remarks that Lombroso finds a "distinctive teratological character from the union of many anomalies in the same cranium . . . . Those anomalies seem to him to result from errors in development of the foetal cranium, or from diseases slowly evolving from the nervous centres." Pick (1986, 80) in passing makes reference to Jules Dallemagne, a contemporary and detractor of Lombroso's work, stating he "rejected Lombroso's obsession with tabulating the superficially monstrous, (his 'teratology' as Dallemagne put it)." In a lengthy piece on the death of Lombroso, Kenny (1910, 221) mentions the early nineteenth century evolutionary biology of Geoffrey St.

Hilaire (discussed below) and nonchalantly stipulates, "Lombroso, in the pages of *L'Uomo Delinquente*, essayed to create an equally scientific teratology of the abnormalities of men's moral nature." In his Preface to his *Man of Genius* from 1896 (v, vii–viii), Lombroso clearly situates his work within the realm of this medical subfield:

> But recent teratological researches . . . have shown that the phenomena of atavistic retrogression do not always indicate true degradation. . . . Hailes, in a much praised essay on genius in art, maintains that genius is a continuation of the conditions of ordinary life; thus, as we all write prose we must all have a little genius. But how then does it happen, Brunetière rightly objects, that one individual alone becomes a great painter or a great poet? And how is it that so many philosophers affirm, and quite truly, that genius consists in an exaggerated development of one faculty at the expense of others?
>
> The man of genius is a monster, say others. Very well, but even monsters follow well-defined teratologic laws.

And again in chapter 1 (1896, 2):

> Even genius, the one human power before which we may bow the knee without shame, has been classed by not a few alienists as on the confines of criminality, one of the teratologic forms of the human mind, a variety of insanity.

In his introduction to his daughter's book on his work, Lombroso writes:

> Thus, by reducing the penal problem, its solution was rendered easier, just as the study of embryology has in a great measure solved the apparently strange and mysterious riddle of teratology (Lombroso 1911, xvii).

The view that the atavist was not a fully formed or developed human being, a life form that was not fully evolved, a defective human being, followed from the medical knowledge of the day, infused with evolutionary ideas drawn from the work of Jean-Baptiste Lamarck, Ernst Haeckel, and Charles Darwin. Lombroso's fetishizing of the bodies of criminals was to detect the defects that made them monsters. Thus measuring body parts was not to inductively produce an ideal type, the criminal, but to chart the deviation of criminals' bodies from the medical norm following deductive inference. David Horn concurs, noting Lombroso focused on "monstrous reversions in modern humans" (2003, 32, 41). As quoted in Horn (2003, 32), Giuliano Pancaldi argued that Lombroso applied "teratological and embryological concepts to psychological phenomena" in an attempt to demonstrate a connection between criminality and animality. Mary Gibson and Nicole Rafter (2006, 17), in their discussion of Lombroso's *Criminal Woman* indicate, too, that Lombroso held female criminals to be "true monsters."

In the late nineteenth century at the same time Lombroso posits his theory of atavism, teratology as a medical subfield was established (see Ballantyne 1895, 1897, 1902; Barrow 1971; Ujházy et al. 2012). Barrow argues the modern medical study of monstrosities begins with the work of French naturalist Etienne Geoffroy Saint-Hilaire, "the first experimental teratologist of any note" (1971, 125). Saint-Hilaire's 1822 text, *Philosophie Anatomique des Monstruosités Humaines*, about human malformation, was drawn from experiments he had performed on chick embryos. Etienne Saint-Hilaire's son, Isidore Geoffroy Saint-Hilaire, produced, *Histoire générale et particulière des anomalies de l'organisation chez l'homme et les animaux* (1836) on the characteristics of teratology (of which the latter term was coined by him). The Saint-Hilaires' path-breaking work informed the work of Gabriel Madeleine Camille Dareste's five principles of experimental teratology published in 1877 and Dareste's 1891 text *Recherches sur la production artificielle des monstruosités: ou, Essais de tératogénie expérimentale*. All of these texts were pivotal for shifting explanations of birth defects away from those based on superstition and the supernatural—from metaphysics—to more materialist explanations (see Ballantyne 1897). It is almost certain the nineteenth century transformation of medicine and particularly developments in teratology shaped Lombroso's view of atavists as monsters. Mary Gibson (2002, 20) notes Lombroso was "an indefatigable reader of several languages and . . . drew on a large and international body of literature not only in medicine and penology but also history and linguistics." Engaged in medical jurisprudence and having had medical training that included study with a known teratologist (Wolfgang 1961, 362), Lombroso would have been familiar with these seminal texts. Indeed, Lombroso speaks of Saint-Hilaire the elder in his Preface to MacDonald's (1892) textbook, *Criminology*.

For medical practitioners of Lombroso's day, monsters where not metaphorical or mythological, they were real. Dunglison's *Medical Lexicon* of 1853 and 1876 (Dunglison and Dunglison) defines "monster" as, "Any organized being, having an extraordinary vice of conformation, or a preternatural perversion of every part, or of certain parts only" (1853, 569; 1876, 664). The later edition adds that a monster is "anything strange." The varied classifications indicate that "malformations" and "defects" are what distinguish a monster or "teras" as it is in Greek from a normal person. The study and production of a discourse on terata (the plural of "teras") is termed "teratology." Teratology in the 1800s concerned a discourse, description, and/or doctrine of monsters (Dunglison 1853, 848). The atavist—that criminal type Lombroso is most famous for, described in detail in Lombroso's five editions of *Criminal Man* and around which he produced the doctrine of criminal anthropology—was a monster within Lombroso's teratology.

Ballantyne is considered an important figure for furthering the transition within teratology from metaphysics to a materialist, scientific empiricist aetiology of monsters (Barrow 1971). At the time Lombroso was writing, J. W. Ballantyne was finishing his texts on fetal pathology (1902, 1904). This large work was preceded by his 1897 text on the various historical accounts of teratogenesis (the production of monsters) in an effort to move medicine away from what he viewed as folklore, fiction, and supernatural understandings. There existed several types of medical monsters and a great many "teratogenic theories" (Ballantyne 1897, 1) to explain their cause. Ballantyne (1897, 11) laments there are still those, including physicians, who are given to superstition and belief in supernatural explanations, too ready to characterize abnormal infants as monsters without explanation of their condition or want to understand it. After reviewing all theories of monstrosity (i.e., teratogenesis), past and present, he (1904, 235) presents his own synthesized schemata of "Terata (Monstrosities and Anomalies)." Below I reproduce Ballantyne's taxonomy to give some idea of the state of the art of teratological knowledge of which Lombroso would have surely been aware.

A. Monosomatous (a single individual involved).
- I. Pantosomatous (the anomaly affects the whole or nearly the whole body).
  - (a) Dwarfism (microsomia).
  - (b) Giantism (macrosomia).
  - (c) Hemi-hypertrophy and Hemi-atrophy.
- II. Merosomatous (the anomaly affects only a part of the body).
  - (a) Partial Macrosomia and Microsomia of various Parts.
  - (b) Spinal Column and Contents, Anomlies of.
  - (c) Cranium and Contents, Anomalies of.
  - (d) Face and Sense Organs, Anomalies of.
  - (e) Neck and Constituent Parts, Anomalies of.
  - (f) Thorax and Contents, Anomalies of.
  - (g) Abdomen and Pelvis and Contents, Anomalies of.
  - (h) Limbs, Anomalies of.
  - (i) Annexa (Placenta, Cord, Amnion), Anomalies of.
- III. Heterotaxic (the anomaly affects only the arrangement of the parts of the body) (Ballantyne 1904: 235).

The idea here is not that Lombroso followed Ballantyne's scheme but that Lombroso's concern with what he believed were observable physical defects indicating atavism and criminality can be seen as a concern with what Ballantyne outlines as Merosomatous. In measuring, comparing, arranging, and classifying the parts of criminals' bodies, most famously their skulls, Lombroso adhered to a teratological taxonomy of defect detection. Although *Criminal Man* was published in 1876 and Ballantyne's taxonomy was published in 1904, because Ballantyne is simply synthesizing already existing ideas about teratogenesis (from the seventeenth century and later), it stands to reason that his scheme captures well the ideas that Lombroso put to use.

Lombroso's first criminal type, the atavist, is a category of monstrosity, a "teratological type" (see Ballantyne 1904, 241). Lombroso's atavists were discerned as a class and became central to campaigns of societal protection and defense, especially important in an era of unsettled debate over the Southern Question concerning the ideal Italian subject and that of Italian nationality. If medicine is about protecting men and women against illness (Shyrock 1969) and atavism was a disease, it would seem self-evident that atavists were teratogens that threatened a healthy polity and ought to be eliminated. If atavism was a "species of illness," then the criminality of the atavist was itself a species of social ill (Shyrock 1969). Disease in the criminal body made the criminal body a disease in the political body.

CONCLUSION

Lombroso was an "influential figure for medical positivism . . . among the first to consider criminality, in men and women, as a phenomenon worthy of scientific study" (Mazzarello 2011, 100). Lombroso's view of "criminal man" was consistent with the medical subfield of teratology and his contribution to criminology was to bring medical jurisprudence and the field of teratology to bear on the study of and construction of "criminal man" as a political, moral, and medical problem. He appears in the history of criminology as a character in an origin myth but was not concerned with "criminogenesis" *per se* but rather "teratogenesis." Lombroso's Atavistic Man, an incorrigible genetic throwback incapable of following the rules, is a monster suffering from a congenital disorder; and criminal anthropology, as a teratology, is a science of monster detection. By implication this makes Lombroso a real-life Van Helsing. Given the teratological orientation of Lombroso's work, the standard view of criminology's origins ought to be revisited.

NOTES

1. The account of Lombroso as a monumentally important figure for modern criminology is so prevalent that it has passed into the criminological common sense, thus it has become part of the "standard view" of criminology's origins. Gibson's

(2002, 2006, with Rafter 2006) and Rafter's (1997, 2006a and b, 2008, with Posick and Rocque 2016) work on Lombroso has done much to ossify this claim. Gibson and Rafter (2006, 3) claim that Lombroso's, *Criminal Man*, is "the founding text of criminology." Rafter, Posick and Rocque (2016, 70) claim Lombroso "was undoubtedly the most significant . . . figure in the entire history of criminology." Intellectual histories, such as by Wolfgang (1961) and Jeffrey (1959), situate Lombroso as the father of modern criminology. Goff's (1986) article on sociological and psychiatric explanations of crime in the early twentieth century, as another example, ignores the important contributions of an antecedent French positivist sociological tradition but includes those of criminal anthropology. Garland (1985, 109), in his "critical account of the formation of criminology at the end of the nineteenth century" does not claim for Lombroso the status of the first scientific criminologist but does hold that it was only after the appearance of his text, *L'Uomo Delinquente* in 1876 that criminology developed into a "programme of investigation and social action." Criminologist Anthony Walsh (2003, 2), in his review of Gibson's book on Lombroso, *Born to Crime*, also relates the view that Lombroso is the father of criminology. Lindesmith and Levin's (1937) early twentieth century criticism of the "myth" of Lombroso's founding status suggests his place in the standard view has long been entrenched.

2. Medical jurisprudence is a field of medicine, not law, which deals with how medical science can be brought to bear on legal problems (Clark and Crawford 1994). For example Lombroso's idea that innate biological defects compelled people to engage in criminal conduct challenged directly the Classical School's conception of free will, rational calculation, and moral responsibility and hence also the legal precepts founded upon these classical ideas. Teratology "is an old human concernment," as Kalter (2010, 1) elaborates, which entails "the search for the causes of human prenatal maldevelopment."

3. See Jeffrey (1959) for the classic treatment of criminology's history as a battle between "classicism" and "positivism." See also Garland (1985) for his history as a contrast between a biomedical positivist criminology and the rationalism of classicism.

4. The French contribution to positivist criminology is largely overlooked (see Shichor 2010).

5. Positivism as a form of empiricism is a philosophy of science that holds all scientific knowledge must be verifiable and must be derived from the senses. Auguste Comte argued that we could only attain true knowledge through science, not through metaphysics or religion. Positivism as a method of producing scientific knowledge requires the use of both *a priori* knowledge (axioms or truths that are held to simply exist and from which one can deduce an hypothesis) and *a posteriori* knowledge (produced and verified via sensory experience and interpreted through reason and logic). Positivism at the time of Lombroso was espoused by many, including the influential English philosopher and sociologist Herbert Spencer, who also promoted evolutionist theory.

6. According to Mazzarello (2011), Lombroso read Darwin but did not understand him. It is likely he read Charles Darwin's *On the Origin of Species* with Herbert Spencer's "Social Darwinism" in mind. Many suggest it was a combination of Spencer, Darwin, the degeneration theory of Benedict Morel, and "recapitulation" theory of

arrested development promoted by Ernst Haeckel that informed Lombroso's views (Gould 1996; Mazzarello 2011, 98; Rafter, Posick and Rocque 2016, 78–79). As Spencer's views were informed by Lamarckian evolutionary theory and Haeckel's views were informed by Morel's social degeneration theory (also influenced by Lamarckism), they would have been largely incompatible with Darwin's views. French naturalist Jean-Baptiste Lamarck emphasized "use inheritance" (that traits developed and strongly used in adapting to environments are passed down as others wither and are eventually lost). This idea is seen in the work of phrenologists such as Johann Spurzheim who believed the more a faculty of the brain was utilized the larger it would get and, in turn, a corresponding region on the skull would be pronounced. The inconsistency in Lombroso's thought—the elements of Morel and Haeckel, on the one hand, and Darwin's views, on the other—manifests what Pick (1989, 112) and others have observed as Lombroso's confusion: "His conception of evolution was not Darwinian as such (although he did read Darwin), but a conflation of contemporary biological and anthropological ideas from many authors such as Moleschott, Morel, Haeckel, Broca and Spencer." Lombroso's eclecticism led to a logical problem that hampered his criminal anthropology, namely a "flawed concept of evolution" (Nye 1976, 350). Rafter et al. (2016, 80) echo this in their study of Lombroso, stating "his thinking about the causes of crime was massively incoherent." Lombroso's views that "atavism" (inherited criminality) was a degenerative condition and that criminals were human beings who had experienced an arrested development *in utero* are derived in large part from Haeckel's notion of "recapitulation" but he did not adopt, or only weakly adopted, the "French Lamarckian tradition (with its stress on use-inheritance and hence environmental agency)" in favor of "an Italian strand of Darwinism (stressing racial struggle, selection, elimination, regression" (Pick 1989, 113; see Gould 1996 on Haeckel; see Horn 2003 and Pick 1989 on Lombroso's degeneration theory).

7. See Conrad and Schneider (1992).

8. See Yea (2016) for her analysis of Lombroso's influence on the French novelist Émile Zola.

9. Darwin had recently published his monumentally important *The Origin of the Species*, and Herbert Spencer had coined the term "survival of the fittest" and argued for what would become known as Social Darwinism. Additionally, medicine was undergoing professionalization, sociology was in its infancy, and physics and chemistry were undergoing paradigmatic change.

10. Physiognomy is the moral interpretation of facial features and was important to the development of phrenology, the study of the skull for how it made manifest inner moral and intellectual characteristics of the individual (Twine 2002). Anthropometry is the comparative and quantitative study of the measurements of the human body (see Gould 1996). Later editions of Lombroso's famous book, *Criminal Man*, did look toward environmental and social triggers of criminality as he felt pressured by the French as well as his colleagues Enrico Ferri and Rafaele Garofalo to include these. Lombroso's staunchest opponents were the French positivists who argued (without dismissing biology) that social and environmental conditions played a key role in the genesis of crime (Gatti and Verde 2012; Nye 1976; Shichor 2010). Belgian Adolphe

Quetelet and Frenchman André-Michel Guerry installed "moral statistics" as the use of aggregate data to map crime by variables such as age, sex, race, poverty, and education, among others, thus inventing the "cartographic school" of "social physics" (later "sociology"). They understood causes of crime to be largely environmental and societal. Quetelet also invented the concept of "average man" and thus in some regard helped usher in a fledgling sociology of deviance. This "French School," a coalition of French scholars unified against criminal anthropology, which included Gabriel Tarde and Alexandre Lacassagne, was largely responsible for the waning of criminal anthropology (see Nye 1976). In the standard view it is the work of Charles Goring that is presented as responsible for the eventual discrediting of the Italian School.

11. For an interesting discussion of Lombroso, see Montessori (1913), who elaborated what is now referred to as the Montessori method of education. Based on Lombroso's later understanding of the socio-biological nature of degeneration—the "Lombrosian doctrine" as she (1913, 8) called it—Montessori (1913, 9) argued, "Now, if it is not yet in our power to achieve a social reform based on the eradication of degenerative causes—since society can be perfected only gradually—it is nevertheless within our power to *prepare the conscience* for acceptance of the new morality, and by *educational* means to help along the civil progress which science has revealed to us." This is clearly about the constitution of what is considered to be the ideal citizen.

12. As Gibson states, "Lombroso's radically new approach to the issue of crime came primarily from his training in medicine rather than law" (2002, 19); and so even into the early twentieth century in Italy, "In the academic world, criminology remained a subdiscipline within medical schools, assuring a continuing emphasis on the biological origins of crime" (Gibson 2002, 129).

13. In 1893 Arthur MacDonald published his four-hundred-plus-page *Abnormal Man: Being Essays on Crime and Education and Related Subjects* through the US Bureau of Education.

14. One of three main explanations of monstrosity on offer in the late nineteenth was germ theory—atavism was thought to be due to "a primitive defect in the germs" where "germ" is defined as "the rudiment of a new being" (Dunglison 1853; Dunglison and Dunglison 1876).

REFERENCES

Arata, Stephen D. 1990. "The Occidental Tourist: 'Dracula' and the Anxiety of Reverse Colonization." *Victorian Studies* 33, no. 4: 621–645.

Ballantyne, J. W. 1895. *The Diseases and Deformities of the Foetus: An Attempt Towards a System of Ante-Natal Pathology*. Volume II. Edinburgh: Oliver and Boyd.

———. 1897. *Teratogenesis: An Inquiry Into the Causes of Monstrosities*. Edinburgh: Oliver and Boyd.

———. 1902. *Manual of Antenatal Pathology and Hygiene, The Foetus*. Edinburgh: William Green & Sons.

———. 1904. *Manual of Antenatal Pathology and Hygiene*, The Embryo. Edinburgh: William Green & Sons.

Barrow, Mark V. 1971. "A Brief History of Teratology to the Early 20th Century." *Teratology* 4, no. 2: 119–29.

Becker, Peter and Richard Wetzell. 2006. "Introduction." In *Criminals and Their Scientists: The History of Criminology in International Perspective*, edited by P. Becker and R. Wetzell, 1–24. New York: Cambridge University Press.

Beirne, Piers. 1995. "The Use and Abuse of Animals in Criminology: A Brief History and Current Review." *Social Justice* 22, no. 1: 5–31.

Carrier, Nicolas and Kevin Walby. 2014. "Ptolemizing Lombroso: The Pseudo-Revolution of Biosocial Criminology." *Journal of Theoretical and Philosophical Criminology* 6, no. 1: 1–45.

Cassata, Francesco. 2011. *Building the New Man: Eugenics, Racial Science and Genetics in Twentieth-Century Italy.* New edition [online]. Budapest: Central European University Press. http://books.openedition.org/ceup/697.

Claeys, Gregory. 2017. *Dystopia: A Natural History*. Oxford: Oxford University Press.

Clark, Michael and Crawford, Catherine, eds. 1994. *Legal Medicine in History*. Cambridge: Cambridge University Press.

Conrad, Peter and Joseph Schneider. 1992. *Deviance and Medicalization*, expanded edition. Philadelphia: Temple University Press.

Dager, Katey, 2014. "Reverse Colonization as a Function of Criminal Atavism in Bram Stoker's Dracula." *Emergence: A Journal of Undergraduate Literary Criticism and Creative Research* 5: 51–64.

De Quiros, C. Bernaldo. 1912. *Modern Theories of Criminality*. Boston: Little, Brown, and Company.

DeLisi, Matt. 2012. "Revisiting Lombroso." *The Oxford Handbook of Criminological Theory*, edited by Francis T. Cullen and Pamela Wilcox, 5–21. New York: Oxford University Press.

Dunglison, Robley. 1853. *Medical Lexicon: Dictionary of Medical Science*, ninth edition. Philadelphia: Blanchard and Lea.

Dunglison, Robley and Richard Dunglison. 1876. *Medical Lexicon: Dictionary of Medical Science*. London: J.A. Churchill.

Ellis, Havelock. 1890. *The Criminal*. London: Walter Scott.

Ellwood, Charles A. 1912. "Lombroso's Theory of Crime." *Journal of Criminal Law and Criminology* 2, no. 5: 716–23.

Garland, David. 1985. "'The Criminal and His Science: A Critical Account of the Formation of Criminology at the End of the Nineteenth Century." *British Journal of Criminology* 25(2): 109–137.

Gatti, Uberto and Alfredo Verde. 2012. "Cesare Lombroso: Methodological Ambiguities and Brilliant Intuitions." *International Journal of Law and Psychiatry* 35: 19–26.

Gibson, Mary. 2002. *Born to Crime: Cesare Lombroso and the Origins of Biological Criminology*. Westport, CT: Praeger.

———. 2006. "Cesare Lombroso and Italian Criminology." In *Criminals and Their Scientists*, edited by P. Becker and R. Wetzell, 137–158. New York: Cambridge University Press.

Gibson, Mary and Nicole Hahn Rafter. 2006. "Introduction." In C. Lombroso, *Criminal Man*, 1–36. Durham, NC: Duke University Press. (Original work published 1876 and 1897.)

Gilman, Sander. 1997. "Review of *Der falsche Körper Beiträge zu einer Geschichte der Monstrositäten*."*Medical History* 41, no. 1: 119–20.

Goff, Colin. 1986. "Criminological Appraisals of Psychiatric Explanations of Crime: 1936–1950." *International Journal of Law and Psychiatry* 9: 245–60.

Gould, Stephen Jay. 1996. *The Mismeasure of Man*. Revised and expanded edition. New York: W.W. Norton and Company.

Harrowitz, Nancy A. 1994a. "Lombroso and the Logic of Intolerance." In *Tainted Greatness: Anti-Semitism and Cultural Heroes*, edited by N. Harrowitz, 109–26. Philadelphia: Temple University Press.

———. 1994b. *Antisemitism, Misogyny, & the Logic of Cultural Difference: Cesare Lombroso and Matilde Serao*. London: University of Nebraska Press.

Horn, David. 2003. *The Criminal Body: Lombroso and the Anatomy of Deviance*. New York: Routledge.

Jacobsen, Michael Hviid and Anders Peterson. 2016. "Contours of a Cinematic Criminology: Distillation, Dramatization, Distortion and Anecdotal Data." In *Framing Law and Crime*, edited by C.J.S. Picart, M.H. Jacobsen, and C. Greek, 401–431. Lanham, MD: Fairleigh Dickinson University Press/Rowman & Littlefield.

Jeffrey, Clarence Ray. 1959. "The Historical Development of Criminology." *Journal of Criminal Law and Criminology* 1: 3–19.

Kalter, Harold. 2010. *Teratology in the Twentieth Century Plus Ten*. New York: Springer.

Kenny, Courtney. 1910. "The Death of Lombroso." *Journal of the Society of Comparative Legislation* 10, no. 2: 220–28.

Kuhn, Thomas. 1996. *The Structure of Scientific Revolutions*, third edition. Chicago: University of Chicago Press.

Kurella, Hans. 1911. *Cesare Lombroso: A Modern Man of Science*. New York: Rebman Company.

Lindesmith, Alfred and Yale Levin. 1937. "The Lombrosian Myth in Criminology." *American Journal of Sociology* 42: 653–71.

Lombroso, Cesare. 2006. *Criminal Man*. Translated with an introduction by M. Gibson and N. Rafter. Raleigh, NC: Duke University Press.

———. 1911. "Introduction." In Gina Lombroso, *Criminal Man, According to the Classification of Cesare Lombroso*, xi–xix. New York: G.P. Putnam's Sons.

———.1898. "Regressive Phenomena in Evolution." *The Monist* 8, no. 3: 377–83.

———. 1891/1896. *Man of Genius*. New York: Charles Scribner's Sons.

Lombroso, Ceasar and William Ferrero. 1895. *The Female Offender*. New York: D. Appleton and Company.

Lombroso, Gina. 1911. *Criminal Man, According to the Classification of Cesare Lombroso*. New York: G. P. Putnam's Sons.

MacDonald, Arthur. 1890. "Review of Havelock Ellis, *The Criminal*." *The American Journal of Psychology* 3, no. 3: 395–97.

———. 1892. *Criminology*. New York: Funk & Wagnalls Company.

Marshall, Bridget. 2000. "The Face Of Evil: Phrenology, Physiognomy, and The Gothic Villain." *Hungarian Journal of English and American Studies* 6, no. 2: 161–72.

Mazzarello, Paul. 2011. "Cesare Lombroso: An Anthropologist Between Evolution and Degeneration." *Functional Neurology* 26, no. 2: 97–101.

Monachesi, Elio D. 1936. "Trends in Criminological Research in Italy." *American Sociological Review* 1, no. 3: 396–406.

Montessori, Maria. 1913. *Pedagogical Anthropology*. Frederick A. Stokes Company.

Nye, Robert. 1976. "Heredity or Milieu: The Foundations of Modern European Criminological Theory." *Isis* 67, no. 3: 334–55.

Olson, Greta. 2013. *Criminals as Animals: From Shakespeare to Lombroso*. New York: deGruyter.

Piamonte, Stephanie. 2015. "The Criminological Imagination and the Promise of Fiction." In *C. Wright Mills and the Criminological Imagination: Prospects for Creative Enquiry*, edited by Jon Frauley, 241–54. Farnham, UK: Ashgate Publishing.

Pick, Daniel. 1986. "The Faces of Anarchy: Lombroso and the Politics of Criminal Science in Post-unification Italy." *History Workshop Journal* 21, no. 1: 60–86.

———. 1988. "'Terrors of the Night': Dracula and 'Degeneration' in the Late Nineteenth Century." *Critical Quarterly* 30, no. 4: 71–87.

———. 1989. *Faces of Degeneration*. New York: Cambridge University Press.

Rafter, Nicole. 1997. *Creating Born Criminals*. Chicago: University of Illinois Press.

———. 2006a. "Cesare Lombroso and the Origins of Criminology: Rethinking Criminological Tradition." In *The Essential Criminology Reader*, edited by S. Henry and M. Lanier, 33–42. Boulder, CO: Westview Press.

———. 2006b. "Criminal Anthropology: Its Reception in the United States and the Nature of Its Appeal." In *Criminals and Their Scientists*, edited by P. Becker and R. Wetzell, 159–82. New York: Cambridge University Press.

———. 2008. *The Criminal Brain: Understanding Biological Theories of Crime*. New York: NYU Press.

Rafter, Nicole and Per Ystehede. 2010. "Here Be Dragons: Lombroso, the Gothic, and Social Control." *Sociology of Crime, Law and Deviance* 14: 263–84.

Rafter, Nicole, Chad Posick and Michael Rocque. 2016. *The Criminal Brain: Understanding Biological Theories of Crime*, second edition. New York: NYU Press.

Roberts, Mark. 2008. *The Mark of the Beast: Animality and Human Oppression*. West Lafayette, IN: Purdue University Press.

Ross, Alex. 1996. "The Shock of the True." *The New Yorker*, Aug 19, 70–77

Ruggiero, Vincenzo. 2003. *Crime in Literature: Sociology of Deviance and Fiction*. New York: Verso.

———. 2015. "Balzac and the Crimes of the Powerful." *Societies* 5: 325–38.

Sagarin, Edward. 1980. "In Search of Criminology Through Fiction." *Deviant Behavior* 2, no. 1: 73–91.

Saint Hilaire, Etienne Geoffroy. 1822. *Philosophie Anatomique des Monstruosités Humaines*. Paris: Rignoux.

Schmid, David. 2010. "True Crime." In *A Blackwell Companion to Crime Fiction*, edited by C. J. Rzepka and L. Horsley, 198–209. Oxford: Wiley-Blackwell.

Seidman, Steven. 2013. "Defilement and Disgust: Theorizing the Other." *American Journal of Cultural Sociology* 1, no. 1: 3–25.

Shichor, David. 2010. "The French–Italian Controversy: A Neglected Historical Topic in Criminological Literacy." *Journal of Criminal Justice Education* 21, no. 3: 211–28.

Shryock, Richard H. 1969. "Empiricism Versus Rationalism In American Medicine, 1650–1950." *Proceedings of the American Antiquarian Society* 79, no. 1: 99–150.

Simon, Jonathan. 2006. "Positively Punitive: How the Inventor of Scientific Criminology Who Died at the Beginning of the Twentieth Century Continues to Haunt American Crime Control at the Beginning of the Twenty-First." *Texas Law Review* 84: 2135–72.

Twine, Richard. 2002. "Physiognomy, Phrenology and the Temporality of the Body." *Body & Society* 8, no. 1: 67–88.

Ujházy, Eduard, Mojmír Mach, Jana Navarová, Ingrid Brucknerová, and Michal Dubovicky. 2012. "Teratology—Past, Present and Future." *Interdisciplinary Toxicology* 5, no. 4: 163–68.

Vrettos, Athena. 1995. *Somatic Fictions: Imagining Illness in Victorian Culture*. Stanford, CA: Stanford University Press.

Walsh, Anthony. 2003. "The Holy Trinity and the Legacy of the Italian School of Criminal Anthropology." *Human Nature Review* 3: 1–11.

Warkany, Josef. 1977. "History of Teratology." In *The Handbook of Teratology, Vol 1 General Principles of Etiology*, edited by James Wilson, 3–74. New York: Plenum Press.

Wilson, Jeffrey. 2015. "The Word Criminology: A Philology and a Definition." *Criminology, Criminal Justice, Law & Society* 16, no. 3: 61–82.

Wolfgang, Marvin. 1961. "Pioneers in Criminology: Cesare Lombroso (1835–1909)." *The Journal of Criminal Law, Criminology, and Police Science* 52, no. 4: 361–91.

Yea, Jennifer. 2016. *The Colonial Comedy: Imperialism in the French Realist Novel*. New York: Oxford University Press.

Zimmern, Helen. 1898. "Criminal Anthropology in Italy." *Popular Science*, April, 743–60.

Chapter Three

Vampire Fictions and the Conflation of Violent Criminality with Real Vampirism

A Practical Overview

John Edgar Browning and DJ Williams

INTRODUCTION

This chapter takes as its primary examples DJ Williams's (2017) article in the *Journal of Forensic Sciences* entitled, "Self-Identified Vampirism and Risk for False Positives: A Case Example of Team Homicide and Implications for Forensic Behavioral Science," a study examining a particular court case in which experts draw fallaciously upon occult religious discourses to implicate real (or human) vampirism as an explanation for certain violent crimes; and Williams and John Edgar Browning's (2016) chapter in *The Criminal Humanities: An Introduction (Criminal Humanities & Forensic Semiotics)* (ed. Michael Arntfield and Marcel Danesi) entitled, "Looking Inside the Coffin: An Overview of Contemporary Human Vampirism and Its Relevance for Forensics Professionals," a study that examines how forensic professionals can benefit from scholarship in Real Vampire Studies. This chapter builds upon these works by examining the media's conflation of fictional vampire narratives with real vampirism to characterize certain violent criminals and the subsequent effect this has had on the real vampire community. After briefly summarizing the general characteristics of the real vampire community, this study analyzes particular recent examples of real/reel vampire conflation by the media and then uses ethnographic data collected from real vampire communities to help illustrate its long- and short-term effects on outside perceptions of real vampirism.

GOTHIC CRIMINOLOGY: VIOLENT CRIMINALS AS VAMPIRES

For Caroline Joan "Kay" S. Picart and Cecil Greek (2007), the public's "ongoing fascination with evil, as simultaneously repellant and irresistibly attractive, both in the Hollywood film, criminological case studies, popular culture and even public policy," has given rise to what they term "Gothic criminology," an area of study in which are given particular importance the themes of "blood lust, compulsion, fear, godlike vengeance, and power and domination" (11). Gothic criminology, "[r]ather than assuming that film and the media tell us little about the reality of criminological phenomena," serves to recognize the "complementarity of critical academic and aesthetic accounts of deviant behavior as intersecting with public policy in complex, nonreductive ways" (ii). Picart and Greek use "Gothic criminology"[1] as a framework for mapping "the complex interactions between the 'real' and the 'reel' in the flow of Gothic metaphors and narratives regarding criminological phenomena that populate not only popular culture but also academic and public policy discourses" (see Picart, Jacobsen, and Greek 2016, 11). In short, "Gothic criminology" mythologizes figures like the serial killer "as a Gothic construction" (40), and in the process it

> gesture[s] towards an account that moves in between the realms of Gothic fiction and film, which entertains its horrified and fascinated readers with unreal horrors attendant upon a realistically/cogently imagined fictional world, and factual cases (e.g. of stalkers, serial murderers, terrorists, rouge cops) framed in Gothic terms, which are essential to plotting the social construction of where evil resides within modernity. (Picart and Greek 2007, 11)

For example, films like *Silence of the Lambs* (1990), *Immortality* (1998), and *Hannibal* (2001) demonstrate how the vampire and serial killer are able to blur seamlessly into one other, exploiting the vampire's "mythic power" and demonstrating in the process the "'natural' slippage from the realms of the natural/'cinema verite' to the supernatural/mythic [which] is what enables the Gothicization of the serial killer as vampiric" (Picart and Greek 2009a, 40, 48).

Similarly, in Bram Stoker's 1897 novel, Count Dracula, like the serial killer, "kill[s] out of an overpowering compulsion, and in similarly periodic and patterned ways" (Picart and Greek 2009b, 97), blurring in distinct yet overlapping ways Stoker's Gothic novel with the Count's bloodthirsty fifteenth-century namesake: Vlad Tepes ("the Impaler"). Son of Vlad Dracul, Prince Vlad Dracula (1431–1476) ruled in what is now Romania during the 1400s, renown then, as today, for the creative ways in which he tortured and impaled—then publicly displayed—tens of thousands of people during his brief reign(s) (see McNally and Florescu 1972 [1994]). Similarly, Countess Erzsébet ("Elizabeth") Báthory (1560-1614), referred to also as the "Blood Countess" or "Female Dracula," lived at Castle Sarvar in Hungary. Hers were particularly sadistic and inventive methods for torturing and killing, but it was her practice of capturing peasant girls, killing them, and afterwards bathing in their blood that led to her being labeled as a human vampire (see McNally 1983). Historical nuances of Vlad Tepes, and perhaps arguably that of Erzebet Báthory, loosely helped in shaping not only Bram Stoker's Gothic classic, but more recent contemporary vampires as well.

Influenced by *Dracula* and the subsequent proliferation of vampire fiction, there have been numerous violent homicide cases, many involving serial murder, wherein the particular offenders have been designated by the media and/or professionals as being vampires. Many cases where a vampire identity has been assigned, such as offenders who murdered victims and drank their blood, are obvious. German serial killer Peter Kurten, born in 1883, committed at least nine murders, was sexually aroused by blood, and reportedly drank blood from the severed jugular veins of his victims (Hickey [2013] 2016, 381). Also in Germany, between 1919–1924, Fritz Haarman, referred to as the "Vampire of Hanover," tortured, sodomized, and murdered homeless young boys by biting through their throats (Newton 2006, 107–8). Both Kurten and Haarman were known to have engaged in multiple paraphilia, including hematolagnia and necrophilia. Another vampire serial murderer, John Haigh, lived in the south London (Great Britain) area where he killed victims and drank their blood before dissolving their bodies in a forty-gallon vat of sulfuric acid (Newton 2006, 108–9). During the 1980s, Richard Ramirez, the "Night Stalker," shot to death numerous victims around Los Angeles. Ramirez cut some his victims' throats and during a preliminary court appearance remarked, "I've killed twenty people, man. I love all that blood" (Newton 2006, 218–19).

Interestingly, some serial homicide offenders have been considered vampires primarily for features apart from blood-drinking. In fictional accounts, vampires typically have been presented as being White, male, upper-class, highly intelligent, charming, and heterosexual, and in recent decades vampires of popular culture have become increasingly sexualized. Criminologists like Eric W. Hickey ([2013] 2016) have pointed out that the typical demographic profiles of fictional vampires have, purposely or not, bled into interpretations of violent serial murderers, thus promulgating myths that serial murderers are White; possess above-average intelligence; have high body counts; cannot stop killing; are necessarily sexually motivated; and tend to be biologically robust. In reality, 20 percent of serial murderers, overall, are Black (approximately 50 percent in recent years); nearly 17 percent are female; most have fewer than eight victims; most have average intelligence; motivations vary; and many go for extended periods of time without killing (Hickey [2013] 2016, 5–6). According to Julie B. Weist (2011), law enforcement, including the FBI, have much to gain, including positive reputation and increased public funding, by capitalizing, though likely unintentionally, on popular serial murder myths that have strong roots in vampire fiction (158).

It is not surprising, then, that some have labeled serial murderers such as Ted Bundy to be vampires. Bundy murdered dozens of women and was convicted in one particular case from bite marks matching his teeth, yet he was handsome, well-educated, articulate, and charming—sharing many of the same easily recognizable traits as modern fictional vampires. Like fictional vampires, Bundy assumedly killed based on an uncontrollable compulsion, yet a careful recent analysis of evidence shows his homicidal process reflected killing as an intentional leisure activity (Williams, Thomas, and Arntfield 2020). Although we often conflate serial homicide (real cases) with vampirism (fiction), both vampire and Gothic representations sometimes may be applied to other types of homicide, including mass murder (Arntfield and Danesi 2017, 129–30). Curiously, just as the highly feared vampires of ancient times were shapeshifters, there do not seem to be specific essential criteria for categorizing modern (violent offender) vampires.

ROLE OF LEISURE CULTURE IN HOMICIDE FANTASY DEVELOPMENT, PLANNING, AND EXECUTION

From a Gothic criminology perspective, not only does the "reel" powerfully shape public and professional interpretations of "real" homicide offenders, but broader leisure culture (including film), especially popular culture, influences the ways in which many homicides are conceived, planned, and carried out. In other words, while some particularly violent criminals are assigned the label of "vampire" or some other monster by media, the public, or professionals, other offenders selectively adopt a vampire persona, or some other notorious identity based on fictional work, prior to or during the initial commission of their violent crimes. Of course, some homicide offenders, such as Dennis Rader, the Bind-Torture-Kill (BTK) serial murderer, intentionally create a unique identity that will be echoed and spread by the media, thus inciting widespread panic and terror. Just as Picart and Greek (2007) pointed out that fact (the "real) and fiction ("reel") cannot be completely separated, we emphasize that the personal and social also always remain entangled, especially within the broad context of leisure culture (13–14).

In discussing extreme forms of violence, including murder, as a form of "mephitic" leisure experience, Chris Rojek (1999) pointed out that some serial murderers purposely seek out intense emotional (pleasurable) experiences that do not occur in everyday life (30). Rojek (1999) further noted that fantasy content adopted by many offenders is a salient feature of mainstream leisure (through film, crime fiction, etc.) and that homicidal fantasies and preparatory acts occur in leisure time and space. Indeed, a recent exploratory study found that four common leisure themes—serial homicide as a game; murder for thrills and intense sensations; murder for simple fun and enjoyment; and murder as a unique form of personal celebration—are present in a large number of diverse types of serial homicide cases (Williams, Thomas, and Arntfield, in press).

Consistent with research from Gothic criminology and leisure science, Michael Arntfield and Marcel Danesi (2017), from a perspective rooted in literary criminology and forensic semiotics, presented a diverse array of homicide cases, including both serial and mass murder, to illustrate how the writings of specific homicide offenders reflect particular works of literary fiction and crime drama, which then shaped the commission of offenders' actual crimes. Arntfield and Danesi (2017) observed that serial and mass murderers often understand their crimes as particular narratives, which they sometimes are compelled to document prior, during, or after their crimes. Several well-known serial murderers, who have reveled in fame and celebrity-like status, have reflected themes associated with monsters and evil. For example, H. H. Holmes, who owned and operated a hotel in Chicago in the late 1800s, tortured and murdered numerous guests. Holmes created his own Gothic narrative, with a central theme of evil and apparently including monsters and vampires, which played out in his "Murder Castle" (113).

Arntfield and Danesi (2017) observed that several serial murderers have claimed to be monsters of one variety or another, which allows offenders to enjoy particular power over people, avoid taking responsibility for their crimes, and also seek sympathy from others. Holmes, for instance, claimed to be born "with the devil inside me" (113); Rader claimed to be "possessed with demons" (118); while David Berkowitz in a letter to police wrote, "I am a monster" (120).

In addition to notable serial homicide cases where the "reel" and the "real" have been conflated within broader leisure culture, one fairly recent, highly sensationalized vampire homicide case stands out, among others, as having lasting impact on common (mis)interpretations, both professional and otherwise, of self-identified vampirism. In 1996, sixteen-year-old Rod Ferrell of Kentucky bludgeoned to death the parents, Richard and Ruth Wendorf, of one of his friends. Ferrell and his small circle of friends frequently played role-playing games focused on vampires, and subsequently formed their own "Vampire Clan," of which Ferrell was the leader (see Miller et al. 1996). According to Miller et al. (1996), a "V" sign surrounded by circular marks, representing each member of the clan, was burned into the victims' bodies (216). This case led to heightened concern, which continues today, by clinical and law enforcement professionals that the effects of such role-playing games include Satanic cult activity and ritualistic violence. As with the previous homicide cases cited herein along with many others, while broader leisure experiences—such as role-playing games, film, music, and so forth—shape the planning and commission of specific violent crimes, such leisure activities do not cause them. Meanwhile, scholars have determined that widespread fears of cult activity and ritualistic violence are not valid, but are largely due, instead, to moral panic (see Laycock 2015). As much or possibly even more so than any other modern violent homicides, the Rod Ferrell case has contributed to widespread fears, overgeneralizations, and misunderstandings concerning the diverse forms of contemporary self-identified vampires (or "real vampires").

CONTEMPORARY SELF-IDENTIFIED VAMPIRES AND COMMUNITY HISTORY

The "real vampire community" comprises people who consume human and/or animal blood (sanguinarian), absorb psychic energy (psychic vampire or psi-vamp), or both (hybrid) out of a need that, according to them, begins to manifest around puberty and results from their bodies' inability to produce natural, subtle energies. They claim to be given neither a choice nor the freedom to change this condition, and should they refrain from feeding on blood or energy, their bodies respond by feeling weak and experiencing an overall diminished health.

Real (or human) vampires do not generally sleep in coffins, nor do they claim to live forever. Indeed, they diffuse

> beyond the realms of film and literature in which popular culture has traditionally situated them. Real vampires are living people, generally leading what may be deemed everyday lives, and who, according to what [Browning] and other scholars have been able to ascertain, appropriate the figure of the vampire and adapt it for self-identificatory purposes. This, however, they do only after—in many cases, years after—the compulsion to take blood or energy arises. Even still, this is not to say that some of the fictional vampire's more obvious cultural and socio-historical dimensions in film and literature are not reflected in real vampires. (Browning 2015, par. 13)

Although the term "real vampire community" did not see regular use until the late 1990s, Browning further adds (2015), referring then primarily to a network of online message boards, chat rooms, and email groups, a vastly disjointed network of people who self-identified as vampire had been in existence by that point for at least two decades (par. 4). In the 1970s, people who openly or secretively identified as vampire, or who experienced the self-described physiological symptoms noted previously, began to attend the same themed social gatherings, enabling the process of networking with one another as well as with blood and energy donors to begin. These themed social gatherings included, among others, *Dark Shadows* conventions and other vampire fiction and film fan organizations; bondage and S&M events attended by blood fetishists and other, often willing, blood donors; and Goth clubs. Self-printed newsletters (i.e., 'zines) also began to appear during this period, and they were an essential first step towards merging into one interconnected community the individual and groups of real vampires peppering the United States (par. 4).

Among the first research organizations dedicated to the study of vampires was the Count Dracula Fan Club (later The Vampire Empire) in 1965. Headed by Dr. Jeanne Keyes Youngson, this organization was originally dedicated to vampire fiction and film, but when Youngson began receiving letters from real vampires in 1970–71, the organization's studies were extended and led Youngson to publish in a casebook some of her more fascinating correspondence with members of the community (Browning 2015c, par. 5). Another notable early researcher was Stephen Kaplan, who in 1972 formed the Vampire Research Center in Suffolk County, New York, where he supervised a "vampire hotline." Kaplan received numerous phone calls, and although the majority of them were pranks, he did document several real vampires; on several occasions, he even made actual house calls to conduct one-on-one interviews, reporting his findings in a book entitled *Vampires Are* (1984). Other important figures emerged like Martin V. Riccardo, who founded in 1977 the Vampire Studies Society and printed a quarterly newsletter entitled *Journal of Vampirism*. The Vampire Information Exchange emerged in 1978 and published the *Vampire Information Exchange Newsletter (VIEN)* for almost 30 years. A number of other pertinent studies followed in the 1980s and 1990s, from folklorists like Norine Dresser, researchers and paranormalists like Rosemary Ellen Guiley, journalists like Carol Page, and academic criminologists like Katherine Ramsland (par. 5).

The 1990s saw an especially significant expansion of the real vampire community. Following the popularity of *Interview with the Vampire* (1976), *The Vampire Lestat* (1985), and *The Queen of the Damned* (1988), Anne Rice conventions began to emerge on the scene at this time, providing closeted and unaffiliated real vampires new opportunities to socialize and network. Equally, if not more, profound in its importance during this period was the publication White Wolf's *Vampire: The Masquerade*, in which was laid the ground rules for a vampire role-playing game (Browning 2015c, par. 5). This text provided, if inadvertently, a social space within which real vampires could congregate and network openly, and it introduced to them a lexicon of conventions, terms, protocols, and identifiers that they eventually adapted for their own needs. What emerged is the predominant real vampire identity we see today. However, to help grow their community, it is the Internet to which they turned next.

In the past, real vampires existed in small pockets or as isolated individuals dependent upon geographically close fan conventions and low-circulation newsletters for communication. Beginning in the 1990s, the Internet helped to dissolve these geographic limitations and made print correspondence an obsolete form by opening up vastly more efficient e-forums, chat rooms, and e-communication.

The mid-2000s through 2010s also saw new scholarship treating real vampirism, not only from academic scholars and writers like Drs. Joseph P. Laycock (2009, 2010, 2016, 2018), DJ Williams (2013, 2015, 2016, 2017), John Edgar Browning (2015c, Williams and Browning 2016),[2] and Mark Benecke (2015), but from actual members of the community itself as well. While Williams and Browning (2016) have focused primarily on the creative, therapeutic, self-liberating, and anti-normative nature of real vampirism and its history, as we will explain momentarily, chief among Laycock's (2009, 2010) studies in the field have been examinations into socio-religious aspects of the community and refuting problematic socio-religious writings on the real vampire identity.

WHO ARE REAL VAMPIRES: RESEARCH WITH THE VAMPIRE COMMUNITY(IES)

Browning's entree into Real Vampire Studies began with his intensive ethnographic fieldwork in New Orleans (2009–2011), a vampire community decimated by Hurricane Katrina, and supplementary ethnographic work in Buffalo, New York (2011–2013). His aim was to situate real vampirism in tandem with film, fiction, and other categories in which popular culture has traditionally situated monstrous figures, then consider afterwards how the figure of the vampire has been appropriated by and adapted to the real vampire community. Browning (2015c) also explores what he terms "defiant culture," a means by which vampire self-identification can potentially achieve some measure of empowerment through resisting "normalcy" by critiquing and challenging the power structures that re/produce it. In sum, a "defiant culture," argues Browning (2015c), manifests its "own deviance through the act of defiance for its own sake, in this case, the conscious use of a negative identifier like 'vampire'" (par. 29).

Williams's professional experience as both a former forensic social worker and as an interdisciplinary researcher (leisure studies, sex science, forensic behavioral science) informed his work in criminology and forensic behavioral science, which together helped to illustrate that many forms expressive crime takes can be explained as types of deviant leisure.[3] However, Williams found that numerous forms of deviant leisure (e.g., consensual bondage-discipline-sadomasochism [BDSM] and real vampirism) are neither criminal nor substantially dangerous if practiced ethically, and what's more may be understood, in many cases, as healthy forms of leisure.[4] It is also worth noting that Browning and Williams, researchers who have spent considerable time with local real vampire communities, have reported feeling generally safe and without significant risk while conducting their research.

Much demographic diversity exists across the vampire community and in its behaviors and practices, As such, while psychological science has much to offer the field in understanding real vampirism, other disciplines can add important knowledge, and indeed already do. We therefore emphasize avoiding relying on narrow or hasty interpretations of real vampirism. The community's rich diversity and variation has and should continue to invite scholars from different disciplines and theoretical orientations to explore this interesting topic.

VAMPIRE CASES AND THE NEED FOR DISENTANGLEMENT: A CRITICAL, MULTIDISCIPLINARY APPROACH

Because of the rich diversity and complexity associated with self-identified vampirism, it is essential that legal and forensic professionals take a critical, multidisciplinary approach to investigating specific cases involving vampires (Williams and Browning 2016, 130). We propose that the following caveats be kept in mind. Experts should be aware of how normalizing discourses fused with powerful sociocultural narratives concerning vampires shape, often unknowingly, "official" interpretations of such alternative identities and practices. Professionals should recognize that specific vampires often interpret their alternative identities in a unique way, thus consciously respecting personal subjectivity is necessary. It is important, then, that professionals do not rely on generalizations from other, high profile, media cases of extreme violence committed by specific self-identified vampires, for example, the Rod Ferrell or Mathew Hardman cases.[5] Instead, forensic investigators should simply apply the usual techniques for assessing violence potential, including a consideration of prior incidents of violence and possible chronic patterns of lack of empathy and violating the rights of others. Investigators should also ask numerous questions concerning how an individual self-identifies as a vampire; how she/he came to identify (awakening); whether the person is or has been part of a vampire community; what specific vampiric practices the person has engaged, or currently engages, in; who is involved (i.e., other vampires, donors, black swans[6]); and so on. Rather than simply assessing deviance around identities and practices, we argue that forensic investigators should be evaluating basic ethical aspects of vampire practices (i.e., clear communication, consent of participants, ethic of care, risk management) (see Williams et al. 2014), along with standard considerations for violence as mentioned above.

BRIEF CASE EXAMPLES: CONSIDERING RISK FOR FALSE POSITIVES AND FALSE NEGATIVES

The legitimate search for justice within the context of violent crime detection involves being aware of the continual risk for making false positive or false negative errors. In assessing violence, we do not want to declare a person or group as dangerous when, in fact, they are not (false positive). At the same time, it is important to not overlook violent criminal behavior, or its likelihood, when such detection is warranted (false negative).

Williams was recently peripherally involved with a homicide case in Los Angeles where Edward and Melissa Hope Garcia brutally murdered Herbert Tracy White in a hotel room. White had met the Garcias days before the murder at a Chase Bank in Hollywood; offered to provide support if the Garcias were interested in getting sober; and eventually checked them into a hotel (see Gerber 2015). After a brief struggle in the hotel room, the Garcias bound their victim with duct tape; cut his face multiple times; stabbed him twice (fatally) in the neck, and dismembered the body (*People v. Edward Garcia, Jr.*, June 15, 2015). Although the Garcias admitted to the killing and dismemberment, legal professionals rightly attempted to determine a motive for the homicide, particularly given the extremely violent nature of the crime. Apparently, Mr. White had made sexual advances toward Mrs. Garcia, and it was clear that both offenders had used a substantial amount of methamphetamine at the time of the murder. A consultant hired by the prosecution strongly believed that the motive centered on ritualistic vampirism. This interpretation of evidence included that the victim was bound, the sole weapon used was a knife, the particular positioning of the torso and limbs, postmortem decapitation, the dismemberment was not a counter-forensic measure, and obviously the high degree of blood loss. The consultant believed that the offenders were "real vampires," rather than "dabblers," and testified that real vampires regularly engage in secretive ritualistic violence. However, despite that such an explanation may seem reasonable at face value to many, a thorough consideration of available research on self-identified vampirism, including the growing literature that we have cited herein, illustrates that there is no evidence connecting real vampirism to violence. As discussed earlier, real vampires seem to be rather ordinary and generally law-abiding citizens, who rightfully have feared being misinterpreted based on conflations that are rooted in forensic and psychiatric discourses on deviance. Overgeneralizations, such as illustrated in the case above, increase the likelihood of false positive error while unjustly marginalizing citizens who have adopted a particular meaningful alternative identity. Although it remains somewhat unclear what the primary homicidal motive was for the Garcias, professional explanations relying on narrow theoretical perspectives and incorrect assumptions about vampires do not contribute to justice (Williams 2017, 819).

Several years earlier in a separate case, Williams received a call from an FBI investigator regarding a detained individual who was suspected by law enforcement authorities of the international kidnapping and possibly killing of young children. The FBI had intercepted a cryptograph journal from the suspect, and when asked about the meanings of its contents, the suspect explained that he was no public threat, but simply was a member of the vampire community. He claimed that his communications were benign and had, quite understandably, been misinterpreted, but that the phrases and directives therein simply reflected vampire jargon used within his alternative community. However, during background investigation it was discovered that this individual had a strong interest in pedophilia, along with a history of violence, including physically and sexually abusing his stepchild. Further questioning and additional investigation by the authorities revealed that the suspect was neither a member of, nor had association with, a legitimate vampire community. In fact, he knew very little about self-identified vampire groups or communities, and his subsequent alibis (e.g., he was expressing specific local cultural vampiric beliefs) were inconsistent and not supported by relevant cultural evidence. In this extremely rare case, the evidence pointed toward the conclusion that it was very likely that this individual was attempting to avoid criminal conviction and subsequent incarceration by claiming to have a legitimate alternative identity. Indeed, after months of further investigation, this offender was convicted of multiple violent crimes, including homicide, in which he had been a suspect. While false positive errors are far more likely to occur than false negatives, this case is an excellent example of good collaboration and thorough investigation, using multidisciplinary expertise, by various law enforcement personnel.

CONCLUDING REMARKS

The common cultural conflation of fictional vampire narratives with self-identified real vampirism and actual forensic cases, recognized via Gothic criminology, remains highly problematic for several reasons. The unintentional relying on fictional narratives for (mis)interpreting actual crime case is misleading and can create unwarranted widespread fear and panic, along with additional harm, while contributing little, if anything, to preventing crime and achieving justice. At the same time, scholars of the real vampire community have reported that both fictional vampire narratives and violent crime cases (separately and combined) are peripheral and largely irrelevant to understanding the real vampire community, despite the common tendency among both media and professionals to conflate these separate phenomena. It is not surprising, then, that contemporary research has found that real vampires remain reluctant, and rightly so, to disclose their vampire identities to well-intentioned, but uninformed, helping professionals.[7] If the tremendous diversity of vampires is to be understood and social justice realized, then a broad, multidisciplinary, scholarly approach must be promoted and applied.

NOTES

1. Although Picart's and Greek's respective uses of "Gothic criminology" overlap in their writings, they also differ. For example, Picart applies Gothic criminology to amp out the "social construction of crime and the nature of criminality, focusing specifically on the proliferation of Gothic tropes and *mise-en-scene* in the media's accounts, often fluctuating between fact and fiction and teratological rhetorics (i.e., 'monster talk')" (Picart 2014, 173). Picart continues:

> [My] work thus far has remained focused principally on tracking evolving representations of a particular type of "monster"—serial killers—along the registers of race, class, gender and sexuality. What the general body of Picart's work has striven to show is that these registers (of race, class, gender, and sexuality) of "real"/"reel" serial killers, result in different narratives. For example, Hannibal Lecter, a fictional character with affinities to Jeffrey Dahmer and Ted Bundy, is cinematically depicted as a hyper-intelligent, classy, heterosexual white male cannibal associated with the image of the glamorous vampire (with his hypnotic gaze; dark, swirling cape; and rakish Borsalino hat). In contrast, a lesbian serial killer, Aileen Wuornos, is cinematically depicted as metaphorically similar to

the Frankensteinian Creature—white trash eternally in search of love and companionship. (Picart, Jacobsen, and Greek 2016, 11)

2. See also John Edgar Browning, "Real-Life Vampires Exist, and Researchers Are Studying Them," *Discover Magazine*, March 26, 2015, http://blogs.discovermagazine.com/crux/2015/03/26/real-life-vampires-exist/#.XdNcpL97n7A; Browning, "Life Among the Vampires," *The Atlantic*, October 31, 2015, https://www.theatlantic.com/health/archive/2015/10/life-among-the-vampires/413446/; and Browning, "What I Learned Studying Real Vampires," *Discover Magazine*, May 17, 2018, https://www.discovermagazine.com/health/what-i-learned-studying-real-vampires.

3. See DJ Williams, "Functions of Leisure and Recreation Activities within a Sexual Assault Cycle," *Sexual Addiction and Compulsivity* 12 (2005): 295–309; Williams, "Forensic Leisure Science: A New Frontier for Leisure Scholars?" *Leisure Sciences* 28 (2006): 91–5; and Williams and Gordon J. Walker, "Leisure, Deviant Leisure, and Crime: Caution: Objects May Be Closer Than They Appear," *Leisure/Loisir* 30 (2006) 193–218.

4. See DJ Williams, "Social Work, BDSM, and Vampires: Toward Empowering People with Non-Traditional Identities," *Canadian Social Work* 15 (2013): 10-24; and Williams, "From Purple Roots to Dark, Sexy, and Diverse: The Past, Present, and Future of Deviant Leisure," in *Leisure Matters: The Present and Future of Leisure Studies*, ed. Gordon J. Walker, David Scott, and Monika Stodolska (State College, PA: Venture, 2015).

5. See Miller et al., 1996; and Dawn Perlmutter, "The Forensics of Sacrifice: A Symbolic Analysis of Ritualistic Crime," *Anthropoetics* IX, no. 2 (Fall 2003/Winter 2004): subsection 20.

6. A "black swan" is a non-vampire who is friendly towards, knowledgeable about, and may be romantically partnered with someone in the real vampire community. A black swan may also frequent vampire nightclubs and may serve as a donor.

7. See DJ Williams and Emily Prior, "Do We Always Practice What We Preach? Real Vampires' Fears of Coming out of the Coffin to Social Workers and Helping Professionals, *Critical Social Work* 16, no. 1 (2015): 79–92.

REFERENCES

Arntfield, Michael, and Marcel Danesi. 2017. *Murder in Plain English: From Manifestos to Memes—Looking at Murder Through the Words of Killers.* New York: NY: Prometheus.

Benecke, Mark, and Ines Fischer. 2015. *Vampyres Among Us: A Scientific Study into Vampyre Identity Groups and Subcultures*. 3 vols. Thüringen: Edition Roter Drache.

Browning, John Edgar. 2015a. "Life Among the Vampires." *The Atlantic*, October 31. https://www.theatlantic.com/health/archive/2015/10/life-among-the-vampires/413446/.

———. 2015b. "Real-Life Vampires Exist, and Researchers Are Studying Them." *Discover Magazine*, March 26, 2015. http://blogs.discovermagazine.com/crux/2015/03/26/real-life-vampires-exist/#.XdNcpL97n7A.

———. 2015c. "The Real Vampires of New Orleans and Buffalo: A Research Note Towards Comparative Ethnography." *Palgrave Communications* 1, no. 15006: doi .org/10.1057/palcomms.2015.6.

———. 2018. "What I Learned Studying Real Vampires." *Discover Magazine*, May 17. https://www.discovermagazine.com/health/what-i-learned-studying-real -vampires.

Gerber, Marisa. 2015. "Closing arguments expected in L.A. hotel dismemberment trial." *Los Angeles Times,* June 18. http://www.latimes.com/local/lanow/la-me-ln -closing-arguments-dismemberment-trial-20150618-story.html.

Hickey, Eric W. [2013] 2016. *Serial Murderers and Their Victims,* seventh ed. Boston, MA: Cengage Learning.

Laycock, Joseph P. 2015. *Dangerous Games: What the Moral Panic over Role-Playing Games Says about Play, Religion, and Imagined Worlds.* Oakland, CA: University of California Press.

———. 2016. "Reply to 'Do We Always Practice What We Preach?' Real Vampires' Fears of Coming of the Coffin to Social Workers and Helping Professionals." *Critical Social Work* 17, no. 2: 83–89.

———. 2010. "Vampires as an Identity Group: Analyzing Causes and Effects of an Introspective Survey by the Vampire Community." *Nova Religio* 14, no. 1: 4–23.

———. 2018. "Vampirism: Modern Vampires and Embattled Identity Claims." *The Supernatural in Society, Culture, and History*, edited by Dennis Waskul and Marc Eaton, 177–89. Philadelphia, PA: Temple University Press.

McNally, Raymond T. 1983. *Dracula Was a Woman: In Search of the Blood Countess of Transylvania.* New York, McGraw-Hill.

McNally, Raymond T., and Radu Florescu. [1972] 1994. *In Search of Dracula: The History of Dracula and Vampires*. Boston: Houghton Mifflin.

Miller, Thomas W., Lane J. Veltkamp, Robert F. Kraus, Tim Lane, and Tag Heister. 1996. "An Adolescent Vampire Cult in Rural America: Clinical Issues and Case Study." *Child Psychiatry and Human Development* 29, no. 3: 209–19.

Newton, Michael. 2006. *The Encyclopedia of Serial Killers,* second ed. New York, NY: Checkmark Books.

Perlmutter, Dawn. Fall 2003/Winter 2004. "The Forensics of Sacrifice: A Symbolic Analysis of Ritualistic Crime." *Anthropoetics* IX, no. 2, subsection 20.

Picart, Caroline Joan "Kay" S. 2014. "Media Myths Regarding Serial Killers: A Gothic Criminology." *The Poetics of Crime*, edited by Michael Hviid Jacobsen, 173–91. Farnham, U.K.: Ashgate.

Picart, Caroline Joan "Kay" S., and Cecil Greek. 2009a. "The Compulsions of Real/Reel Serial Killers and Vampires." *Draculas, Vampires, and Other Undead Forms: Essays on Gender, Race, and Culture*, edited by John Edgar Browning and Caroline Joan "Kay" S. Picart, 37–62. Lanham, MD: Scarecrow Press.

———. 2007. *Monsters in and Among Us: Toward a Gothic Criminology.* Madison, NJ: Fairleigh Dickinson University Press.

———. 2009b. "When Women Kill: Undead Imagery in the Cinematic Portrait of Aileen Wuornos." *Draculas, Vampires, and Other Undead Forms: Essays on Gen-

der, Race, and Culture, edited by John Edgar Browning and Caroline Joan "Kay" S. Picart, 93–114. Lanham, MD: Scarecrow Press.

Picart, Caroline Joan "Kay" S., Michael Hviid Jacobsen, and Cecil Greek. 2016. "Introduction: Attempting to Frame Law and Crime: An Experiment in Interdisciplinary Commensurability." *Framing Law and Crime: An Interdisciplinary Anthology*, edited by Caroline Joan "Kay" S. Picart, Michael Hviid Jacobsen, Cecil Greek, 1–24. Lanham, MD: Fairleigh Dickson University Press.

Rojek, Chris. 1999. "Abnormal Leisure: Invasive, Mephitic, and Wild Forms." *Society and Leisure* 22, no. 1: 21–37.

Wiest, Julie B. 2011. *Creating Cultural Monsters: Serial Murder in America.* New York, NY: CRC Press.

Williams, DJ. 2006. "Forensic Leisure Science: A New Frontier for Leisure Scholars?" *Leisure Sciences* 28: 91–5.

———. 2015. "From Purple Roots to Dark, Sexy, and Diverse: The Past, Present, and Future of Deviant Leisure." *Leisure Matters: The Present and Future of Leisure Studies*, edited by Gordon J. Walker, David Scott, and Monika Stodolska. State College, PA: Venture.

———. 2005. "Functions of Leisure and Recreation Activities within a Sexual Assault Cycle." *Sexual Addiction and Compulsivity* 12: 295–309.

———. 2019. "Is Serial Sexual Homicide a Compulsion, Deviant Leisure, or Both? Revisiting the Case of Ted Bundy." *Leisure Sciences*, March 28. https://tandfonline.com/doi/abs/10.1080/01490400.2019.1571967?src=recsys&journalCode=ulsc20.

———. 2017. "Self-Identified Vampirism and Risk for False Positives: A Case Example of Team Homicide and Implications for Forensic Behavioral Science." *Journal of Forensic Sciences* 62, no. 3: 819–21.

———. 2013. "Social Work, BDSM, and Vampires: Toward Empowering People with Non-Traditional Identities." *Canadian Social Work* 15: 10–24.

Williams, DJ, and Emily Prior. 2015. "Do We Always Practice What We Preach? Real Vampires' Fears of Coming Out of the Coffin to Social Workers and Helping Professionals." *Critical Social Work* 16, no. 1: 79–92.

Williams, DJ, Jeremy N. Thomas, Emily E. Prior, and M. Candace Christensen. 2014. "From 'SSC' and 'RACK' to the '4Cs': Introducing a new framework for negotiating BDSM participation." *Electronic Journal of Human Sexuality* 17: http://www.ejhs.org/volume17/BDSM.html.

Williams, DJ, Jeremy N. Thomas, and Michael Arntfield. "An empirical exploration of leisure-related themes and potential constraints across descriptions of serial homicide cases." *Leisure Sciences* 42, no. 1: 69–84.

Williams, DJ, and John Edgar Browning. 2016. "Looking Inside the Coffin: An Overview of Contemporary Human Vampirism and its Relevance for Forensics Professionals." *The Criminal Humanities: An Introduction,* edited by Michael Arntfield and Marcel Danesi, 117–34. New York: Peter Lang.

Williams, DJ, and Gordon J. Walker. 2006. "Leisure, Deviant Leisure, and Crime: Caution: Objects May Be Closer Than They Appear." *Leisure/Loisir* 30: 193–218.

Part II

CONTAGION, MONSTROSITY, ETHICS

Chapter Four

A Double-Tap "Lilith Moral Panic" in Israel, 2014

How Labeling Others as "Monsters" Conceals Their Victimization

Orit Kamir

INTRODUCTION: ISRAELI "LILITH MORAL PANIC"

Sometimes communities are seized with an overwhelming dread that a monster lurks in their shadow, creeping around in their midst, and threatening their most precious and vulnerable values, customs, and members—and thus their very existence as they know and cherish it. The fear is frequently exaggerated and the blame misplaced. As early as 1972, sociologist Stanley Cohen (1980) dubbed this phenomenon "moral panic" and its victims "folk devils" (see also Goode and Ben-Yehuda 1994a and 1994b; Garlan 2008). This chapter examines a recent case in point, illustrating the dynamics of a specific type of moral panic I label "Lilith moral panic" after the archetypal female monster of Jewish folklore.

Typical of a patriarchal society in distress, Lilith moral panic brings the community together around a marginalized woman—or class of women—personified as a dangerous monster. The communal targeting, demonizing, and assault of this creature channels the panic and defuses it, functioning as a "witch-hunt backlash" in the service of maintaining conservative, gender social order. On occasion, social institutions—such as the judiciary or health care—are enlisted to hunt the foe, the monstrous tools they develop taking root and corrupting the systems they administer. When the monster is finally defeated and destroyed, society seems cleansed of its distress and can return to normalcy, resuming its routines.

In a previous study, I formulated and presented this type of gendered moral panic via an examination of several historical misogynous outbursts (Kamir 2001, pp. 51–67). Here, I present a contemporary Israeli episode that exhibits the same symptoms. The framing and analysis laid out here suggest a possible fusion of underlying gender- and national-based existential anxieties.[1]

In the summer of 2014, the Israeli media became fixated on reports that a 38-year-old woman was raping hundreds of boys in the southern town of Kiryat Gat, possibly infecting them with HIV. Portrayed as a deviant, child-endangering monster on the loose, the story both fascinated and outraged the public. The legal system played into the moral panic in two ways. Adopting an irrational interpretation of the criminal code, the prosecution accused the woman of sodomy (despite the fact that she was the one penetrated), and a conservative Member of Knesset (Israel's Parliament) introduced a highly controversial bill that expanded the definition of rape to include unwelcome seduction of a man by a woman. The sensationalist preoccupation with what was construed as monstrous child molestation disguised the true reality: dozens if not hundreds of adolescents were systematically taking advantage of a mentally- and socially-challenged woman as parents, teachers, and social workers turned a blind eye.

Immediately after this affair had faded into obscurity, another "monstrous Other" aroused public righteous indignation—Haneen Zoabi, an Israeli-Palestinian MK.[2] As Israel's Jewish public held its breath in the hope of discovering three youngsters who disappeared from Israeli settlements in the occupied West Bank alive, Zoabi refused to refer to those responsible as "terrorists" (Hovel 2104; Zonszein 2014). Her instant vilification in the Israeli media as a sick, monstrous figure diverted attention from her claim that the conditions of Israeli occupation might have driven desperate Palestinians to commit such an act.

The "Lilith moral panic" these events encapsulated, generated by patriarchal distress, metamorphosed into a national-based witch-hunt, eventually merging with public anxiety and fervor over the Israeli military operation against Gaza that took place in the summer of 2014.

The chapter opens with a brief introduction of the ancient Lilith legend. It then offers a concise account of the patriarchal crisis that gave rise to the Lilith moral panic in the summer of 2014. This is followed by a depiction of the events framed here as the double-tap Lilith moral panic and its legal aspects. The conclusions drawn suggest that the hysterical "monsterification" of the Kiryat Gat woman and MK Haneen Zoabi concealed their gendered victimization.

THE LILITH MYTH

In Jewish mythology, Lilith is a murderous, vampiristic, baby-snatching monster with a woman's body and bird's wings who lures men and has intercourse with them by "riding" them, sometimes also drinking their blood and eating their flesh (see in greater length Kamir 2001, pp. 19–42, 49–50). She also devours babies she snatches from their mothers' arms. Originally Innana, the prehistoric Sumerian Great Mother Goddess, Queen of Heaven and Earth, under the new monotheistic patriarchy she became a demoness.[3]

Ancient Jewish mythologists furnished Lilith with a narrative to explain her monstrosity (Yassif 1984): in the beginning of time, in the Garden of Eden, God created Adam and Lilith together as siblings and man and wife. One day, Adam wanted to lie on top of Lilith. When Lilith objected, Adam responded violently. Pronouncing the sacred name of God, Lilith gained the ability to fly. Roaming the world, she found Satan, whom she discovered to be a more potent and satisfying lover than Adam. When Adam complained to God that his woman had flown off, he sent three angels to find and fetch her back. She, however, retorted that, according to his own law, having had intercourse with another male she could not return to her husband.

Conceding her point, God created Eve out of Adam's rib, thus making her subordination clear. At the same time, he sent the angels back to Lilith, forcing her to generate enough offspring so that 100 of them might die daily and turn to dust as payback for the earth God had used to create Lilith. Lilith was now independent, as well as smart, strong, resourceful, with the power to fly and assume various guises. As a demoness, she seduced Adam and his sons into begetting her monstrous offspring, spitefully killing Eve's children. Enticing men, she was irresistibly alluring; devouring children, she was heinous. Many Jews kept amulets in their homes warning her—in the name of the three angels—to stay away.

Countless variations of this powerful myth have circulated in the Judeo-Christian world for millennia, with "fatal attraction" films constituting one familiar example. I believe that the myth and its demonized—monstrous—female protagonist are inseparable from Western collective cultural unconscious. When Adam's rule of Eve appears to be challenged and threatened, communities imagine that Lilith is in their vicinity. They then unconsciously seek her in an attempt to rid their world of her menacing presence, thereby restoring patriarchal equilibrium and conservative peace of mind. These instances, sometimes cruel and bloody, are Lilith "moral panics" whose real-world victims are marginalized, disempowered women constructed as Lilith monsters.

ISRAELI PATRIARCHAL SOCIAL ORDER IN DISTRESS

Despite Israel's pride in its progressive gender egalitarian ethos, its lack of separation between Church and State subjects women to gender-discriminatory religious laws of marriage and divorce, compounding the militaristic nature of Israeli society with its strong masculine bias (Halperin-Kaddari 2004). In 1998, Israel passed a law defining sexual harassment as an offense against human dignity, restriction of liberty, infringement of privacy, and gender discrimination (Kamir 2003). It prohibits six behaviors, defined as criminal offenses, as well as civil torts and employment infractions. While significantly affecting social norms, it also led to waves of backlash that burst out in particular when central public figures were accused, charged, and prosecuted for harassment.

The summer of 2006 (June–July) marked a significant moment in this development, with the President and Minister of Justice both being accused of sexual harassment. The complaints eventually resulted in prosecution, conviction, and incarceration (Kamir 2008). The public debate over the two affairs was heated, many expressing the fear that "open season" had been declared on men, with women abusing their newly gained legal rights to target and persecute powerful men. That same summer (June 28), Israel invaded Lebanon, launching a five-month military operation/war. During the second half of 2006, public debate focused heavily on both militarism and sexual harassment.

A similar phenomenon occurred eight years later in the summer of 2014. During the first months of 2014, the Israeli public sphere was mesmerized by two disturbing sexual phenomena: adolescent gang rapes and complaints of sexual assaults committed by public figures. One of the country's most popular male singers was interrogated, together with his father, in connection with the systematic sexual abuse of underage fans (Kubovitch 2013). Although the criminal case was closed because the complainants refused to testify, the media and social networks were flooded with extreme responses, from disgust and indignation to fear of "manhunts" (*Haaretz* 2014).

Around the same time, a new Israeli film made its debut in cinemas around the country. Written by Rona Segal and directed by Jonathan Gurfinkel and reportedly inspired by true events, *Six Acts* portrays a group of adolescent males toying with a female classmate who, in her desperate attempt to belong, lets them take advantage of her. Powerful and almost documentary in its realistic exposé of Israeli youth, the film generated fierce debate about parental roles, alleged young-female promiscuity, and rape culture at large (Littman 2013).

On March 25, 2014, the media reported that the police were investigating a gang rape committed by seven adolescents on a thirteen-year-old girl (Kubovich 2014a). The boys' parents and lawyers insisted that the sexual interactions were consensual, and that the young woman was playing fast and loose and ruining the lives of boys from upstanding families. Social media exploded with confusion and outrage on all sides.

A day earlier, the media had reported a sexual harassment charge against the Minister of the Interior, a prominent candidate campaigning for the office of President (Kubovich and Hovel 2014). Aware that the complaint would not lead to charges because the alleged harassment had occurred fifteen years earlier, the woman chose to file it in order to influence the Interior Minister's political campaign. With many of his supporters abandoning him, he withdrew his candidacy two months later. His wife, a familiar public figure in her own right and host of a popular radio show, led the uproar against women who, making accusations that cannot be properly scrutinized in a court of law, ruin honorable men and their families (Kaplan Sommer 2015; *Haaretz* 2015).

In the midst of this scandal, in May 2014, an additional presidential candidate supported by many opposition party members was implicated in a sexual harassment affair. According to the media, he had paid off his housekeeper to stop her from filing a complaint against him (Kubovich 2014b). This news aroused further frustration and confusion, some claiming that the housekeeper was a blackmailer and that no man was safe.

I suggest that these frequent reports of the systematic sexual abuse of girls on the one hand and sexual accusations against public figures on the other elevated the levels of patriarchal distress to a breaking point, paving the way for a "Lilith moral panic," in the wake of which patriarchal social order and its reassuring morals were restored. In the epic struggle to rid itself of the monstrous Lilith endangering and corrupting young boys, the community saved and purified itself, exonerating adolescents and men at large of sexual predation and parents and teachers of negligence by construing them as helpless victims of a diabolical female with supernatural powers.

The following narration of the events of summer 2014 suggests that the "Kiryat Gat woman," as she was referred to by the media, served as the perfect "Lilith distraction" until the kidnapping of three youngsters from the Jewish settlements in the West Bank turned MK Haneen Zoabi into a more suitable candidate.

MORAL PANIC PHASE I: A LILITH MONSTER IN KIRYAT GAT

On May 28, 2014, the Israeli media reported that the parents of hundreds of teenage boys in the south of Israel had discovered that their sons were having sexual encounters with a thirty-eight-year-old woman from Kiryat Gat.[4] The worried parents had their children tested for AIDS, filed complaints against the woman with the police, and demanded that the authorities require that she also be tested. The woman was immediately arrested. She agreed to be tested and asked to see a psychiatrist, who later determined that she was responsible for her actions (Siedler 2014a, 2014b).

From the moment the information was released, Israeli radio stations, newspapers, and social media were saturated with speculation, rumor, fear, and outrage. Piecing together bits of data, self-assigned analysts disseminated the hypothesis that the woman—whose twelve-year-old daughter had been removed from her by the authorities—was avenging herself on society by corrupting and infecting as many young boys as she could (Siedler 2014a). Her obsession with her uncontrollable, deranged sexual desire for young boys made her stalk them, lure them to her apartment, and have repeated intercourse with them. In this way, she seduced hundreds if not thousands of youngsters from the area, who were apparently helpless to resist her beguilements. Ever new speculations were reported on the news, the topic becoming the talk of the country.

On June 1, 2014, all the news programs reported that the "Kiryat Gat woman" was HIV negative (Siedler 2014c). Rather than diminishing the huge, pornographic interest in her sexual escapades, however, public criticism now directed itself at the local welfare services. Having known of what was happening for five years, they had done nothing to stop it (Baltman 2014). Neighbors, relatives, and worried citizens participated in countless public discussions, venting their concern and anger.

On June 5, 2014, a popular Israeli internet newspaper, *Ynet*, published an interview with one of the boys. Garnering much attention, his testimony included the following narration:

> "The first time I heard of her was in Grade 5. Classmates were with her and said it was like in movies we saw. I didn't go, but heard the stories, and we joked a lot about them." Two years ago, when he was approximately 12, Amit [alias] decided to be "one of the guys" and have his first sexual experience. "A friend said that I was the only one not to have been with her. He laughed and said that I was the only one in the whole of Kiryat Gat, so I said—why not. I wanted to go anyways. He called her from school, said he had a friend, and set up a time and place. We didn't go to her apartment because she said she lived at someone's and couldn't meet there, but she set up a place and we went there Friday night." (Levi 2014 [author's translation]).

Typical of many of those told by other boys involved in the affair, Amit's story supports the argument made by the defense—namely, untreated wretchedness rather than a woman abusing innocent boys. Amit and other boys described how they beat, humiliated, and made fun of the woman:

> I arrived there with two classmates. She laughed with us and straight away we went to her bed. I was stressed out because it was my first time, and I didn't

> want my friends to watch me. She laughed as well, and my friends went to wait in the living room. She took off my clothes and hers, lay on the bed and told me to come. She touched me there, and then I lay on top of her. I felt like in a blue movie. Then I left the room and my friends came in together (chuckles). They stayed in there much longer than me, but I got the idea. (Levi 2014)

Amit's next meeting with the woman exemplifies the way in which the adolescents abused her:

> We were three friends, not the ones that first brought me there, we went into her home and a friend of mine said to her, "Quick, you whore, go to the room." I laughed sillily [sic], although I also felt badly. But she laughed and we all went to the room, where she immediately took her clothes off. I sat watching as my friends did her together. They cursed and beat her. First just on her butt, but then my friend slapped her over the face. She said "No," but he laughed and said, "Shut up, whore." The funny thing was that she laughed as well, and they did her like in a blue movie, and when they were through they sat aside and I came in. They watched, but I no longer cared, because I knew what to do. I also did a girl from my class. When I was doing it to her they cursed her, called her whore, and told her to give me a blow job. She did everything and I laughed hard. When I was done, they wanted to go again. She said she was out of strength, so my friend cursed her and said he would do it fast. She refused, so he threw something at her, I can't remember what. We were about to leave and she said OK, we could do another round. I think she was still hot, but had to leave the apartment or something, I don't know. So we each did it to her and left. When we left, I threw her shirt at her and said: "This is the last time you say no to us." It was nothing, and she laughed too. From there we went to buy something to drink and went to the park. (Levi 2014)

This testimony prompted some of the participants in the public debate to claim the woman was a victim, calling upon the welfare services to come to her aid (Landsman 2014; Kamir 2014). Most of the voices in the public sphere continued to express righteous indignation at her depraved, inhuman, harmful conduct, however. The southern branch of the general attorney's office thus swiftly filed criminal charges against her (Siedler 2014d). Claiming that she constituted a public threat, the prosecution demanded her detention until the end of the legal proceedings (ibid.). She was charged with committing criminal sexual acts against dozens of children, motivated by a compulsive drive to derive sexual satisfaction from intercourse with minors. The prosecution claimed that the woman used tender children as tools in the service of her insatiable lust (ibid.). She was thus officially framed as revoltingly monstrous.

MORAL PANIC PHASE II: A PALESTINIAN LILITH

The charges against the "Kiryat Gat woman" were brought on June 11, 2014. The following night, three Israeli teenagers were reported missing from Jewish settlements in the occupied West Bank. Between June 13 and June 30, 2014, when their bodies were found, Israeli media focused solely on their wellbeing, speculation regarding their whereabouts, and reports of the search for them (Kubovic, Harel et al. 2014). The "Kiryat Gat woman" was completely forgotten.

On June 16, 2014, MK Haneen Zoabi was interviewed on Tel Aviv radio in connection with the missing adolescents. Zoabi is the first Palestinian woman (and Israeli citizen) to be elected to the Israeli Knesset as a member of an Arab party (Balad). Single, short-haired, childless, and blatantly outspoken (by Israeli standards with respect to Palestinian Israeli citizens), she quickly became very unpopular among Israeli Jews. Her active, high-profile involvement in the Gaza flotilla in 2010, which included blunt criticism of the Israeli naval blockade of the Gaza Strip, her presence on a ship sailing from Turkey to Gaza, and her fierce condemnation of the Israeli army's attack of the ship, made her the most hated woman in Israel (Strickland 2015).

In the radio interview, Zoabi asked:

> Is it strange that people living under occupation and living impossible lives, in a situation where Israel kidnaps new prisoners every day, is it strange that they kidnap? They are not terrorists. Even if I do not agree with them, they are people who do not see any way to change their reality, and they are compelled to use means like these. (Hovel 2104; Zonszein 2014)

In contemporary Israeli Hebrew, the label "terrorist" is tantamount to "menacing monster." Palestinians labeled as such are considered by many Israeli Jews to be "two-legged animals"—that is, inhuman beasts innately programmed to kill. In stating that Palestinians who kidnap Israelis are not terrorists but desperate victims of the Israeli occupation, Zoabi claimed that they were not monsters but human beings, motivated by human feelings, political aspirations, and offenses against their human dignity and rights.

By widespread Israeli standards, such a statement constitutes treason—so unspeakably outrageous that it renders the speaker herself a monstrous, inhuman, bloodthirsty foe.[5] Not surprisingly, immediately following the interview Israel's then Minister of Foreign Affairs, Avigdor Lieberman, thus declared: "Not only are the kidnappers terrorists but Haneen Zoabi is a terrorist too. . . . The fate of the kidnappers and the fate of the inciter who encourages kidnapping, Haneen Zoabi, should be the same" (Harkov 2014).

In the wake of this interview, Israeli ministers, MKs, and other public figures competed to find the harshest words to condemn her (Harkov 2014), their zealous, derogatory epithets being repeatedly reported in great detail in on-the-hour national news broadcasts. This marked the official "open season" on Zoabi. Social media exploded with hate speech directed towards her, internet and Facebook pages named "Zoabi the Whore" gaining vast numbers of "likes" and sharing. The outspoken, unmarried, childless Palestinian woman was described as a cold-blooded, man-hating, child-threatening lesbian. People wished gang rape and torture upon her and she received hundreds of death threats (Lis and Kubovich, 2014a). In an op-ed published on June 25 in *Haaretz* (Israel's equivalent of the *New York Times*), Emilia Cohen called the affair a witch-hunt:

> The many responses on Facebook [to Zoabi's interview] did not attempt to address the content of her statement—an easy thing to do—but attacked her sexually: "Haneen Zoabi you need a black man with a dominant organ to shut you up[;]" "it's time to take the whore and stick her in a whore house;" "she is waiting for 72 Sudanese virgin-men to do her a favor;" "a frustrated old blue-stocking;" "Zoabi, suck my dick"—are just some of the expressions that flooded the net. A man, even an Arab, would never receive such responses. (Facebook posts, in Cohen 2014 [author's translation])

Significantly, as this communal fear and hate show was taking place, the digital newspaper *nrg* reported on June 17, 2014, that a woman in Nahariya was suspected of having sexual encounters with numerous young boys (Strauss 2014). The story was not picked up because the public and its conventional and social media all were too busy fearing, hating, and demonizing Zoabi. By the end of July 2014, Zoabi had been suspended from the Israeli Knesset for six months for her alleged support of terror (Lis 2014).

Shortly after the bodies of the three kidnapped youths were discovered, Israel launched Operation Protective Edge in Gaza (July 18, 2014). As Israeli media and social networks became preoccupied with the war, public interest in Haneen Zoabi significantly waned. Chauvinistic nationalists now channeled their misogynous anxiety and hatred in a new direction: Israel's southern enemy. The right-wing social media circulated explicit sexual slogans expressing militaristic views—the most telling perhaps being that calling on Israeli Prime Minister Benjamin Netanyahu, to "fuck" Gaza without any holding back: "Bibi, this time come inside" (Basol 2104).[6]

This violent sexual imagery suggests that, for some Israelis, the Gaza war served as an outlet for their aggressive, militant desires towards the menacing Lilith. Hamas-controlled Gaza, which has long been construed in Israel as a monstrous and threatening force, was portrayed by some in the summer of

2014 as a demoness that must be repelled by forceful penetration. The "Kiryat Gat woman," Haneen Zoabi, and Gaza all merged into a monstrous entity that had to be "fucked senseless" by the Israeli army. Through this gendered image, Operation Protective Edge could serve as a means of addressing the patriarchal distress aroused during the course of 2014.

LEGAL PANIC

In an earlier study (Kamir 2001, 60–67, 175–203), I suggested that Lilith moral panics sometimes induce legal systems to fight monstrous creatures with equally monstrous legal tools that occasionally linger on long after the panics have passed. In 2014, Israeli law-and-order authorities contributed to the double-tap Lilith moral panic in several deeply disturbing ways. Fortunately, the relatively short time within which the panic faded—probably due to the war in Gaza—appears to have prevented the perpetual corruption of the legal system by alarmed responses.

The first of the latter was the decision to charge the "Kiryat Gat woman" with several counts of sodomy. In Israeli criminal law, "rape" is defined in section 345 of the criminal code (1977) as non-consensual vaginal penetration, including any vaginal penetration of girls under 14. Section 347 defines "sodomy" as non-consensual oral or anal sexual penetration, including that of under-14-year-olds. Other non-consensual sexual acts that do not involve penetration and are meant to arouse or gratify the actor or humiliate the victim are labeled "indecent conduct" (sections 348–349). The Law for the Prevention of Sexual Harassment (1998) redefined "indecent conduct" as sexual harassment.

By all accounts, the Kiryat Gat woman allowed adolescents to penetrate her vaginally, orally, and anally, sometimes touching their genitals to stimulate them, her consent to penetration not always being free (as required by the Israeli criminal code). According to the Israeli criminal code, in relation to boys younger than fourteen, she should have been charged with indecent conduct/sexual harassment. Any adolescents over twelve who penetrated her without her free consent should have been charged with rape and/or sodomy—as she repeatedly requested, filing rape complaints with the police (Siedler 2014h).

In order to justify the charge of sodomy, the prosecution fabricated a monstrous legal construction, accusing her of *causing* the youngsters to sodomize her. Section 350 of the Israeli criminal code states that a person may be charged with committing a sexual offense if he or she *caused* the offense to be committed. This is clearly meant to apply to a person who caused another to rape, sodomize, or commit indecent conduct upon an unwilling victim.

The logic behind this legislation is that anyone who causes another to commit such conduct should be held responsible for the sexual offense as though he or she committed it themselves. This section is completely irrelevant in the case of someone who caused another person to penetrate her own body. Had the "Kiryat Gat woman" penetrated her body herself, there would clearly be no offense; causing another to do so thus cannot constitute one either. Put differently, such conduct has no victim, no organ being penetrated without its owner's free consent.

Nevertheless, apparently seeking to please the public, the prosecution used this outrageous legal construction to initiate cruel legal proceedings that set a dangerous precedent—namely, that any complainant of rape could be charged with rape herself, if the accused argued that she *caused* him to penetrate her. At the same time, none of the youngsters were charged with rape, sodomy, indecent conduct, or sexual harassment while the woman's complaints were totally ignored.

Riding the moral panic, Amnon Levy, a conservative MK, revived a legislative bill designed to expand the definition of rape to include any case in which a woman causes a man to penetrate her without his free will (Bender 2014). Although the bill had originally been supported by the Ministry of Justice, it was dropped when MKs understood that it would deter rape victims from filing complaints: women who alleged that they had been raped could face the counter-charge that they had *caused* the men to penetrate them and thus be liable themselves.[7]

As the moral panic evaporated, so did the proposed backlash bill and irrational charges of self-inflicted sodomy. On March 12, 2015, newspapers reported that a Beersheba court had accepted a plea bargain: the "Kiryat Gat woman" admitted committing seven indecent acts on minors and was sentenced to eighteen months in jail. She was also ordered to undergo psychological treatment, which she had long requested (Siedler 2105).

The outrageous, panicky legal treatment of Haneen Zoabi left an even deeper scar on Israel's democratic tissue. In mid-June, the police recommended investigating Zoabi for incitement over her claim that the kidnapping of three Israeli teens from a West Bank hitchhiking post was not a terrorist act (Lis and Kubovitch 2014b). A month later, they recommended that she be charged with the offense (Lior and Khoury 2104). Around the same time, she was suspended from the Israeli Knesset for six months, immediately appealing to the Supreme Court to overturn the decision (Lis 2014). In a mind-boggling move, the Supreme Court approved her suspension, stating that by refusing to call Palestinian kidnappers of Israeli teens "terrorists," Zoabi "went too far" and could reasonably be understood as supporting and encouraging terror (Hovel 2015). Four of the Supreme Court justices did not perceive Zoabi's suspension as interfering with her freedom of speech or right as an MK to express her political views and represent her voters. The single dissenting voice was that of Justice Salim Joubran, the only Palestinian (with Israeli citizenship) on Israel's Supreme Court (Hovel 2015).

A year later, however, in December 2015, when the moral panic was long over, the panicky criminal accusation evaporated with it. Without much ado, the legal authorities dropped the charges of incitement (Khoury 2015).

CONCLUSION

Over the course of the summer of 2014, the Israeli media reported the victimization of two women. Frail and disempowered, the "Kiryat Gat woman" was systematically exploited, humiliated, beaten, and raped by dozens of unruly adolescents. Parents, teachers, and social workers all looked the other way, enabling the continuation of the traumatizing abuse and the socialization of young Israeli Jews into conduct patterns of aggressive machismo. Haneen Zoabi, a female representative of an oppressed ethnic minority, was likewise delegitimized, suspended from office, and targeted by an unprecedented wave of gendered hate speech. Israeli ministers, MKs, and many participants in the public discourse threatened, incited against, humiliated, and insulted her in every possible way, frequently in gendered and sexual forms. Both these events were extreme cases of violent victimization exhibiting clear symptoms of gender discrimination, with the two women falling prey to overt sexual harassment.

Despite close, continuous scrutiny of both cases, however, neither officialdom nor the social media portrayed the events as victimization.[8] In both cases, the "monsterification" of the women disguised this circumstance, depicting them as dangerous, threatening aggressors rather than victims.

Israel's Basic Law: Human Dignity and Liberty (1992), the country's Bill of Rights, determines the equal worth of all human beings, promising basic human rights for all. However, monsters are inhuman, without any intrinsic value. Not sharing in human dignity, they are not entitled to basic human rights or decent, respectful treatment. As evil, menacing foes, they are inherently suspect, and all means for dealing with them are thus justified.

This chapter suggests that both the "Kiryat Gat woman" and MK Haneen Zoabi were rendered monstrous in the course of a double-tap Lilith moral panic that seized Israel in the summer of 2014. In a period of patriarchal distress, the two women served as scapegoats for communal anxieties. They were used to restore collective self-assurance by being construed in terms of the archetypal monstrous female, whose legendary presence explains corruption and turmoil, and the struggle against whom unites social forces in protection of their core.

The archetypal Lilith is extremely powerful in her combination of uncontrollable female sexuality and sharp, cutting wisdom and eloquence. One way of disempowering her is via a divide-and-conquer strategy—the slicing of her multifaceted image into two partial, paler, more manageable ones. The "Kiryat Gat" woman was portrayed as a voluptuous, insatiable, child-devouring nymphomaniac; Haneen Zoabi was depicted as an uncontrollably smart, strong, ruthless, "masculine" adversary. Together, they constituted an overpowering mythological Lilith. Separated, they could be caricatured, humiliated, and burnt on the stake. United, they might have conquered; divided they fell.

In the summer of 2014, instigated by patriarchal distress, moral panic in Israel took on nationalistic attributes, finally dissolving into militaristic aggression. While the panic dissipated, as all panics tend to do, and most of the monstrous legal instruments enlisted for the battle dissolved, Israeli patriarchy, nationalism, and militarism were redeemed and fortified. Monstrous Lilith was defeated. Female sexuality was once again cut off from wisdom and strength, with aggressive manly combat conquering all.

NOTES

1. A Hebrew version of this paper, written in August 2014, was rejected that October by the journal of the Israeli Anthropological Association, which had initially solicited it, due to the critical political undertones of the gender-nation connection. A revised Hebrew version was rejected in September 2017 by a law review for "crude language, unsuitable for publication" (both correspondences, in Hebrew, kept by the author). It was finally published, after lengthy negotiations, a year later.

2. Approximately 20 percent of Israel's citizens are Palestinian. Other Palestinians, including those who live in Gaza and the West Bank, are not Israeli citizens.

3. Lilith's Greek doppelgänger is Lamia, an incarnation of the prehistoric Libyan Great Mother Snake Goddess, Queen of Heaven and Earth (Edwards 1991, p. 208). According to the Olympian mythologists, Lamia was originally the beautiful Queen of Libya, beloved (raped?) by Zeus. When Hera, Zeus's jealous wife, killed all she bore Zeus, Lamia's pain transformed her into an ugly, old baby snatcher (Hera being the protectress of childbirth and children, Lamia threatened her protegées). Finally, she became a beast and went to live in a cave (Lederer 1968, p. 62). Lamia and Innana/Lilith appear to have merged in the Western unconscious imagination.

4. Kiryat Gat is a "development town"—i.e., built in the 1960s on the periphery to settle newcomers, frequently from Arab countries. These cities often suffer from high unemployment rates and governmental neglect.

5. Then Knesset Interior Committee chairwoman Miri Regev (Likud Beytenu) said: "Hanin Zoabi is a traitor and should be deported to Gaza . . . once a traitor, always a traitor" (Harkov 2014).

6. Basol—a Palestinian Israeli citizen—notes that Palestine as a whole and Gaza in particular are both referred to in the Arab media as a bride who, rather than spending her wedding night with her Arab savior/groom, is raped by Zionists (Basol 2014).

7. Supporting the initiative, the Ministry of Justice argued that existing legislation prevents the prosecution of a woman who caused a man to penetrate her, hence the need for explicit legislation. I participated in the Knesset discussions, arguing against the proposed bill. The prosecution's charges against the "Kiryat Gat woman" interpreted the criminal code in clear contravention of the Justice Department's own express stance regarding the draft bill.

8. The striking exceptions were the few voices, primarily expressed in *Haaretz* (see, for example, Landsman 2014; Kamir 2014).

REFERENCES

Baltman, Daniel. 2014. "Officials Knew Woman Was Having Sex With Teenagers." *Haaretz*, June 9, http://www.haaretz.com/israel-news/.premium-1.597661.

Basol, Jenan. 2014. "Gaza's Sexists." *Haaretz*, 4 August, https://www.haaretz.co.il/gallery/mejunderet/.premium-1.2396709 (Hebrew).

Bender, Arik. 2014. "Who Is Opposed to a Law Incriminating Women of Rape?" *Maariv*, June 26, www.maariv.co.il/news/new.aspx?pn6Vq=E&0r9VQ=FKDGD.

Cohen, Emilia. 2014. "The Witches Haneen and Ortal." *Haaretz*, June 25, https://www.haaretz.co.il/opinions/.premium-1.2359297 (Hebrew).

Cohen, Stanley. 1980. *Folk Devils and Moral Panics: The Creation of the Mods and Rockers*. Oxford: Martin Robertson.

Edwards, Carolyn McVicker. 1991. *The Storyteller's Goddess: Tales of the Goddess and Her Wisdom from around the World*. San Francisco: Harper.

Goode, Erich and Nachman Ben-Yehuda. 1994a. *Moral Panics: The Social Construction of Deviance*. Oxford: Wiley.

———. 1994b. "Moral Panics: Culture, Politics, And Social Construction." *Annual Review of Sociology* 20: 149–71.

Haaretz. 2014. "Eyal Golan Accuses Ashkenazi Reporters of 'Dancing on His Blood.'" *Haaretz*, April 3, https://www.haaretz.com/israel-news/1.583673.

———. 2015. "Embattled Minister's Wife Blasts Meretz Leader: 'If Only I Was a Terrorist, She'd Love Me.'" *Haaretz*, December 19, https://www.haaretz.com/israel-news/1.692727.

Halperin-Kaddari, Ruth. 2004. *Women in Israel: A State of Their Own*. Philadelphia: University of Pennsylvania Press.

Harkov, Lahav. 2014. "Zoabi: Kidnappers Are not Terrorists, They're Fighting Occupation." *Jerusalem Post*, June 17, http://www.jpost.com/Pillar-of-Defense/Zoabi-Kidnappers-are-not-terrorists-theyre-fighting-occupation-359609.

Hovel, Revital. 2014. "High Court Rejects MK Haneen Zoabi's Petition to Overturn Suspension." *Haaretz*, October 12, http://www.haaretz.com/israel-news/.premium-1.630845.

———. 2015. "Israel's Supreme Court Justifies MK Zoabi's Suspension From Knesset." Haaretz, February 11, http://www.haaretz.com/israel-news/1.642039.

Kamir, Orit. 2001. *Every Breath You Take: Stalking Narratives and the Law*. Ann Arbor, MI: University of Michigan Press.

———. 2003. "Dignity, Respect and Equality in Sexual Harassment Law: Israel's New Legislation." *New Directions in Sexual Harassment Law*, edited by Catharine MacKinnon & Reva Segal, 561. New Haven: Yale University Press.

———. 2008. "Law, Culture and Society in the Case of Haim Ramon: Israel's Indecent Conduct Offense, Relevant Social Norms and a New Proposed Sexual Offenses Law." *Hamishpat Law Journal* 13: 289–340 (Hebrew).

———. 2014. "Hunting the Witch from Kiryat Gat." *Haaretz*, June 15, https://www.haaretz.co.il/opinions/.premium-1.2348841 (Hebrew).

Kaplan Sommer, Allison. 2015. "The Rise and Fall of the Ultimate Israeli Power Couple." *Haaretz*, December 20, https://www.haaretz.com/israel-news/1.692940.

Khoury, Jack. 2015. "MK Zoabi Reaches Plea Deal, Will Not Be Charged With Incitement." *Haaretz*, December 10, http://www.haaretz.com/israel-news/.premium-1.691234.

Kubovich, Yaniv. 2013. "Eyal Golan Is Top Israeli Singer Embroiled in Underage Sex Scandal." *Haaretz*, November 20, https://www.haaretz.com/israel-news/1.559105.

———. 2014a. "Nine Youths Arrested on Suspicion of Sexually Assaulting 13-year-old Girl." *Haaretz*, March 25, https://www.haaretz.com/israel-news/.premium-1.581827.

———. 2014b. "Sheetrit Signed Secret Deal With Fired Housekeeper Over Sexual Harassment." *Haaretz*, June 12, https://www.haaretz.com/israel-news/1.598299.

Kubovich, Yaniv and Revital Hovel. 2014. "Israeli Minister Silvan Shalom Accused of Sex Offense." *Haaretz*, March 24, https://www.haaretz.com/israel-news/.premium-1.581580.

Kubovich, Yaniv, Amos Harel, Yair Etinger, Chaim Levinson, Barak Ravid, Gil Cohen, and *Haaretz*. 2014. "LIVE UPDATES: Israel Searches for Teens Kidnapped in West Bank, Day 3." *Haaretz*, June 15, https://www.haaretz.com/israel-news/1.598771.

Landsman, Carolina. 2014. "The Banality of Injustice." *Haaretz*, June 13, http://www.haaretz.com/opinion/.premium-1.598556.

Lederer, Wolfgang. 1968. *The Fear of Women*. New York: Harcourt Brace Jovanovitch.

Levi, Shai. 2014. "A 14-Year-Old: I Sat There as My Friends Did Her Together." www.mynet.co.il/articles/0,7340,L-4527147,00.html (Hebrew).

Lior, Ilan and Jack Khoury. 2014. "Israel Police Recommends Putting Arab PM on Trial." *Haaretz*, August 19, http://www.haaretz.com/israel-news/.premium-1.611325.

Lis, Jonathan. 2014. "MK Zoabi Suspended from Knesset Plenum for Excusing West Bank Kidnap." *Haaretz*, July 27, http://www.haaretz.com/israel-news/.premium-1.607838.

Lis, Jonathan and Yaniv Kubovich. 2014a. "MK Zoabi Gets Knesset Bodyguard Amid Wave of Threats Against Her: Police, Prosecutors Checking Whether she Violated Law against Incitement in her Remarks about Recent Kidnapping." *Haaretz*, June 18, http://www.haaretz.com/israel-news/.premium-1.599654.

———. 2014b. "Police Open Investigation against MK Haneen Zoabi for Incitement: Balad MK has been under Fire for Saying the Kidnapping of the Three Israeli Teens was not Terrorism." *Haaretz*, July 25, http://www.haaretz.com/israel-news/.premium-1.607234.

Littman, Shani. 2013. "'Six Acts': Power and Sex Among Israeli Teens." *Haaretz*, 5 December 2014, https://www.haaretz.com/israel-news/culture/leisure/.premium-1.561882.

Siedler, Shirly. 2014a. "Disturbed Woman Arrested after Allegedly Sleeping with Hundreds of Boys." *Haaretz*, May 30, http://www.haaretz.com/israel-news/.premium-1.596193.

———. 2014b. "Kiryat Gat Woman in Teen Sex Scandal Fit to Stand Trial." *Haaretz*, 30 May, http://www.haaretz.com/israel-news/.premium-1.597279.

———. 2014c. "Israeli Woman in Teen Sex Scandal not HIV Carrier." *Haaretz*, 1 June, http://www.haaretz.com/israel-news/.premium-1.596610.

———. 2014d. "Israeli Woman Indicted for 'Causing Minors to Commit Sodomy on Her.'" *Haaretz*, June 11, http://www.haaretz.com/israel-news/.premium-1.598230?=&ts=_1503261294680.

———. 2014h. "The Sex Scandal in Kiryat Gat: Public Defense Filed Rape Charges on Behalf of Suspect." *Haaretz*, June 3, https://www.haaretz.co.il/news/law/.premium-1.2339099 (Hebrew).

———. 2015. "Plea Bargain Confirmed for Resident of Kiryat Gat Accused of Indecent Conduct with Minors: Will Serve 18 Months." *Haaretz*, March 12, http://www.haaretz.co.il/news/law/1.2587811.

Strauss, Yair. 2014. "Nahariya: A Woman Suspected of Having Intercourse with 13 Year Olds." *nrg*, June 17, www.nrg.co.il/online/1/ART2/586/291.html (Hebrew).

Strickland, Patrick. 2015. "Q&A: Hanin Zoabi – Israel's 'Bad Arab.'" *Aljazeera*, February 11, http://www.aljazeera.com/news/2015/02/qa-hanin-zoabi-israel-bad-arab-150202072900248.html.

Yassif, Eli. 1984. *The Tales of Ben Sira in the Middle Ages: A Critical Text and Literary Studies*. Jerusalem: Magnes (Hebrew).

Zonszein, Meirav. 2014. "The Knesset v. Zoabi: Israeli Arab MK's Politics Put on Trial." *Haaretz*, September 12, https://972mag.com/trial-over-zoabi-suspension-turns-political/99770/.

Chapter Five

Evil-by-Proxy and Everyday Monsters

Toward a Moral Sociology for Overcoming the Passive Observation of Evil

Michael Hviid Jacobsen

INTRODUCTION[1]

When I was recently visiting colleagues in Liverpool (UK), a young man lost his life under violent and tragic circumstances. I was staying in a hotel not far from the hustle and bustle of the famous nightlife district in the city. Upon waking up one morning, I discovered from the local *Liverpool Echo* newspaper that a young man—Anthony Condron (29)—had been beaten to death in a bar not far from my hotel. Based on police reports, several people had been present in the bar at the time of the "altercation," which the local media described as an utterly "unprovoked assault." Condron had been on a night out with his partner and friends before his life was ended on the floor of a music club. Subsequently, three young local men were arrested and charged with manslaughter. The next day, I was out in town myself, and when turning the corner to the (in)famous Matthew Street I witnessed, first-hand, a brutal fistfight between a bunch of young men—in which particularly the image of an aggressive guy yelling "I am going to f****** kill you!" to his opponents stayed with me afterwards. Presumably, and luckily, no one was seriously hurt during this particular incident, but the spectacle of a group of young men deliberately wanting to hurt each other in the midst of a crowd of unresponsive and slightly encouraging spectators prompted me to write this piece.

Obviously, these two stories do not tell us anything conclusive about the character of the nightlife of a particular city; neither does it only reveal something about particular people being present in the particular circumstances reported above. In fact, it could probably have been in almost any city in any country in the world. However, it does perhaps tell us of something of a more general nature, namely that we are all, in different degrees of physical proximity, spectators to incidents involving harm to and evil-doing towards others. Even though the death of another human being (such as the case with Anthony Condron above) is always something extraordinary, episodes like these are unfortunately far from special cases or unlikely events. Stacked on my office desk, I have several newspaper clippings from the past few years bearing witness to the fact that people are being harassed, bullied, mutilated and even killed with non-interfering observers present. Obviously, this is far from new. When African-American people were lynched in public in the United States during the aftermath of the civil war, when people were hurried down dark corridors to end their lives in stuffy gas chambers in concentration camps during World War II or when ethnic cleansings were being performed in the Balkans in the 1990s, there were often hundreds or even thousands of passive onlookers who did not intervene. But why did they not intervene? Why did they not voice their objections or try to stop the misdeeds? The same goes for television viewers watching starvation, mutilation and war crimes committed against innocent people. Why do they not turn their anger and resentment into action? Why do they not start pestering their elected politicians to intervene? Why do they accept that evil is part of life? Obviously, *some do something*, but—let us face it—most remain passive observers in these situations. We can probably all agree that those who actively commit such heinous acts of violence and murder are somehow inhuman monsters who should be persecuted and punished for their actions, but they still remain aberrations from the norm. So even though their actions are indeed atrocious, this group of people is nevertheless a minority. But how about all those who both directly and indirectly witness human suffering and pain and do nothing? Are they exempt from moral judgment? How can we accept their (and our own) passivity? Why are they not motivated or impelled to intervene? These are some of the questions to be explored further in this chapter.

This chapter is concerned with delineating and discussing the rise and the consequences of the so-called "spectator society." In the chapter, I want to introduce and explore the notions of "evil-by-proxy," "everyday monsters" and "techniques of passivation." By drawing kaleidoscopically and admittedly unsystematically on the conceptual apparatuses of, for example, "adiaphorization," "liquid modernity," "moral blindness," "unconditional moral responsibility" (Zygmunt Bauman 1993), "unresponsive bystanding" (Bibb Latané and John M. Darley 1970), "techniques of neutralization" (Gresham M. Sykes and David Matza 1957), the "visibility of evil" (Lewis A. Coser 1969/1988), "postemotionalism" (Stjepan G. Meštrović 1997), "distant suffering" (Luc Boltanski 1993), "states of denial" (Stanley Cohen 2001) and "compassion fatigue" (Keith Tester 2001), as well as many other relevant sources of inspiration, the chapter seeks to develop an understanding of the social processes supporting the rise of a "spectator society." The chapter argues that passivity vis-à-vis harm-doing and suffering is socially contagious creating, at the micro-level as well as at the macro-level, the perfect conditions for the perpetuation of actual evil. The chapter deals with two different levels of "evil-by-proxy"—at the microsociological level, the chapter revisits and discusses the "bystander effect" or the "spectator mentality" based on some classic studies of the Holocaust atrocities and the murder case of Kitty Genovese, and, at the macrosociological level, the chapter will discuss how the media in contemporary liquid-modern society contributes to "compassion fatigue" and to the passive observation of "distant suffering." The chapter thus argues that the "monster" is perhaps not only the perpetrator of actual evil, but also that we are all potentially "everyday monsters" by passively watching and accepting acts of evil. Due to the scope and complexity of these matters, the chapter only promises to provide a selective sketch of a sociological understanding of the topics of "evil-by-proxy," "everyday monsters" and "techniques of passivation" as well as, towards the end, to suggest an—admittedly tentative—framework for moral action.

"EVIL-BY-PROXY"—THOUGHTS ON THE "BYSTANDER EFFECT"

Conventionally, sociology has not been prone to investigate the topic of evil, presumably due to the normative connotations of the notion of "evil." Moreover, because evil is seen as so difficult to narrow down conceptually as well as to capture empirically, sociologists—with a few exceptions—have been more than happy to hand over the topic to moral philosophers, theologians and to their colleagues in social psychology departments (Lemert 1997; Lyman 1989). As American sociologist Stanford M. Lyman once noted: "Evil seems to be too great, too impersonal, and too absurd to be a serious concern for sociological concern. Its very omnipresence, grossness and grotesqueries defy and transcend the sociological imagination" (Lyman 1989:1). Moral philosophers, theologians, social psychologists and lawmakers have been keen to specify different types of evil such as "natural evil," "moral evil," "pure evil" and so on. Incarnations of so-called "pure evil" are often depicted in the mass media as being personified by serial killers, mass murderers, school shooters, sexual predators, pedophiles, terrorists and others who deliberately harm or inflict pain on other people. However, one of the pathways through which evil can also be understood to enter the social world is perhaps through the so-called "bystander effect"—a phenomenon loaded with historical, sociological and psychological evidence (see, e.g., Barnett 1999; Clarkson 1996; Staub 2003). When discussing the so-called "bystander effect," or what in this chapter will be labeled "evil-by-proxy" or the "spectator mentality," one can—at least—consult two by now classic and authoritative sources.

When describing the predicament of the Jewish population during the Holocaust, Austrian-American political scientist and historian Raul Hilberg (1992) proposed the first of these understandings of the role of the bystander. In his scenario, there were three groups of people involved in the events: the victims, the perpetrators and the bystanders. Hilberg described this latter group as those who *could* have done something in order to prevent the fate of the Jews but nevertheless refrained from acting. So even though the bystanders did not directly inflict any harm themselves, they had knowledge of and at times even bore witness to what went on, but felt too powerless to prevent it. The bystanders—individuals as well as nation states—thus did not harm the victims, but at the same time they did nothing to stop the harm being done by others, because they did not themselves want to be harmed by the Nazi perpetrators (Hilberg 1992:xi). In Hilberg's analysis of the bystander effect, he thus pointed out that the bystanders might have made a difference had they dared to intervene and help the hapless victims. Hilberg distinguished between two different ways in which the bystanders could have acted in order to help the victims and two different types of helpers. According to him, one's assistance to victims may be short-lived and relatively risk-free for oneself, on the one side, and, on the other, it may be more sustained and risk-inducing—and thus by helping the victims one might be putting oneself in a dangerous situation. Moreover, Hilberg differentiated the "selective helpers" who involve themselves in helping out only specific individuals or groups from those armed with a more universalistic mentality who want to help everyone in need (Hilberg 1992:212–214). Hilberg's contention is therefore that the many bystanders were in fact complicit and culpable in the events that took place prior to and during the Holocaust atrocities, because they *did not help* the victims; and even though *some* did indeed help (and often placed themselves at great risk for doing so), the vast majority did not.

The second classic source for understanding the bystander effect is the much publicized and debated description of the so-called "Kitty Genovese case" referring to the murder of the twenty-eight-year-old American bar manager Kitty Genovese in Kew Gardens, New York City, in 1964. She died from repeated stab wounds inflicted by her attacker, Winston Moseley, and it is estimated that the dirty deed (consisting of numerous deadly stab wounds, rape and eventually theft from a dying person) lasted at least half an hour before Genovese eventually died. Several books have subsequently speculated and sought to clarify—even though the actual circumstances of the murder case are still a matter of controversy—why so many people in a densely populated area apparently heard Kitty's screams for help (and some also reporting seeing her being assaulted) and nobody did anything, nobody came to her rescue, which might in the end have saved her life. Inspired by the Genovese case and relying on social-psychological research, American scholars Bibb Latané and John M. Darley (1970) in their ground-breaking book on the so-called unresponsive bystander stated that one reason might be that deep down "passivity is contagious": when everybody present (and especially if many people are present) is turning their backs or shrugging their shoulders, nobody intervenes. Even though there has continued to be a lot of controversy within social-psychological research (especially based on studies using controlled experiments and questionnaire methods) concerning how to interpret and extrapolate from the Genovese case—and not least due to the highly tenuous and inconclusive character of the available evidence—the primary outcome of the case has often been critically to point to the self-sufficiency and blasé attitude of modern urban living and the way in which a cultural insensitivity towards the suffering of others has gradually spread throughout society. We will return to this point later in the chapter.

The Holocaust and the Genovese cases both undoubtedly point to some important lessons to be learned for a sociology concerned with evil. First and foremost, they were not one-off events. There are indeed strong parallels between what Hilberg specifically described in connection to the Holocaust with what later took place in the Balkans and Rwanda in the 1990s and most recently in Syria. There are also certain parallels between the Kitty Genovese case and the grisly murder of Liverpool toddler James Bulger, who was abducted, tortured and killed with his mutilated body left on the railway line by two ten-year-olds in 1993 (Levine 1999), not to mention the manslaughter of Anthony Condron detailed in the beginning of the chapter. Even though these events are in many respects unique historical testimonies of concrete individuals acting in specific ways in concrete circumstances, they still share the same factor that *someone* had knowledge of or perhaps even heard and saw what transpired without intervening. Thus, neither the Holocaust atrocities nor the Genovese murder was an entirely exceptional case (although the magnitude and expediency of the mass killings in the concentration camps is almost beyond historical comparison). So despite their unique sets of individuals, sequences of actions and circumstances, they are nevertheless still paradigmatic cases of so many other similar or relatively similar incidents—historical or individual—in which people have been molested and murdered whilst being witnessed by passive bystanders. Even though the bystanders in the Holocaust events, in the Kitty Genovese case and elsewhere (at times only a very few individuals, at other times millions of seeing, hearing and knowing people) *in themselves* did nothing to harm the victims, their inaction nevertheless did not prevent evil from being carried out. This is therefore what can be described as "evil-by-proxy." Australian philosopher Raimond Gaita once proposed that "actions are evil by proxy when they result in evil states of affairs" (Gaita 1991/2004:65). Gaita's point is indeed well put, however I am here rather inclined to suggest that "evil-by-proxy" is a term more appropriately reserved for all those *inactions* that result in evil-doing to others (and the denial of this evil-doing) and especially inactions that—had they been turned into action—might *perhaps* (obviously we will never know for sure) have prevented evil from materializing in the first place. Let us, in the following sections, turn our attention to some of the social mechanisms and cultural factors of modern and liquid-modern society that seem to produce—or at least do not seem to prevent—evil-by-proxy from occurring.

SOLID MODERNITY AND ADIAPHORIZATION—CUTTING THE CHAIN OF EVIL INTO BITS AND PIECES

Earlier we saw how "evil-by-proxy" is a term here reserved for the outcome of the inactions of spectators to different kinds of human suffering—suffering that *may* have been prevented or at least alleviated by a more active approach on behalf of the unresponsive bystanders. According to Polish-British sociologist Zygmunt Bauman, modern society (in his terminology "solid modernity"; Bauman 2000) and particularly the modern organizational structure (which Max Weber described as a "bureaucracy" [Weber 1922/2004]) was well-suited to silence the "inner voice of conscience" that people might feel whenever confronted with evil, injustice or suffering. Those working in such organizations were, still in Weber's memorable terms, "men of order," who had a "passion for bureaucratization," and who were warmed by a "cold rationality." First of all, according to Bauman (1994), in such organizations the main problem becomes one of "floating responsibility"—in a highly structured chain of command everybody will always point upwards and thus exempt themselves of responsibility for any wrongdoing (and those at the top will claim that they themselves did nothing or knew nothing about what their subordinates did). Secondly, modern organizations routinely reject any association with topics of "good" and "evil." All that matters is to keep the organization or business running as smoothly as possible and according to the overall scheme of things. All in all, Bauman observed that the "modern organization is a contraption designed to make human actions immune from what the actors believe and feel privately" (Bauman 1994:10). Such organizations, relying as they do on duty and blind loyalty, place people in what Stanley Milgram (1963) once called an "agentic state" in which they do not feel (or rather are not expected or allowed to feel) personally responsible for the outcome of their actions (or, we might add, inactions). Morality, empathy and compassion thus give way to rationality, expediency and procedural correctness. This is all part and parcel of the bureaucratic ethos.

Elsewhere, Bauman (1995) specifically proposed the tortuous notion of *adiaphorization* to account for the emptying of action of moral content in modern society, instead making the assessment of actions (or inactions for that sake) a matter of, for example, efficiency or technical precision. According to Bauman, adiaphorization refers to the cutting of sequences of action into small separate units, thereby blurring the unbroken line of consequences leading from one action to another, eventually excusing the acting individual for the actions/inactions gone before and after what he or she personally did (Bauman 1995:133–134). Moreover, adiaphorization also reduces the victim or suffering person to a set of easily identifiable traits or negatively constructed characteristics (for example, the "Jew" or "refugee") thereby diminishing the very humanity of the victim. The outcome of adiaphorization processes is nothing less than moral indifference and dehumanization. Adiaphorization is thus the label used to describe:

> the stripping of human relationships of their moral significance, exempting them from moral evaluation, rendering them "morally irrelevant." Adiaphorization is set in motion whenever the relationship involves less than the total person, whenever the object of the relationship is a selected aspect . . . since it is only the *full* relationship, a relationship between spatially and temporally *whole* selves, that may be "moral," that is embrace the issue of responsibility for the other. Preventing the looking from turning into seeing is . . . a major mechanism of adiaphorization (Bauman 1995:133–134).

Such adiaphorization processes abounded in modern society—pregnant as it was, in Hannah Arendt's words, with "totalitarian tendencies"—and they played a significant role in bystanding, not only within organizations and corporate businesses but also in everyday life. They made many human bystanders into assembly-line cogs in machines of murder and mutilation in which these individuals perhaps did not themselves press the button or pour the Zyklon B down the hatches and ventilation holes, but they nevertheless, in many minor ways, contributed to keeping the process running in an unobstructed manner. In his critically acclaimed book on the modern preconditions for the Holocaust exterminations, Bauman thus quoted American Holocaust scholar Henry L. Feingold on how it all proceeded in a seemingly innocent way:

> [Auschwitz] was also a mundane extension of the modern factory system. Rather than producing goods, the raw material was human beings and the end-product was death, so many units per day marked carefully on the manager's production charts. The chimneys, the very symbol of the modern factory system,

> poured forth the smoke produced by burning human flesh. The brilliantly organized railroad grid of modern Europe carried a new kind of raw material to the factories. It did so in the same manner as with other cargo. In the gas chambers the victims inhaled noxious gas generated by prussic acid pellets, which were produced by the advanced chemical industry of Germany. Engineers designed the crematoria; managers designed the system of bureaucracy that worked with a zest and efficiency more backward nations would envy. Even the overall plan itself was a reflection of the modern scientific spirit gone awry. What we witnessed was nothing less than a massive scheme of social engineering (Feingold quoted in Bauman 1989:8).

In many ways, there was a strange sense of normality about it all. Adiaphorization processes (of which the Holocaust was but one extreme example)—characterized as they were by bureaucratic chains of command, a concern with technical solutions and industrial output as well as a machine-like approach to human life—also made it possible to exempt the millions of bystanders from any feelings of shame, guilt or remorse, because the processes were designed in quite similar ways to many other ordinary types of factory production. The bystanders in this highly organized system of human mass murder could always claim that none of them pressed the trigger or pushed the victims into the innocently labeled "showers." However, whether they were functionaries stamping a ticket with Auschwitz as the final destination, architects designing railroad systems and blueprints for work camps, soldiers zealously guarding the perimeter of the concentration camps, foremen organizing daily production plans in the camps or members of the *Sonderkommando* cleaning up the crematoria after use, they *did* see the victims, they *did* contemplate the character of their work, they *did* speculate about the smoke rising from the crematorium chimneys, they *did* smell the strong odor of burning human flesh and so on. But they still *did not* intervene. They were all a classic case of unresponsive bystanders blindly following orders and obeying their superiors. And remember, this was far from just a Holocaust incidence—Stalin's purges of dissidents and Mao's "Cultural Revolution" shared an eerily close resemblance in the way in which mass murder was effectively carried out in the age of solid modernity—indeed, in Eric Hobsbawm's words, a "century of extremes" (Hobsbawm 1994).

There are so many testimonies from survivors of the concentration camp system who were incapable of understanding how so many presumably "good people" either participated in the processes of dehumanization and extermination or did nothing to prevent it. Based on his research on Nazi Germany in the 1930s and again after World War II, American sociologist Everett C. Hughes (1962) once answered the question of why "good people do dirty work" by insisting that processes of distancing from the actions one performed, dissociation from fellow human beings, the existence of small secret societies of those who knew but did not react, feelings of loyalties and discipline, fear of retaliation and a host of other explanations could help account for the apparent smoothness with which so many were killed without widespread objections. Almost simultaneously with the publication of Hughes's piece, Hannah Arendt (1962) famously and in great detail described the eerie banality or normality of evil (exemplified through the trial of Adolf Eichmann), by showing that evil is not necessarily dressed in extraordinary or recognizable garments, but is often practiced by those functionaries, foot soldiers and others who willingly follow orders without objecting. So apparently "good people," it seems, often commit "bad deeds" without bad conscience, because they are capable of somehow normalizing and neutralizing whatever they did. The same, one might suspect, may also be the case with those who witness—directly or indirectly—the suffering of others through the media.

LIQUID MODERNITY AND MEDIATED SUFFERING—EVIL AS SPECTACLE

Even though the newspaper, radio, camera and cinema (with its weekly news reels) were indeed all invented and available to the public by the time of the Holocaust (and were thus capable of documenting the atrocities to a reading, hearing and watching audience), the media landscape and its ability to instantaneously reach and capture us all 24/7 has changed quite dramatically since then, not the least with the invention of the internet and the proliferation of the mobile phone. The media is not only a Fourth Estate as so often described within political science theory, it now also becomes a fourth party—besides perpetrator(s), victim(s) and bystander(s)—in the way in which violence and evil are being communicated and received outside the immediate context of suffering to a potentially worldwide audience. Today, we have thus all become "global bystanders" and "eye witnesses to the wrongs done to human beings everywhere in the world. We do not just hear of evil—we see evil being done" (Bauman 2010:96). The face-to-face of solid modernity is now being supplemented (and perhaps increasingly replaced) by the face-to-interface on the internet.

British sociologist Anthony Giddens (1990) once spoke of "disembedding" as an integral part of the transformation of modernity, claiming that events are now lifted out of the immediacies of their time-and-space–bound confines and into a new global context—and in this way also evil is being disembedded from its actual crime scenes and is dispersed and proliferates online. We can now watch and re-watch it again and again: videos of the decapitation of captivated journalists and aid workers, suicide bombings, executions, plane crashes, fatal car accidents and other unspeakable extremities are immediately available for those who seek out this kind of violent voyeurism. The so-called society of the spectacle once envisaged by French philosopher and writer Guy Debord (1970) has now moved well beyond even his wildest imagination. With the society of the spectacle, or the "spectator society," everything can in principle become spectacular: sex, politics, sport, evil, suffering and even death (see, e.g., Jacobsen 2016). Unsurprisingly, in such a "spectator society" a "spectator mentality" prevails—and at times evil even seems to become entertainment—and as a consequence the spectacular no longer seems to move us as we have already become accustomed to witnessing and observing all kinds of human misery without much moral outrage or emotional distress. Croatian-American sociologist Stjepan G. Meštrović (1997) once claimed that we now live in a "postemotional society" in which our emotions are being manufactured, manipulated and McDonaldized by the media, and this means that we are unable to muster any genuine, deep or lasting sense of, for example, empathy or sympathy that would make us susceptible to the suffering of others. We are simply deprived of real feelings and, even worse, are unable to tell the real ones from those artificially induced. Add to this what American feminist theorist Judith Butler (2009) has called "grievability": that we seem to have developed a highly selective sense of which kinds of lives we deem valuable—the loss of which should be mourned—as against those millions of lives that we deem invaluable and thus also ungrievable.

The important role played by the media in communicating evil and suffering has been the concern of a growing body of literature over the years. For example, in his influential book *Distant Suffering* (1993) French sociologist Luc Boltanski discussed the "spectacles of suffering" made available to television viewers around the world. By differentiating between two types of response to suffering—"pity" motivated by an abstract universalism and "compassion" relying on a local particularism—Boltanski laid bare some of the main dilemmas of the humanitarian movement. It was his point that spectators of distant suffering *could* become activated, first by feeling "indignant" and then by starting to "speak," to themselves and to others, of what they have witnessed, thereby perhaps being able to influence public opinion. In Boltanski's words: "we must maintain an orientation towards action, a disposition to act, even if this is only by speaking out in support of the unfortunate" (Boltanski 1993:153). Even though Boltanski's book did not contain any ready-made prophylaxis against distant suffering, he recommended that we orient ourselves to the present—to the presently felt and witnessed suffering—instead of being preoccupied with past or future injustices. British sociologist Stanley Cohen, in his book *States of Denial* (2001), has pointed out how denial is a common strategy used in many situations in everyday, political and social life, but that denial becomes particularly problematic when it ignores the suffering of others. By developing a catalog of different "states of denial" as well as separating different "types of bystanders" from each other (such as "internal bystanders," "external bystanders" and "bystander nations"), Cohen provided a useful vocabulary for understanding why people—individually as well as collectively—do not react when knowing about or being confronted with the suffering and tragedy of others. He also used the term "everyday bystanders" to account for all those who in everyday life—observing bullying in the schoolyard, harassment in the workplace or other types of offensive behavior—are discouraged to react in order to stop the unfolding situation. To Cohen, the problem with denial was that we would almost always be able to rationalize it away by referring to so many seemingly "good excuses" for not intervening. Also in several acclaimed books, Greek media and communications scholar Lilie Chouliaraki has pointed out how humanitarianism today finds itself between a rock and a hard place (Chouliaraki 2006, 2013). The reason for this, she suggests, is that we now live in "post-humanitarian" and neoliberal times in which the displayed concern for the suffering of others (as expressed, for example, by "caring" Hollywood celebrities, Facebook and Twitter one-liners, charity rock concerts or the wearing of the fashionable wrist bands) is often just another way of showing off ourselves to others. Conviction and vision have been replaced by choice—we *choose* to engage in such "good causes" because it makes *us* feel good, but not the least because it makes *us* look good. Our displayed concern for the suffering and vulnerable others, as Chouliaraki claims, is therefore "ironic" if not downright narcissistic as it has no connection with any genuine or deep-seated interest in understanding or alleviating the actual and mainly structural causes of suffering, and, at the end of the day, it has very little lasting impact on the actual course of events in the world.

All in all, the admittedly rather gloomy picture here painted of the role of the media in contemporary society makes it quite clear that liquid modernity—like its solid-modern predecessor—has its own fair share of adiaphorization processes, which blur not only the causes and consequences of the suffering of others but ultimately also dilute the responsibility for what takes place and for what could be done to prevent it. Boltanski's (1993), Cohen's (2001) and Chouliaraki's (2006, 2013) observations above also indirectly raise the tricky question: who are the real monsters? Since we—or at least many of us (perhaps a silent majority)—at a safe distance are apparently capable of witnessing and consuming the suffering of others on the television screen without being severely distraught or immediately propelled into action, we are in many ways not just "everyday bystanders," as proposed by Cohen, but perhaps even "everyday monsters," who, although we would never ourselves directly inflict any pain on others, as spectators, nevertheless, still allow it to take place. In fact, as Zygmunt Bauman insisted, "there is an affinity between 'doing evil' and 'non-resistance to evil'" (Bauman 2009:138). So how is it even possible for such "everyday monsters" to sleep at night with clear consciences?

ON THE TURNING AWAY— REVISITING THE "TECHNIQUES OF NEUTRALIZATION"

A thought-provoking song by Pink Floyd is titled "On the Turning Away" (1987). The lyrics of the song deal with the way in which we—the well-off in the Western world—seem so easily to turn away from the pain and suffering of other less fortunate people, particularly "the weak and the weary," "the pale and downtrodden" and "the coldness inside." As we have seen above, solid modernity predominantly employed one type of adiaphorization technique that would cut sequences of action (in the production factory as well as in the concentration camp) into bits and pieces resulting in nobody claiming responsibility for the process as such or for the outcome of events, finally resulting in the effacement of the human face of the victims. With the coming of liquid modernity (and not the least with its increasing mediatization of our experience of the world), a second and updated type of adiaphorization technique is now put into action. When human suffering becomes mediatized and is framed within a media (and entertainment) universe of charity shows, collections, donations and national lotteries, it somehow loses some of its ability to touch us. We have seen it all so many times before—and once again the human face of the victims is effaced. Increasingly, instead of trying to make a difference ourselves, we gladly allow others—always smiling semi-voluntary charity collectors in the street, professional campaign managers and television celebrities—to provide us with a sense of absolution. The consequence is the general loss of moral sensibility and the ability and willingness to make a difference ourselves. The $10 donation in the collection box can keep us complacent and guilt-free for quite a long time. Slowly and securely, "compassion fatigue," as British sociologist Keith Tester (2001) called it (a term conventionally reserved for the dwindling compassionate engagement over time of professionals working with trauma victims), creeps in. Eventually, we even become sick and tired of seeing all the suffering and sense that nothing can really repair the situation—not even our petty donations and charities.

More than sixty years ago, an important essay was published dealing with so-called "techniques of neutralization." Written by two American sociologists, Gresham M. Sykes and David Matza (1957), the theoretically informed piece outlined several ways in which people accused of deviance or illegitimate acts (e.g., delinquents) would respond in order to neutralize the moral implications of their actions. Sykes and Matza specifically mentioned the following neutralizing techniques: "denial of responsibility," "denial of injury," "denial of the victim," "condemnation of the condemners" and "appeals to higher loyalties." According to the authors, such techniques would—at least temporarily—allow the offender to justify, to himself as well as to others, why he acted in a specific way (e.g., breaking the law) and relieve him—at least temporarily—from feelings of responsibility or complicity. Later, others have supplemented Sykes and Matza's catalogue with more techniques used to "silence" the conscience of offenders (see, e.g., Bryant et al. 2017; Henry and Eaton 1999:21–22). However, instead of talking about these "techniques of neutralization" in connection to accusations of active wrongdoing by perpetrators (but simultaneously being inspired by them), within the specific context of this chapter it would perhaps be more useful to speak of "techniques of passivation" that refer to the many often quite ingenious and inconspicuous ways in which people avoid engaging with or taking responsibility for the suffering of others. According to American sociologist Lewis A. Coser (1969/1988) in a classic piece, there are two identifiable types of spectator mentality that may be used whenever one is watching war scenes, atrocities and suffering on the television from the safety of one's own sofa. The first mentality is simply a matter of turning the blind eye, denying that any wrongdoing has taken place at all or pretending that one did not know. However, according to Coser, at some point, this strategy becomes untenable not the least due to the never-ending news reports and media coverage of real events of suffering (and we have to bear in mind that his analysis was made almost half a century ago when the media were still far from as omnipresent in social life as today). As Coser stated: "Publicity, powerfully aided by the recent communication revolution, brought the evidence of illegitimate violence into every living room and thus made previous denial mechanisms inoperative. . . . The revolution in the communication system of the last few decades has made the operation of the mechanisms of denial ordinarily relied upon by 'good people' much more difficult" (Coser 1969/1988:226–230). This new situation—one that perhaps temporally overlaps with the aforementioned shift from solid to liquid modernity—therefore leads to the invocation of the second type of mentality described by Coser as the denial of the humanity of the victims: one simply stops regarding those who suffer as individual human beings of flesh and blood who can feel the pain inflicted upon them, or one stipulates that it probably is not so bad after all. Coser concluded that this proposed shift in mentalities, in his view, could risk leading to an increasing brutalization of everyday life, because we—ordinary people and decision-makers alike—would stop regarding the visibility of evil and the suffering of others as something standing out of the ordinary (Coser 1969/1988:231).

As mentioned, today the media play a significant role in the way we comprehend and react towards events around the world. This also goes for our knowledge of and response to disasters, wars, famines and other man-made or natural catastrophes. Internationally renowned Polish correspondent Ryszard Kapuściński—who throughout his career reported from many hotspots around the world—in his book *Lapidarium III* (1997) once described how human suffering in the Third World was deliberately hidden from or neutralized by the Western television audience through spectacularly staged charity shows, collection campaigns and the like, whose main purpose paradoxically is to show the suffering, promote feelings of sympathy and solidarity and not the least to instigate action in the shape of "payment." Kapuściński spoke of three ways in which the real suffering of others was being blurred through the media, which has a lot in common with Cohen's previously mentioned mentalities/strategies. First, those suffering and starving are being depicted as individuals who actually have the option to act in order to counteract their situation of need—and thus, in the final instance, their suffering is to be blamed on their own laziness and passivity. Second, their suffering is reduced only to a matter of lack of food, so viewers are being seduced into believing that the problem can be solved merely by providing enough food supplies—which obviously only solves the superficial problem regarding acute survival, but which reduces the more complex and lasting problems in developing countries to one single and solvable dimension (which then requires donations). Third, television viewers in the West are routinely presented with images of destruction, killings, illnesses, refugees, poverty, starvation and so on from all around the world (but particularly from less developed countries), but only seldom—if ever—is the connection explicitly made that it in fact is often weapons from Western-controlled arms factories that are used in conflicts or that the existence of suffering and need is often due to the exploitation of the local population by multinational or governmental agencies supported by the West. In this way, it seems as if suffering is something the sufferers have brought unto themselves, and we can then pretend that it is acceptable not to feel any sympathy or to do anything about it (Kapuściński 1997).

So, at first glance, it seems as if these so-called "techniques of passivation" of the bystanders are as varied and may seem as innocuous as the classic "techniques of neutralization" used by the perpetrators. The different "techniques of passivation" mentioned above (and there are many more of them in the relevant research literature) provide us with some hints as to why people do not intervene when others are in danger or need help. Several justifications (or excuses)—some good, believable and legitimate, others more dubious, contestable and less flattering—may be at stake depending on the actual situation; particularly whether one is physically co-present with the perpetrator and the victim (as in the Condron case), whether one can hear and perhaps also see someone in distress from a certain distance (as in the Genovese case), whether one has knowledge that wrongdoing to others is taking place but lacks concrete firsthand evidence (as in the Holocaust case) or whether one is observing the mediatized suffering and pain through the television screen (as mentioned by Boltanski, Tester, Coser, Kapuściński, Cohen and many others). However, based on the above I think it is possible to summarize a number of specific reasons—some of which have by now been tested in classic and recent empirical studies (see, e.g., Latané and Darley 1970; Fischer et al. 2011; Liebst, Heinskou and Ejbye-Ernst 2018)—that can help us understand the bystander's lack of intervention: fear of retribution from the perpetrator(s), lack of knowledge/certainty, incapacity/inability, insensitivity (forgetting, neglecting or denying the humanity of the victim), denial and/or delegation of responsibility (others must take action—this is not my business/problem!) and, last but not least, indifference. The language of passivity can thus seemingly be spoken in many different tongues. Maybe the banality and normality of *doing evil*, of which Arendt (1962) wrote, has now in liquid-modern society been supplemented by the banality of *witnessing evil*. But perhaps one of the worst things of being a victim is the gnawing suspicion that *someone could have done something*. Remember the murder of Josef K—the progenitor of Franz Kafka's famous novel *The Trial*—who on the final page of the book is brutally executed in a remote quarry (in Kafka's words "like a dog") by two men, his main concern being that somebody did perhaps—in a window from afar—witness his death: "Who was that? A friend? A good person? Somebody who was taking part? Somebody who wanted to help?" (Kafka 1925/2015:160). Josef K did not live to find out.

TOWARD A MORALITY OF RESPONSIBILITY—FROM "SPECTATORS" TO "ACTORS"

As mentioned at the beginning of this chapter, just as sociology conventionally has had very little to say about evil, so it has also (and quite possibly for the self-same reasons) largely avoided the topic of morality, once again satisfied to relinquish the investigation of such an elusive phenomenon to moral philosophers and theologians. However, perhaps sociology, after all, has something of importance to say about how we may not only understand but also address the bystander problem as sketched in this chapter. Looking at the many complex causes of the problem with passive, unresponsive, apathetic or indifferent bystanders—whether in a solid-modern world of face-to-face killings in concentration camps or in a liquid-modern "spectator society" in which acts of violence are increasingly mediated and almost instantaneously mediatized—it becomes obvious that it is well beyond the scope of this chapter to provide a *solution* to such a problem. Was such a solution anywhere in the offing, it would probably already have been tried and tested. Here we shall therefore briefly discuss some of the different ways in which the problem of the bystander can be approached before ending up with a somewhat radical *suggestion.*

In Luc Boltanski's (1993) aforementioned analysis, he proposed two basic ways in which the spectators of "distant suffering" could decide to react: they could either *refuse* the request to commit themselves or they could *accept* it. If they chose the former approach, then they might rely on some of the previously mentioned "techniques of passivation" in order to quench their potential for bad conscience. If they chose the latter approach, acceptance, then Boltanski believed that two options were available: "paying" or "speaking." Where payment is similar to what we previously described as the charity carnivals of occasional donations made to good and deserving causes, then speech is concerned with objecting openly to the injustice by appealing to politicians to take action. According to Boltanski, speaking is thus a political act—aimed at challenging and changing the conditions causing the pain and suffering one has seen. However, in neither "paying" nor "speaking" is the spectator *personally* requested to *do something* (apart from paying and speaking), and, as Boltanski therefore pointed out: "No one ever suggests, for example, that the spectator should drop everything and take himself to the unfortunate's side" (Boltanski 1993:17). So instead of *doing something oneself,* the task of responding to one's moral outrage or emotional discomfort at the sight of suffering is thus subtly transferred to intermediaries such as politicians or relief organizations. *They should do something*—we are taxpayers after all! In this way, personal moral responsibility either is made a matter of paying indulgences or is being delegated and outsourced to others.

Following this, another way of trying to deal with distant suffering and indirectly with the problem of unresponsive bystanders is to appeal to and invoke higher principles such as "restorative justice," "restorative action" and "human rights." Obviously, these longstanding and praiseworthy notions have greatly contributed to the reduction of need and to a sense of justice in the world. However, the problem with such notions is that they seem to work primarily *after* the damage is already done—often in connection to persecuting and punishing the perpetrator(s) or in rehabilitating the victim(s). Moreover, human rights are abstract formulations needing humans of flesh and blood in order to be turned from valiant ideas to actual practice: *someone* needs *to do* something, not just talking about rights, obligations, gold-plated principles and responsibilities. That *someone* will often be official agencies and organizations—mediators of our moral responsibility that are put in the world to act on our behalf—which may paradoxically end up reinforcing our role as unresponsive bystanders. After all, it is a contradiction in terms to claim that one's *personal* moral responsibility can be passed on to someone else.

Yet another way of dealing with the problem of bystander passivity (at least in directly observable emergency situations) has been through the so-called "Bad Samaritan laws" within many different legal contexts. For example, the Danish Criminal Code §253 states that it is punishable by law not to assist people in emergency situations if this assistance does not involve any grave danger to oneself. This thus establishes "a duty to give reasonable emergency assistance to persons in grave and immediate peril when this assistance could be given easily, without risking harm to oneself and without neglecting one's other duties" (McIntyre 1994:158). The peculiar thing about these "Bad Samaritan laws," however, is that they may sometimes seem to go against actual police advice. For example, a frequent recommendation —and probably in many cases also a wise one as well—made by police representatives whenever someone has witnessed, for example, street violence is to calmly observe but *not to intervene* (this is, after all, a police matter). Although there are indeed good reasons not to interfere in such events (not the least due to one's own safety as a spectator/witness), there are, however, at least three problems associated with the recommendation merely to stay put. First of all, one could *perhaps have prevented* any harm or damage done by the perpetrator in the first place or at least have reduced the severity of the situation (this will obviously always remain unknowable just as will the evidence for the opposite claim). Second, one would have let the victim know that he or she was not alone, and even though that knowledge might not have prevented harm-doing, it could have reassured the victim, as in Franz Kafka's story above, that someone did not only *see* but did in fact also *care*. Third, and for the point of this chapter perhaps most importantly, as numerous studies have shown, *passivity breeds passivity*. If any perpetrator can rest assured that *no one*—individual or collective—will intervene in misdeeds, then we have let evil and evil-by-proxy loose on the world without any practical or moral restraints. It is obviously impossible to extrapolate from witnessing emergency situations to the mediated distant suffering around the world. However, at the end of the day, "Bad Samaritan" laws like these testify to the fact that personal moral responsibility cannot be legislated.

So are there any remaining possibilities available for dealing more directly with the bystander problem? According to American philosopher and conceptual artist Adrian M. S. Piper (1991), witnessing the suffering of others can in principle lead us in two extreme directions—either into "self-absorption," in which one is utterly unmoved by and incapable of empathizing with the suffering other due to one's cynical self-concern (as was perhaps the case with Chouliaraki's [2006; 2013] "ironic spectators" above), or into "vicarious obsession," in which one becomes almost paralyzed due to an overwhelming identification with and sympathy for the suffering. Neither extreme seems to spur the actor into any action—on the contrary, both extremes lead to a solidification of passivity. There is, however, also another option open. Returning to the writings of Zygmunt Bauman, and particularly to his lifelong devotion to teasing out the moral implications of the human condition, one will discover the bricks and mortar needed for a moral sociology concerned with how to embrace the responsibility for the suffering of the other whether close by or far away. Obviously, this is neither the time nor the place to dig deep into Bauman's moral sociology (for more, see, e.g., Bauman 1989, 1993), but stated briefly, Bauman proposes a sociological perspective stressing a *personal and unconditional moral responsibility for the Other*—no matter who or where this Other is—as the best, and perhaps the only, bulwark against adiaphorization and the accompanying "moral blindness" that has come to characterize our society (Bauman and Donskis 2013). Bauman's moral sociology is heavily indebted to the phenomenological philosophy of Emmanuel Lévinas (1969, 1985) with his emphasis on the unconditional responsibility for the Other, which is actualized by the presence of the "Face" of the Other—a Face symbolizing the innate humanity and vulnerability of another human being. This Face of the Other lays claim to and commands the actor to engage and to assist (Burggraeve 1999). *Being-for-the-Other* is thus substituted for merely *being-with-the-Other*, and one's moral *responsibility* takes precedence over other commitments, duties or obligations. This responsibility of Lévinas and Bauman—unconditional, interminable and non-negotiable as it is—cannot be offloaded, shared, pawned, delegated, taken away or shifted on to the shoulders of others (Bauman 1993:250). Because it is *my* responsibility and *mine* alone, it is and must remain burdensome, at times even verging on ethical tyranny (e.g., by insisting on our responsibility to act as our brother's keepers and claiming that "thou must help thy neighbor"), but without this responsibility, excuses, rejections, disclaimers and ingenious techniques of passivation will be invoked in order to avoid it. As in Lévinas's writings, Bauman's understanding of moral responsibility ultimately also rests on a proximity to the Other, and he admits that such a Levinasian morality of proximity faces certain problems in a world increasingly characterized by actions and observations made at a distance (Bauman 1999). Therefore, such a morality of unconditional responsibility necessarily needs to be coupled to an ethically motivated politics of commitment on a global scale, but, as Bauman admits, such a politics of commitment is still found missing.

To summarize, in Bauman's view, in order to transform passive and unresponsive spectators into morally responsible actors, we need to bridge the many abysmal gaps between the seeing, the knowing and the doing/acting (Bauman 2009). Obviously, this is easier said than done. Moreover, one may also object that it is too much to ask of people that they should all be do-gooders all the time, potentially towards everybody and ultimately with a willingness *to sacrifice oneself* and *to die for* the (unknown) Other. To Bauman (1992:210), however, this is the fundamental nature of all morality. When discussing the bystander problem, one might perhaps want to consider moderating this radical perspective into a claim that one's responsibility extends as far as one does "not allow the Other to be harmed" or does "not let the Other die," but to Bauman (and Lévinas) this will not suffice. It is thus evident that Bauman does perhaps not provide a *practical or realistic prophylaxis for solving the bystander problem*, but he does propose that we need to understand that only an unconditional and personal responsibility for alleviating the Other's suffering can ultimately claim to be moral. After all, there is nothing like a sense of personal moral responsibility to spur people into action.

CONCLUSION

This chapter has sought to develop some—perhaps trivial, perhaps provocative, depending on the reader's own predilection and temperament, but most definitely tentative—ideas about what has been teasingly termed "evil-by-proxy." As is shown in the chapter, this is not evil deliberately perpetuated or performed by so-called "monsters" or "predators" who strive to harm other people. Evil-by-proxy is rather the descriptive term invoked here in order to capture the passivity of evil or the evil of passivity that means that actual evil—violence, killing, torture or human suffering in general—is observed yet not acted upon or prevented by the observers, the "everyday monsters," who through different "techniques of passivation" excuse and exempt themselves from action. Evil-by-proxy, as described in this chapter, is an everyday thing. Perhaps particularly in a society in which human suffering and violence is more than ever before a mediated and mediatized phenomenon, a world in which the mass media report and reproduce heretofore unparalleled amounts of spectacles of human suffering and pain (either actual or fictional), evil-by-proxy becomes something that many—perhaps even most—of us somehow participate in. Under the right (or perhaps rather the wrong) circumstances, maybe we all have the capacity for doing evil (Zimbardo 2007), or maybe we don't, but most of us—for various reasons shown in by now numerous psychological, criminological and sociological studies—still mostly refrain from doing so. However, most of us do have the capacity for witnessing evil-doing and doing nothing about it—and most of us actually do this. In this way, we are all, in each our seemingly innocent way, small "everyday monsters," who rarely actively pursue evil, but who nevertheless tolerate it by turning the blind eye and thus allowing it to take place. As the chapter also discussed, there are many different (and apparently also many good as well as bad) reasons why people who become aware of or directly or indirectly witness evil refrain from intervening in order to help the victim(s)—whether they are right in front of them or thousands of miles away: fear, lack of knowledge, lack of resources, the delegation of responsibility or plain indifference were some of the reasons briefly mentioned. Most of these reasons for refraining to act in order to alleviate suffering or prevent assaults may seem quite reasonable and innocent (apart perhaps from the last one). However, whether one or the other reason motivates inactivity and passivity, its consequences are the same for the victims.

The purpose of the chapter has not been to point the finger, to preach morality or to insist that we should all parade as everyday saints or heroes wearing a halo of charity and self-sacrifice. In fact, the attentive reader might also quite reasonably ask what the author himself has ever done to prevent actual evil from occurring or evil-by-proxy from gaining ground. Does he himself practice what he preaches? Instead of making this an ethical quarrel between the reader and the author, the main purpose of the chapter has rather been to discuss—through the use of different theoretical lenses—the topic of "evil-by-proxy" and its concomitant idea of "everyday monsters" and "techniques of passivation" as concepts useful for understanding different—and perhaps also overlooked—aspects of evil. Despite their descriptive intention, the concepts obviously beget moral questions of possible complicity as well as of ethical tyranny. So even though there has been no intention in the chapter to blame people for their passivity or to climb on a high horse, descriptive concepts almost unavoidably always invite normative discussion.

In a world in which millions watch and re-watch (again and again) the slaughtering and suffering of other people at a safe distance behind their television screens, there is however no safety in numbers for the victims. In conclusion to this chapter, we might thus paraphrase Zygmunt Bauman's contention from his book on the Holocaust by saying that it does not matter *how many* refrain from intervening to help, but it matters that *someone* does not, and thus, as Bauman insisted, "evil is not all-powerful. It can be resisted" (Bauman 1989:207). Following this lead, he also once so poignantly suggested that "one can recognize a moral person by their never quenched dissatisfaction with their moral performance; the gnawing suspicion that they were not moral enough" (Bauman 1994:45). The alternative to a bystander is neither a superhuman nor a hero—it is to be a moral person. Obviously, at the end of the day, the descriptive concepts of "evil-by-proxy," "everyday monsters" and "techniques of passivation" raise a number of moral questions to the reader such as: could you have done more, should you do more, do you feel good about yourself, and did you do enough? I think these open-ended questions—as seen through Bauman's aforementioned depiction of the moral person—are an appropriate way to end this chapter.

NOTE

1. Some of the ideas presented in this chapter were first proposed in Jacobsen and Tester (2008).

REFERENCES

Arendt, Hannah. 1962. *Eichmann in Jerusalem: A Report on the Banality of Evil*. Harmondsworth: Penguin Books.

Barnett, Victoria J. 1999. *Bystanders: Conscience and Complicity During the Holocaust*. New York: Praeger.

Bauman, Zygmunt. 1989. *Modernity and the Holocaust*. Cambridge: Polity Press.

———. 1992. "Postscript: 'To Die For…' or Death and Morality," in *Mortality, Immortality and Other Life Strategies*, 200–210. Cambridge: Polity Press.

———. 1993. *Postmodern Ethics*. Oxford: Blackwell.

———. 1994. *Alone Again—Ethics After Certainty*. London: Demos.

———. 1995. *Life in Fragments: Essays in Postmodern Morality*. Oxford: Blackwell Publishers.

———. 1999. "The World Inhospitable to Levinas." *Philosophy Today*, 43 (2):151–167.

———. 2000. *Liquid Modernity*. Cambridge: Polity Press.

———. 2009. "From Bystander to Actor." *Journal of Human Rights*, 2:137–151.

———. 2010. "Media, Bystanders, Actors," in Gorana Ognjenovic (ed.): *Responsibility in Context: Perspectives*, 95-102. Dordrecht: Springer.

Bauman, Zygmunt and Leonidas Donskis. 2013. *Moral Blindness—The Loss of Sensitivity in Liquid Modernity*. Cambridge: Polity Press.

Boltanski, Luc. 1993. *Distant Suffering: Morality, Media and Politics*. Cambridge: Cambridge University Press.

Bryant, Emily et al. 2017. "Techniques of Neutralization and Identity Work Among Accused Genocide Perpetrators." *Social Problems*, https://doi.org/10.1093/socpro/spx026.

Burggraeve, Roger. 1999. "Violence and the Vulnerable Face of the Other: The Vision of Emmanuel Levinas on Moral Evil and Our Responsibility." *Journal of Social Philosophy*, 30 (1): 29-45.

Butler, Judith. 2009. *Frames of War: When Is Life Grievable*? London: Verso.

Chouliaraki, Lilie. 2006. *The Spectatorship of Suffering*. London: Sage Publications.

———. 2013. *The Ironic Spectator: Solidarity in the Age of Post-Humanitarianism*. Cambridge: Polity Press.

Clarkson, Petruska. 1996. *The Bystander—An End to Innocence in Human Relationships?* London: Whurr Publications.

Cohen, Stanley. 2001. *States of Denial: Knowing About Atrocities and Suffering*. Cambridge: Polity Press.

Coser, Lewis A. 1969/1988. "The Visibility of Evil," in *A Handful of Thistles: Collected Papers in Moral Conviction*, 225–232. New Brunswick, NJ: Transaction Books.

Debord, Guy. 1970. *Society of the Spectacle*. Boston: Black & Red.

Fischer, Peter et al. 2011. "The Bystander-Effect: A Meta-Analytic Review on Bystander Intervention in Dangerous and Non-Dangerous Emergencies." *Psychological Bulletin*, 4: 517–537.

Gaita, Raymond. 1991/2004. *Good and Evil: An Absolute Conception* (2nd Edition). London: Routledge.

Giddens, Anthony. 1990. *The Consequences of Modernity*. Cambridge: Polity Press.

Henry, Stuart and Roger Eaton, eds. 1999. *Degrees of Deviance: Student Accounts of Their Deviant Behavior* (2nd Edition). Salem, WI: Sheffield Publishing Company.

Hilberg, Raul. 1992. *Perpetrators, Victims, Bystanders: The Jewish Catastrophe, 1933–1945*. New York: Harper Collins.

Hobsbawm, Eric. 1994. *The Age of Extremes: A History of the World, 1914–1991*. New York: Vintage Books.

Hughes, Everett C. 1962. "Good People and Dirty Work." *Social Problems*, 10 (1): 3–11.

Jacobsen, Michael Hviid. 2016. "'Spectacular Death'—Proposing a New Fifth Phase to Philippe Ariès's Admirable History of Death." *Humanities*, 5 (19): 1–20.

Jacobsen, Michael Hviid and Keith Tester. 2008. "Ondskabens senmoderne svøbe—en sociologi om passiv observation og aktiv overvindelse af ondskab" ["The Late Modern Scourge of Evil—A Sociology of the Passive Observation and Active Conquest of Evil"], in Sara Normann Thordsen and Helle Dam Sørensen (eds.): *Ondskab—et politisk begreb* [*Evil—A Political Concept*], 71–100. Århus: Aarhus Universitetsforlag.

Kafka, Franz. 1925/2015. *The Trial*. New York: Tribeca Books.

Kapuściński, Ryszard. 1997. *Lapidarium III*. Warszawa: Czytelnik.

Latané, Bibb and John M. Darley. 1970. *The Unresponsive Bystander: Why Doesn't He Help?* New York: Prentice-Hall.

Lemert, Edwin M. 1997. *The Trouble with Evil—Social Control at the Edge of Morality*. New York: State University of New York Press.

Lévinas, Emmanuel. 1969. *Totality and Infinity: An Essay on Exteriority*. Pittsburgh: Duquesne University Press.

———. 1985. *Ethics and Infinity: Conversations with Philippe Nemo*. Pittsburgh: Duquesne University Press.

Levine, Mark. 1999. "Rethinking Bystander Nonintervention." *Human Relations*, 52: 1133–1155.

Liebst, Lasse S., Marie B. Heinskou and Peter Ejbye-Ernst. 2018. "On the Actual Risk of Bystander Intervention: A Statistical Study Based on Naturally Occurring Violent Emergencies." *Journal of Research in Crime and Delinquency*, 55 (1): 27–50.

Lyman, Stanford M. 1989. *The Seven Deadly Sins: Society and Evil*. New York: General Hall Publishers.

McIntyre, Alison. 1994. "Guilty Bystanders? On the Legitimacy of Duty to Rescue Statutes." *Philosophy and Public Affairs*, 23: 157–191.

Meštrović, Stjepan G. 1997. *Postemotional Society*. London: Sage Publications.

Milgram, Stanley. 1963. *Obedience to Authority: An Experimental View*. New York: Harper.

Piper, Adrian M. S. 1991. "Impartiality, Compassion and Modal Imagination." *Ethics*, 101: 726-757.

Staub, Ervin. 2003. *The Psychology of Good and Evil: Why Children, Adults and Groups Help and Harm Others*. Cambridge: Cambridge University Press.

Sykes, Gresham M. and David Matza. 1957. "Techniques of Neutralization: A Theory of Delinquency." *American Sociological Review*, 22 (6): 664–670.

Tester, Keith. 2001. *Compassion, Morality and the Media*. Buckingham: Open University Press.

Weber, Max. 1922/2004. "Bureaucracy." *The Essential Weber—A Reader*, edited by Sam Whimster, 245–249. London: Routledge.

Zimbardo, Philip. 2007. *The Lucifer Effect: Understanding How Good People Turn Evil*. New York: Random House.

Chapter Six

Monstering Madness

Criminal Lunatics in Broadmoor 1863–1913

Lucy Williams, Sandra Walklate,
and Barry Godfrey

This chapter explores the ways in which inmates at Britain's first (and, until the twentieth century, only) Criminal Lunatic Asylum, Broadmoor Hospital in Berkshire, were interpreted and represented in the popular press. Taking a small sample of inmates across the institution's first half century, we use biographical and crime-related data taken from patient casefiles at Broadmoor, and contemporary newspapers sourced from online digital archives, in order to assess which facets of each patient's case and crime were highlighted by the press, and for what purpose. Broadmoor patients, suffering from mental illness, were quickly subject to processes of monstering by Victorian newspapers, which seized upon the opportunity to portray these patients as subjects of both moral and mental degeneration. We investigate the construction of Broadmoor "monsters" in the popular press, and illustrate their divergence from the real, and often tragic, lives of the Broadmoor patients.

MONSTERING AND MADNESS: CRIMINAL LUNATICS IN BROADMOOR (1863–1913)

In 1861 an escaped convict dramatically cornered and confronted a young boy in a darkened graveyard:

> A fearful man, all in coarse grey, with a great iron on his leg. A man with no hat, and with broken shoes, and with an old rag tied round his head. A man who had been soaked in water, and smothered in mud, and lamed by stones, and cut by flints, and stung by nettles, and torn by briars; who limped, and shivered, and glared, and growled; and whose teeth chattered in his head (Dickens 1861, 1–2).

In this well-known story, Charles Dickens wrote that Abel Magwitch threatened the young boy with having his heart and lungs torn out, and his liver roasted and eaten:

> Now, I ain't alone, as you may think I am. There's a young man hid with me, in comparison with which young man I am an Angel . . . That young man has a secret way pecooliar [sic] to himself, of getting at a boy, and at his heart, and at his liver. It is in wain for a boy to attempt to hide himself from that young man. A boy may lock his door, may be warm in bed, may tuck himself up, may draw the clothes over his head, may think himself comfortable and safe, but that young man will softly creep and creep his way to him and tear him open (Dickens 1861, 3–4).

Dickens's caricature of hardened and violent criminals keyed directly into intertextual cultural references that predominated in Victorian society, and Dickens toyed with established and emerging conceptions of the criminal "other" in many of his works, but the form of expression is intriguing (Collins 1995). Depicted more as flesh-eating monster than man, Magwitch seems more at home in the pages of a tale of horror than a story about love and rejection, as *Great Expectations* is. The existence of men who become, or act like, monsters has long been debated. Stephen Asma describes the history of monsters as a concept and as an embodied collection of fears and anxieties about "others"; exploring archival and literary historical sources, Asma demonstrates that the "otherness" of monsters is merely the shadow of ourselves, that their monstrous qualities collectively symbolize all that humanity should shun because they are the antithesis of humanity (Asma 2009; Athens 2012). Alexander Hinton works a similar vein when he asks whether those who are capable of great evil are humans or really monsters. Whither humanity when thousands and thousands are killed in gas chambers or in the killing fields (Hinton 2016)?

The question of what constitutes humanity, and therefore inhumanity, and whether the term "monsters" should be applied to people who fall outside the normal bounds of humanity has long fascinated writers and poets. Recently, Alex Sharpe has also discussed how the law deals with categories of people who have ambiguous identities or who resist falling into neat socio-legal categories.[1]

Here, we look to the legal and social boundaries between criminality and madness by examining some of the inmates at Britain's first (and, until the twentieth century, only) Criminal Lunatic Asylum, Broadmoor Hospital in Berkshire. We use biographical and crime-related data taken from patient casefiles at Broadmoor, and contemporary newspapers sourced from online digital archives, in order to assess which facets of each patient's case and crime were highlighted by the press, and for what purpose. Broadmoor patients, suffering from mental illness, were quickly subject to processes of monstering by Victorian newspapers, which seized upon the opportunity to portray these patients as subjects of both moral and mental degeneration. We investigate the construction of Broadmoor "monsters" in the popular press, and illustrate their divergence from the real, and often tragic, lives of the Broadmoor patients.

This chapter argues that processes of othering are as visible in Victorian society's treatment of particular kinds of criminals as they are in literary depictions of monsters such as Mary Shelley's *Frankenstein* and Robert Louis Stevenson's *Mr. Hyde*. It uses historical data to examine how newspapers at that time "monstered" violent men and infanticidal women, and also the counteracting processes of "de-monstering," which seemed to appear from the 1860s in medical and legal debates. The chapter also focuses on the creation of an institution especially designed to contain and treat society's "monsters" partly due to the criminal justice system's inability to process people who did not fall into neat conceptual and legal categories (e.g., Foucault 2003 and Sharpe 2007a, 2007b, 2009). The chapter uses evidence taken from the patient files of Broadmoor Hospital in Berkshire to explore the subtle undermining of the monster narrative by Victorian psychologists and health-care professionals; and concludes by briefly exploring how psycho-medical theories influenced proto-criminological theory. In essence we trace the history of monster-making and monster-unmaking with regard to criminals in the mid- to late Victorian period. We will begin this journey by returning to the soaking-wet, bandaged and bloody, fearful figure of Abel Magwitch.

Despite his entrance as a violent madman preying on a scared young boy in a foggy graveyard, Magwitch is eventually revealed at the end of *Great Expectations* as a benevolent benefactor, a convict who "made good" in the Australian colonies following a sentence of transportation for his crimes. Not a monster then. The grotesque way Dickens describes him in the opening chapter, however, was not far removed from the daily portrayal of convicts, or those who were conditionally released early from their sentence of penal servitude to be "at-large" in respectable society (Bailey 1993; Davis 1980; McGowan 1990; Sindall 1987). Convicts and criminals were all subject to pejorative comment in the press for the whole Victorian period, really as one would expect. People who break the law are seldom lionized as heroes. Many contemporary descriptions, however, emphasized the monstrous, seemingly inhuman and animalistic characteristics of street-dwellers, thieves, and robbers.[2] From 1888 the newspapers wrote of a "Spectre" that stalked East London, a "phantom" of the slums (*Punch Magazine* 1888). Both Judith Walkowitz and Marie-Christian Leps have described how stories woven around the

Whitechapel murders both contributed to and were located within existing subterranean dialogues—Jack the Ripper and his work personified sexual danger and license, social pollution, the biological and moral degeneration of the species, and religious "deviance" (Walkowitz 1992; Leps 1992). Jack the Ripper was also the embodiment of fictional gothic terrors that were current in the popular imagination—the similarity between Jack the Ripper and Bram Stoker's "Dracula" are unmistakable (Godfrey 2001). While some criminals—Jack the Ripper, convicts "at large"—were singled out for special condemnation, many criminals were condemned strongly in print and public opinion. The "monstering" of criminals was part of a long-term process in the daily newspapers, which depicted them as atavistic brutes, sub-humans, whose development was retarded, and who were not the same as the citizens of normal society. They were the "others" in society, outside (and against) reasonable civil society. Some of the most lurid descriptions and most vigorous condemnations were reserved for mothers who had been charged with murdering their children.

Little discussed, there is a character often in Magwitch's shadow. Whilst still criminally active, Magwitch began a relationship with a seemingly mentally unstable woman, Molly, who later was acquitted at the Old Bailey because the members of the jury were convinced that she did not possess the physical strength to have strangled the victim. The story then relates that Molly had given birth to Magwitch's daughter. Molly told Magwitch that she had destroyed the child, and as far as Magwitch knew, his daughter had indeed died (Dickens 1861, 334). Whether she did in fact attempt to commit infanticide is never clarified in the book (Cellier 2013). Nevertheless, like Magwitch, the reader is convinced that Molly was capable of the most heinous and violent crimes. Molly was fictional, but the many real women who were tried for infanticide received strong condemnation in the press. As Adina Ciugureanu noted, "When a woman opposes the patriarchal world, . . . she becomes an object of ridicule, a grotesque figure, a monster, a stereotype pitted against that of the angel of the house" (Ciugureanu 2011, 354). When a woman perverts her "natural function" as a caring mother in the very worst way, she could expect little sympathy from Victorian newspapers.

Harriett Parker, for example, was described as "a repulsive, downcast looking woman" when she appeared at the Old Bailey on January 31, 1848, charged with the murder of two children (*Morning Post* January 3, 1848). The victims, seven-year-old Amina, and her five-year-old brother, Robert, were fathered by Harriett's lover, Robert Blake. Despite both being married to other people, Parker and Blake had cohabited together as man and wife for the previous three or four years (*Morning Post* January 3, 1848). On New Year's Eve, Robert Blake had returned to the home they shared in St. Lukes,

London, commanded Harriet to ready the supper and prepare water so that he might wash and get ready for a trip to the theater. Harriett, who had expected to accompany Blake to the show was then shocked to hear that Blake was taking another woman, Jane Jones (identified in several reports as a local prostitute). Incensed, Harriett proceeded to follow Blake, Jones, and their friend Hewlett, around several drinking establishments, before Blake disappeared with Jones, and spent the night away from home. At around four the next morning, Harriett handed herself into police custody, having smothered both of Blake's children who had been left in her care. She had, apparently, no other motive, other than to exact revenge on Blake for his infidelity. Newspapers nationwide were quick to seize on the grizzly double murder of children, not only due to the rarity of a woman murdering two non-infant children but also because Blake and Parker's domestic situation made for the perfect scandal.

The newspapers highlighted her lack of compassion from the outset, as well as her jealous nature, and her desire for cold-blooded revenge (*Exeter and Plymouth Gazette* January 8, 1848). "The woman in a fit of jealousy proceeded to the bed where the children lay fast asleep and by pressing her hands on the throats of the poor innocents, she suffocated them almost instantly . . . she was in her perfect senses at the time she committed the dreadful act." (*Birmingham Journal* January 8, 1848). After the inquest, when Parker was committed for trial, the papers referred frequently to her lack of remorse (*Hereford Journal* January 12, 1848; *Caledonian Mercury* January 13, 1848; *Dorset County Chronicle* January 13, 1848; *Bradford Observer* January 13, 1848; *London Evening Standard* February 5, 1848; *Globe* February 14, 1848; *Evening Mail* February 21, 1848). She was portrayed as cold and calculating, firm and unafraid. Not the traditional feminine ideal—a weak passive woman in need of protection (perhaps most especially from a jury)—but, instead, a bold and confident woman who knew exactly what she was doing. She was thus positioned as an inhuman monster capable of grotesque acts of violence:

> She gloried in what she had done...The wretched woman, when brought into the court, walked boldly into the dock, and having coolly surveyed the numerous assemblage in the court, seated herself...The prisoner then rose from her seat, pointed to Blake and Jones said, "Him and that woman there has been the cause of all our misfortune, and the death of the children lies at their door". . . Her firmness astonished everyone in court. . . . The demeanour of the miserable outcast since her condemnation has been in every respect becoming of the awful position in which she is placed (*Northampton Mercury* January 15, 1848.

No mercy was forthcoming, and she was hanged (*Morning Post* February 22, 1848).

DE-MONSTERING?

While it would be foolhardy to contend that Victorian newspapers did not reflect then-contemporary sensibilities, there were other opinions beginning to emerge, particularly with regard to infanticide. Nineteenth-century juries were increasingly sympathetic to the plight of women who had been forced into desperate acts through poverty, or by ruthless and exploitative men (Emsley 2010, 104–5; Williams 2016, 84–90; Jackson 2002, 1–18; Rabin 2002, 73–93). Moreover, some of the women in the dock could appear manifestly and obviously to be experiencing severe mental instability. The courts found *mens rea* (the intention was formed in her mind to commit the offence) and fitness to plead as an issue *de facto* if not *de jure*. Sharpe comments that "in the context of a history of the English legal category monster, it is the body, not the mind that proves to be the ultimate bedrock of what it means to be human" (Sharpe 2009, 101). However, it was the mind that increasingly came to predominate in legal discussions.

The Criminal Lunatics Act of 1800 stated that anyone found to be insane at the time they committed their crime would be detained "at Her Majesty's Pleasure," which ensured that a route was found for those who might otherwise escape punishment due to lunacy. Martin Weiner intimates that this was a concern at a time when the number of psychiatric cases and the number of institutions in which to put them were both growing, and when medical defenses were also on the increase in the courts (Weiner 1990, 86–87). If that was indeed the case for the 1800 Act, it was in the mid-century when this "control reflex" would come into its own.

Daniel M'Naghton was a Scottish wood turner who was charged in 1840 with murdering a man he had mistaken for Prime Minister Sir Robert Peel. After his acquittal on grounds of insanity as per the 1800 Act, he was transferred from Newgate Prison to the State Criminal Lunatic Asylum at Bethlem Hospital in London. Following his acquittal, the House of Lords asked a panel of judges a series of hypothetical questions about the defense of insanity. The principles expounded by this panel came to be known as the M'Naghten Rules (although if these rules had been applied to his own case, M'Naghten would actually have been convicted). When the tests set out by the Rules are satisfied, the accused may be adjudged "not guilty by reason of insanity" or "guilty but insane."

If we take the example of infanticide, for which insanity was commonly invoked as both an explanation for the crime and, in the later nineteenth century, a legal defense, there was a complex nexus of factors including law, social expectation, the context of the offense, defendant identity, and penal disposal which ultimately determined the leniency with which the crime was treated in both the courts, press, and penal institutions. Ann-Marie Kilday cites evidence for a mid-century "moral panic" surrounding child killing, reflected in an increase of indictments for infanticide in the period (Kilday 2013). Likewise, Hillary Marland suggests that by the 1860s, infanticide had been found as prevalent as at any other time in history (Marland 2004, 168). During the same period, Roger Smith tells us, insanity pleas drawing on medical testimony about defendants' state of mind as evidence was also growing steadily (Smith 1981). Insanity defenses of this nature had been relatively unheard of just decades before (Smith 1981). The link between the two was by no means a coincidence. However, rather than ushering in an age of leniency across the board, the shift in the treatment of infanticide defendants re-created a "gendered leniency" for the crime, present in the eighteenth century and which "became even more explicit by the Victorian era" (Kilday 2013, 124). By then, explanations of criminality shifted away from solely moral failings towards medical explanations of heredity and psychological abnormality, and women's crimes, especially infanticide, became interpreted differently (Zedner 1991, 309). Medical responses to infanticide in the late nineteenth century, allowed criminals, like infanticidal women who challenged social and cultural norms, to be dealt with as "mad" rather than "bad," and allowed legal responses which were more in line with the scientific, rational, and philanthropic spirit of the age, and the persistent rhetoric of women as the weaker sex, than the brutal bloody code of ages past.

More than any other kind of insanity used as a defense against an infanticide charge was puerperal insanity—an illness now recognized as post-natal depression. Puerperal insanity was a specifically female affliction, and when deployed in court could lead to acquittal, or a vastly reduced sentence for what was technically a capital crime (Marland 2004, 171). Marland contends that the insanity defense plea—specifically women's puerperal insanity in the case of child murder—not only satisfied "many of the ambiguities surrounding infanticide," but also "mediated between the wrath provoked by high levels of child murder and the sympathetic approach towards the mothers who committed the crime" (Marland 2004, 172).

Of course, the leniency shown in successful insanity pleas in infanticide cases was not indicative of a unilateral shift towards the medicalization of crime. Weiner argues that unlike their female contemporaries, men could only risk pleading insanity for murders (of either adults or children) as a last-ditch attempt to escape a murder conviction. Male insanity had the potential to see a defendant detained for the rest of their lives at Broadmoor, whereas women who killed their children found the defense of temporary insanity "increasingly successful" as the nineteenth century progressed (Weiner 1990, 270). With women able to key in to shifting medical ideas about the impact of pregnancy on the body and the trauma of birth on the mind in order to support claims of temporary insanity, men could not rely on the same medical precedents, leaving little on which they could pin defenses of temporary mental breakdown.

Though a notable tension remains amongst researchers as to the overall impact of the nature of insanity in the criminal trial and its benefits, and detractions for defendants, what is clear is the way in which ideas about criminal insanity in this period were as socially constructed as they were medical. Marland's claims for the mediating function of puerperal insanity in infanticide cases could easily be broadened out for other forms of insanity. In a select number of circumstances, medical and psychological analyses of crimes allowed for both society and the law to reconcile shocking crimes with reformative, even therapeutic, penal outcomes, and for the public to reconcile monstrous actions with the often complicated plight of people responsible for them.

Trials were not the only part of the criminal justice system grappling with the medicalization of crime. New understandings of insanity and mental well-being had a significant impact on the carceral landscape too. The increasing attention given to criminal lunacy in the mid-century and the creation of an institution for the reception of the criminally insane had a profound effect on how some of Britain's most serious criminals were treated and perceived, as evidenced in, for example, the creation of Broadmoor—Britain's first hospital for the criminally insane.[3]

For the first year of its operation, 1863, only women were resident, but men were subsequently transferred from 1864 onwards. M'Naghten became one of the first male inmates. In the Victorian period, men would outnumber women at Broadmoor by about four to one; men also served longer periods of time in the Hospital, and whereas one in three women was discharged before death, only one in five men would be discharged before they died in Broadmoor. The environment at Broadmoor was and still is, secure, but also therapeutic, a legacy of Superintendent Dr. William Orange. The regime Dr. Orange established was lauded for its results and for its humanity (Stevens 2013, 2014). There was an entrenched regime of exercise, fresh air, and occupational work. No doubt the system grated on many, and it restricted liberty and restricted access to friends and family for hundreds of people for many years; however, the system was not designed to punish individuals in the way that the convict prison did.

Obviously preferable to the gallows, Broadmoor was also a better environment for the troubled men and women sentenced to penal servitude in the convict prison system.[4] For example, Ann Griffin was convicted of the crime of arson (Berkshire Archives D/H14/D2/2/2/331/1). Tried at York Assizes, she received fifteen years' penal servitude. Her prison record described her as: “A woman of violent temper and a more than average physical strength. Is unwilling to submit to authority and has recourse to violence with a view to gaining her own ends” (Penal Record on Transfer from Millbank September 2, 1881). Her medical record stated that she appeared to have a “Violent and unrestrained temper, sometimes seems quite crazy. Fights with her fellow prisoners whenever she has the opportunity. A woman of large frame and muscular development. Does not sleep well. Wants nourishment—promises to behave well” (Berkshire Archives D/H14/D2/2/2/331/1). Over the next few years she broke many prison rules—destroying her cell furniture, destroying her clothes, shouting, displaying insolence, swearing, and so on—and received heavy punishment in return. She was stripped naked, her head shaved, chloroformed, restrained in a straitjacket on many occasions, and for long periods of time (Ibid.). The Prison Medical Officer stated: “This woman is (whether sane or insane) most assuredly a demonised termagant and requires firm and continuous repression” (Ibid.). A month later he recommended that she should be removed to Broadmoor (Ibid.). As stated earlier, Broadmoor had a more therapeutic approach, with the aim of bringing about mental stability and re-entry to society, rather than punishment, and the environment was much more appropriate for women like Ann Griffiths, and also for Ann Nicholls who was admitted to Broadmoor in 1871 for pouring vitriol into the mouth of her young baby (Report on Ann Nicholls, January 30, 1878, Berkshire Archives D/H14/D2/2/2/188/1).

After Nicholls had been under therapy for two years, her husband asked Dr. Orange if he could appeal for discharge on grounds that his wife was now well, and that they intended to emigrate to Germany. Dr. Orange replied that there was little prospect of success in the request. After further petitions for freedom, Dr. Orange commented:

> Ann Nicholls has not, to my knowledge, shown any sign of mental aberration or depression during that time in an equitable and even cheerful frame of mind, and at work in the laundry. She is sane and appears to have been so for several years, and I believe that, under ordinary circumstances, she might without insurmountable risk, be discharged to the care of her husband who is prepared and anxious for her to share the comforts of his home in America. No doubt, if she again became pregnant and had children (being 38 years of age) there would be risk of relapse (more or less temporary) into insanity so that at such periods, special care and attention would have to be exercised (Report on Ann Nicholls, January 30, 1878, Berkshire Archives D/H14/D2/2/2/188/1).

On February 9, 1878, Ann was discharged and shortly afterwards left England bound for New York (Ibid.). In April, her husband wrote back to Broadmoor thanking them for their kindness and care. He wrote: “Rest assured that I shall faithfully observe and carry out the conditions upon which she was released for my own comfort and duty will ever prompt me that way. She is now in the best of health and it will be my greatest earthly aim to keep her so." (Ibid.). In 1880, living in Pittsburg with husband Richard, she gave birth to a son (Ibid.).

Not everyone was able to leave the Hospital and make a new life abroad. A quarter of Broadmoor's residents were discharged to their families when the Hospital decided that they were ready to go. Thirty percent were removed to other asylums as pauper lunatics, or to Rampton in Nottinghamshire, which provided an overflow facility from 1912. Forty-five percent died at Broadmoor.[5] Most of those who died had become effectively institutionalized, having spent decades in Broadmoor's care; Mary Ann Parr, for example.

Born 1830 in Derbyshire, Mary Ann Parr was a "blind pauper inmate" of the Bingham workhouse by the time she was fourteen years old (Berkshire Archives D/H14/D2/2/2/1). She was still living in the workhouse when the *Nottinghamshire Guardian* reported that:

> The greatest excitement was occasioned in the village of Bingham last week by the announcement that a murder of a very revolting description had been committed in the Union Workhouse—the criminal being a female inmate called Mary Ann Parr, the victim her illegitimate female child. The unnatural mother appeared to have resolved upon destroying her unfortunate infant and from the time of its birth had refused to give it the breast, and neglected and ill-treated, and . . . by the wretched woman's own confession, had wilfully murdered it . . . [a fellow inmate stated]. She had not prepared for it, would not say who the father was . . . she had plenty of milk for the child, but would not let it suck. We had to put the child to her breast by force. I told her Monday last that if it did not suck it would die. She replied "Let it die." (*Nottinghamshire Guardian,* December 16, 1852).

Several women from the workhouse stated in depositions that Mary was sane; that she was warned about smothering the baby; and that she had confessed to her crime shortly afterwards (Berkshire Archives D/H14/D2/2/2/1). The surgeon was not convinced the child had been deliberately smothered but Mary confessed: "I did smother the child against my breast. I took the child to my breast at first to suckle it. I then squeezed it against my breast on purpose to take away its life, and when I saw it was dead I was frightened. I was not exactly sure it was dead till my mistress told me." (*Nottinghamshire Guardian,* December 16, 1852).

The *Derby Mercury* further explained:

> The prisoner is a woman of an exceedingly low development, and her blindness gives an expression to the countenance of extreme silliness. She unites with

> her apparent craziness, however, a low cunning, and, when she found that the law was likely to execute justice, she made an attempt to scale the workhouse wall and escape—a design which she failed to consummate (*Derby Mercury*, December 15, 1852).

She was tried at Nottingham Assizes on March 3, 1853, and found guilty of the willful murder of her ten-day old daughter (Berkshire Archives D/H14/D2/2/2/1). Her death sentence was commuted to transportation for life, and she was removed to Broadmoor (Berkshire Archives D/H14/D2/2/2/1). The Hospital Admission register stated she was "suicidal. Believes that everybody is her enemy. Constantly dreaming of murders. Complains of pains in her head and is most obstinate and intractable disposition. No education. Temperate. Church of England" (Berkshire Archives D/H14/D2/2/2/1). Nearly thirty-years later, the notes made by Dr. Orange noted that Mary was "much enfeebled. Occasionally irritable, quarrelsome and excited. Present state indifferent. She is mentally unsound. Not suitable for workhouse, having been 32 years in Bethel and Broadmoor. No friends" (Berkshire Archives D/H14/D2/2/2/1). She died in Broadmoor at 4.55 a.m., July 31, 1900, of chronic kidney disease; she had been kept in Broadmoor for forty-seven years.[6]

MONSTERING, PSYCHIATRY, AND CRIMINOLOGY

As David Garland (2002, 18) has lucidly argued, the seventeenth and eighteenth centuries abounded with explanations of criminal monsters from falling into bad company; having bad blood, being too fond of drink; to being driven by greed, lust, or despair, often supported by reference to Providence or the will of God. Indeed it was not until the nineteenth century that these rudimentary explanations for deviance began to be transformed into explanations informed by empirical investigation. Prominent in this search for an empirically supported evidence base for criminal monsters was the work of Cesare Lombroso. Lombroso's book, *Criminal Man*, published in 1876, and his other major work with Guglielmo Ferrero, *Criminal Woman*, first published in 1893, established the foundational thinking for what is now recognized as Criminology (Rafter and Gibson 2004). Interestingly Lombroso was, amongst other professions, a psychiatrist working mostly in prisons though his earliest work was based on soldiers rather than prisoners. Much of his theorizing emanated from the documentary evidence and notes on inmates and patients increasingly available consequent to the growth in prisons and asylums like that of Broadmoor during the eighteenth century. All of these bolstered the emergent disciplines of both Psychiatry and Criminology. Importantly many of these ideas were underpinned by Social Darwinism.

The influence of Darwinism on Lombroso's ideas in particular and the intellectual debates of the nineteenth century more generally has been widely discussed (see for example, Rafter and Gibson 2004). In pressing this point Eagle Russett (1989, 63) states: "Women and savages, together with idiots, criminals and pathological monstrosities, were a constant source of anxiety to male intellectuals in the late nineteenth century." Russett adds that this anxiety could be discerned in four Darwinist principles underpinning the emergent sciences of the nineteenth century within which it is possible to trace the birth of early criminology. In all of those sciences it was the Darwinian law of biogenetics that was most influential. This law stated: "ontology recapitulates phylogeny." In other words every individual organism revisits the development of its species within its own developmental history. This principle of recapitulation was one of the unifying and organizing principles of Lombroso's work properly termed as criminal anthropology. Assuming that the process of recapitulation usually produced biologically normal individuals, Lombroso envisaged the criminal as a throwback, an atavistic degeneration, to an earlier biological ancestry. Indeed, the tendency for criminals to mark themselves with tattoos led Lombroso to argue that this was evidence of their closer relationship with "savages." ("Savages" were deemed to be located at an earlier point in the development of the human species on the Darwinian evolutionary scale.) Lombroso introduced the concept of atavism to explain their abnormality, that is, their criminality.

The concept of atavism was also applied to females and children. Consequently, the idea of the "atavistic criminal" served a double helping of inadequacy to the female criminal. It is important to note that in general terms Victorian science viewed women as a "developmental anomaly" (Eagle Russett, 1989, 74). In particular, the biogenetic laws presumed the ultimate stage of evolutionary development was that reached by the white, Caucasian male and this presumption rendered the criminal woman particularly problematic. For Lombroso and Ferraro the female criminal was a "monster": she constituted both a throwback to an earlier species type as well as being arrested in her development as a member of her species. Thus the Darwinian principle of biogenetics deployed by Lombroso and Ferraro placed males and females (children and savages) on different points on the evolutionary scale. The greater development of the male (reflected in the greater variability in the male of any species, they believed) was likely to produce a greater variation in atavistic degeneration. Whereas the greater conservatism (less variability), alongside the arrested development of the female of the species, resulted in her degeneracy (for the purposes of this discussion her criminal behavior) being all the more problematic when it occurred.

Thus the *Origin of the Species* by Charles Darwin published in 1859 dovetailed with the emergence of the asylum and the associated record keeping that made it possible for the emergent disciplines of psychiatry and criminal anthropology empirically to investigate and challenge the more salacious visions of the criminal monsters reported on in the press. It did this up to a point. While, on the one, hand Lombroso, for example, "proposed humanitarian alternatives to incarceration for so-called occasional criminals, or those driven to crime by bad environment, and he became an ardent champion of special medical institutions for the criminally insane" (Gibson 2006, 2); on the other hand, the endorsement that bodily types (whether that be the size of the jaw or the shape of the head) or the presence of tattoos, marked the criminal from the non-criminal, and did little to assuage popular visions of the criminal monster whether they were male or female. Indeed this was particularly telling for the female criminal, especially in cases of infanticide. As Annie Cossins (2015, 3) points out:

> The nineteenth century discourse on the sexed female body emerged from an expanding and competitive media which, in exaggerating the characteristics of the infanticidal murderess for entertainment value, also "educated" the public and the depravity of the working classes in general and morally debased women in particular.

All of these were further endorsed in the emergent anthropological criminology in defining the criminal woman as "doubly deviant," offending both her species type and the wider norms of society. This is a definition of woman being "doubly deviant" continuing contemporary relevance as illustrated by the widely reported cases and responses to, for example, notorious British child murderers.

CONCLUSION

Did monsters live in Broadmoor? The psychological and medical staff who worked there clearly did not think so. Nevertheless, the wider public, supported in their view by a punitively minded and sensationalistic newspaper industry, continued to think so. The high walls at Broadmoor were designed to keep inmates in, but also to keep sight of the therapeutic regime away from prying local eyes. The regime introduced by Dr. Orange served many inmates well, particularly infanticidal women, and their relatively quick release back into society posed little risk to the general public. Indeed, it was less costly than keeping them locked up in a convict prison for years. However, Broadmoor's story is not one of continual development towards a therapeutic nirvana. The institution has had its scandals, and exposées in the 1980s showed that inmates were regularly physically and mentally abused. This confirmed the public's long-held view that it was an unregulated and chaotic "madhouse." It is entirely possible abuses had long been present at Broadmoor, and that some inmates were sorely ill-used in the Victorian period. Historical investigation of the institution can reveal the truth. However, the idea of Broadmoor, and its successes with infanticidal women shows that this was an important development in the treatment of mental instability, and an important site for the "de-monstering" of those society had cast as the greatest of villains.

NOTES

1. In discussing legal responses towards the hermaphroditic body, Sharpe notes that English law never problematized ambiguous gender identity in the way that Foucault suggests French law did (see Sharpe 2007a: 395; also see Sharpe 2007b; 2009).

2. Young female offenders being termed "Viragoes" in Victorian Manchester, for example, see Davies 1999; or common thieves possessing animalistic low-cunning according to social investigator Henry Mayhew 1861/1996: 431.

3. Berkshire Records Office holds the records on behalf of Broadmoor Hospital and makes many of the records of patients and admissions registers available for public access, subject to certain exemptions (see the Department of Health's *Guidance for Access to Health Records Requests* 2010, and the 2016 protocol issued by Berkshire Records Office). Broadmoor records can be viewed at the Berkshire Record Office, although photography is restricted. All inactive patient records are held by Broadmoor Hospital for a minimum period of thirty years and access is generally granted under the "100–year rule." This means that any records of a patient who died more than one hundred years ago can generally be accessed.

4. Weiner implies that M'Naghton was rarely applied, that cases which tried to extend its provisions failed, and that capital cases were seldom reprieved by showing evidence of insanity (just twenty capital cases were respited for insanity in 1881; Weiner 1990: 90–91).

5. Figures based on a sample of 1885–1888 extracted from Broadmoor Admission Registers, Berkshire Archives.

6. Berkshire Archives D/H14/D2/2/2/1. Some other residents were housed at Broadmoor for over sixty years, one woman being resident in the Hospital for nearly seventy-years.

REFERENCES

Andrews, Jonathan. 1998. "Case Notes, Case Histories, and the Patients Experience of Insanity at Gartnavel Royal Asylum, Glasgow, in the Nineteenth Century." *Social History of Medicine*, 11, 2: 255–281.

Appignanesi, Lisa. 2009. *Mad, Bad and Sad: A History of Women and the Mind Doctors from 1800 to the Present*. Virago: London.

Asma, Stephen. 2009. *On Monsters: An Unnatural History of Our Worst Fears*. Oxford University Press: Oxford.

Athens, Lonnie. 2012 "Virulency." *Speaking of Monsters; A Teratological Anthology*, edited by Caroline Joan Picart and John Edgar Browning, 153–156. Basingstoke, Palgrave Macmillan.

Bailey, Victor. 1993. "The fabrication of deviance: 'dangerous classes' and 'criminal classes' in Victorian England." *Protest and Survival: The Historical Experience: Essays for E. P. Thompson*, edited by John Rule and Robert Malcomson, 221–56. London: Merlin.

Brown, George. 1917. Presidential Address to the Royal College of Physicians, *British Medical Journal*, 27, Volume IV: 257.

Cellier, Sien. 2013. "'The Monstrous Feminine' Female Abjection in the Works of Charles Dickens. Master's unpublished dissertation submitted in partial fulfilment of the requirements for the degree of "Master in de Taal- en Letterkunde: Engels," University of Ghent.

Chaney, Sarah. 2016. "No 'Sane' Person Would Have Any Idea: Patients' Involvement in Late Nineteenth-century British Asylum Psychiatry." *Medical History*, 60, 1: 37–53.

Ciugureanu Adina. 2011. "The Victim-Aggressor Duality in Great Expectations." *Partial Answers: Journal of Literature and the History of Ideas*, 9(2): 347–361.

Collins, Phillip. 1995. *Dickens and Crime*. Palgrave Macmillan: Basingstoke.

Cossins, Annie. 2015. *Female Criminality: Infanticide, Moral Panics and the Female Body*. London: Palgrave-Macmillan.

Davies, Andrew. 1999. "These viragoes are no less cruel than the lads: Young women, gangs and violence in Late Victorian Manchester and Salford." *British Journal of Criminology*, 39, 1: 72–89.

Davis, Jennifer. 1980. "The London garotting panic of 1862." *Crime and the Law: The Social History of Crime in Western Europe since 1500*, edited by V. A. C. Gatrell et al. London: Europa.

Dickens, Charles. 1861/2011. *Great Expectations, 3 Volume Set: Great Expectations: The First Edition, 1861 Volume 1*. Cambridge University Press Re-issue.

Eagle Russett, Cynthia. 1989. *Sexual Science: The Victorian Construction of Motherhood*. Cambridge, Mass: Harvard University Press.

Emsley, Clive. 2010. *Crime and Society in England, 1750–1900*. Harlow, Essex: Longman.

Foucault, Michel. 2003. *Abnormal: Lectures at the College de France 1974–1975*, translated into English by Graham Burchell. London: Verso.

Garland, David. 2002. "Of crime and criminals: The development of criminology in Britain." *The Oxford Handbook of Criminology*, edited by M. Maguire, R. Morgan and R. Reiner, 2–50. Oxford: Oxford University Press.

Gibson, Mary. 2006. *Criminal Man*. Durham NC: Duke University Press.

Godfrey, Barry. 2001. "Jack the Ripper and fin de siecle anxiety: 'Re-positioning agency.'" *Newsletter Moderne*, March: 24–27.

Hinton, Alexander Laban. 2016. *Man or Monster?: The Trial of a Khmer Rouge Torturer*. Durham: Duke University Press Books.

Jackson, Mark. 2002. "The trial of Harriet Vooght: Continuity and change in the history of infanticide." *Infanticide. Historical perspectives on child murder and concealment, 1550–2000*. Ashgate: Aldershot.

Kilday, Anne-Marie. 2013. *A History of Infanticide in Britain c. 1600 to the Present*. Basingstoke: Palgrave Macmillan.

Leps, Marie-Christine. 1992. *Apprehending the Criminal: The Production of Deviance in Nineteenth-Century Discourse*. Durham, NC, and London: Duke University Press.

Marland, Hilary. 2004. *Dangerous Motherhood: Insanity and Childbirth in Victorian Britain*. Basingstoke: Palgrave Macmillan.

Mayhew, Henry. 1861–4/1996. *London Characters and Crooks*, edited by Christopher Hibbert. London: The Folio Society.

McGowan, Randall. 1990. "Getting to know the criminal class in nineteenth-century England." *Nineteenth Century Contexts*, 14, 1: 33–54.

Rabin, D. 2002. *Infanticide. Historical perspectives on child murder and concealment, 1550–2000*, edited by Mark Jackson. Aldershot: Ashgate Publishing.

Rafter Hahn, Nicole and Mary Gibson. 2004. *Criminal Woman, the Prostitute and the Normal Woman*. Durham, North Carolina: Duke University Press.

Scull, Andrew. 2012. *Hysteria. The Disturbing History*. Oxford: Oxford University Press.

Sharpe, Andrew N. 2007a. "Foucault's Monsters, the Abnormal Individual and the Challenge of English Law." *Journal of Historical Sociology*, 20, 3: 384–403.

———. 2007b. "Structured like a Monster: Understanding Human Difference through a Legal Category." *Law Critique* 18: 207–228.

———. 2009. "England's Legal Monsters." *Law, Culture and the Humanities* 5: 100–130.

Shepherd, Jade. 2016. "'I am very glad and cheered when I hear the flute:' The Treatment of Criminal Lunatics in Late Victorian Broadmoor." *Medical History*, 60, 4: 473–91.

Showater, Elaine. 1987. *The Female Malady: Women, Madness and English Culture, 1830–1980*. London: Virago.

Sindall, R. 1987. "The London garrotting panics of 1856 and 1862." *Social History*, 12, 3: 351–9.

Smith, Roger. 1981. *Trial by Medicine: Insanity and Responsibility in Victorian Trials*. Edinburgh: Edinburgh University Press.

Stevens, Mark. 2013. *Broadmoor Revealed. Victorian Crime and the Lunatic Asylum*. Barnsley: Pen and Sword.

———. 2014. *Life in the Victorian Asylum: The World of Nineteenth Century Mental Health Care*. Barnsley: Pen and Sword.

Walkowitz, Judith R. 1992. *City of Dreadful Delight: Narratives of Sexual Danger in Late-Victorian London*. London: Virago.

Watson, Stephen. 1994. "Malingerers, the 'Weakminded' Criminal and the 'Moral Imbecile': How the English Prison Medical Officer Became an Expert in Mental Deficiency, 1880–1930." *Legal Medicine in History*, edited by Michael Clark and Catherine Crawford, 223–241. New York: Cambridge University Press.

Weiner, Martin. 1990. *Reconstructing the Criminal: Culture, Law and Policy, in England, 1830–1914*. Cambridge: Cambridge University Press.

Williams, Lucy. 2016. *Wayward Women. Female Offending in Victorian England.* Barnsley: Pen and Sword.

Wise, Sarah. 2013. *Inconvenient People: Lunacy, Liberty and the Mad-Doctors in Victorian England.* London: Vintage.

Zedner, Lucia. 1991. "Women, Crime, and Penal Responses: A Historical Account." *Crime and Justice* 14.

Part III

MONSTERS IN REEL/REAL LIFE

Chapter Seven

The Purge, or Law of the Universal Monstrous

Matthew Sorrento

At first glance, *The Purge* film series (2013–2015) offers a vision of human monstrosity that's at once striking—so pervasive and immediate—and convenient, even banal, in the films that portray legally sanctioned criminals that don monstrous "masks" to perform the abnormality. And yet, of the recent horror film series, the films offer the strongest premise for widespread terror at the hands of humanity. By presenting a near-future, dystopic United States in which crime is legal for one night (a twelve-hour span) per year, the series presents a telescoped version of a horror movie apocalypse outside of the worn zombie narrative. *The Purge* thus follows the general trend of extremism in the horror film.[1] And yet, with the apocalypse condensed to a twelve-hour narrative span (described later), the series also invokes and revises tropes of the disaster movie.[2] Numerous films concern humanity's impending disaster in scenarios that flirt with mass destruction and personal disaster.[3] For example, instead of presenting a large group in peril (the motif in traditional disaster films), "character disaster" films telescope the torment to one character, in a reformed disaster scenario, to reflect the dread of a mass threat (Sorrento 2013). In apocalyptic horror films, the monstrous appears as a threat able to take *us*, that is, the innocents, over. If strong enough, one or a group of us may rise as the chosen ones, saviors of humanity to fight off plague or rampant infection.

As a hybrid of several film genres, the first entry of *The Purge* series (2013) structurally employs home invasion, a style that blends the horror and crime film genres.[4] By presenting a version of the traditional family unit overcome by invaders, the home invasion film invokes a threat to home and security, essentially a challenge to the status quo, on a small-scale level, to prove its strength and defeat a threat to its social order. Though far from the standard conservative horror film, the astute revision of home invasion in

The Purge—as the film's premise works with horror apocalypse and disaster motifs—presents humanity as universally monstrous, with everyone ready to attack and the victims with little hope for their own salvation (in a different circumstance, these same people could turn monstrous). The film's "device" offers direct social commentary, as a new reigning political party, *The New Founding Fathers of America* (NFFA), allows citizens to purge their criminal instincts they would otherwise express regularly while NFFA rids society of the "undesirable" working class and underclass. *The Purge* motif can yield a variety of related narratives; along with the series' original trilogy, an origin-themed prequel (*The First Purge*) was released in summer 2018. That a home invasion was the choice for writer-director James DeMonaco in the 2013 series opener was obviously budgetary, since the project required mostly just one filming location. Though in the process *The Purge* refashioned the home invasion to present even the putative saviors of the tradition (the victims turned avengers) as forms of the human monster. While monster studies argue the monster to be a reflection of the human self and our fears (Surrette 2007, 199; Grant 2018, 18), *The Purge* series clarifies its potential in all of us.

In the three films that make up *The Purge* series, the monstrous is realized as universal via mandate and citizens' willingness to embrace it. In this chapter I discuss how the use of genre hybridity in the series—blending in particular apocalyptic horror and, interchangeably, home invasion and street hunter narratives[5] to result in a revisionist disaster film—offers a unique portrayal of the monstrous in humanity. I'll first detail how the history of the monstrous onscreen in the United States—from supernatural to human, in the horror film, along with use of the gangster invasion film—has led to crime/horror hybridity in *The Purge* series. Then I will discuss how each film develops the conceit of all humanity as monstrous. In unpacking this genre revision offered by the series, I then analyze how the films depict the safety mandate of libertarianism—now surging under the policies and rapacious challenges to law of the Trump administration—as fallacious, as libertarianism is at the root of the legal philosophy behind the ruling NFFA, which mandates the annual Purge.

ON THE "MONSTROUS" IN HORROR

Ever since the popularity of Alfred Hitchcock's *Psycho* (1960) helped establish the slasher film as a trend by the 1970s (Thomson 2009, 128), the human monster is familiar onscreen. But at the birth of sound cinema, this was hardly so.[6] In aiming to terrify viewers in the early 1930s, Universal Studios adapted the gothic novels *Dracula* by Bram Stoker (novel, 1897; film, 1931) and *Frankenstein* by Mary Shelley (novel, 1818; film 1931). The studio's choice for supernatural threats to normality offered a sense of security, as the monstrous was something removed from humanity, and often the product of a remote gothic castle. And hence, in this narrative a community based on traditional family values rises to defeat the monster by the narrative's end (Wood 2003, 65–66; Williams 2014, 12). With the couple Jonathan Harker (David Manners) and Mina (Helen Chandler) ascending castle stairs at the end of Tod Browning's *Dracula* (1931), a coming marriage and family is implied, even if the monster's relative (in the film's sequel, *Dracula's Daughter*, 1936) would return to face the same kind of defeat. Similarly, friends and family offer a "toast to the house of (Dr.) Frankenstein" at the close of this 1931 film—after the Creature has been defeated in a burning windmill—assuring prosperity for the traditional family unit in the making. As Dracula represents a racial outsider, as an eastern European man of means moving to London (who feeds on/infects women), and Frankenstein, an economic outsider (dressed in laborer's clothes), Robin Wood, using psychoanalytic/Marxist theory, argues that society's repressed—made monstrous in the process—assaults on normality only to be defeated and endorse the status quo (2003, 65-66). Occasionally perceptive films, like *The Devil and Daniel Webster* (1941), reflect on the past and future of horror and dynamic portrayals of the monstrous (Williams 2000). Nevertheless, the gothic outsider dominated on the 1930s–40s US screen.

Though the horror film had its changes—switching out gothic monsters for atomic age ones, or alien invaders, by the thick of the Cold War/arms race/space race in the 1950s—Robin Wood notes a major revision of horror coming in the 1970s. He cites *Psycho* as a major transformative work since it implicates the traditional American family as the source of horror, that which transforms man, Norman Bates (Anthony Perkins), into psycho killer/human monster, and thus revealing human beings as the true "tormentors and butchers" (Wood, 2002, 150). Soon after, *Night of the Living Dead* (1968) presented humanity as monstrous as the living dead attacking them (a conceit that's been worn out by the zombie craze in pop culture). This groundbreaking film underscores familial breakdown in the form of the disintegrating one (the Coopers, played by Marilyn Eastman and Karl Hardman), soon eaten/destroyed by their infected daughter. Similarly, the brother and sister who arrive to the house at the beginning (Judith O'Dea and Russell Streiner) eventually reflect the traditional American family consuming itself, as the infected brother breaks through the protected door to get his sister (Williams 2014, 135–36). Even more important to Wood thus is *Texas Chain Saw Massacre* (1974), which presents the family unit—Leatherface's—as a completely monstrous entity. As a truly progressive horror film, *Texas Chain Saw* reflects the traditional family unit's monstrosity (Wood 1979, 32). This film clarified the classic horror film's endorsement of an institution that represses alternate family units, economic and political outsiders, women, and racial groups outside the normalized White Anglo-Saxon Protestant presence.

The appearance of the human monster in the horror film—thanks to some earlier examples in European cinema (1960's *Eyes Without a Face* and 1955's *Diabolique*)—offered a new threat and, thus, potential for political commentary.[7] The most popular ensuing trend regretfully missed the opportunity for such comment. The slasher films of the 1970s and 1980s reflect mostly conservative values in their portrayal of a human killer preying on a small group of teenagers in either a remote location (*Friday the 13th*), where suburbanites go for a summer outing, or their suburban neighborhood (*Halloween*). This portrayal of the monstrous is mixed between the realistic and supernatural, a cynically convenient blend, and the murders reflect a conservative reaction to sex-equals-death, as the sexually active teens are murdered. A final, virginal girl rises to face the vague threat. In the more interesting series in the cycle, *A Nightmare on Elm Street*, Wes Craven commits his slasher to the supernatural, as he's a haunt in teenagers' collective dreamscape.[8] His weapon, a glove of five knife-talons, reflects his evil snatching as a former child killer, with facial burns reflecting the vigilante justice of the parents years ago when they trapped and burned him alive after he escaped the law on a technicality. In employing the horror movie trope that the monster feeds on a victim's fear,[9] *Elm*'s "final girl" drops her fear to thwart the monster (the best potential in films that always leave the monster reigning at the end for a sequel).[10] He is a repressed monster of a parent's worst nightmare forever haunting other youths. Thus, his survival past episode one into a series reflects the painful memories beyond death.

And yet, Wes Craven's contributions were the sole high points for the slasher to offer insight into the human monstrous.[11] Developments of the serial killer film offered portrayals of the human monstrous via a hybrid of crime-horror. The early trend in this style, the "sex crime film" or "sexual pathology" film (Rubin 1999, 43–4), appeared in the greater trend of social problem film. The latter style consisted of torn-from-the-headlines films from Warner Bros. studios like *I Am a Fugitive from a Chain Gang* (Mervyn LeRoy 1932), *Wild Boys of the Road* (William Wellman 1933), and *Each Dawn I Die* (William Keighley 1939), films often concerning crime and punishment, in some cases wrongful. By the 1950s, the style moved from the safer confines of law and justice/prison to criminals on the loose. *The Sniper*, a 1952 study of a sex murderer (based on criminology research) was an early project by producer Stanley Kramer, who would make big issues his concern throughout his career. Featuring Eddie Miller (Arthur Franz), a serial killer, as a central character, the viewer moves along with him as he moves from victim to victim. Meanwhile, the film reveals his motives and some sympathy for him, while he grows more frail and readying for his eventual capture. The monstrous is not an invader but a first-person perspective, even gathering sympathy at times. Thus, the film serves as an early example of the monstrous lurking in the everyday before *Psycho* popularized the conceit. As a piece of exploitation cinema masked as a prestige production, the film serves viewers on both counts. As an entry on the monstrous in cinema, it offers a glimpse at the universal status of monstrous potential in all humanity.

The Boston Strangler (1968) appeared some years after *Psycho* and during the surge of New Hollywood Cinema, which allowed filmmakers to explore sex and violence more freely (Rubin 1999, 43–4). Also featuring the actions of a serial killer in first person, the film opts for depicting his everyday life, the banality of his actions though he feels the urge to kill and act on it. With a clear moral stance—the film begins with the law's reactions to the killings of Albert DeSalvo (Tony Curtis) and the investigation, led by the noble presence of Henry Fonda—the film clarifies its stance on the deviant subject it holds up close, a definite outsider whose monstrous nature remains enigmatic, even after much study and attention. The final scene, in which DeSalvo responds to the therapist in his own (credible) confusion, tributes the closing of *Psycho.*[12] It has the camera tracking away to trail from Salvo, backed up by padded walls, to offer a surreal closing. A man lost in his own mind, Salvo (informed by Hitchcock) is monstrous by way of a doomed mind, which replaces the supernatural factors of Golden Age monstrosity onscreen.

As if to answer the verity of films like *Boston Strangler* (though with little concern in the style), Leonard Kastle's *The Honeymoon Killers* (1970, based on a real couple) offers a raw, personal (delightfully flawed) portrayal of a con team. The documentary style is relaxed and clean, with the actions of the murderous duo matter-of-fact and, considering the subject matter, all the more haunting. It recalls the docu-noir films popular in the late 1940s–1950s (Sorrento 2016, 248–54) while informed by recent exercises in true crime like *In Cold Blood* (Richard Brooks 1967). That Ray (Tony Lo Bianco), who woos then murders women, chose Martha (Shirley Stoler) as his real, secret wife (they pose as siblings) may have been a ruse (even if he confesses his true love for her), in his need for an accomplice to help catch prey. The path to murder grows surprisingly vivid in a scene of Martha's cold-blooded killing of a girl (offscreen), whose mother was recently their victim. In style of classical Hollywood cinema (Bordwell et al. 1985),[13] this signals their downfall from their roving lives of crime outside the status quo. She soon turns both of them in for him to face the electric chair. She has reached the bleakest depths with the child killing, and finds some redemption as a penitent human monster, even if jailed and facing execution, like Ray. Meanwhile, Ray remains his ordinary little self who has all the while been capable of killing, with even the kind of glimmer surviving in Norman Bates (post-arrest) unlikely.

The everyday banality, minus the gothic flair of Bates's psychosis, of *The Honeymoon Killers* years later worked into a bleaker vision of a citywalker/monster in *Henry: Portrait of a Serial Killer* (John McNaughton 1986/released 1990). Some victimization appears in this rendition of the human monster: he was an abused youth whose memories of the incidents (if we trust them to be true) are as shifting as his fantasies of rape and murder. His attacks in the film are shocking, but equally disturbing is the portrayal of his routine life in between killing and drifting. A dedicated video nasty, the film offers insight into the psychological drive for Henry. After he kills an electronics fence and takes away a camcorder, Henry (Michael Rooker) and his partner, the impulsive letch Otis (Tom Towles), have a means of recording their crimes (like the killer in Michael Powell's *Peeping Tom* [1960]). When they replay them over, we have a reflection of the repeated fantasies in Henry's mind, his engine of violent obsession leading to urges realized.[14] Though offering commentary on the psychology of horror and the monstrous, horror films often channel progressive notions of women and gays only to reaffirm them as monstrous, as in the serial killer themed hit *The Silence of the Lambs* (1991) (Sharrett 1996, 257). The 1990s serial killer cult classic *Se7en* (David Fincher 1995) formats the serial killer as an allegorical agent. In a series of killings reflecting the Seven Deadly Sins, the killer ("John Doe," Kevin Spacey) possesses the power to consume one of his investigators (by killing the police officer's wife before they apprehend him) and meeting the killer's wish to be executed by the police officer, for Rage (the final sin) to play out. While Henry lives on, killing anything that comes too close, *Se7en*'s killer is a monster so powerful that he punishes his investigator and removes due process from the equation.

THE "OTHER" MONSTER INVADING THE HOME

The opening film in the *Purge* series (2013) came in the wake of extremist violence in American cinema post–9/11. This release also works off a trend of home invasion films. The style presents a middle-class home, as an example of complacent modern family values, violated by a break-in/takeover. In the traditional films of the classical Hollywood (1930s–40s, specifically), to prove their communal strength, the family rises to defend their home/safety and defeat the intruder (discussed further below). Recent films in the style (*The Strangers* 2008; *Trespass* 2011; *Knock Knock* 2015) either reveal weaknesses in the family (in *Knock Knock*, the male's weakness is sexual temptation, while in *Trespass*, the father sells off prized heirlooms, due to his business failures) or a visceral downbeat sentiment (in *The Strangers*, the family killed for the criminals to repeat the process). The break-in is a common motif for high-concept crime cinema, stemming back to D.W. Griffith's 1909 short film, *The Lonely Villa*, and featured in classics like Hitchcock's *Dial M for Murder* (1954), Terence Young's *Wait Until Dark* (1967), and Michael Mann's *Manhunter* (1986). But the home invasion telescopes the break-in/takeover for the entire narrative, for the victims to rise up against their violators.

While structurally devised as a home invasion film, *The Purge* takes inspiration from the recent trend of New Extremism that originated in France, then spread to other European nations (Horek and Kendall 2011) before American films post-9/11 incorporated some of its techniques in genre films blending with arthouse treatments of cinema (Sorrento 2013). As a home invasion film, *The Purge* holds a special connection to one work of New Extremism, Michael Haneke's *Funny Games*, originally a 1997 film made in Austria before the director remade it in the United States in 2007.[15] It's something of a metacinematic study of the home breached, with the invading youths breaking the fourth wall and able to rewind their narrative to repair their victims' attempts to escape. It presents viewer awareness of a long-running tradition in cinema first popularized as a subgenre of the 1930s gangster film, the gangster home invasion.

The classical gangster film, which was popularized by the Depression-era hits *Little Caesar, The Public Enemy* (1931), and *Scarface* (1932), presents a monstrous aberration of humanity for our delight. With the central character a gangster, the film presents his rise into the top of an organization and his downfall (killing) by police or rival hoods. Each gangster is an outsider racially set apart from the White Anglo-Saxon Protestant identity (Italian or Irish American), while Tony Camonte, as played by Paul Muni, appears as a reptilian threat to the public. Capable of cold-blooded murder from the film's start, Camonte realizes a megalomaniacal (and masturbatory) delight when firing for the first time a Colt Thompson Submachine Gun, ripping holes in the poolhall wall (and multiplying the sure-shots of that game) in glee.

While these early gangster films covered various crimes by the gangster and cohorts, tales of gangsters on the lam became popular (Mason 2002, 67; quoted in Sloninowski 2016, 13). One version is the gangster raid film, in which one or more gangsters invade a home or family business to take over and take hostages. The style telescopes the gangster experience into one crime, with the safety of the hostages in question. It depicts the "monstrous outsider" up closer than the broader classical style, to see his abuse and violation of the family, and what he manages through manipulation. While offering viewers the delight of watching a hood at work (one whom, according to mandates of the Production Code ["Motion Picture" 1930]), would have to be punished by the film's end), the gangster raid served as a call for the victims of the home, those representing the traditional family unit to rise and defeat the threat, thus asserting the strength of family values. In essence, it is the classical horror film redressed and slightly revised, with a non-urban home invaded, beyond the urban-ethnic (Catholic, Italian, or Irish) associations of the 1930s gangster film.

The 1936 film *The Petrified Forest* (Archie Mayo, based on a 1935 Robert E. Sherwood stage play of the same name) uses a gangster invasion of a roadside diner to assert the willpower of the owner-family threatened.[16] A drifter and failed writer, Alan (Leslie Howard), stirs the artistic sensibilities of the owner's daughter Gabrielle (Bette Davis). The head gangster, Duke (Humphrey Bogart), eventually grants Alan's wish to be shot so his insurance can go to Gabrielle to find her mother in France. It's a sacrifice that offers insight and experience to Gabrielle, while the hoods escaping with human shields are caught with ease offscreen, the news of which is delivered by a phone call. The 1944 dark comedy *Arsenic and Old Lace* (based on a 1941 play by Joseph Kesselring) is a clever revision that's aware of the conservative treatment in *Forest*. With the family no longer the picture of moral strength, the film presents the Brewster family of Brooklyn (an American mainstay, as descendants of the Mayflower) descending into madness. Aunts Abby (Josephine Hull) and Martha (Jean Adair, both to Cary Grant's Mortimer Brewster) have been luring lonely aged bachelors to poison them with elderberry wine. Meanwhile, Mortimer's brother Jonathan (Raymond Massey) returns home a murderer on the run from the police. Jonathan is accompanied by his plastic surgeon/mad scientist/"creator" (Peter Lorre), who botched his accomplices' facial procedure to make him look like Frankenstein's monster. This character notes the gangster raid's overall connection to the 1930s gothic horror film in light of Wood's theory of the "return of the repressed."[17] In "invading" not a house of moral fortitude by a madhouse, Jonathan folds his comical monstrousness into that of his aunts by burying his recent victim in their basement/makeshift crypt.

John Huston's *Key Largo* (1949), based on a 1939 play by Maxwell Anderson, with Bogart now a victim and Edward G. Robinson, star of the *Little Caesar* (1930), as the invading gangster echoes the gothic connections of the style, with Robinson like a beast haunting the prisoners of the stormy tropical house. Robert Siodmak's *The Killers* (1946) serves as the most threatening and insightful reflection on the gangster raid in question, even if comprising only 20 minutes of the film's screen time.[18] This time based on a terse 1927 short story by Ernest Hemingway, the father of the hardboiled style, the film uses the source's invasion of a roadside lunch counter, by two gangster/hitmen looking to execute the Swede (a wonderfully understated Burt Lancaster, in his debut), to launch a noir investigation into his death (an insurance investigator wonders why he didn't run). A German émigré who fled Nazism to France then later to Hollywood in 1939, director Siodmak crafts a bleak film of chiaroscuro lighting and claustrophobia, executing the expressionism from his homeland that had become part of the noir style. The two hitmen arrive to a diner that, in graphic representation of the set of tight walls and a low ceiling, transforms into a coffin-like prison once they command their plans. Grotesque in their causal threats, they turn a small business into their home-base for a hit completed minutes later. With the low ceilings (usually left out in 1940s set design) in the production design to highlight the oppression, the film offers little hope for the Swede, lying in wait in his nearby apartment, with fate against him. Nick Adams (Phil Brown) rushes to warn him, which only confirms the Swede's acceptance of his fate. When unloading their bullets into the Swede, the hitmen unleash a nightmarish thunderstorm of light, the kind of expressionist flourish that stays just this side of realism while capturing a death sentenced by the underworld. With the opening narrative concluded, the film turns to insurance agent Jim Reardon's (Edmund O'Brien) investigation, motivated to discover why the Swede accepted his fate. Reardon's trail brings about the slow mystery unraveling in a Dashiell Hammett or Raymond Chandler, with noir-style flashbacks to the Swede's earlier life and wrong turns.

THE MONSTROUS INVADING THE MONSTROUS: *THE PURGE*

In the wake of New Extremism (in the twenty-first century), the American film tradition of the gangster invasion film has remained a mainstay for filmmakers to present a picture of normality in home life turned nightmarish. The opening entry in the *Purge* series uses the gangster raid genre to present the motif of societal monstrosity. As the narrative choice for the first entry on a political satire in a planned series, the home invasion was budgetary, with the film restricted mostly to one set (the home invaded). The series had bigger aims once a larger budget was available (depending on the first entry becoming a hit) (DeMonaco 2014).

The film's premise concerns a dystopian near-future United States in which the NFFA had ratified the 28th Amendment of the Constitution to legalize an annual event called The Purge, on March 21–22 from 7 p.m. to 7 a.m., when all crimes are legal and emergency services are suspended. To protect the NFFA, certain government officials, in a ranking system at 10 or higher, are immune from the Purge; weapons from Class 4 and below are allowed (five sections to 28th Amendment described all of this). Violation is punished by hanging (described in Section 5), an ironic, primitive form compared to the widespread violence of automatic weapons. Two incidents referred to in the film's universe (though fictitious)—the Queensbridge Incident and Covina Alley murders—were fake ones set up by NFFA to foster an overthrow of the government. The NFFA touts that the Purge has plummeted both crime and unemployment to 1 percent. Though presented as an organic means to "clean" society, the NFAA sends out its own agents to kill those of lower socioeconomic status. This sets the tone of the empowered preying on the economically and racially disenfranchised happening throughout the United States. The production wisely exploited a website (http://www.newfounders-america.org/founders) and social media to popularize the fictional concept of the NFFA and its twelve-hour event. As satire, the concept indicates reductive principles of government opposed to progress. Especially in the film's target scope is libertarianism, which will be a focus at the end of this chapter.

Responses to *The Purge* film have focused on immediately obvious social frameworks, namely social Darwinism apparent in the films.[19] With criticism limited to discussing the film as satire in response to the current economic crisis and government shutdown, these readings miss stronger implications: that the situation represents the monstrous extent of humanity, especially in the current political climate. These satire-based readings restrict cinema to be fleeting entertainment and not the permanent commentary that it is, often on ideology. The New Founding Fathers obviously try to connect themselves to the original ones, much like how the US Right Wing "Tea Party" and libertarian party co-opted the *Don't Tread on Me* Gadsden flag of the American Revolution (Schartz 2014).

The first entry of the series uses the gangster invasion tradition to reflect the Purge's influence over action and morality—the family invaded, in the earlier tradition, would rise and defeat threat—since the family itself is infected by politics of the New World Order. While nullity in the raided family is nothing new (see Polanski's *Cul-de-Sac*, *Trespass,* and *Knock Knock*), *The Purge* advances beyond familiar weakness to legal mandate for consuming others to maintain normalcy. *The Purge* is categorized as dystopian horror though its connections to the crime genre are clear. As a hybrid crime-horror-disaster pic, the apocalyptic-themed film realizes the highest potential in political commentary. As a device, the Purge indicates widespread mayhem, though the films portray just selected incidents. Though it offers no dread as the result of scientific advances, *The Purge* realizes the potential of science fiction–horror in its widespread terror beyond the localized style of other horror films.[20]

Following a brief overview of the NFFA and the Purge "holiday," on Purge Night, 2022, the film centers on the home of James Sandin (Ethan Hawke), an upper-middle-class security salesman (shaped by the premise of security and threat) and his family: wife, daughter, younger son. Soon becoming a target for Purge raiders, who don Halloween-style masks reflecting a new Day of Death (to ignite spring) and "perform" it, Sandin admits to his wife that their home's premier security system is designed to deter more than stop a forceful entry. The pack of rich-kid raiders (twenty-somethings) eventually brings heavy machinery to rip off the reinforcements to the Sandin home. Purgers plan ahead for a year, with the wealthy ready to take on the like.

But the initial target of the youth-gone-mad isn't the Sandins. They chase a young African American (Edwin Hodge, titled "Bloody Stranger" in this film) to the affluent Los Angeles suburb. Escaping them for a time, he reaches the Sandin home for help and sanctuary. This character comes off as a plot device, the kind that is used in several films to unpack politics of white Americans. Nevertheless, he proves to have a larger impact in the narrative. By writing him into the second and third installments (now as Dante Bishop), DeMonaco uses the character to thread the three films together, while the character's role as a hero turns eventually into mad rogue avenger (in *The Purge: Election Year*, 2016).

Charlie lets in the "Bloody Stranger," who has managed to kill one of the Purgers chasing him. Once inside, he escapes an armed James during a confrontation with his daughter's boyfriend (who snuck in before the system was first engaged for the night). The home now has two trespassers: one a threat to family values (the teenage boyfriend at odds with the "law of the father") and the other a socioeconomic victim opposing their affluent security. When the Purgers arrive outside, they demand via the security camera that the victim be returned to them, threatening the family's security if they fail to do so. Deciding to give him up to the Purgers, James has his wife, Mary (Lena Headey), torture him with a letter opener to get him back out of the house. Here the victims of the raid, themselves turning monstrous (in line the revisionist horror movie tradition: see the victims-turned-hostile of a zombie raid in a farmhouse in *Night of the Living Dead*, 1968), implore the Law of the Purge's execution. As a racial outsider, the stranger reflects the current government's legacy as well at the original founding fathers' (Fuchs 2013), thus indicating a tradition of racism now reformatted into a new type of aggression and annihilation. With the film afraid of committing to this conceit completely, the family decides to keep and protect the "stranger," before he escapes in the house where the lights/power have been cut off (a modern-horror landscape, where his safety is still in question). Their choice reflects the film's quick attempt to restore family values and have viewers side with the family.

The Purgers soon invade, by ripping off the house's metal protection, and their hunt begins. A cavalry of relief comes from the neighbors, along with approaching daylight (to signify some hope), who save the Sandins, and thus suggest that familial relations, from another dimension of the narrative, will in fact be the salvation. The twist, then, is that the neighbors (crime film victims as monsters) have killed the putative Purgers to reclaim that right upon the Sandins, out of jealousy of preying on their fear (marketing security product) and revenge, now that the house is exposed. Soon, the "bloody stranger" appears (rather conveniently) to kill one of the neighbors and hold another at gunpoint, thus waiting out the Purge. The nationwide siren noting the Purge's end resolves the conflict (the neighbors casually walking home, along with the stranger) and offers another irritating convenience, highlighting the seams in the melodramatic narrative that is more probing in its thematic construct.

That the monstrous casually disperse back to their daily lives, to prepare for next year's holiday, underscores their monstrous presence. In *The Purge,* as in everyday life in the United States, the monstrous resides within a complacent middle-class exterior. Jordan Peele's *Get Out* (2017), which became a runaway hit and a contender for several Academy Awards (winning Best Original Screenplay), addresses the lives of African Americans being body-snatched, with brains of dying whites implanted in them, to reflect the oppression of the powerful and the inheritance of their ideas into the oppressed. Peele presents a severe example of marginalization and, hence, absolute control. *The Purge* indicates a widespread threat of annihilation and while less concerned with the psychology of oppressed (coming from a white director instead of a black one), implicating the widespread psychology of the oppressors instead. With both films dabbling in dystopic tropes—Peele's more in science fiction than the *Purge*'s political nightmare—they reflect the nightmares behind H.G. Wells's call for fascism and totalitarian rule in *Things to Come* (1936), in which an evolved micro-society, Wings of the World/World Communications, gains control of the world after chemical warfare ("wandering sickness") consumes most of the population. Wells's belief that, in some cases, fascism is good (in his idea of "Liberal Fascism") indicates the elite's power to oppress when control is established. Wells wished for such, as Europe was headed to World War II (which he uncannily predicts in his film). Peele and DeMonaco note another kind of fascism in culture happening for some time in the United States.

The Purge also recalls John Carpenter's *They Live* (1988), which could work as a prequel to the former film. As the monstrous (in this case, alien) beings are discovered masked as middle-class yuppies, with their mind-control messages hidden just beneath marketing materials, a working class revolt takes them on to expose them and remove their brainwashing means.

Now exposed, *The Purge* could be the monstrous reclaiming control by downing the working class revolt: have them buy in to the annual night of the hunt endorsed and sold by the elite. The famous fight scene in *They Live*, in which John Nada (Roddy Piper) forces (Keith David) to put on the special sunglasses, that is, the way to see the hidden monstrous, reflects the rejection of ideology to break free from its façade, which in the *Purge*'s case is the bloodthirsty draw of one night to kill. In light of this, the most we can hope for is another revolution, anarchy to a society free of the chains of the law of the monstrous.

HUNTING/BUTCHERY IN THE STREETS— *THE PURGE: ANARCHY*

The second film (2014) doesn't present such. Knowing that the first film didn't deliver the widespread mayhem that the concept promises, DeMonaco, armed with a bigger budget (from the success of the first film), moved the Purge away from the home to the streets. (The question of revolt against the NFFA is taken up in the final installment of the trilogy: *The Purge: Election Year*, discussed below.) Urban hunts often take place in crime cinema proper, as in Walter Hill's *The Warriors* (1979), though some gang members attacking the title gang are gothic in nature. A more monstrous presence in an urban hunt is something like a serial killer in *Henry*, though hybrid horror films, such as *Predator 2* (1990), use the urban landscape rife with gang warfare for a human hunt.[21]

One year following the events of part one, the Purge has been deemed a success while potential victims rush to protect themselves for this year's twelve-hour hunt, again focusing on Los Angeles. A working class Latino family takes the focus, as waitress Eva Sanchez (Carmen Ejogo) returns home to her teenage daughter. Her father, terminally ill, submits to the monstrous soon approaching as he sneaks out into a limousine: in a deal for $100,000 to be paid to his daughter, he has sold himself to wealthy Purgers, who will sacrifice him in the safety of their home (how the wealthy prefer to do it). The monstrous has effectively shorn a family of security even before their ritual begins. In this way, the home is ripped of its security at the onset and the monstrous law creates victims instantly. The mother and daughter are soon attacked by their letch of a superintendent (a potential victim as monster), in which ownership of their home also undermines their security. (Later, when Eva and her group take refuge in the home of Eva's friend, Tanya [Justina Machado], her sister attempts to Purge Tanya for sleeping with her husband.) The attack is halted by a pro-Purge paramilitary group who brings them to their boss, Big Daddy, who rides in the back of a tractor trailer with a heavy artillery machine gun to mow down Purge victims. With an American flag ball cap, sunglasses, and white apron, he reads as hunter-*cum*-butcher feeding his bloodthirst. As a man of means roaming the streets to kill, he's the film's vision of the monstrous as government-funded entrepreneur who sends out minions to poach prey. At the narrative's end, after he has chased down the man who has helped Eva (Leo, billed as "the sergeant," who returns in *Purge: Election Year*), Big Daddy notes that the NFFA, concerned that Purgers focus too much on other middle-class members against whom they have grudges, have deployed murder squads to hunt the lower classes better.

Upon escaping Tanya's house, the group is captured by a gang of Purgers that brings them to a ceremonial hunt in a makeshift sports theater (the "slave hunt" having returned to popularity with the film *The Hunger Games* [2012] though prominent since *The Running Man* [1987]). The upper class, behind protective glass, will bet and delight in the victims hunting each other. The random hunters on the streets, some on ripping-loud motorbikes to reflect the surging thrill of the hunt, are cyphers of the severe murder wielded by Big Daddy, the family that "hired" Eva's father, and the group holding the hunt to the death—the entitled the most monstrous, and, as in American capitalism, those honoring the wealthy who emulate their actions. The upper class discuss weapons as elegant commodities, thus establishing the means of gun worship, as in actual American society.

The "Bloody Stranger" from the first film, here named Dwayne, with a team that is part of an anti-Purge campaign (indicated by online protests earlier in the narrative) saves the group from the hunt, and sergeant reaches his goal through the night—the home of the man who killed his son while driving inebriated. With his monstrous nature possible via the law, he withholds killing the man, becoming a source of hope until he's shot (non-fatally) by Big Daddy, who has tracked him down and delivers the news of the NFFA's recruiting butchers like him. Big Daddy is killed by another survivor (the man Leo spares), but the monstrous is held at bay only until next year's Purge.

COUNTERREVOLUTION—*THE PURGE: ELECTION YEAR*

Always keen on exploiting premise for effect, the series released its third installment to underscore the controversial election between Hillary Clinton and Donald Trump. The critiques of the former are nearly as renowned as the strong case against the latter. But needless to say, the uber-capitalist reality TV show star who won represents a monstrous backlash to progressivism, what commentator Van Jones called a "whitelash" against the nation's first black president, Barack Obama (Ryan 2016). The political environment was ideal for a film centered on a campaign of a woman senator for president, Senator Charlie Roan (Elizabeth Mitchell), running in opposition to the NFFA (an opening scene shows her family as victim of it in her youth, with her the only survivor). The NFFA, led by their candidate Minister Edwidge Owens (Kyle Secor), remove immunity for politicians on the approaching Purge night. This quick modification shows the weakness of political opposition to the oppressive monstrous body, but also that of constitutional rights, especially in the hands of powers professing its value. With Roan obviously in jeopardy, her protectors prove under the control of the monstrous in power. Members of the security force let in a paramilitary group, led by the neo-nazi Danziger (Terry Serpico) donning a confederate flag (the series now clarifying the racist goal of the Purge), through security to get Roan. As a trained hunter aiming to halt political revolution/freedom from fascism, he exemplifies the extremity in the Purger's monstrous evolution, following the truck-bound machine-gun butcher in *Anarchy*. By breaching her protection, the security allows the monstrous to invade, like a home-invasion-meets-monster-attack. Leo Barnes, one in security not compromised (and returning from *Anarchy*), saves Roan and moves her to the streets; hence, the film repeats the urban chases of the second film.

They retreat to a small grocery led by a man, Joe (Mykelti Williamson), who learns, earlier in the narrative, that he could no longer afford Purge insurance for his store, thus deciding to guard it himself. As a small business owner, Joe contributes to non-corporatized commerce to serve community and not executives wanting to grow, consume small businesses like this one, and reach an infallibility by offering reduced prices that the underclass cannot resist. By enacting the annual Purge, the NFFA acts as a megacorp that in mere hours consumes small business while sales of weaponry for slaughter surge.

While holed up in the store, Joe, Roan, and the others are targeted by a group of teenage girls. Their association to teen culture appears earlier in the narrative when, in private school uniforms, they are caught trying to steal candy; now they return for revenge ("I want my candy!" they scream to show their delight in violence and the reward). The crime of shoplifting quickly surges into armed raiding, as the law allows youth to balloon into the monstrous. Returning in ceremonial dress for the Purge (gowns with the typical mad-looking Halloween masks, and even their car is dressed in Christmas lights, a holiday signifying nothing but excessive consumption), they represent over-matured youth consumers empowered to destroy. They are teens consumed by their need to consume, as they embrace the codes of NFFA eagerly when they should be negotiating uncertainties of adulthood. Their desires reflect a specific monstrosity of late capitalist United States.

Like the Purgers in *The Purge* and others in *Anarchy*, these teens reflect how consumerist culture tempts and reprograms the middle class. Oppressed by their own fears of economic uncertainties, they direct it toward the disenfranchised (a struggling business owner). Considering their affluence in dress and transportation, these teens are members of the upper-middle-class family (the source of security in classical Hollywood horror). Thus, macro-conservative values now reprogram youths into the monstrous, whereas the oppressive Law of the Father is the original source.

After an EMT helps to take out the attacking girls and their reinforcements, the group's escape leads to more chasing in the streets. When they find an anti-Purge hideout (dark like the electricity-deprived points of attack throughout the series), it's led by Dante Bishop (the "Bloody Stranger" of the first film and savior in the second, continuing the leadership role). Bishop wants to assassinate Minister Owens to end the Purge. The obsession shows monstrous potential now in Bishop, the hope compromised for a time and showing the breadth of the universal monstrous. Their fortress broken, Roan is stolen away and taken to a Purger ceremony to assassinate her. In the Catholic imagery, *Election Year* uses formal ritual to reflect the ritualistic wear of the Purgers in the streets. It clarifies the rituals behind the killing-game in *Anarchy*. The religious ceremony of *Election Year,* situated in a cathedral, notes the obvious ties to corruption of government and worshiping bodies. The film aims to close the trilogy with Roan surviving her assassination to free other victims and win the election to end the Purge, only for violent uprisings of NFFA members to ignite throughout the country. It seems a fast and convenient, two-headed resolution by the filmmakers: restoring order for it to be threatened. But by implying that the monstrous have informally assembled (news reports in the film don't clarify how they have done so) to attack others daily in the streets, the Purge now occurs sporadically and continuously, leaving society in thrall, if not direct victims, and warfare imminent.

THE MENACE: LIBERTARIAN ANARCHY

The *Purge* trilogy progresses from horror in the home, to the city streets, and then against an emerging government opposing the NFFA. In developing thus, the series invokes the roots of the oppressive body (in the household) to unveil how oppression, to a greater extent, extends throughout American society. The NFFA have added a holiday of violence to market a visceral version of freedom, nearly absolute in the freedom to kill. This concept and evolution of the Purge critique right-wing libertarianism,[22] in its implications of no assistance or safety from the governing body. Though putatively a small time frame (twelve hours a year), the long-term effects of the annual Purge show how the lack of help affects the safety and livelihood of others. It's as common as the random/continual riots closing *Election Year*.

The immediate issue when connecting right-libertarianism with the series is the political philosophy's "non-aggression principle"—that you are allowed absolute freedom from government interference as long as you do not infringe on the safety of others (Hamowy 2008, xxi; Rose 2013). Taken at face value, this would prevent a Purge from ever occurring. Libertarian theorist Gerard Casey argues that most killing is done by the state (Casey 2012, 32–3), but does not acknowledge how non-social policies adversely affect the livelihood and wellbeing of the underclass, leading to its slow death. As depicted in the series, for the one night of the year the lack of support that results from absolute freedom impinges on the livelihood and safety of the underclass. In a nation supporting economic inequality and prejudiced action related to race, gender, and sexual preference/sexual identity, the privileged classes have no interest in helping the oppressed out of their state. Securing themselves in libertarian entitlement, these privileged citizens indirectly harm and oppress. The Purge invokes all this damage as a condensed, fiercely boiling metaphor—putting a face to the damage that is done, in spite of an official non-aggression stance. Big Daddy, the machine-gun butcher of *Anarchy*, may be the most vivid representation (in spite of the implications of Danziger's power), though the NFFA governing body, largely off screen, looms the most. While libertarians ensure safety of the underclass but refuse to use resources to help them (calling taxation theft [Casey 2012, 1], since they don't want to support the society that helps them build wealth), the home security system (a motivating factor of the first film) is their dream industry. They believe in safety for all yet prepare for attacks upon themselves, since they distrust the motivations of the underclass. The racist and classist ideas of these extreme conservatives produce the violence of the Purge, while their policies of inaction create violence in inaction.

Libertarians believe that the citizen shall make no contact with the state and hence, would reject a new amendment for the Purge as outrageous. And yet, their philosophy merely assumes the safety of all, without arguing for law and justice through a closely watching governing body. By limiting government, libertarian philosophy ignores discussion of funding for the police/law and order. The beliefs reflect the lack of police assistance and other first responders on Purge night—instead of funding enforcement, let the Purge weed them out. The libertarian discourse concerns protection of self and private property, while their lifeways result from an idealist's form of capitalism, wide open trade, in which their concept of isolation is actually detrimental for business. Supposedly all deals are negotiated in this form of free trade, but in reality this kind of capitalism serves the needs of big business ownership. Thus, the privileged class aims to trade amongst itself, while employing the underclass in servitude. If taxation, as a form of theft by "criminal" government bodies, "aggresses against the free exchange of goods and services" (Casey 2012, 3), then the series presents the entitled violently striking back at the underclass for needing the assistance from the capitalist system that relies on them as producers (workers) and consumers. With no public funds, the privileged class of libertarians would control wealth while privately funding the policing, which would be a thug body oppressing the underclass (very common already) in service of their criminal bosses. This reality directly opposes the libertarian assumption that leadership exploits the poor (Casey 2012, 33), and not the free market.

The concept of libertarian freedom really means fascism at the cost of the underclass. The attempted Purging by the neighbors in the first film, even if against others of the middle class, is really an attempt to secure themselves from the underclass. The Purgers outside the Sandin home, when they demand to have the "Bloody Stranger" back, embody this preying upon the underclass (in which the Sandins partake when they torture him). Overall, the first film shows this monstrous mentality occupying the middle-class home, at the cost of outsiders from the underclass; the second, owning the home and streets (via government-funded butchers); and the third, suppressing political opposition and striking back, as widespread mobs, after being voted out. The series results from a careful hybridization of crime-horror resulting in a kind of disaster film, an apocalyptic vision very immediate.

NOTES

1. Critic David Edelstein has described the post–9/11 trend of horror as "torture porn" (see Edelstein 2006), which, if derogative, points to a general trend of extremism in horror.

2. Though disaster is common in end-of-the-world films like *2012*, I should note that actual disasters are of little concern, as events such as Hurricane Katrina get little attention, aside from the documentary *When the Levees Broke* (Spike Lee 2006). In 2017, damage in Houston, Texas (Hurricane Harvey), the state of Florida (Hurricane Irma), and that resulting from the 2017 Central Mexico Earthquake will likely get little attention onscreen in coming films.

3. Christopher Sharrett (2012) notes the American mind has difficulty imagining its own disaster, and when it does it casts such as apocalyptic and unique to America.

4. Like the gothic horror films of the early 1930s, in which a supernatural outsider invades a small community, the gangster invasion films of the late 1930s onward present a criminal invading into the middle-class home (both trends are discussed further in later sections).

5. See *Predator 2* (1990) as an example of a science fiction–horror film that uses a hunt in the urban streets as a narrative device.

6. Though Gary D. Rhodes (2018) details that early silent horror was largely non-supernatural.

7. As Steven Schiender (2000, 169-70) notes, monsters in various forms reflect psychological fears, though they remain largely consistent in effect.

8. In following *Psycho*'s title cards clarifying the time and place of realistic horrors to come, the slasher film cycle of the 1970s ties films to everyday dates (Halloween, Friday the 13th) and locations (set in everyday "Haddonfield, IL" or "Elm Street").

9. In Michael Winner's earlier supernatural horror *The Sentinel* (1977), demons force a new guard of the gates of hell, who is charged with protecting humanity, to commit suicide before she can take the post.

10. Here, the monster survives, evidenced by his locking the top of a teen's convertible while snatching away the final girl's mother through a nearby front door.

11. Though credited for spearheading the 1970s slasher film in *Halloween*, John Carpenter established a strong conservative strain by having teens that express themselves sexually get murdered soon after. He has jokingly acknowledged (Marriott 2004, 185), "I didn't mean to put an end to the sexual revolution!"

12. It features Norman's mother speaking in voice-over (i.e., in Norman's mind), while the camera moves in to him in his cell, the white background transferring him into a netherworld of the mind. Hitch's fascinating editing of three superimposed images—Norman, a quick flash of his dead mother's mummified skull, and the chain pulling out his victim's car (the transition to the next scene)—reflects the haunting of Norman by his madness, while pulling at/draining his humanity.

13. Peter Bogdonavich's *Targets* (1968) is another compelling example of serial killer cinema possible in the New Hollywood.

14. By portraying the most extreme scene (home invasion/family murder) via their camcorder videotape, the filmmakers implicate us in the action (Picart and Greek, 2007, 235). The movie-in-a-movie device here owes much to Michael Powell's perceptive *Peeping Tom* (1960).

15. Haneke always wanted a US setting for his original 1997 version (Koehler 2008, 55–57).

16. The gangster invasion was popular on the stage where constraints of theatrical sets were used to add to the tension.

17. In a referential joke, Boris Karloff played the role in the original stage version. See also Warner Bros.'s *The Return of Dr. X* (Vincent Sherman 1939), a mad-scientist horror film starring Bogart as a blood-seeking corpse (really against type!) who's chased and shot down like that studio's early 1930s gangster.

18. Art films in the 1960s and 70s offered unique revisions of the home invasion, such as Roman Polanski's *Cul-de-Sac* (1966) and Larry Cohen's *Bone* (1972)—for the latter, see Williams, 2015, 83–7.

19. For a response to part one, see Moore 2013, and to part three, Patterson 2016. See also Ardiarta 2017.

20. Sobchak, Vivian, *Screening Space: The American Science Fiction Film* (New Brunswick: Rutgers University Press): 29–30.

21. As star Danny Glover noted, the Predator—an alien now just a preying monster—is attracted to such an environment as a pure hunter, though the genus of beast found itself in the jungle in the first film (1987) of the series. See "Creating" 2005.

22. In simplified terms, that "men should be treated as autonomous individuals, free to make their own decisions regarding how to live their lives . . . as long as their decisions are made freely and do not directly harm their fellow men" (Hamowy 2008, xxi).

REFERENCES

Ardiarta, Faisal Agata. 2017. *The Representation of Social Darwinism in James DeMonaco's* The Purge: Anarchy (2014). Thesis, Universitas Sebelas Maret. Accessed May 1, 2018. https://eprints.uns.ac.id/34046/.

Bordwell, David, Janet Staiger, and Kristin Thompson. 1985. *The Classical Hollywood Cinema: Film Style and Mode of Production to 1960*. New York: Columbia University Press.

Casey, Gerard. 2012. *Libertarian Anarchy: Against the State.* London: Continuum.

"Creating the Ultimate Hunter." 2005. Featurette on *Predator 2* DVD, 20th Century Fox.

DeMonaco, James. 2014. "Interview: *Purge: Anarchy*." Interviewed by Matt Barone. *Complex,* July 14. Accessed June 1, 2018. https://www.complex.com/pop-culture/2014/07/interview-james-demonaco-the-purge-anarchy.

Edelstein, David. 2006. "Now Playing at Your Local Multiplex: Torture Porn." *New York Magazine,* February 6. Accessed June 1, 2018. http://nymag.com/movies/features/15622/index1.html.

Fuchs, Cynthia. 2013. "*The Purge* Violently Explores the Mayhem of Order." *PopMatters,* June 7. Accessed June 2, 2018. https://www.popmatters.com/172300-the-purge-the-mayhem-of-order-2495749975.html.

Grant, Barry Keith. 2018. *Monster Cinema.* New Brunswick, NJ: Rutgers University Press.

Hamowy, Arnold. 2008. *Encyclopedia of Libertarianism.* New York, NY: Sage Publications.

Horeck, Tanya C. and Tina Kendall, eds. 2011. *The New Extremism in Cinema: from France to Europe*. Edinburgh: Edinburgh University Press.

Koehler, Robert. 2008. "*Funny Games*." *Cineaste* 33.2. Accessed September 9, 2018. http://www.cineaste.com/articles/funny-games.htm.

Marriott, James. 2004. *Horror Films.* New York, NY: Virgin Books.

Mason, Fran. 2002. *American Gangster Cinema, from* Little Caesar *to* Pulp Fiction. New York, NY: Palgrave MacMillian.

Moore, Roger. 2013. "*The Purge*: Morality Tale Binges on Violence and Plot Lapses." *Chicago Tribune*, June 6. Accessed April 5, 2018. http://www.chicagotribune.com/entertainment/movies/sc-mov-0605-purge-20130606-story.html.

"The Motion Picture Production Code (Published March 31, 1930)." Accessed November 14, 2018. https://www.asu.edu/courses/fms200s/total-readings/MotionPicture ProductionCode.pdf.

Patterson, John. 2016. "*The Purge: Election Year*—a Shlocky Alternative to Clinton Versus Trump." *The Guardian,* July 11. Accessed March 5, 2018. https://www.theguardian.com/film/2016/jul/11/the-purge-election-year.

Picart, Caroline Joan "Kay" S. and Cecil Greek. 2007. "The Compulsion of Real/Reel Serial Killers and Vampires: Toward a Gothic Criminology." In *Monsters In and Among Us*, edited by Caroline Joan "Kay" S. Picart and Cecil Greek, 227–255. Madison, NJ: Fairleigh Dickinson University Press.

Rhodes, Gary D. 2018. *The Birth of the American Horror Film*. Edinburgh, UK: Edinburgh University Press.

Rose, Julie L. 2013. "Review of *Libertarian Anarchy* by Gerard Casey." *Philosophical Reviews,* June 24. Accessed February 2, 2018. http://ndpr.nd.edu/news/libertarian-anarchy-against-the-state/.

Rubin, Martin. 1999. "The Grayness of Darkness: *The Honeymoon Killers* and Its Impact on Psychokiller Cinema." In *Mythologies of Violence in Postmodern Media,* edited by Christopher Sharrett, 41–64. Detroit, MI: Wayne State University Press.

Ryan, Josiah. 2016. "'This Was a Whitelash': Van Jones' Take on the Election Results." *CNN*, November 9. Accessed November 8, 2017. https://www.cnn.com/2016/11/09/politics/van-jones-results-disappointment-cnntv/index.html.

Schwartz, Hunter. 2014. "States Where You Can Get a 'Don't Tread On Me' License Plate." *Washington Post*, August 15. Accessed April 14, 2018. https://www.washingtonpost.com/blogs/govbeat/wp/2014/08/25/states-where-you-can-get-a-dont-tread-on-me-license-plate/?noredirect=on&utm_term=.9f4e90c8b6b8.

Sharrett, Christopher. 1996. "The Horror Film in Neoconservative Culture." In *Dread of Difference*, edited by Barry Keith Grant, 253–276. Austin: University of Texas Press.

Sharrett, Christopher. 2012. "Extremely Loud and Incredibly Close." *Film International* January 24. Accessed February 2, 2018. http://filmint.nu/?p=3969.

Sloninowski, Jeannette. 2016. "All for Naught: the American Gangster Film in the 1950s." In Sloninowski, Jeannette and Jim Leach, editors, *The Best Laid Plans: Interrogating the Heist Film*, 11–29. Detroit: Wayne State University Press.

Sobchak, Vivian. 1999. *Screening Space: The American Science Fiction Film*. New Brunswick, NJ: Rutgers University Press.

Sorrento, Matthew. 2013. "Last Man (With)Standing: the Character-Disaster Film," *Film International* 11.3–4: 36–48.

Sorrento, Matthew. 2016. "Documenting Crime: Genre, Verity, and Filmmaker as Avenger." In *Framing Law and Crime*, edited by Caroline Joan "Kay" S. Picart, Michael Hviid Jacobsen, Cecil Greek, 243–266. Madison, NJ: Fairleigh Dickinson University Press.

Schneider, Steven. 2000. "Monsters as (Uncanny) Metaphors: Freud, Lakoff, and the Representation of Monstrosity in Cinematic Horror." In *Horror Film Reader,* edited by Alain Silver and James Ursini, 167-192. New York, NY: Limelight.

Surrette, Raymond. 2007. "Gothic Criminology and Criminal Justice Policy." In *Monsters in and Among Us*, edited Caroline Joan Picart and Cecil E. Greek, 199–226. Madison, NJ: Fairleigh Dickinson University Press.

Thomson, David. 2009. *The Moment of Psycho.* New York, NY: Basic.

Williams, Tony. 2000. "Is the Devil American? William Dieterle's *The Devil and Daniel Webster.*" In *Horror Film Reader*, edited by Alain Silver and James Ursini, 129–149. New York, NY: Limelight.

Williams, Tony. 2014, 1996. *Hearths of Darkness: The Family in the Horror Film.* Jackson, MS: University of Mississippi Press.

Williams, Tony. 2015, 1998. *Larry Cohen: the Radical Allegories of an Independent Filmmaker*. Jefferson, NC: McFarland.

Wood, Robin. 1979. "The American Family Comedy: from *Meet Me in St. Louis* to *The Texas Chainsaw Massacre.*" *Wide Angle* 3.2: 5–11.

Wood, Robin. 2002. *Hitchcock's Films Revisited.* New York, NY: Columbia University Press.

Wood, Robin. 2003. *Hollywood from Vietnam to Reagan . . . and Beyond.* New York, NY: Columbia University Press.

Chapter Eight

Contrasting Depictions of Medical Serial Killers

Doctors Pétiot and Shipman from the Manic to the Mundane

Steve Greenfield

ABSTRACT

The portrayal of serial killers, on film, television and via streaming services, has developed to encompass fiction, docudrama and documentary. New dramatic works have been produced and old cases retold to fuel a seemingly insatiable audience desire and construct a blurring of more traditional genre boundaries. This changing dynamic was noted by Picart and Greek who applied a framework of gothic criminology to the "monstrous" and explored this altered relationship between fact and fiction. "That is not to say there is no such thing as 'fact,' or that 'fact' and 'fiction' are the same thing: rather, it is to point out that fact and fiction do not form a simple binary, especially in media depictions" (Picart 2016, 319). A serial killer, due to the extent of the crimes committed almost automatically, for the viewer, appears with a cloak of "monstrosity." Within this trope there exists a more specific group of medical practitioners who kill either patients or others. These stories and the portrayals are highly troubling as someone sworn into a profession to save lives moves to a polar opposite—a serial murderer. It is this leap, from savior to slaughterer that renders the behavior even more inexplicable and disturbing to the audience. Motive thus becomes an imperative to provide some semblance of reassurance, that this abnormal deviancy can be explained if not completely understood. This chapter focuses on the depiction of two such figures: Dr. Marcel Pétiot and Dr. Harold Shipman were both medical practitioners and contemporaneously notorious serial killers. It considers two specific films; the French film *Docteur Pétiot* (1990) and the British television film *Harold Shipman: Doctor Death* (2002). The former is set during the Second World War in Paris and covers the killings, by Dr. Pétiot, of those seeking to escape the German occupation. The latter film dramatizes the case of the English general practitioner, Dr. Harold Shipman, who murdered at least 215 of his patients in the north of England over a long period. The two films offer contrasting perspectives on motive and behavior but contain similarities in terms of the method of killing and personality traits. Both were revered and respected medical professionals within their communities which presents a frightening vision. Pétiot seems to fit squarely into the definition of a dramatic cold-blooded killer, motivated purely by greed whilst Shipman, Britain's most prolific serial killer, is a very different proposition. Shipman defies traditional classification; his motivations are unknown and unsubstantiated and his killings mundane. If greed is not a motivating factor then can he be categorized as a mercy killer, a trope that permits some sympathy? However Shipman is neither an angel of mercy nor motivated by greed and so is set apart from the usual categorization of medical professionals who kill. This chapter explores the extent to which a prolific but undramatic serial killer fits into the serial killer portrayal and the concept of the "monstrous." One perspective is that the sheer ordinariness of killing, by a doctor, constructs a more frightening and disturbing vision that his comparator, Dr. Pétiot, whose motivation is clear and his killing visually dramatic.

INTRODUCTION[1]

Both Dr. Marcel Pétiot and Dr. Harold Shipman used their chosen profession to carry out a large number of murders. The sensational nature of their crimes has led to a wide range of books, academic articles and audio-visual works.[2] *Docteur Pétiot* (1990) is a French film directed by Christian de Chalonge starring Michel Serrault in the lead role for which he received a EuropaCinema award for best actor. *Harold Shipman: Dr. Death* (2002) was produced by ITV and Yorkshire TV as a TV movie directed by Roger Banford and featuring James Bolam as the GP (general practitioner). The timing of the release of the Shipman film was heavily criticized as it appeared to be premature, given an official Public Inquiry into his activities was underway. The film was not critically well received but does offer a visual perspective on the horrific events that took place. It is the portrayal of the two characters in the films that are the central focus for this chapter. Both Pétiot and Shipman were eventually prosecuted for their murderous acts, Pétiot in Paris, France, in 1946 and Shipman in Preston England, in 2000. Pétiot was convicted of twenty-six counts of murder and Shipman fifteen with one additional count of forgery relating to a will. Both are suspected of many more deaths that were not prosecuted largely due to evidentiary problems. Shipman's forgery suggested that financial gain could provide a rationale, yet this was a solitary instance and other examples of Shipman acquiring small pieces of property were minor and not considered to be a motivating factor. It was this act of forgery that led directly to his downfall and occupies a significant early scene in the film. However far from clarifying any motivation his sheer ineptitude adds to the mystery. As Smith noted: "It seems to me that Shipman could not rationally have thought that he would get away with Mrs. Grundy's estate. The whole venture was grossly incompetent. Discovery was inevitable" (Smith, Volume 1, Chapter 13, 13.16). In Pétiot's case the bodies were dismembered and some parts burned or dissolved in quick lime. Ironically it was the lawful process of cremation that destroyed much of the forensic evidence of Shipman's acts. Furthermore, there were concerns about whether any additional trial could be fairly conducted given the publicity surrounding the first one. Pétiot was sentenced to death and beheaded on May 25, 1946, whilst Shipman was sentenced to fifteen terms of life imprisonment with a judicial recommendation that he never be released (*R v. Shipman*). However on January 13, 2004, Shipman was found hanged in his cell at Wakefield prison.

The scale and enormity of Shipman's crimes and the vast publicity led to the setting up of an independent inquiry by the Secretary of State for Health (Smith 2003). It is difficult to comprehend the sheer volume of Shipman's killing as Gilleard notes: "One of the twentieth century's most prolific mass murderers (in one year, 1997) he was responsible for 6% of *all* the homicides in England and Wales" (Gilleard 2008, 89). The other key feature of Shipman's killing was that his victims were almost exclusively old people. Whilst originally the inquiry's findings were to be made public, the hearings were scheduled to be private, which angered the families who consequently sought judicial review of this decision.[3] As a result of the legal challenge, a formal Public Inquiry was established, under Janet Smith that commenced work in February 2001 with public hearings commencing in 2002. The Smith Inquiry eventually produced a huge six volumes of material. Volume One, *Death Disguised* (Smith 2002), covered the number of killings and the time period over which he killed. Volume Two, *The Police Investigation* (Smith 2003a), analyzed the failed police investigation into Shipman that had been undertaken in 1998. Volume Three covered *Death Certification and the Investigation of Deaths by Coroners* (Smith 2003b), Volume Four dealt with *The Regulation of Controlled Drugs in the Community* (Smith 2004a) and Volume 5 covered *Safeguarding Patients: Lessons from the Past—Proposals for the Future* (Smith 2004b). The Sixth, *Final Report*, was published in January 2005 (Smith 2005).

The Smith Inquiry was a comprehensive attempt to understand how so many killings could take place seemingly unnoticed for so long. However the terms of reference didn't require an investigation into Shipman's motives or any relevant psychological factors. Smith, though, opted to explore this dimension both to assist the inquiry in its second phase and, perhaps more importantly, for both the public and the victims as she noted it: "might assist them in coming to terms with what has happened" (Smith 2002, 13.177). The fundamental problem was the lack of any psychiatric assessments of Shipman as he refused to cooperate with the Inquiry resulting in a huge knowledge vacuum. He clearly couldn't be forced to participate, and Smith ruled out interviewing the members of his family. Whilst the inquiry team had access to his medical and prison records, these offered little additional insight. Without any understanding or indication of motive or the ability to create intention, the film makers had an undeniable problem—how to produce a visually dramatic film. It would have been impossible given the sensitivities to stray too far from the "known" facts. Demonstrating the motive for Pétiot's killing was far simpler given his theft of both money and property from those he murdered which is dramatically highlighted in the film. This chapter first reviews the development of films based around serial killers and murderers who are also medical professionals and the problems with dramatizing real-life events before setting the films and the characters in the context of a gothic criminology framework.

CINEMATIC SERIAL KILLERS AND MEDICAL PRACTITIONERS WHO KILL

There are two distinct sources for the cinematic portrayal of serial killers aside from the numerous documentaries and docudramas.[4] First the purely fictional of which the most prominent is the character of Hannibal Lecter who first appeared in the novels of Thomas Harris starting with *Red Dragon* (1981), followed by *The Silence of the Lambs* (1988), *Hannibal* (1999) and *Hannibal Rising* (2006). These successful books led to five films: *Manhunter* (1986), *The Silence of the Lambs* (1991), *Hannibal* (2001), *Red Dragon* (2002) and *Hannibal Rising* (2007).[5] This was followed by an NBC Television series *Hannibal* which ran for three seasons between 2013 and 2015. In 2003 the American Film Institute named Lecter, as played by Hopkins, as the number one film villain.[6] The film also introduced into popular culture the concept of criminal profiling through the characters of both Lecter and Clarice Starling.[7] Fiction films based on real-life serial killers have developed as a group on a spectrum through docudrama to the purer form of documentary. A subgroup with the trope of serial killers portrays murderers within the medical profession as either doctors or nurses. The obvious crossover is with Lecter whose occupation was a forensic psychiatrist. The portrayal of the medical profession has attracted analysis with examples following the type of work carried out on law films. Flores's widespread survey of physicians in the movies sought to answer six questions:

1. What are the most common demographic attributes of movie physicians, including specialty, type of practice, gender, ethnicity and race?
2. What are the major themes?
3. How are medical researchers portrayed?
4. How are the issues of compassion and materialism handled?
5. What are the major ethical issues addressed?
6. Has the cinematic portrayal of physicians over the decades changed or largely remained the same? (Flores 2002, 636).

Flores only included films with a doctor as the main character with 505 films initially listed and later reduced to 131 for detailed analysis.[8] Flores's discussion mirrors some of the concerns about negative lawyer portrayals expressed by legal commentators such as Asimow (2000) who suggests that the negative portrayals of lawyers were clearly noticeable in the 1980s and 1990s:

> The benign treatment of lawyers from the beginning of the sound era until the 1960s began to change during the 1970s. During that decade, as well as the 1980s and 1990s, typical lawyer portraits turned strongly and consistently negative. Thus, of the 71 fictitious lawyer films of the 1990s, the lawyer or lawyers in 37 of the films were bad; in an additional 9 films, there were one or more bad lawyers along with some good ones (the "mixed" category). Thus, 65% of the films of the 1990s had at least one bad lawyer. Similarly for the 1980s—in 38 fictitious lawyer films, the lawyer or lawyers in 18 were bad; in an additional 8 films, there were one or more bad lawyers along with some good ones. Thus 68% of the movies of the 1980s had at least one bad lawyer. In short, in about two-thirds of the fictitious lawyer films of the 1980s and 1990s, there is at least one negatively portrayed lawyer (Asimow 2000, 569).

Flores also highlights this specific period as one of increasing negative portrayals of doctors:

> Negative cinematic portrayals of physicians are on the rise. The past five decades have seen a steady increase in the proportion of movies that portray physicians negatively, culminating in about half of all 1990s films depicting physicians in a negative light. The 1990s movie physician all too often is portrayed as egotistical, materialistic, uncaring, and unethical (Flores 2002, 656).

There are obvious caveats to this type of work. First, how identified "negativity" may be construed subjectively by the audience or by individual members of the audience; there may not be a common or shared view. Secondly, the extent to which one negative character is overshadowed by another more positive portrayal. By overcoming hostility and prejudice, the leading character is able to stand even taller, what might be termed the Atticus effect. There is also the well-worn trope of the individual cathartic experience that provides a route for personal redemption.[9] Thirdly, the impact on the audience of such portrayals is clearly uncertain and whether it extends to a more negative public perception of the profession and its practitioners. Clearly for a significant period lawyers and doctors occupied a revered position in society and this status was duly reflected in the contemporary films. It is possible that the creation of more multi-dimensional characters beyond the simplistic good/bad is more about the screen writing and the desire to produce more "interesting" roles than it is about producing negative imagery or reflecting a declining public confidence.

One of the key themes identified by Florin he terms "Egotism and God Complexes," which has a long cinematic history going back as far as *The Raven* 1935 (Flores 2002, 654). This is a clear trait of the character in both films. Shipman is shown as aloof and somewhat arrogant with a clear view that he knows best and he operates a traditional hierarchical relationship to his patients. The majority demure to him although there are one or two examples of relatives who are critical of the care he is providing, which clearly riles Shipman. Indeed in an artificially created scene, when discussing Shipman's motive with the local vicar DI Stan Egerton remarks:

> "I think that's what I see when I look in those eyes I think the Doctor reckons he is the supreme being that he has the ultimate power over life and death" (*Shipman* 2002).

However Shipman was clearly not carrying out "mercy killings" as not all his victims were terminally ill. As Gilleard (2008) notes his treatment of those facing death enabled him to obtain the morphine that he used to kill all his victims. If Shipman had a god complex, it wasn't informing his decisions about who to kill. Pétiot also exhibits the characteristics of a doctor who knows what is best for his patients and has little time to discuss the treatment with those who visit his surgery. Those he is intending to kill are portrayed clearly as obstacles to obtaining financial gain rather than connected to any more individualized motive.

TRUE STORIES, DRAMATIZATION AND "TRUTH"

One of the key debates—in film and the law and other areas that utilize true stories as the basis of audio-visual works—is the extent to which "dramatic license" is acceptable. In order to produce the necessary tension or drama, events may be edited or even created and the truth "bent." Many critically acclaimed films are founded on such stories, see *inter alia*: *Let Him Have It* (1991), *In the Name of the Father* (1993), *The Hurricane* (1999), *10 Rillington Place* (1971) and *Breaker Morant* (1980). There is, though, an obvious question with such events, especially those rooted in the past, as to what the "truth" actually amounts to. On a superficial level two contrasting approaches to the value of such films, beyond entertainment, can be identified. The question can be constructed as follows: what do such films contribute to our understanding of the historical events and to what extent does inaccurate detail matter? This debate coalesced around the film portraying the Guildford Four and the Maguire family, Jim Sheridan's *In the Name of the Father* (1993). Pallister outlined the concerns of inaccuracy:

> In fictional film there can be no dissent from the view that the facts should not get in the way of a good story (although the myriad absurdities in the court scenes, straight out of LA Law, are inexcusable) (Pallister 1994).

In his survey Flores notes three types of medical inaccuracy: "(1) unrealistic depictions or views of physicians or their practice; (2) scientifically unsubstantiated therapeutic interventions; and (3) factual errors" (2002, 643). One danger is that the inaccuracy becomes the primary point for discussion causing the entertainment dimension to be sidetracked. However not all reviews of *In the Name of the Father* (1993) raised the issue and instead focused on the directing and acting.[10] There is a question whether film, as a medium itself, contains the necessary detail for the work to be viewed as having intrinsic historical merit. Jarvie takes the view that it is inherently limited:

> Film is not the material of history. Documents are the material of history. At best, film is a visual aid. It is very nice to see and hear dead people, see places as they were, the state of technology and so on; film may be a useful check on interpretation, but it is not essential and not necessarily enlightening" (Jarvie 1978, 378).

If films have limited historical importance, in the way described by Jarvie, added dramatic events or interpretations might have little significance; however, Pallister argues that inaccuracy might have an impact on the broader issue:

> But *In the Name of the Father* regrettably also plays fast and loose with the context of an event that not only retains a high profile in the public mind, but is actually still the subject of a judicial inquiry by Sir John May (Pallister 1994).

Given the timescale and importance of the official inquiry, this is a legitimate concern if it could result in a lessening of critical analysis of either the process or findings. The May Inquiry issued a Final Report in June 1994 after the film had been released. Put succinctly the argument runs that the errors in the film become the focus and a distraction from the real-life events. Art not so much mimics life but replaces the events with a dramatic interpretation. This view has greater legitimacy the closer the release of the film to any parallel development in the "real" case. There is an alternative claim that the films promote an understanding of broader issues. Writing on *In the Name of the Father* (1993) and *Let Him Have It* (1991), Greenfield and Osborn noted:

> What makes the films important is not found in a semantic debate about minutiae of detail, but rather through a wider view of the films' worth in terms of raising consciousness or awareness of the issues that pervade the two films—police brutality and capital punishment (Greenfield and Osborn 1996, 1198).

Films such as *Let Him Have It* (1991), *10 Rillington Place* (1971), *Dance with a Stranger* (1985) and notably *Pierrepoint* (2005) inform the contemporary audience that capital punishment was, until 1965, part of the British criminal justice system. They also raise issues around the fallibility of the criminal justice process and the potential for miscarriages of justice to occur, a theme highlighted by films such as *In the Name of the Father* (1993). The clear significance of *Let Him Have It* (1991) was to place the Derek Bentley case back into the public spotlight even if some of the factual detail was compromised for dramatic impact.

Harold Shipman: Doctor Death (2002) was released after the Smith Inquiry was instigated and during the period of its tenure which places it within the "contemporaneous parameters" of the criticisms of *In the Name of the Father* (1993) rather than the older issues portrayed in *Let Him Have It* (1991). As Gallagher (2002) in his review of the film notes: "There is a question over whether this is cashing in on a horrific story, and whether drama has a right to examine topics that are still fresh." That events were ongoing also raises questions about how the film would be received by relatives as well as the public; and with the Shipman case the relatives made up a very large and inevitably diverse group. The company claimed to have acted with care and sensitivity and issued a statement: "Yorkshire Television and ITV have sought throughout to be very sensitive towards the relatives of Shipman's victims and in particular have taken great care in dealing with the relatives of those portrayed in the film with consideration and respect. We do believe that our broadcast scheduling is timely and appropriate and do not propose therefore to postpone it."[11] Relatives were invited to a prescreening though the timing of the release caused controversy with one noting:

> I don't think the makers of the programme have been in touch with any of the relatives—they have not been in touch with me. I cannot agree with the timing of the programme. It is getting very close to the time when the inquiry is likely to say if other patients who died were victims of Shipman and this programme will be going out at the same time. I think that is deliberate timing by the television company (BBC 2002).[12]

If relatives or the general public audience were expecting some critical insight into Shipman's motives they were to be disappointed; there was nothing new to add. In some ways showing this lack of understanding of motive added to the overall feeling of disconcertion.

ROUTINE AND ERRATIC KILLING

On an initial reading the two films seem to offer a contrasting approach to medical serial killing. Shipman is routine and methodical and Pétiot, impulsive and erratic; however, deeper analysis offers an alternative perspective. The films are very different in terms of script, production and direction; it would be surprising if they weren't given the obvious distinctions in geography and the time period. The most obvious initial difference is the political context to Pétiot with the occupation of Paris by the German army and the action being taken against the Jewish community. It is this latter activity that provides the opportunity for Pétiot to set up his clandestine smuggling practice. Thus the background to *Pétiot* (1990) is of a disrupted society overwhelmed by violence, terror and fear. The opening scene of the film highlights the political dimension as a newsreel is being shown bemoaning the Jewish Problem and the incursion of Jews into French society. The next film he views is *Hangman's Castle* a classic gothic horror film but its lack of authenticity displeases Pétiot, who storms out. The contrast with *Shipman* (2002) is stark as the film opens with a fundraising scene for the doctor's practice: "Dr. Shipman's patient fund." Shipman is shown with his wife at the center of his community clearly well liked. This is a stable, well-established practice with a respected medical professional who cares for his patients. However the following scene immediately establishes the dark side to Shipman in the exercise of his profession. An elderly patient, Ivy, attends the surgery early and enters the consulting room; she is portrayed through the interaction between the doctor and the receptionist as something of a "nuisance." Whilst Ivy disrobes, Shipman searches for her medical file, pauses for a moment and then seems to make a deliberate decision. He opens his desk drawer, takes out a death certificate, fills in the cause of death and then administers his patient a fatal injection. He closes the door to the side room and bizarrely continues to see his other patients with Ivy's body a few yards away. This creates a series of opposites within the narrative. Shipman the friendly lovable community doctor is juxtaposed with Shipman the "matter of fact" uncaring killer. He isn't shown as particularly cold or ruthless or with any specific motive—he seems to kill Ivy merely because he can. The viewer is left puzzled by his act: is it just because he sees her as a nuisance or is there some deeper as yet unexplained motive? It seems so implausible from the bonhomie in the first scene that he could kill and then carry on with overseeing his patients. When he eventually calls the receptionist after what appears to be about an hour he explains: "She's died on me." The killing is left unexplained so the viewer is left to try to reconcile a caring, considerate doctor and an uncaring, cold-hearted motiveless killer.

Dr. Pétiot also appears with contradictory personality traits within the different aspects of his somewhat chaotic life. He is shown dealing with his patients whom he often seems to use as a reason to leave something else he is doing. He is also seen counselling those frightened Jews who are fearful for their lives under the Nazis and wish to escape, and Pétiot offers them the possibility of safe passage to Argentina. He arranges a rendezvous at his own office for both of them to await the people "smuggler." The victim is told to bring just one suitcase and once on Pétiot's premises is told a vaccination is required before the refugee can embark on the journey, otherwise there is a risk of being turned back. The victim concurs and is duly given a lethal injection; Pétiot pretends someone is calling and locks him in a room and secretly monitors his death. Whilst this might be seen as obtaining gratification in line with some of the cinematic portrayals of serial killing, it appears as a more pragmatic matter. Once the victim is dead, the body can be disposed of.

During the day Pétiot deceives some of his patients, listening in to them griping about their complaints in the waiting room in order to then effect an impressive diagnosis. He seems to not care much about them almost in line with Shipman's "nuisance" yet he shows his compassionate side when dealing with a bedridden young girl. He is seen refusing payments and seems unconcerned about receiving money from his usual patients. Yet he is clearly portrayed as motivated by money that drives him to kill those trying to escape Paris. There is a distinction between Pétiot the physician during the day seeing patients and generally busying himself and the figure who comes out at night. This is the time when he conducts his other enterprises, flitting around to various meeting points and arranging secret rendezvous. He seems to relish the darkness itself and explains to the family of the sick child, "It's nearly night time. I love that, I love the night." He adds, "I'm like a cat, I can see in the dark." The abiding image is of Pétiot furiously pedaling his bike through the deserted misty streets hurrying towards yet another dastardly act. He appears to have two distinct parts to his character that are tied to light and darkness, giving the film a strong semblance of horror. There are echoes of Jekyll and Hyde with the killer Pétiot unshackled from his normal behavior as a physician unrestrained as a killer but afterwards returning to care for his patients. When he opens the case of the evacuee he has killed, there is a "heady recklessness" as he throws the money around the room.[13] This is not a cold, planned, careful response—more of a celebration of his achievement.

Shipman is very much a creature of daylight as we see little of him at night; his surgery and home visits take place during the day. He is shown calmly killing another patient, but the emphasis in the film then shifts to concerns about the sheer number of deaths within Shipman's practice being expressed by both a young undertaker and a group of doctors from another practice.[14] These concerns are referred to the coroner who then informs the police to commence an investigation. The brusque police response is dealt with in several short scenes with a finding that nothing was untoward and that the paperwork was in order. The police are clearly wary about investigating a well-respected doctor. It is then the murder of Kathleen Grundy and her daughter's investigation of the origins of the forged will that lead to his eventual arrest. The daughter, Angela Woodruff, is shown confronting one of the two witnesses to the will, "Paul." In a hard to believe scene, at a pet shop named "Monkey Business," she identifies a reluctant Paul by a tattoo of his name on his neck. The police reopen the investigation into Shipman, as there is now clear evidence of wrongdoing and the coroner gives permission for Kathleen Grundy's body to be exhumed. Gradually everything unravels; Shipman's past criminal acts are revealed with a suggestion that he has a problem with drug dependency. There is a distinct shift in the portrayal of Shipman post-arrest and particularly after he is charged and interviewed. During the initial questioning Shipman is shown to be cunning and deceitful, inventing a story, based on forged patient records, that Mrs. Grundy was drug dependent and had caused her own death. When Pétiot is being sought by the police after the fire at his offices that reveals the extent of his crimes, he demonstrates cunning to avoid arrest despite the police and army searching for him. Eventually though he is tricked into revealing himself and captured.

The method of killing, by lethal injection, is common to both doctors but Shipman's victims seem to be selected entirely at random whilst there is a clear purpose to Pétiot's killing. Shipman is very calm and matter of fact, moving slowly through the film; his life has a slow steady pace bound by a clear routine of daily surgeries. Pétiot is manic, charging from place to place seeing patients when he wishes and more concerned with his other nefarious activities. Pétiot has the physical problem of disposing of the bodies whilst Shipman merely signs off the paperwork and the undertakers destroy the evidence through cremation. He manages to convince relatives, for their own good, not to require a postmortem which might reveal the poisoning. The film creates an expectation that Pétiot will kill; once his *modus operandi* is established, the viewer knows the victim will be killed. Because there is no logic or pattern to Shipman's killing, they are more erratic; whilst Pétiot is killing to a defined plan. There is terror inherent within Shipman as the audience knows, and knew before they came in, that Shipman not only has the capacity to kill but has killed on a large scale. We just don't know exactly which of his patients he will choose to kill at what time. Each Shipman killing produces a new shocking event. Overall when comparing the two films, what originally seems random is planned and vice versa. The sheer mundanity of Shipman's killing and his normal characteristics draw comparisons with Arendt's account of Adolf Eichmann at his trial in Israel: "Despite all the efforts of the prosecution, everybody could see that this man was not a 'monster,' but it was difficult indeed not to suspect that he was a clown" (Arendt 2006, 54). Furthermore, Eichmann had been examined by psychiatrists who certified him as "normal" (Arendt 2006). This description of Eichmann's crimes as the "banality of evil" applies equally to Shipman both in terms of his appearance and seemingly motiveless crimes. Whether Shipman would have been viewed as "normal" had he been interviewed by a psychiatrist is unknown, but superficially he seemed a diligent and careful medical professional.

SHIPMAN & PÉTIOT MEDICAL MONSTERS AND GOTHIC CRIMINOLOGY

As part of their work exploring gothic criminology, Picart and Greek identified: "two monstrous figures in contemporary popular culture whose constructions blur into each other, and who most powerfully evoke not only our deepest fears and taboos, but also our most repressed fantasies and desires: the serial killer and the vampire as creatures compelled to kill" (Picart and Greek 2003, 40). *Dr. Pétiot* (1990) fits squarely into this group of films, at times overlapping between both the serial killer and the vampire as a creature of the night. The scene at his office where partly dismembered bodies are found points to a level of blood lust—he seems to relish not just the destruction of the bodies but the process itself. *Shipman* (2012) is problematic; he is constructed as an evil monster not the least because of the sheer number of killings. Contemporaneously he is just an ordinary, unexciting figure going about his work and his killings reflect this mundanity. The film has no dramatic dimension around any of the killings—his murders are shown as part of his daily life. It is as if he is administering a routine procedure, only this injection results in death. The visible emotions are those of the bereaved, and once, Shipman, when he effects a breakdown whilst in custody though this is shown as a cynical attempt to avoid further questioning. Despite attempts to label him a "monster," for example, through the use of the title *Dr. Death*, this seems to lack objective authenticity. It is the sheer number of killings that we know about rather than the method or motive or his personality that leads to the conclusion that he *must* be a monster. How else can his character be framed, given the volume of murders and the length of time over which he carried them out? A doctor who kills to reduce suffering may be termed a mercy killer whilst a doctor who kills so many without reason defies description. So if he is not a monster, what is he?

The most obvious link from *Shipman* (2012) is to a broader interpretation of gothic criminology that encompasses the concept of the banality of evil (Picart and Greek 2007). Within the film there is a constructed passage where the concept of "evil" and its existence is discussed. Gallagher, in his review, is scathing of this scene: "Toward the end Hazeldine's character talks at length to a priest (Gareth Thomas) and the scenes are simply dreadful. It is not dialogue, not conversation, not debate, it is a list of points that the script could not fit in anywhere else" (Gallagher 2002). It can be understood as being introduced to initiate some discussion of motive though arguably is rather shallow. The two participants are the local vicar, Reverend Denis Thomas, and the police officer leading the investigation, DI Stan Egerton. It takes place in a room at the church over a drink and they discuss Egerton's puzzlement as to Shipman's motive which draws in some philosophical observations. The Reverend commences with the only clear evidence of a motive of fraud:

> DT: You sure it's not just greed pure and simple?
>
> SE: That will was a one off—as far as we know—all right here might have been a few bits and bobs of tatty jewelry and a few quid here and there but . . . that's not what this is about.

Financial motivation is thus immediately dismissed and the whole issue of the forged will discarded so the police officer attempts to broaden the discussion into a debate around nature and nurture:

> SE: Can a man be born evil?
>
> DT: Then he wouldn't be responsible for his actions would he? No I have to be believe that he was created good.
>
> SE: So he chose to be a mass murderer same as you chose to be a vicar?
>
> DT: Closeted child, over achiever from an early age, his mother gets cancer when he's a teenager and he watches the doctor come and give her injections of

morphine to ease the pain. Who knows what that does to a young impressionable mind? She dies in agony when he is 17 and he spends the whole night running alone in the rain.

SE: With all due respect, bollocks, there's thousands of kids go through much worse than he ever did, granted some of them turn out bad or mad. I come across that type every day but they don't end up like that warped bastard, do they?

This short exchange attempts to probe into the background of Shipman's relationship with his mother and speculates on his chosen method of killing and his relationship to morphine. The police officer introduces the notion of Shipman as a born psychopath but this is contradicted by the Reverend on purely theological grounds. Interestingly, this then shifts to the legal question of the potential for a lack of responsibility due to his unbalanced state of mind and the consequent impact on his free will. The question of how evil is developed is consequently left unanswered though the discussion has crossed spiritual, psychological and legal boundaries. The Reverend moves the conversation to a more traditional explanation:

DT: Is there a sexual dimension to the crimes?

SE: I could understand that, I'd hate it, it would disgust me but at least I'd know what kind of monster we are dealing with.

Again the concept of the monster is raised and in this case what would be a recognizable figure, one driven by perverted sexual desires. This short exchange also stresses the need to know and be able to interpret the behavior within an existing framework. A fundamental question is whether this framework, of the sexually motivated serial killer, is constructed through fact, fiction or a complex mixture. It is extremely unlikely that either figure will have any direct experience of this phenomenon in the real world so it points towards a mediated creation. The discussion shifts to the selection of his victims and the role the doctor plays when he kills:

DT: Why did he kill old ladies?

SE: He killed whoever he could get away with killing The most vulnerable of his patients happened to be mostly old ladies living alone. Who knows? If he worked in the inner city he'd probably be knocking off junkies. You've been around the dying, Denis.

DT: That does come with the turf I'm afraid—you never get used to it.

SE: What kind of person could get pleasure out of watching people die, being there when they take their last breath?

> DT: Sometimes can be a blessing—when the suffering is all over. Could he have believed that somehow he was easing their pain?
>
> SE: Absolutely not; there's no element of mercy here, Denis. I wish there was. Not that I'd ever condone it.

A moral and philosophical question as to the sanctity of life and the acceptability of euthanasia is introduced in order to consider the "mercy killing" dimension which is quickly dismissed.

> DT: I'm sorry, Stan. I'm not being much use, am I?
>
> SE: You're a great help, Denis. It's just a bloody mystery. Did he get some sick gratification from having that power, choosing whether he took a life or saved it playing God?

What is of great interest in this scene is that it explores a whole range of possible motives ordinarily attributable to a serial killer. They commence with money and raise the question of sexual gratification. In quite a bizarre trade off, Egerton adds that whilst a sexual dimension would disgust him at least he could understand what or who he was dealing with. After money and sex are dismissed, they muse over mercy killing before settling on a god complex as the most likely. They also discuss the root cause of his behavior and the Reverend raises his relationship with his mother. This scene draws upon existing knowledge of serial killers beyond the immediate case to seek an explanation. *Shipman* (2012), as a source, is in many ways difficult to classify beyond the unexplained medical serial killer. Bereft of a plausible explanation, we are left to ponder the idea of the mundane evil.

CONCLUSION

In his highly critical review of *Shipman* (2012), William Gallagher pointed out the severe limitations of the script and how the film draws upon the existing knowledge of the viewer rather than creating a dramatic account:

> You get a sense that the story is accurate, that it has stuck rigidly to every detail, but while you would not want fabrication, drama needs more to it than fact and writer Michael Eaton has had his hands tied. This is not drama at all, it is a very long Crimewatch reconstruction. It does not involve us in the story, but trades exclusively on the horror we already feel (Gallagher 2002).

This supports the view of Picart and Greek concerning the lack of a distinct line between fact and fiction. Here we also see the incorporation of different sources of material beyond the script, the very public knowledge of Shipman's acts. *Dr. Pétiot* (1990) is very different, based on crimes committed some fifty years earlier so the contemporary knowledge is largely absent.

Shipman and Pétiot operated in different countries in different time periods with a distinctive set of contextual factors. The common feature was their membership of the medical profession and their mass killing. Superficially, the cinematic Pétiot appears as a clear example of the monstrous figure. He operates in a shadowy nighttime world deliberately out of sight of both the authorities and the public. The disposal of the bodies is similarly horrific, mutilated and dismembered. Picart and Greek's reference to themes within gothic criminology including: "godlike vengeance, and power and domination" resonates with the portrayal of Marcel Pétiot. Pétiot's egotistical narcissism drives the narrative forward at a fast pace and he exerts the power of life and death over those he is charged with helping. There seems to be no limits to his depravity in pursuit of wealth. Greed is the motivating factor. The portrayal of Shipman is dissimilar, involving killing without apparent motive taking place during daylight. That he visits a patient at 8 a.m. is noted. The scene is the security of the willing victim's home. The relationship that is highlighted with Shipman is one of extreme trust and confidence.

As Mr. Justice Forbes, the judge pressing over his trial, noted:

> Each of your victims was your patient. You murdered each and every one of your victims by a calculated and cold blooded perversion of your medical skills. For your own evil and wicked purposes you took advantage of and grossly abused the trust that each of your victims reposed in you. You were, after all, each victim's doctor. I have little doubt that each of your victims smiled and thanked you as she submitted to your deadly ministrations. None of your victims realised that yours was not a healing touch. None of them knew that in truth you had brought her death, death which was disguised as the caring attention of a good doctor. The sheer wickedness of what you have done defies description and is shocking beyond belief.[15]

The language is that of the evil other; without any explanation of motive it becomes a "cold blooded perversion." With Pétiot's victims the contract is financial and rooted in desperation to escape the imminent Nazi horror. *Shipman: Dr. Death* (2012) unfolds slowly and the patient deaths are without additional violence or the victim's knowledge; the distress is that of the relatives. This latter group is largely absent from *Dr. Pétiot* (1990) though at the outset the audience is shown a couple splitting up with the soon to be murdered husband leaving first. The primary difference between the two films is viewer understanding of the rationale for the murders. Pétiot's desire for money and the trappings of wealth are highlighted at various times least not the manic throwing of money round the room. Shipman has but one such example when we see him forging the will though other minor thefts are suggested. Pétiot fuels the fear of the monstrous serial killer, but Shipman presents the audience with an unknown dimension—a serial killer who murders ordinary people in ordinary homes with impunity. The quiet motiveless murdering doctor is in many way a far more disturbing and lasting image.

NOTES

1. For ease of reference, given that both films have the name of the killer in the title, when the name is in italics it refers to the film.

2. King, David. 2012. *Death in the City of Light: The True Story of the Serial Killer Who Terrorised Wartime Paris*, Crown Publishing, New York; Maeder, Thomas. 1980. *The Unspeakable Crimes of Dr. Pétiot*, Boston: The Atlantic Monthly Press; Dominique, Jean-François and Dobrian, Joseph (translator). 2019. *The Butcher of Paris: The Crimes of Dr. Pétiot—And an Indictment of a Nation*, Rex Imperator Publishing; Peters, Carole. 2005. *Harold Shipman—Mind Set On Murder—Why Shipman Killed and Killed Again—The True Story*, England: Carleton Books; Marshall, Natalie. 2016. *Doctor Death: The True Story of Harold Shipman*, CreateSpace Independent Publishing Platform; Clarkson, Wensley. 2005. *Evil Beyond Belief—How and Why Dr. Harold Shipman Murdered 357 People*, Blake Publishing, England.

3. See https://webarchive.nationalarchives.gov.uk/20090808155114/ and http://www.the-shipman-inquiry.org.uk/backgroundinfo.asp The challenge was brought by both the families and media organizations: *Regina (Wagstaff and others) v Secretary of State for Health* and another *Regina (Associated Newspapers Ltd and others) v Secretary of State for Health and another* [2001] 1 W.L.R. 292.

4. See for example the numerous portrayals of Dahmer and Bundy that demonstrate the ongoing public fascination: *Confessions of a Serial Killer: Jeffrey Dahmer* (1994), *The Jeffrey Dahmer Files* (2012), and *Ted Bundy* (2002), *Murderous Minds: Ted Bundy* (2018) and *Conversations with a Killer: The Ted Bundy Tapes* (Netflix 2019).

5. The discrepancy between the four books and five films is explained by the remake of *Manhunter* (1986) with *Red Dragon* (2002). Both were based on the same book, though in *Red Dragon* (2002) the role of Lecter was played by Anthony Hopkins following the commercial and critical success of *The Silence of the Lambs* (1988). The original Hannibal Lecter in *Manhunter* (1986) was played by Brian Cox.

6. Interestingly, Clarice Starling, the FBI agent opposite Lecter, played by Jodie Foster, appeared as number six on the list of heroic Hollywood figures.

7. A number of TV shows have emerged around criminal profiling such as *Mindhunter* (2017), *Cracker* (1993), *Profiler* (1996) and *Criminal Minds* (2005). The latter was a clear success with fourteen seasons showing the attractiveness of the genre.

8. Michael Asimow's broadly comparable survey on lawyer films consisted of some 284 films (Asimow 2000). One has to admire both authors' sheer perseverance.

9. Examples from lawyer films include *The Verdict* (1982) and *Regarding Henry* (1991). Flores cites *Sunchaser* (1997), *Doc Hollywood* (1991) and *The Doctor* (1991) as examples of the transformative trope.

10. See for example Maslin, Janet (1993) Review/Film: In the Name of the Father; The Sins of a Son Are Visited on His Father. https://www.nytimes.com/1993/12/29/movies/review-film-name-father-sins-son-are-visited-his-father.html (last accessed 03/25/2019).

11. https://www.theguardian.com/media/2002/jul/01/broadcasting3 (last accessed 05/02/19).

12. http://news.bbc.co.uk/1/hi/england/2076460.stm_(last accessed 05/02/19).

13. On the development of the relationship between the two sides, see Miyoshyi, Masao. 1996. "Dr Jekyll and the Emergence of Mr. Hyde." *College English,* Vol. 27, No. 6, 470–474.

14. These concerns were noted by the Smith Inquiry:

> When Dr Reynolds made her report to the Coroner, she mentioned two particular grounds for concern. First, she told him that she knew that Shipman, who was a single-handed practitioner, had signed 16 cremation Forms B in the previous three months, whereas the Brooke Practice, with a patient base of 9500, had had only 14 patient deaths during the same period. Shipman had a patient list which was approximately one-third the size of the Brooke Practice list. Moreover, the figure of 16 cremations within his practice would not include: deaths which had occurred in hospital; deaths followed by burial; deaths certified by the coroner and; deaths where Shipman had asked a doctor other than one from the Brooke Practice to complete Form C.
>
> The effect of these factors was that, if Shipman's practice followed the usual pattern, those cremations which members of the Brooke Practice were aware of were likely to represent no more than about 21% at most of Shipman's total deaths during the relevant period. Given the fact that Shipman had a patient list which was approximately a third the size of that of the Brooke Practice, it is apparent that the disparity between the number of deaths of patients in Shipman's practice and in the Brooke Practice was potentially very large indeed. It was this disparity which concerned Dr Reynolds and the other members of the Brooke Practice (Smith, Vol 2).

15. https://webarchive.nationalarchives.gov.uk/20090808214147/http://www.the-shipman-inquiry.org.uk/trialday/asp?day=58.

REFERENCES

Arendt, Hannah. 2006. *Eichmann in Jerusalem*. New York: Penguin Books.

Asimow, Michael. 2000. "Bad Lawyers in the Movies." *24 Nova Law Review*: 533–611.

Byrne, Peter. 1998. "Fall and Rise of the Movie 'Psycho-Killer.'" *Psychiatric Bulletin* 22: 174–176.

Canby, Vincent. 1990. "Review/Film Festival; Murders Most Foul In France's 'Dr. Pétiot.'" *New York Times*. September 23. Accessed March 25, 2019. https://

www.nytimes.com/1990/09/23/movies/review-film-festival-murders-most-foul-in-france-s-dr-Pétiot.html.

Clarkson, Wensley. 2005. *Evil Beyond Belief--How and Why Dr. Harold Shipman Murdered 357 People*. England: Blake Publishing.

Dane, Peter E. 2007. "The Physician at the Movies." *The Pharos* Summer: 40–44.

Deans, Jason. 2002. "Shipman Film 'Timely and Appropriate.'" *The Guardian*, July 1. Accessed March 25, 2019. https://www.theguardian.com/media/2002/jul/01/broadcasting3.

Dominique, Jean-François and Joseph Dobrian (translator). 2019. *The Butcher of Paris: The Crimes of Dr. Pétiot—And an Indictment of a Nation.* Rex Imperator Publishing.

Flores, Glenn. 2002. "Mad Scientists, Compassionate Healers, and Greedy Egotists: The Portrayal of Physicians In the Movies." *Journal of the National Medical Association* 94, (7): 635–658.

Gallagher, William. 2002. "Shipman's Painful Drama." *BBC News*. July 9. Accessed March 25, 2019. http://news.bbc.co.uk/1/hi/entertainment/2117692.stm.

Gilleard, Chris. 2008. "A Murderous Ageism? Age, Death and Dr. Shipman." *Journal of Aging Studies* 22: 88–95.

Greenfield, Steve and Guy Osborn. 1996. "Pulped Fiction? Cinematic Parables of (In) Justice." *University of San Francisco Law Review* 30: 1181–1198.

Jarvie, I.C. 1978. "Seeing Through Movies." *Philosophy of Social Sciences* 8: 374–397.

Jarvis, Brian. 2007. "Monsters Inc: Serial Killers and Consumer Culture." *Crime Media Culture* 3 (3): 326.

Johnson, Bradley R. and Judith V. Becker. 1997. "Natural Born Killers?: The Development of the Sexually Sadistic Serial Killer." *Journal of the American Academy Psychiatry and the Law* 25 (3): 335–348.

Kaplan, Robert. 2007. "The Clinicide Phenomenon: An Explanation of Medical Murder." *Australasian Psychiatry* 15 (4): 299–304.

King, David. 2012. *Death in the City of Light: The True Story of the Serial Killer Who Terrorised Wartime Paris*. New York: Crown Publishing.

Maeder, Thomas. 1980. *Unspeakable Crimes of Dr. Pétiot*. Boston: The Atlantic Monthly Press.

Marshall, Natalie. 2016. *Doctor Death: The True Story of Harold Shipman.* CreateSpace Independent Publishing Platform.

Maslin, J. 1993. "Review/Film: In the Name of the Father; The Sins of a Son Are Visited on His Father." *The New York Times*. December 29. Accessed March 25, 2019. https://www.nytimes.com/1993/12/29/movies/review-film-name-father-sins-son-are-visited-his-father.html.

May, Sir John. 1994. *Final Report.* London Her Majesty's Stationery Office: 449.

Miyoshyi, Masao. 1996. "Dr. Jekyll and the Emergence of Mr. Hyde." *College English* 27 (6): 470–474.

Pallister, David. 1994. "In the Name of the Father." *Vertigo* 1 (3), Spring. Accessed May 2, 2019. https://www.closeupfilmcentre.com/vertigo_magazine/volume-1-issue-3-spring-1994/in-the-name-of-the-father/.

Peters, Carole. 2005. *Harold Shipman--Mind Set on Murder—Why Shipman Killed and Killed Again*—The True Story. England: Carleton Books.

Picart, Caroline Joan "Kay" S. and Cecil Greek. 2003. "The Compulsion of Real/Reel Serial Killers and Vampires: Toward a Gothic Criminology." *Journal of Criminal Justice and Popular Culture* 10 (1): 39–68.

Picart, Caroline Joan "Kay" S. 2006. "Crime and the Gothic: Sexualizing Serial Killers." *Journal of Criminal Justice and Popular Culture* 13 (1): 1–18.

Picart, Caroline Joan "Kay" S. and Cecil Greek. 2007. *Monsters in and among Us*. Madison, NJ: Fairleigh Dickinson Press.

Picart, Caroline Joan "Kay" S. 2016. "Race and Serial Killing in the Media: The Case of Wayne Williams." In *Framing Law and Crime: An Interdisciplinary Anthology*, edited by Caroline Joan "Kay" S. Picart, Michael Hviid Jacobson, and Cecil Greek. Madison, NJ: Fairleigh Dickinson University Press.

Smith, Dame Janet. 2002. *Death Disguised*. TSO: London. Available at https://webarchive.nationalarchives.gov.uk/20090808155110/http://www.the-shipman-inquiry.org.uk/reports.asp

Smith, Dame Janet. 2003a. *The Police Investigation of March 1998*. TSO: London. Available at https://webarchive.nationalarchives.gov.uk/20090808155110/http://www.the-shipman-inquiry.org.uk/reports.asp

Smith, Dame Janet. 2003b. *Death Certification and the Investigation of Deaths by Coroners*. TSO: London. Available at https://webarchive.nationalarchives.gov.uk/20090808155110/http://www.the-shipman-inquiry.org.uk/reports.asp

Smith, Dame Janet. 2004a. *The Regulation of Controlled Drugs in the Community*. TSO: London. Available at https://webarchive.nationalarchives.gov.uk/20090808155110/http://www.the-shipman-inquiry.org.uk/reports.asp

Smith, Dame Janet. 2004b. *Safeguarding Patients: Lessons from the Past—Proposals for the Future*. TSO: London. Available at https://webarchive.nationalarchives.gov.uk/20090808155110/http://www.the-shipman-inquiry.org.uk/reports.asp

Smith, Dame Janet. 2005. Shipman: *The Final Report*. TSO: London. Available at https://webarchive.nationalarchives.gov.uk/20090808155110/http://www.the-shipman-inquiry.org.uk/reports.asp

Walsh, Anthony. 2005. "African Americans and Serial Killing in the Media: The Myth and the Reality." *Homicide Studies* Part 9 (4): 271–278.

Chapter Nine

The Redactasaurus Chronicles

Fear, Consumption and Graffiti in Capital City

Deborah Landry

Government employees push past her, annoyed at her slowed pace. She shelters her eyes, squints, notices marking high up on the side of the building (see figure 9.1). Has that always been there? Perched just over the edge the shadows hang, menacing and yet completely unnoticed. What beastly tale/tail created this grey and red scar blistering out of that weathered stone? What lay beneath these layers of willful destruction?

This chapter draws upon observations I have made over the course of my ethnographic work on graffiti in the City of Ottawa. This critique draws upon Kenneth Burke's Dramatism as we set out on a mystified quest for the fantastic urban aesthetics of security in this capital city of Canada. I offer

Figure 9.1. Photo by the author.

an ironic reading of urban surfaces: the imagery of a monster is invoked to problematize the grotesque absences and violent silences that remain because of the city's War on Graffiti. This case is but one example of many street-level material manifestations of urban planning strategies that haunt us long after the turn of the nineteenth century. This chapter digs under the swaths of black and grey secretions that redact signs of those whose security has been sacrificed in the monstrous service of maintaining the appearance of security for others.

The pulling down of confederate statues across North Carolina during the summer of 2017 (Graham, 2017) is related to the soft policies of social exclusion that this chapter takes up. In Canada, calls to remove the memorialization of Canada's questionable *heroes* similarly rang out after a group of active Canadian armed forces personnel, self-identified members of the racist and misogynist Proud Boys militant collective, disrupted an Indigenous ritual at the foot of an Edward Cornwallis statue on Canada Day (Young, July 5, 2017). Public parks, civic art and statues are shaped by structural collaborations and mundane rituals of everyday social interactions. Many of the chapters in this edited collection offer valuable insight into the ways in which vulnerable persons are rendered inhuman by such generic social mechanisms; this chapter reframes the main antagonist in this capital city chronicle about urban blight, destruction and despair. I offer a moral tale in the spirit of Max Weber's *verstehen*, an approach to understanding human action by taking an empathetic view of the context and the intentions involved (Ferrell, 1997). I consider this problem of "graffiti" through a Cultural Criminological lens, informed by the pragmatic Marxist framework of Kenneth Burke (Overington, 1977). I shine a light on the regulation of taste in Ottawa, which has effectively silenced racialized aesthetics in favor of "defensible aesthetics" (Landry, 2016).

This chapter joins many other texts (Harvey, 1992; Leitner and Sheppard, 2003: Young, 2003; Vigar, Graham and Healey, 2005, Soja, 2010; Jarvie and Friend, 2016) in working towards a compassionate theory about social justice and urban spatiality. Accordingly, the first section of this chapter proposes an unforgetting of Kenneth Burke's theoretical opus as a tool to demystify how graffiti is covered over by the city through a process I identify presently as redaction. The second section outlines the socio-historical foundations of the National Capital Region (NCR) and the structural inequality that bears out in present-day land-based policies, administration and regulatory relationships. The third section ushers the reader into the ruins of the everyday to present the violence concealed by "beautification."

CHRONICLING MONSTERS, MISERY AND GRAFFITI

The Redactassaurus is a symbolic figure that characterizes a seemingly innocuous bundle of federal, provincial and municipal legislations, which re-create exclusionary practices of silencing from our past. The Redactasaurus is a derivation inspired by Jock Young's (2011) Datasaur and Travis Linnemann's (2016) work on redaction and police violence. Extending Charles Wright Mills's *Sociological Imagination* into criminology, Young renders us the image of a T-Rex like figure to express his frustration with the state of orthodox criminological research: the Datasaur imposes its distended belly, bloated with calculations, digestion stunted by a lack of theory. Unmotivated to venture from its comfortable rest, its gangly tail sways inconclusively in the wind. The Redactasaurus similarly represents attempts to harness the persuasive rhetorical power of positivism, making flawed predictions about people and security while planning for an ideology of a utopic future. The task of locating this metaphorical monster requires us to seek out how ideological assumptions are used as data (or motives) to explain urban intervention for the future (Young, 2011: 15–16; Ferrell, Hayward and Young, 2008). Add to this, I pull in Linnemann's work on redaction as "the horrific acts" of state institutions (2016). Black ink covers over large swaths of text that explain what heavy hand the state has had in managing crime. The redactions are manifestations of cultural and political powers, "signifying that which is (un) known" (Linnemann, 2016). It is in the symbolic and literal (un)remembering of human misery where we recognize the Redactasaurus's movements through the city, as malicious destruction.

Graffiti is produced in many contexts and for different purposes; however, there are similar aesthetics and meanings that speak to the historical and political contexts in which it is produced (Ferrell, 1993; Snyder, 2009; Wacławek, 2011; Millie, 2017; Avramidis and Tsilimpounidi, 2016):

> Graffiti is, of course, not a single genre—the term is more of an umbrella to indicate the range of generally unsanctioned texts written onto city surfaces and furniture ranging from apparently random scribbles to elegant street art. The unsanctioned graffiti texts speak to a range of imagined communities that coexist, often unhappily, within the powerful geographies of the mainstream (Carrington, 2009: 412).

While graffiti includes many kinds of public and typically criminalized writing, being young, poor and marginalized is an undeniable characteristic of most graffiti writers (Ferrell, 1993:5). This chapter is concerned with Hip

Hop graffiti, which emerged in the impoverished neighborhoods of Philadelphia and New York City during the early 1970s. Of concern to my analysis is the push to eradicate "graffiti" symbolically and materially, which is not unlike similar attempts in other North American and Australian cities in large part due to the popularity of racist police-centric strategies of the Broken Windows Hypothesis (Rahn, 2002; Halsey and Young, 2002; Young, 2010; McAuliffe and Iveson, 2011). I aim to break this window; my slingshot is aimed at the pro-policing Eurocentric logic that seeps of "beautification" found in the wake of the Redactasaurus.

TO CATCH A REDACTASAURUS: BURKEAN DRAMATISM FOR VISUALIZING MORAL ORDERS

Kenneth Burke is largely overlooked among contemporary social scientists (Mangham and Overington, 1987: 1; Overington, 1977:131; Overington, 2001:94; Thames, 2015) despite Burke's influencing the work of sociologists such as Goffman (1959: 194), C.W. Mills (1959: 215) and Duncan (1962:143-176; 1969). Burke's theoretical framework has much to offer critical socio-legal and cultural criminological research. Dramatism provides a framework that is sensitive to the socio-historical context through which ideological performances—such as policing art preferences—appears natural (Mangham and Overington, 1987: 7). The dialectical approach to reading the social world guides the cultural critic to identify explanatory frameworks; construct ironic terminologies in opposition to expected vocabulary of motives; and offer alternative readings (Overington, 1977:139).

The objects of this inquiry are the statements that explain human actions, which Burke calls motives. Motives are culturally relevant explanations offered up by people and institutions to justify social order (Burke, 1968). This chapter accordingly reveals the vocabulary of motives at work in narratives about urban security, which consistently draw upon pathology and nostalgic nationalism to justify criminalization of "uncivilized" taste and movement. I locate rhetorical motives in urban planning schemes, bylaws, stories recounted by various actors in this drama, and in the absences: "Burke is not simply the analyst of ordering talk; he is also an authority that tells us [. . .] how to find what is missing and how to include that which is omitted" (Overington, 2001: 111; Burke, 1968).

The production of cultural artifacts such as graffiti is not unlike the production of crime legislation, which in turn produces criminalized people and behaviors (Frauley, 2015: 619). These productions are statements about social relationships and power. Rendering a linguistic spin on Emile Durkheim,

Burke argues that power "is a social fact that manifests itself in numerous and complex ways, both physically and symbolically" (Cheney, Garvin-Doxas and Torrens, 1999:137). Discourse is collective production; institutional discourse offers categories of thought, which shape a vocabulary for self-knowledge and identity (Burke, 1968). Burke helps us unpack expected vocabularies of motives: what is beautiful in the city, and why, says who? By identifying these frameworks, we may strategically create social orders that are more humanistic than others (Burke, 1968: 45). Or, stated differently, this Burkean analysis captures the Redactasaurus, reveals the ideological impetus that fuels its destructive capacity, and suggests new ways in which the city might be re-made beautifully just.

STOKING THE EMBERS OF MORAL HYGIENE: A SOCIO-HISTORY OF OTTAWA'S LAND USE LEGISLATION

A British settlement staked out along unceded Algonquin territory, Bytown was settled by Lieutenant Colonel John By who was authorized by the British government to divide up parcels of land along the Ottawa and Rideau rivers (Cross, 1973). This would lay the foundation for a military post and a thriving lumber and pulp industry that would become the City of Ottawa. During his tenure in Canada, the Lieutenant Colonel supervised the construction of the Rideau Canal, largely built by Irish immigrant laborers who were also among those who would have their homes expropriated as part of a public health strategy to deal with problematic urban density, a problem that the municipality would welcome today (Cross, 1973). Several catastrophic fires would tear through the newly incorporated City of Ottawa, providing an opportunity to rebuild the new state capital, at a time when urban spaces were coming to be understood as a collection of land use parcels in need of conservation (Valverde, 2011: 281).

Prime Minister William Lyon Mackenzie-King, elected from 1921–1930 and 1935–1948, visualized a capital city of Canada that would stand in tribute to the fallen soldiers of the war (Picton, 2010: 310). Jacques Greber's urban renewal plans were mandated in 1937 by Mackenzie-King, impressed with Greber's experience in designing urban landscapes in the service of military pomp and authority in France. Most notably, Greber introduced "zoning controls, building codes, public financing and urban renewal policies, and a new set of institutional and legal structures for promoting urban renewal" which would "transform central city locations in major Canadian urban centres" (Picton, 2010: 301–2).

Like many cities during the early part of the nineteenth century, general anxieties about slums and moral health circulated widely. To manage how people moved through urban spaces, cities formally restrained leisure and shopping activities to static places and concrete structures, which created economic and legal hardships for the strolling street vendors and buskers who were once common features of the city (Blomley, 2010). The motive of *pathologically risky populations* was drawn upon to justify strict zoning laws; Greber incorporated intolerance of the working poor into his designs, explicitly seeking to prevent the working-class district from impeding "the beauty of the rocky Mediterranean shoreline for those driving along a proposed seaside roadway" (Picton, 2010: 308). Greber's 1950 Plan for the National Capital similarly pathologized the poor as innately deviant, and their communities as ugly (Picton, 2010: 310). And while he was not directly implicated, Greber's assumptions about the poor reverberated in his plans for France, providing the blueprint and rhetorical motives for the Vichy regime to "cleanse" neighborhoods deemed as "slums," and see to "the deportation of 1,949 Jews to death camps" (Picton, 2010: 309).

The expropriation of lands designed by the Greber Plan consumed over 200 acres of the City of Ottawa's core. The willful destruction of communities created immense housing demands and friction between municipal and federal governments. Ottawa's Mayor, Charlotte Whitton, sought unsuccessfully for resources from the federal planners to create social housing to alleviate the mandated hardships. However, concerns about the National War Monument were prioritized over housing. Suburbs were planned as a key component to these initial designs, placing laborers on the outskirts of the city, separating them from their workplaces by large swaths of forested greenspace. Mayor Whitton decried the distances between where people worked and lived, with little effect on the federal plan (Picton, 2010: 317–18). Before the completion of the Greber plan, the economy collapsed and federal funds and political will to complete it disappeared. Many expropriated lands remained as large parcels of "brownfields," industrial lands and former razed "slums," contaminated from past uses and fire (De Sousa, 2003; Ouseley, 2013). Approximately four decades later—faced with the overwhelming expenses associated with rehabilitating the land for use—the municipality began selling the lands to private developers, which was met with intense public outcry (Bliek and Gauthier, 2007). "The expropriation was exposed as a gigantic disaster" because federal aspirations superseded local concerns, scarring Ottawa's landscape (Picton, 2010: 320, 302). Of greater concern for this analysis, though, is the transfer of large parcels of Ottawa's inner-city to private developers and private police.

The National Capital Region (NCR) was established by the federal government in 1959 to oversee the federal buildings and lands created by the Greber plan in the cities of Ottawa Ontario and Gatineau Quebec. Unlike other capital cities such as Washington DC, however, NCR is not a separate political or administrative entity from the provinces it straddles (Gordon, 2017). Each municipality within the NCR functions as a traditional municipality in line with their provincial mandates and protections under the Canadian Constitution, with some exceptions (Gordon, 2017). Most notably, the NCR maintains the right to affect urban zoning practices within the City of Ottawa. This exceptional right was granted after legal disputes between the municipal, provincial and federal levels, which reached the Supreme Court of Canada (Fullerton, 2005). The NCR introduces yet another level of policing into Ottawa's geography, the National Capital Commission (NCC) conservation officers who police NCR lands (Walby and Hurl, 2014).

Lands that fall under NCR are policed in the spirit of "beautification" by NCC conservation officers, with authority granted under the Criminal Code of Canada (Walby and Lippert 2014). Walby and Lippert (2012) posit a nuanced typology that highlights the complex private and public relationships involved in surveillance and social exclusion on NCC lands. In an effort to maintain "optical consistency," NCC manage homeless populations using dispersion practices—as opposed to banishment or punishment—in the service of risk management (Walby and Lippert, 2012: 2014). Not to be mistaken for an act of benevolence, conservation officers often likened their roles to policing and garbage removal (Walby and Lippert, 2012). Dispersion practices would merely force people to sleep upon private property, whereby sleeping becomes criminal trespassing. Furthermore, Walby and Lippert (2012) trace out a typology of these spatial management, which illustrates the complex relationship between the purpose and nature of the space and the time of day when the spaces can be used.

Practically, this means someone walking in a straight line through town faces multiple levels of sanction—by federal, municipal and provincial police as well as conservation, transit and private security officers—even though the act of walking (or sleeping, or writing graffiti) is phenomenologically the same. Ottawa is a vacillating legal and temporal geography. Metaphorically, these various levels of governance push hot acidic breath on the backs of those who live and labor precariously; this breath is invisible to those whose consuming lifestyles conform to the expected moral order. "Beautification" is the term used to sanitize the act of dislocating poor people, and this indignity is made possible through land use strategies such as conservation policies and zoning legislation (Valverde, 2011; Sylvestre, Damon, Blomley, and Bellot, 2015).

Regulating "unwanted" people through land use practices is a disturbing trend in urban planning (Valverde, 2011: 279). These spatial practices inflict injustices that reflect the morality campaigns of yesterday. For example, Christine Bruckert and Martin Dufresne (2002) note how attempts to eradicate strip clubs by the City of Ottawa failed Supreme Court challenges because the political campaign, or vocabulary of motives, violated *The Canadian Charter of Rights and Freedoms* by attempting to regulate women's bodies. The city revised its strategy, exploiting land use and licensing regimes. Similarly, vagrancy laws were struck down from the *Canadian Criminal Code* in 1972 and effectively replaced by provincial legislations such as *the Ontario Safe Streets Act*, inspired by the misinformed popularity of Broken Windows policing (Chesnay, Bellot and Sylvestre, 2013; O'Grady, Gaetz and Buccieri, 2013; Sylvestre, Damon, Blomley and Bellot, 2015). The first provincial statute against begging, *The Safe Streets Act*, was justified publicly to secure city streets by eradicating unregulated labor, such as squeegeeing and panhandling. Since the contemporary versions of these laws speak to regulating labor and land, they do not sound like the crushing monstrous footfalls of the moral hygiene movement and eugenics legislation in Canada (Adams, 1994).

THE SACKING OF CAPITAL CITY: THE CAPITAL CITY WAR ON GRAFFITI

The urban management and regulatory relationships between federal and provincial and municipal governments have come to bear strange fruit. Today, 89 percent of Ottawa's population lives in the suburbs; further, the average household income in the City of Ottawa, \$104,000, is \$20,000 above the national average (Canada, 2017a). Ottawa is popularly perceived as the safest city in Canada, and crime rates (however imperfect) echo this sentiment (CBC, 2017; Canada, 2017b). However, the relative economic stability and sense of safety does not extend to the city's Black and Indigenous populations who tend to live in the city's center (Canada, 2011; 2016). The reality of racialized and gendered economic disparity is important to this narrative. Provincially mandated municipal amalgamation merely exacerbated social exclusion inherent to the planning of the NCR.

In 2001, the City of Ottawa would be among several Ontario cities forced into amalgamating outlying townships under the *Ontario Municipal Act* (Rosenfeld and Reese, 2003). At the federal level, the newly elected conservative minority government distanced themselves from funding municipal and provincial budgets, forcing municipal governments to depend on public-private partnerships. Add to the financial pressure the global context of post–9/11 anxieties and discourses aligning terrorism, risk and race circulated widely in support of many neoliberal policies and the expansion of surveillance and policing strategies (Althiede, 2006). It was against this political backdrop that the Ontario Conservatives, under Premier Mike Harris, introduced amalgamation policy to address structural deficits in Ontario's largest cities (Fanelli, 2014). The consequences for Ontario residents soon turned deadly due in large part to desperate attempts by both the province and municipalities to cut costs (Fanelli, 2014:12). Deficits only increased when the province cut over 650 million dollars in provincial transfers to municipalities by the end of Harris's second term (Fanelli, 2014; Prudham, 2004).

Meanwhile, back in the capital city, many candidates who were running for election in the newly amalgamated City of Ottawa ran on campaigns that exploited anxieties about urban creep (Barthel, 2002). Constituents in suburban townships correctly suspected they would experience reduced services. And so, it is no coincidence that the City of Ottawa entered a cultural battle against graffiti writers during amalgamation. The charge was primarily led by one city councillor, with the key support of local newspapers: "Mr. Cullen is proposing a War on Graffiti, and is asking city staff to come up with policy recommendations. It might not be the city's first priority, but it's a battle we should fight" (Ottawa Citizen, 2001: D4). The newly elected councillors from suburban townships together with conservative former member of the NCC, Mayor Bob Chiarelli, wasted no time in extending the discourse of public health and civil security to the argument that graffiti was a threat worthy of vigilance; graffiti writers were pathologized as viral infections, whose only cure was eradication (Barthel, 2002; Landry, 2016).

The economic fallout was extensive. Initially, the municipality planned to focus on buffing graffiti surfaces visible from main streets. Summer students were hired to hunt down graffiti on municipal surfaces, and bylaw officers were dispatched to order immediate decontamination by public works (City of Ottawa, 2009; Ottawa-Carleton Police Services Board, 2000). The beastly alliance stormed through the core of Ottawa, eradicating colorful productions that sat peacefully on walls for nearly a decade without prior complaint. Soon, however, the beast consumed the visible graffiti in the relatively small downtown core; and so, the monster began scouring places that were only visible to the most covert graffiti writers. Unsanctioned museums of important graffiti artifacts that remembered a graffiti community that had existed in the city since the early 1990s were desecrated. The campaign had changed in purpose to securing (and justifying) the private and public industry that now grew to feed the Redactasaurus.

Early graffiti abatement efforts were hampered by property owners who did not wish to have surfaces redacted, and unionized Public Works employees who took issue with the City of Ottawa contracting sand blasting and buffing services to private companies that specialized in "graffiti" eradication services (City of Ottawa, 2000). Relationships needed to be negotiated between the multiple levels of government lands. With vandalism laws already on the books, the City of Ottawa turned to criminalizing the ideology of graffiti. Funding to organizations that incorporated the style graffiti in outreach programs was threatened. The city used zoning and signage laws to regulate art; all permanent outdoor murals (and signage) would have to go through an assessment process with the municipality The *Graffiti Management By-law 2008-1* (City of Ottawa, 2001–2017) made it illegal for building owners to have graffiti on their structures, and encouraged citizens to call the city to report any graffiti. This involved an "education campaign" to convince Ottawa's residents of the harm that lurked in the aesthetic of graffiti, but also how to tell the difference between a legal mural and illegal graffiti. Behold the criminalization of taste; property owners who did not paint over municipally unsanctioned artwork were threatened with fines. Local property and business owners expressed understandable frustration with being punished for something that they did not do, which only instigated feelings of resentment towards graffiti writers: "Nail the little donkeys that are doing the damage," suggested Rob Sproule of Ottawa's business advisory committee (CBC, 2017).

VISUALIZING THE REDACTASAURUS RAMPAGE

Prior to amalgamation, few people expressed concern for graffiti, and the city managed incidents in a reactive approach for less than $30,000 a year (Barthel, 2002). By 2008, the municipality was proactively budgeting over $3 million to graffiti abatement, motivated by the ideology that unsanctioned artwork was a threat to potential shopping experiences. Suburban councillor Steve Desroches's comments represented the tone at City Hall: "If you have an area where people notice there may be graffiti and crime, that's an area where they don't want to shop. [. . .] So I think the economic consequences of not going forward with the strategy are a lot worse than spending the money that we're talking about" (CBC, 2017). But was it? Given that there is no evidence to support the hypothesis that graffiti reduces shopping traffic, let us weigh the harmful ramifications of this cultural war.

First, the monster emerges in punches thrown by people graffiti writers ironically call *heroes*: vigilant citizens who threaten people they believe to be graffiti writers. To illustrate, consider this incident drawn from my field notes. Several informants explained a similar violent altercation that unfolded atop a semi-visible building rooftop in a high-end shopping neighborhood that had long been a popular spot for graffiti writers.[1] Bylaw officers had issued ordinances to the building owner for removal several times. Fed up, a few owners organized a reconnaissance, waiting several nights for writers to return. The police were eventually called to contend with the unfortunate young writers who eventually did show, but not before they were physically assaulted by the owners.[2] Responding to a general query about the recent eradication of graffiti in that area, the story was corroborated to me by a pub owner. The restaurateur justified his exceptional support of violence in terms of the city's zero tolerance strategy. While sheepish about violence generally, he explained:

> We really have no choice because we are the ones . . . you know, we get stuck with the tab, right? It's frustrating after a while. It is constant threat and harassment by these bylaw officers if we don't take it down. If the police can't stop [the graffiti writers] and it costs us money, well . . . go for it, you know? Maybe word will spread that it is too dangerous to paint here, right? [3]

Even if one could find logic in sanctioning violence to respond to a relatively minor property offense, this violence extends to young people painting legally too. There are two legal graffiti walls in Ottawa and many sanctioned graffiti spaces across the river in the City of Gatineau (OttawaVeloOutaouais, 2015). Furthermore, spray paint is often used in legal murals. Nevertheless, few "heroes" are familiar with such shifting spatial and material permissions. Consequently, writers are often physically and verbally attacked while painting in legal spaces, or while painting commissioned murals. One former graffiti writer, who runs a business with friends painting commissioned murals in the city, explained it like this:

> They will yell at us from across the street . . . call us lazy . . . dirty punks. They have no clue. I get that. But this is my job. I'm legit now! We went through all the red tape, we jumped through all their hoops. And businesses that pay for us to paint these legal murals, they don't want people calling By-law on them all the damn time because someone thinks it's "graffiti." It's a problem when we are trying to get new clients (Dominique LaRocque, 2015).[4]

Part of the costs the municipality associates with the War on Graffiti is indeed calls made to Ottawa's municipal complaint line. City of Ottawa councillor Rick Chiarelli reported that it costs between $90 and $300 for bylaw officers to respond to calls (CBC, 2011). In many instances, bylaw officers are checking in on legal murals and explaining to the callers what is not graffiti (CBC, 2011).

Second, there are financial consequences for members of Ottawa's arts community. In addition to fostering a broader reluctance to support urban art, as indicated in the previous paragraph, opportunities to make a living as an urban artist and muralist are increasingly restricted to those who are classically trained or willing to claim that they disavow graffiti (Landry, 2016). Graffiti writers who used to work with community outreach organizations were effectively ousted because of the very skill that qualified them for the job in the first place. Any organization dependent on the City of Ottawa for art programming grants was expected to justify their project in terms of urban art that prevents graffiti and, thus, fights crime. House of PainT, an important Hip Hop collective that defended the rights of graffiti artists in Ottawa in their early years, has recently replaced the word graffiti with "urban art" in their annual International Festival, marking a shift away from graffiti towards more professional mural work.[5] This change reflects the ongoing pressure from the City of Ottawa for the organization to denounce *crime* to maintain financial and legal support (e.g., providing permits for the annual outdoor event). Graffiti writers who attempt to make a living in Ottawa become complicit in the disappearance of the word and style of graffiti: it is an "illusion of 'freedom'" given the precariousness of their lives (Bruckert and Dufrense, 2002: 83). This war has turned fools into heroes, turned artists into criminals or conspirators lest they pledge allegiance to the art of crime prevention.

The third consequence is the visual colonization of space. Aesthetics are a key element in discretionary practices of spatial regulation, conservation and public security (Walby and Lippert, 2012: 1019). The recent influx of federal

Figure 9.2. Photo by the author.

funding for urban art that celebrates Canada's 150th year of confederation went, perhaps unsurprisingly, to those artists willing to animate *democratic propaganda:* a visual narrative that highlights Ottawa as a tourist destination, or recalls the military or architectural features of the city (Picton, 2010). The graffiti community and its style were never eradicated, though, and this becomes clear when confronted with charred walls of mismatched black, red and grey scars. Behold the work of the Redactedsaurus, or what is bewilderingly referred to as "beautification" (see figure 9.2):

CONCLUSIONS AND IMPLICATIONS

Jennifer Barthel describes the urban aesthetic of The City of Ottawa as privileged, in that it equates the scouring of unauthorized voices with the ideology of security (2002: 8). The City of Ottawa prefers projects that can promise a defensible aesthetic by whispering sweet nothings about crime prevention in the application and review process (Landry, 2016). It is a suburban aesthetic, supported in large part due to the mandates provided to suburban councillors who vote on issues that rarely impact the townships situated far from the city center. The reasons for the increasingly divergent thinking between suburban and urban residents is complex; however, geographical segregation based on race and class is a key factor (Walks, 2006; Williamson, 2008; Forest, 2012).

Rhetorical and ideological redaction is an offensive extension of historic dispossession; it is a violent forgetting of the insecurity that exists for racialized and economically disadvantaged populations in Ottawa. The narrative of structural disparity is erased, but a wound remains. The racialized quality of the Hip Hop graffiti style is most certainly a key component to these battles and it is not a coincidence that Indigenous youth in Canada are similarly being drawn to the ethics and aesthetics of Hip Hop, which is grounded in resistance to systemic oppression (Skinner and Masuda, 2013; Lashua and Fox, 2006; Buffam, 2011). Urban Indigenous populations are the fastest growing, and youngest, segments of Canadian society (Canada, 2011). In addition to the reasons I outlined in the preceding section, and in the spirit of reconciliation on these stolen lands, I suggest that Canadian municipalities would benefit from reconsidering its use of redaction to regulate urban practices given the reality of who lives in these Canadian cities.

This chapter illustrates how neoliberal legal and social policy contribute to the normalization of moral orders that tell us resistance to the status quo is ugly, and that consumption is beautiful. Keynesian urban planning, characterized by the Gerber Plan (Picton, 2010: 303), coupled with the era of austerity, has brought about legislations akin to those about which the warning

Datasaur (Young, 2011) represented: a science of uncreative calculations, building weak theories about the moral future of the city based on ideological assumptions about why the city is the way it is today, devoid of any consideration for the socio-political history that preceded these streets. Zoning and land use practices seemingly revive the ideologies of moral hygienic movements, resurfacing the city with black spaces and brownfields, calculating the cost of silence today against the imagined futures of consuming urban lifestyles. Witness the criminalization of taste and "low class" performance (Brucker and Dufrense, 2002) executed through capitulations to commerce as security, which contributes to the expansion of potential legal targets for punishment and eradication.

Through Burke's philosophical lens, the Redactasuarus has been seen ransacking the city, leaving "beautification" in its wake. Unsanctioned writing and art is publicly accessible artistic humor, not hidden behind the doors of pretentious galleries; its text open for public viewing and response. It is what Burke (1966) identifies as the comedic response to this tragedy of the modern city. It is an attempt to ironize defensible aesthetics. As Camille Lewis beautifully explains (2008: par 4):

> While tragedy reaches for a beautiful ideal, comedy lampoons the ideal. While tragedy feels guilty for falling short of perfection, comedy juggles the cultural books so that a loss is translated into a win. While tragedy blames a scapegoat for cultural sin, comedy finds that sin in every human being. The Other in tragedy is irreconcilably evil, but in comedy the Other is simply mistaken.

The question remains: now that the beast is revealed, what do we do with it? Carlos Fanelli rightly suggests that there needs to be cultural strategies in place to challenge "the social attitudes about the role of taxation and make the connections between social justice and democracy" (2014: 20). By demystifying the real cost of neoliberal fantasies, it is a worthy attempt to restore municipal coffers and public services of yesterday. However, bylaw legislations, such as the Graffiti Management by-law, persist despite pressures they place on budgets (City of Ottawa, 2001–2017). The willingness of municipalities to budget for the fallout of social exclusion, and indeed foster new industries that will depend on maintaining inequality, is linked to broader cultural attitudes about criminalization and punishment. As such, we cannot deal with these inequalities without also confronting another monster in the room: the normalization of criminalization and dispossession (Carrier and Piché, 2015). I suggest that we must impede pedestrian traffic on our figurative sidewalk, look up and be horrified. Then, I propose that we take a broader aim and organize our response accordingly through localized anti-prison action as *part of* our urban planning involvement, and following these threads in our academic scholarship and pedagogy.

On a final note, it may be helpful to remember the Canadian history on urban renewal projects that demonstrates similarly abhorrent dispossessions, as in the cases of Africville Nova Scotia (Clairmont and McGill, 1999) or the Metis suburb of Rooster Town in Winnipeg (Burley, 2013). Ottawa's forgetting of Indigenous communities deserves closer critical attention and response to these ends. In the shadow of American tensions over President Trump's inability to stand firmly in denouncing Neo-Nazism, Canadians have responded in kind, pulling down statues that commemorate the genocide and colonization of Indigenous people. It is my hope that this chapter might leverage this social turn, and encourage a critical reflection about how urban planning and bylaws are implicated in these symbolic and material exclusionary practices.

NOTES

1. Neil Brahms (pseudonym), interview by Deborah Landry, March 15, 2013, interview 2013F2 transcript; Chris LeBlanc (pseudonym), interview by Deborah D. Landry, June 23, 2012, interview 2012C1 transcript; Ahmed Tariq (pseudonym), interview by Deborah D. Landry, June 30, 2013, interview 2013R2 transcript.
2. Ahmed Tariq (pseudonym), interview by Deborah D. Landry, June 30, 2013, interview 2013R2 transcript; Neil Brahms (pseudonym), interview by Deborah Landry, March 15, 2013, interview 2013F2 transcript.
3. Neil Brahms (pseudonym), interview by Deborah Landry, March 15, 2013, interview 2013F2 transcript.
4. Dominique LaRocque (pseudonym), interview by Deborah D. Landry, August 15, 2015, interview 2015LL1 transcript.
5. Dominique LaRocque (pseudonym), interview by Deborah D. Landry, August 15, 2015, interview 2015LL1 transcript.

REFERENCES

Adams, Mary Lewis. 1994. "In Sickness and in Health: State Formation, Moral Regulation, and Early VD Initiatives in Ontario." *Journal of Canadian Studies* 28(4): 117–130.

Altheide, David. 2006. "Terrorism and the Politics of Fear." *Cultural Studies—Critical Methodologies* 6(4): 415–439.

Avramidis, Konstantinos and Myrto Tsilimpounidi (Eds.). 2016. *Graffiti and Street Art: Reading, Writing and Representing the City*. London and New York: Taylor & Francis.

Barthel, Jennifer. 2002. "The Perceptions of Graffiti in Ottawa: An Ethnographic Study of an Urban Landscape." *Agora: Online Graduate Humanities Journal* 1(2). http://www.humanities.ualberta.ca/agora/articles.cfm?ArticleNo=139

Bellemare, Andrea. 2016. "Wilfrid Laurier University Nixes Prime Minister Statues Project School Will Remove existing Sir John A. Macdonald Statue." *CBC News*, February 12. http://www.cbc.ca/news/canada/kitchener-waterloo/wilfrid-laurier-university-pulls-prime-minister-statues-1.3445652

Bliek, Desmond and Pierre Gauthier. 2007. "Mobilising Urban Heritage to Counter the Commodification of Brownfield Landscapes: Lessons from Montréal's Lachine Canal." *Canadian Journal of Urban Research* 16(1): 39.

Blomley, Nicholas. 2010. *Rights of Passage: Sidewalks and the Regulation of Public Flow*. London: Routledge

Bruckert, Christine and Martin Dufresne. 2002. "Re-Configuring the Margins: Tracing the Regulatory Context of Ottawa Strip Clubs, 1974–2000." *Canadian Journal of Law & Society/La Revue Canadienne Droit et Société* 17(1): 69–87.

Buffam, Bonar. 2011. "Can't Hold Us Back! Hip-Hop and the Racial Motility of Aboriginal Bodies in Urban Spaces." *Social Identities* 17(3): 337–350.

Burley, David G. 2013. "Rooster Town: Winnipeg's Lost Métis Suburb, 1900–1960." *Urban History Review/Revue d'histoire urbaine* 42(1): 3–25.

Burke, Kenneth. 1968. "Dramatism." *International Encyclopedia of the Social Sciences*. New York: Macmillan, 445–452.

———. 1966. *Language as symbolic action: Essays on Life, Literature, and Method.* Berkeley: Univ of California Press.

Canada. Statistics Canada. *Police-reported crime statistics in Canada, 2016*. 2017a. http://www.statcan.gc.ca/pub/85-002-x/2017001/article/54842-eng.htm

———. Statistics Canada. Census families include couple families, with or without children, and lone-parent families. 2017b. CANSIM, table 111-0009. http://www.statcan.gc.ca/tables-tableaux/sum-som/l01/cst01/famil107a-eng.htm

———. Statistics Canada. Juristat. *Victimization of Aboriginal People in Canada, 2014*. 2016. http://www.statcan.gc.ca/pub/85-002-x/2016001/article/14631-eng.htm

———. Statistics Canada. National Household Survey. 2011. Catalogue no. 99-014-X2011041. http://www12.statcan.gc.ca/nhs-enm/2011

Carrier, Nicholas and Justin Piché. 2015. "Blind Spots of Abolitionist Thought in Academia: On Longstanding and Emerging Challenges." *Champ pénal/Penal field*, 12. http://champpenal.revues.org/9162

Carrington, Victoria. 2009. "'I Write, Therefore I Am: Texts in the City." *Visual Communication* 8(4): 409–424.

Castleman, C. (1982). *Getting Up: Subway Graffiti in New York*. Cambridge, MA, and London: MIT Press.

CBC. 2017. "Canadians See Ottawa as the Country's Safest City." *CBC News*, August 23. http://www.cbc.ca/news/canada/ottawa/canada-ottawa-safe-city-poll-2017-1.4258987

———. 2017. "Ottawa Should Spend $2M More to Fight Graffiti: Committee." *CBC News*, May 4. https://www.cbc.ca/news/canada/ottawa/ottawa-should-spend-2m-more-to-fight-graffiti-committee-1.655122.

———. 2014. "Jack Purcell Park Art Honours the Wrong Jack Purcell: Park Named after Hockey Volunteer, not Former Badminton Star." *CBC News,* May 20. http://www.cbc.ca/news/canada/ottawa/jack-purcell-park-art-honours-the-wrong-jack-purcell-1.2648751

———. 2011. "Complaining a Civic Sport in Ottawa," *CBC News*, February 15. http://www.cbc.ca/news/canada/ottawa/complaining-a-civic-sport-in-ottawa-1.976933

———. 2008. "Business Owner Fights City over Removal of Spray Paint: Restaurateur Says It's Art, but Inspectors Deemed It Graffiti." *CBC News,* November 8. http://www.cbc.ca/news/canada/ottawa/business-owner-fights-city-over-removal-of-spray-paint-1.715693

Cheney, George, Kathy Garvin-Doxas and Kathleen Torrens. 1999. "Kenneth Burke's Implicit Theory of Power." In *Kenneth Burke and the 21st Century*, edited by Bernard Brock, 133–150. Albany: State University of New York Press.

Chesebro, James W. 1988. "Epistemology and Ontology as Dialectical Modes in the Writings of Kenneth Burke." *Communication Quarterly* 36(3): 175–191.

Chesnay, Catherine T., Céline Bellot and Marie-Ève Sylvestre. 2013. "Taming Disorderly People One Ticket at a Time: The Penalization of Homelessness in Ontario and British Columbia." *Canadian Journal of Criminology and Criminal Justice* 55(2): 161–185.

Chunn, Dorothy E. and Shelley A. Gavigan. 2004. "Welfare Law, Welfare Fraud, and the Moral Regulation of the 'Never Deserving' Poor." *Social & Legal Studies* 13(2): 219–243.

City of Ottawa. 2001–2017. "Graffiti and Mural Program" *Ottawa.* http://ottawa.ca/en/residents/water-and-environment/green-living/graffiti-and-mural-program

City of Ottawa. 2009. City of Ottawa Act (S.O. 1999, Chapter 14 Schedule E). Available at https://www.ontario.ca/laws/statute/99c14e. Accessed 30 October 2017.

Clairmont, Donald H. and Dennis William Magill. 1999. *Africville: The Life and Death of a Canadian Black Community*. Toronto: Canadian Scholars' Press.

Cross, Michael, S. 1973. "The Shiners' War: Social Violence in the Ottawa Valley in the 1830s." *Canadian Historical Review* 54(1): 1–26.

De Sousa, Christopher A. 2003. "Turning Brownfields into Green Space in the City of Toronto." *Landscape and Urban Planning* 62(4): 181–198.

Duncan, Hugh. 1962. *Communication and Social Order*. New York: Bedminster Press.

Duncan, Hugh. 1969. *Symbols and Social Theory*. New York: Oxford University Press.

Fanelli, Carlos. 2014. *Under Pressure: How Public Policy Is Constraining Ontario Municipalities*. Canadian Centre for Policy Alternatives Ontario, Ryerson University. www.policyalternatives.ca

Ferrell, Jeff. 1997. "Criminological Verstehen: Inside the Immediacy of Crime." *Justice Quarterly: JQ / Academy of Criminal Justice Sciences* 14 (1): 3–23.

———. 1993. *Crimes of Style: Urban Graffiti and the Politics of Criminality*. New York: Garland.

Ferrell, Jeff, Keith Hayward and Jock Young. 2008. *Cultural Criminology: An Invitation*. Thousand Oaks: Sage.

Forest, Benjamin. 2012. "Electoral Redistricting and Minority Political Representation in Canada and the United States." *The Canadian Geographer/Le Géographe Canadien* 56(3): 318–338.

Frauley, Jon. 2015. "On Imaginative Criminology and Its Significance." *Societies* 5 (3): 618–630.

Fullerton, Christopher. 2005. "A Changing of the Guard: Regional Planning in Ottawa, 1945–1974." *Urban History Review/Revue D'histoire Urbaine* 34(1). Urban History Review/Revued'histoire urbaine: 100–112.

Goffman, Erving. 1959. *The Presentation of Self in Everyday Life*. New York: Doubleday Anchor.

Gordon, David. 2017. "Urban History Review Urban History Review Weaving a Modern Plan for Canada's Capital: Jacques Gréber and the 1950 Plan for the National Capital Region." *Urban History Review* 29(2) (March). https://www.erudit.org/en/journals/uhr/2001-v29-n2-uhr0878/1019205ar/abstract/

Graham, David A. 2017. "They Took Old Faithful Down. I Just Can't Believe It." *The Atlantic*, August 15. https://www.theatlantic.com/politics/archive/2017/08/durhams-civil-war-monument-and-the-backlash-to-the-backlash/536889/

Halsey, Mark and Allison Young. 2006. "Our Desires Are Ungovernable: Writing Graffiti in Urban Space." *Theoretical Criminology* 10(3): 275–306.

Harvey, David. 1992. "Social Justice, Postmodernism and the City." *International Journal of Urban and Regional Research* 16(4): 588–601.

Jarvie, James and Richard Friend. 2016. "Urbanization, Inclusion, and Social Justice." In *State of the World: Governing for Sustainability* edited by Worldwatch Institute, 343–353. Island Press/Center for Resource Economics.

Landry, Deborah. 2016. "Defensible Aesthetics: Creative Resistance to Urban Policies in Ottawa." In *Graffiti and Street Art: Reading, Writing and Representing the City*, edited by Avramidis, Konstantinos and Myrto Tsilimpounidi, 216–222. London and New York: Taylor & Francis.

Lashua, Brett and Karen Fox. 2006. "Rec Needs a New Rhythm Cuz Rap Is Where We're Livin'." *Leisure Sciences* 28(3): 267-283.

Leitner, Helga and Eric Sheppard. 2003. "Unbounding Critical Geographic Research on Cities: The 1990s and Beyond." *Urban Geography* 24(6): 510–528.

Lewis, Camille K. 2008. "Publish and Perish?: My Fundamentalist Education from the Inside Out." *KB Journal* 4(2) (Spring). http://www.kbjournal.org/lewis

Linnemann, Travis. 2016. "On Black Spaces: Death, Denial, Exorcism and Erasure." *New Directions in Critical Criminology*. Conference Proceedings held at University of Tennessee, Knoxville.

Lippert, Randy K. and Kevin Walby. 2014. "Municipal Corporate Security, Legal Knowledges, and the Urban Problem Space." *Law & Social Inquiry: Journal of the American Bar Foundation* 39(3): 720–39.

Mangham, Ian and Michael Overington. 1987. *Organizations as Theatre: A Social Psychology of Dramatic Appearances*. New York: Wiley.

McAuliffe, Cameron and Kurt Iveson. 2011. "Art and Crime (and Other Things Besides . . .): Conceptualising Graffiti in the City." *Geography Compass* 5(3): 128–143.

Millie, Andrew. 2017. Urban Interventionism as a Challenge to Aesthetic Order: Towards an Aesthetic Criminology. *Crime, Media, Culture* 13(1): 3–20.

Mills, Charles W. 1959. *The Sociological Imagination*. New York: Oxford University Press.

Mitchell, Don. 2003. *The Right to the City: Social Justice and the Fight for Public Space*. New York: Guilford Press.

O'Grady, Bill, Stephen Gaetz and Kristy Buccieri. 2013. "Tickets . . . and More Tickets: A Case Study of the Enforcement of the Ontario Safe Streets Act." *Canadian Public Policy* 39(4): 541–558.

Ottawa Citizen. 2001. "Let's Get Rid of Ottawa's Graffiti Pollution." August 15: D4.

Ottawa-Carleton Police Services Board. 2000. "Item 5: Presentation on 1999 Graffiti Removal Project." In *Minutes of Ottawa-Carleton Police Services Board Meeting 17 April 2000*. Ottawa City Hall: Champlain Room. https://app06.ottawa.ca /calendar/ottawa/archives/rmoc/Police_Services_Board/17Apr00/Psm17APR.html

Ottawa-Carleton Police Services Board. 2000, April 17. Meeting of the Ottawa-Carleton Police Services Board: Champlain Room, Ottawa City Hall.

OttawaVeloOutaouais. 2015. "Bike Tour of Graffiti Walls around Ottawa and Gatineau." *OttawaVeloOutaouais*. October 9. https://ottawaveloooutaouais.com /2015/10/09/bike-tour-of-graffiti-walls-around-ottawa-and-gatineau/

Ouseley, Mark. 2013. "Capital Brownfields: An Assessment of Brownfield Planning Policy in the City of Ottawa, Ontario." Master's Dissertation, University of Waterloo.

Overington, Michael. 2001. *Rhetorics and Sociology: Responsibility and Science*. Halifax: 42+1 Inc.

———. 1977. "Kenneth Burke and the Method of Dramatism." *Theory and Society* (4)1: 131–156.

Picton, Roger M. 2010. "Selling National Urban Renewal: The National Film Board, the National Capital Commission and Post-war Planning in Ottawa, Canada." *Urban History* 37(2): 301–321.

Prudham, Scott. 2004. "Poisoning the Well: Neoliberalism and the Contamination of Municipal Water in Walkerton, Ontario." *Geoforum; Journal of Physical, Human, and Regional Geosciences* 35(3): 343–59.

Rahn, Janis. 2002. *Painting Without Permission: Hip Hop Graffiti Subculture*. Westport: Bergin & Garvey.

Rosenfeld, Raymond A., and Laura A. Reese. 2003. "The Anatomy of an Amalgamation: The Case of Ottawa." *State and Local Government Review* 35(1): 57–69. Los Angeles: Sage Publications.

Skinner, Emily and Jeffrey R. Masuda. 2013. "Right to a Healthy City? Examining the Relationship between Urban Space and Health Inequity by Aboriginal Youth Artist-Activists in Winnipeg." *Social Science & Medicine* 91: 210–218.

Snider, Laureen. 2003. "Captured by Neo-liberalism: Regulation and Risk in Walkerton, Ontario." *Risk Management* 5(2): 27–36.

Snyder, Greg. 2009. *Graffiti Lives*. New York: New York University Press.

Soja, Edward W. 2010. *Seeking Spatial Justice*. Minneapolis: University of Minnesota Press.

Stern, Karen B. 2013. "Graffiti as Gift." In *Mortuary and Devotional Graffiti in the Late Ancient Levant*, edited by Michael L. Satlow, 137–157. Oxford: John Wiley & Sons.

Sylvestre, Marie-Eve, William Damon, Nicholas Blomley and Celine Bellot. 2015. "Spatial Tactics in Criminal Courts and the Politics of Legal Technicalities." *Antipode*, 47(5): 1346–1366.

Thames, Richard, H. 2015. "Unforgetting a Tradition: Kenneth Burke, Karl Marx and Aristotelian Naturalism." *Russian Journal of Communication* 7(1): 116–124.

Valverde, Mariana. 2011. "Seeing Like a City: The Dialectic of Modern and Premodern Ways of Seeing in Urban Governance." *Law & Society Review* 45(2): 277–312.

Vigar, Geoff, Stephen Graham and Patsy Healey. 2005. "In Search of the City in Spatial Strategies: Past Legacies, Future Imaginings." *Urban Studies* 42(8): 1391–1410.

Walks, R. Alan. 2006. "The Causes of City–Suburban Political Polarization? A Canadian Case Study." *Annals of the Association of American Geographers* 96(2): 390–414.

Wacławek, Anna. 2011. *Graffiti and Street Art*. London: Thames & Hudson.

Walby, Kevin and Chris Hurl. 2014. "Policing Urban Natures: Conservation Officer Work in Ottawa and Toronto, Canada." *International Journal of Urban and Regional Research* 38(4): 1476–90.

Walby, Kevin, and Randy Lippert. 2012. "Spatial Regulation, Dispersal, and the Aesthetics of the City: Conservation Officer Policing of Homeless People in Ottawa, Canada." *Antipode* 44(3): 1015–33.

Williamson, Thad. 2008. "Sprawl, Spatial Location, and Politics: How Ideological Identification Tracks the Built Environment." *American Politics Research* 36(6): 903–933.

Young, Allison. 2010. "Negotiated Consent or Zero Tolerance? Responding to Graffiti and Street Art in Melbourne." *City* 14(1 & 2): 99–114.

Young, Jock. 2003. "Merton with Energy, Katz with Structure: The Sociology of Vindictiveness and the Criminology of Transgression." *Theoretical Criminology* 7(3): 389–414.

Young, Jock. 2011. *The Criminological Imagination*. Cambridge: Polity Press.

Young, Leslie. 2017. "Who Are the 'Proud Boys' Who Protested an Indigenous Ceremony in Halifax?" Global News, May 5. http://globalnews.ca/news/3576666/who-are-the-proud-boys-who-disrupted-an-indigenous-ceremony-in-halifax

Part IV

LAW, WAR, AND MONSTROUS DISCOURSES

Chapter Ten

Human Trafficking, Empathy for Victims, the Tool of Eradication

DW Duke

The term *human trafficking* conjures a variety of images, ranging from drugged sex slaves standing on a stage while being auctioned to the highest bidder to women kept captive in a disease-infested brothel providing sex for ten to twelve hours in a day. For many Americans the only perspective of human trafficking derives from media portrayals as in the motion pictures *Taken* (2008) or *Trafficked* (2017). With images of girls drugged and sold into slavery by an elite subculture, the temptation is to dismiss these victims as persons in their proper place because of their promiscuous past or their poor social choices. Stereotyping and casting them aside with the subconscious conscience-pacifying antidote, *they are reaping what they have sown,* is perhaps society's way of ignoring this inconvenient crisis.

Today discussions of human trafficking typically focus on the twenty-first-century phenomenon with little or no consideration of the history of this condition. However, placing human trafficking in an appropriate historical perspective demonstrates that this is nothing more than ancient slavery juxtaposed against a modern society. Dismissing trafficking victims as monsters and dregs of society, allows us to ignore their plight. But what causes certain classes of citizens to acquire the moniker *monster*, the grotesque undesirables who deserve nothing more than subjugation to slavery? Understanding that human trafficking is repackaged ancient slavery in a modern context may help us overcome prejudices that cause us to look the other way, seeing those trapped in its clutches as freakish monsters who don't deserve our asylum or assistance.

As shown in this chapter's discussion of the *Dred Scott* case *Dred Scott v. Sanford,* 60 US 393 (1857), during the slave era, black persons were viewed as subhuman beings justifiably in their proper place as slaves. We have since learned that this racism was wrong and immoral.[1] Nevertheless, today we find another blind spot that allows society to dismiss trafficking victims the same way previous societies dismissed persons because of their race. That blind spot is to identify the victims of trafficking as immoral people suffering the fate caused by their poor choices and their wickedness. This blind spot serves as an obstruction that prohibits the development of empathy without which there is no understanding of the suffering and the need for change.

I had an opportunity to observe this phenomenon personally several years ago. The story involves an organization that works with the US Office of Refugee Resettlement. However, because of death threats and protests that have occurred the organization will remain anonymous for protection of its employees and will only be identified as ICA. At approximately 4:30 p.m. on Friday, June 27, 2014, a call came into ICA's office located in Temecula, California, an entity of which I serve as co-president. On the other end of the line was an officer from the Department of Homeland Security's (henceforth, DHS) enforcement division, who said, "We really need your assistance. We have looked far and wide and ICA keeps coming up as the organization best equipped to handle a massive influx of refugees from South America. We would like to transport them to the border patrol detention center in Murrieta, California, next week and then to your office so you can serve as the reception center. Will you help us get them to their final destinations? Many of them are victims of trafficking and some are escaping cartels. They have walked from El Salvador, Nicaragua and Honduras. They are almost all children well under the age of ten."

After conducting our own investigation to confirm that the information from DHS was correct, we spent the weekend preparing for a massive influx of refugees consisting of 140 every two days. Finally, on July 1, 2014, the first buses arrived, carrying 140 children to the Homeland Security detention center in Murrieta, California. After traveling 1,400 miles to the United States, many on foot, with many dying along the way, they believed they had finally found a community that would care for them. That is what they had been told by Homeland Security who had made the arrangements with ICA. Instead, when they arrived in Murrieta, they were met with angry violent protestors and news cameras. Some of these protestors were carrying Confederate flags and signs with rattlesnakes that said, "Don't Tread on Me" and "These Colors Don't Run." These little children, already traumatized by seeing people in their own community murdered by high power weapons wielded by the cartel, and many of whom had seen their own loved ones die as they made their way to the "Promised Land," now saw pick-up trucks with gun racks and high powered rifles parked at the side of the road. They saw signs saying, "Get out and go home." Many of the protestors pounded and spat on the windows of the bus. Though they could not speak English, hate is a universal language and curse words are understood in any language. Although the buses had to turn around and leave the detention center, DHS later brought the children to the ICA office at 4:00 a.m. in secrecy so the office could process them and send them on their way. Processing involved interviewing them and we learned that most had been sent by their parents or relatives to keep them from falling victim to human trafficking.

What struck me in observing this occurrence was the reality that these children, most of whom were under the age of six years, were seen by the media and the public as "them," the "undesirables," the people we don't want in the United States. Despite the knowledge that these traumatized children would be returned to their homeland where they would likely be trafficked, or worse, many Americans were willing to turn their backs on them. How could this happen? It happened because the children were viewed as monsters —foreigners who don't belong here. This image was fueled by the media who reported that the children might be carrying diseases such as scabies and tuberculosis, allegations of which were false.[2]

In this chapter, we will explore the thread of slavery through modern trafficking in our effort to identify some of the factors that historically allowed slavery to flourish. What mechanism allows certain members of society to acquiesce and even participate in this atrocity? What causes the "us versus them" mentality that allows society to view certain segments of the population as deviant monsters undeserving of even the most basic human rights. By looking at the roots of slavery and the conditions that allowed it to exist for centuries, as well as the efforts to abolish it, this chapter aspires to develop a clearer view of modern slavery and how we can successfully eradicate it.

Human trafficking, assuming a wide variety of forms, currently imprisons an estimated 21 million victims, according to the International Labor Organization,[3] and as many as 40 million by some researchers.[4] The same source states that 71 percent of slaves are women and children (Free the Slaves 2020) and that human trafficking generates $150 billion in revenue per year (Free the Slaves 2020).

A paramount question is, *why do we find such a disparity in the estimates of the number of victims of human trafficking?* Are methods of calculation really that distinct? The reason is that those trapped in its clutches are the unseen voiceless victims who, in the eyes of the world, do not exist. They lack connections and methods for making their imprisonment known to the outside world. Hence, it is difficult to identify and track these slaves which accounts for the wide range of estimates of the number of trafficking victims.

Trafficking assumes a variety of forms. Comprising one of best-known single categories is the female sex slave industry and, for this reason, this chapter focuses on female victims of sex slavery. Siddharth Kara, author of the book *Sex Trafficking: Inside the Business of Modern Slavery* (2009), spent decades researching sex trafficking in various parts of the world by traveling to distant locations and interviewing prostitutes and studying the culture. He notes that due to historic factors, modern trafficking has been facilitated most in four geographic regions—South Asia, East Asia, Central Europe and Eastern Europe (Kara 2009, 25). These historic demographics, namely extreme poverty, severe gender bias and acute minority disenfranchisement, often shape the nature of trafficking today and have been exacerbated by economic globalization (Kara 2009, 25). We find this phenomenon in Thailand where prostitution was legal from the fourteenth century until the mid-twentieth century.[5] Prior to the twentieth century Thailand encouraged prostitution and heavily taxed this industry (Boonchalaski and Guest 1994, 3). In 1996 Thailand passed the 1996 Prevention and Suppression of Prostitution Act B.E. 2539 (1996).[6] This act was a project of the National Policy and Plan of Action for the Prevention and Eradication of the Commercial Sexual Exploitation of Children. Eliminating the trafficking of children is a priority of the government of Thailand today with three primary objectives: (1) preventing children under the age of eighteen years from entering into commercial sex work, (2) prohibiting luring, threatening, exploiting and using violence in commercial sex the business, and (3) imposing severe penalties for those who participate in prostitution of minors and punishment for government officials who are negligent or who ignore their duties to compel compliance with statutes designed to eliminate child prostitution.[7]

According to Kara, at the high end of the sex industry in Thailand are women working in strip clubs designed for tourism in an area of Bangkok called Patpong (Kara 2009, 154–155). Most of the girls in this category are not coerced (Kara 2009, 155); more commonly, these girls are pressured by their parents to earn money to support the family (Kara 2009, 155). In Thai society the duty to care for parents falls to the youngest unmarried daughter and commercial sex is typically the most lucrative, and often the only way, to earn the money necessary for this task (Kara 2009, 155). Though they also engage in sex, it is generally conducted off premises (Kara 2009, 155). Competition is fierce for this high-end commercial sexual activity because many others are ready to replace them. The girl must achieve a certain level of income for the club owner or she will be replaced (Kara 2009, 155). The more celebrity a woman achieves, the less likely she will be forced into the lower forms of trafficking (Kara 2009, 156). Behind the high-end commercial sex industry in Thailand are the tens of thousands of women and children who are literal slaves in the underworld of Thailand's sex industry (Kara 2009, 156). These slaves serve as cheaply as $5 for two or three hours of sex; they are the victims of the truest form of modern slavery (Kara 2009, 156). In recent years, Thailand has begun to see a decline in the number of sex workers, not simply because of the passage of the 1996 Prevention and Suppression of Prostitution Act, but also because of increased enforcement efforts largely the result of international pressure.[8] Thailand is not unique as a nation where sex trafficking still flourishes, but it is one of the most widely known because of its tourist industry.

Sex slavery is only one form of human trafficking, though it is the most widely known. Forced manual labor, often coupled with physical and sexual abuse, is rampant in many parts of the world and comprises approximately 50 percent of slaves in the world today.[9] In some cultures, such as Cambodia, parents commonly sell their children to the highest bidder.[10] In my own work with international refugees and adoptions, I have encountered a number of situations where women would willfully became pregnant to give birth to children they could sell. This differs from surrogate parenting in that with surrogate parenting, the new parents are already known to the mother and one of them usually has a biological connection to the child. In contrast, simply selling the child typically results in the child going to a complete stranger who may have sinister interests.

Another form of human trafficking is child soldiering. In this form of slavery, children are conscripted into the military at a very young age and are forced to engage in military activities against opposition forces. According to Child Soldiers International, forty-six countries still recruit and train children under the age of eighteen to serve in combat.[11] Surprisingly, even Britain is among the nations that allow recruits as young as sixteen years of age.[12]

Illegal adoptions also account for a significant number of trafficking cases. This form of trafficking often provides a segue into the other forms of trafficking mentioned above. Sometimes the unlawful adoption is accomplished by falsified documents claiming a parental relationship to the child. Sometimes it is accomplished by identifying an abandoned child and simply purchasing that child from those in control of the child such as an orphanage. China has been particularly problematic because of government participation in seizing children then placing them for adoption.[13] Thus, the Hague Convention on the Protection of Children and Co-operation in Respect of Intercountry Adoption was a multinational effort to eradicate illegal intercountry adoptions that concluded in 1993. The Convention places strict guidelines on the manner in which intercountry adoptions are conducted in an effort to protect the children. The United States signed the Convention in 1994 but it did not go into effect in the United States until 2008.[14] Additionally, child marriage is now considered a form of human trafficking. Most prevalent in nations where child marriages are a religious or social tradition, the International Labour Organization estimates that 15 million children are trapped in child marriages today.[15]

THE DEVELOPMENT OF ANTI-SLAVERY LEGISLATION IN BRITAIN

The previous section addressed modern slavery commonly known as human trafficking and examined some forms of operation. This section notes how society has historically attempted to eliminate slavery and hopefully gains insight into ways of fighting trafficking today. This section also considers the ethnocentrism that allows various societies to ignore slavery by seeing their victims as monsters who are receiving their just rewards.

The fifteenth century marked the beginning of the European slave trade in Africa with the Portuguese transporting Africans to Portugal and selling them as slaves.[16] In 1562, the British joined the slave trade in Africa.[17] The development of plantation colonies increased the volume of the slave trade.[18]

In the late 1700s, a moral outcry against slavery began to surface in Europe. Britain, who had been the European leader in the slave trade, became the primary area of focus to end slavery. In 1772 the landmark case, *Somerset v. Stewart* (1772) 98 ER 499, was heard in the Court of King's Bench by Lord Mansfield (William Murray, First Earl of Mansfield) who found that slavery was unsupported in common law in England and Wales (*Somerset v. Stewart*, 510). And since there were no statutes authorizing slavery, Lord Mansfield concluded that there existed no legal support for slavery in England and Wales (*Somerset v. Stewart*, 510).

In Somerset, a slave owner named Charles Stewart had purchased an African slave named George Somerset in the colonies (*Somerset v. Stewart*, 499). Stewart returned to England in 1769 bringing Somerset with him (*Somerset v. Stewart*, 499). Somerset escaped in 1771 but was recaptured in November of that year and imprisoned on a ship called *Ann and Mary* bound for Jamaica (*Somerset v. Stewart*, 499). On June 22, 1772, in response to a writ of habeas corpus, Lord Mansfield delivered his opinion that in the absence of legal support for slavery in either common law or in statutes, Somerset had to be released and could not be forcibly removed to another country (*Somerset v. Stewart*, 510). The Somerset case resounded throughout Europe as the first judicial decision to strike a serious blow to the slave trade. It became a symbolic torch for the Abolitionists who, for the first time, began to sense support for their position in the judiciary.[19]

In 1781 a significant event caused outrage resulting in another case that struck a blow against slavery. A British slave ship called the *Zong*, while transporting slaves, began experiencing slave deaths due to illness, in part caused by an insufficient supply of water on the ship. To keep the sickness from spreading to other slaves in passage the captain ordered 133 men and women, who had become ill, to be thrown overboard resulting in their drowning.[20] Under British law at the time, if the deaths resulted from efforts to save the lives of the crew, then insurance could be compelled to pay the loss but if the deaths resulted naturally or by illness, then insurance could not be compelled to pay. In *Gregson v. Gilbert* (1783) 3 Doug KB 232, also heard by Lord Mansfield, the court determined that the deaths were not necessitated to save the crew and for that reason, there was no coverage under the policy of insurance issued to the ship (*Gregson v. Gilbert*, 234). The court determined that the cause of the illness was an insufficient supply of water which was the fault of the captain who had not only failed to load an adequate water supply but could have stopped at numerous ports to obtain water along the way (*Gregson v. Gilbert*, 233-234).

With these two decisions Lord Mansfield likely accomplished more to end the European slave trade than any act by any other single person. His opinions demonstrated something not commonly seen in Europe at that time, that is, they demonstrated empathy and compassion toward Africans. What caused Lord Mansfield to develop empathy toward a people who were hated and despised by others in his culture? What was the mechanism that triggered empathy which in turn spread through the nation like a breath of fresh air? At a time when Africans were considered subhuman, why did Lord Mansfield see them differently?

Perhaps the trigger of empathy was caused by an event in Lord Mansfield's personal life an account of which is provided in *Belle: The True Story of Dido Belle; The Slave Daughter and the Lord Chief Justice* (Byrne 2001). In Byrne's account Lord Mansfield had a nephew named Sir John Lindsay, a ship captain (Byrne 2001, 15–16). In 1761, while in the West Indies, Lindsay became involved with an African slave woman named Maria Belle who bore him a child, named Dido Elizabeth Belle (Byrne 2001, 22). The record is unclear what became of Maria but given that Captain Lindsay appeared in England without her presence (Byrne 2001, 85–88), it is possible she had passed away during childbirth or shortly thereafter. Since Lindsay could not raise Dido on a ship, he took her to Lord Mansfield, his great uncle, to raise her (Byrne 2001, 85–88). Lord Mansfield, and his wife, Lady Mansfield, took Dido into their home where she was raised as a member of the family (Byrne 2001, 88, 97). They were also raising another white niece from another nephew who was the same age as Dido though it is unknown which of the girls was taken in first (Byrne 2001, 85–89).

Dido bonded with her aunt and uncle and they grew to love her as much as their other niece and both nieces were frequently doted on by Lord Mansfield (Byrne 2001, 96). Was it the relationship with Dido, his niece, that ultimately allowed Lord Mansfield to overcome prejudice against Africans? Was it his emotional attachment to her and his observation of her emotional attachments to others combined with her superior cognitive abilities that allowed him to overcome his prejudice and to see Africans as human beings and not as sub-human creatures? Was this the result of empathy that he had developed? If so, in like manner, can people today overcome prejudices against trafficking victims and become empathetic to their plight?

The Society for Effecting the Abolition of Slavery was formed in England in May 22, 1787, as the culmination of years of work by abolitionists consisting largely of Quakers.[21] After a century of efforts by British citizens to end slavery, one of the first efforts by Parliament to legally abolish slavery was the British Parliament Slave Trade Act of 1807.[22] The Act proved ineffective because, while it prohibited individuals from participating in the slave trade, it did not outlaw slavery. Those who already owned slaves could keep them. Nonetheless, even though the Act was ineffective in ending slavery, it was important in swaying public opinion concerning its evils.[23] Finally, in 1833, Britain passed the Slavery Abolition Act of 1833, which officially ended slavery in Britain.[24] The Act provided for compensation to slave owners in exchange for the release of their slaves (ISB 2020). Inasmuch as Britain had been a leader in the slave trade, the abolition of slavery impacted the slave trade throughout all of Europe. Were these efforts to eliminate slavery in England fueled by the decisions of Lord Mansfield discussed above? Perhaps the empathy he exhibited as expressed in his opinions became the standard of thought throughout England and eventually Europe and beyond.

THE ABOLITION OF SLAVERY IN AMERICA

After the abolition of slavery in Britain, slavery continued to thrive in the United States. The US Supreme Court rendered the infamous *Dred Scott v. Sanford,* 60 US 393 (1857) decision which held that African Americans were not citizens within the meaning of the Constitution; and further, lacked standing to sue for redress of grievances (*Scott v. Sanford*, 407–410). This also meant that an African American lacked standing to sue to prove that he is free person of color (*Scott v. Sanford,* 407–410). In its ruling the US Supreme Court demonstrated a lack of empathy for African people who were seen by the court as less than human. The text of the *Dred Scott* decision reveals with shocking clarity the monster moniker of the slave which prevented empathy for the victim of slavery. The views expressed by the majority of the court embodied the view of slaves that had persisted in America since the establishment of the colonies.

Dred Scott, the plaintiff in the case, was a slave owned by John Emerson who resided in Missouri (*Scott v. Sanford 60 US 393,* 457). In 1843 Emerson took Scott to Louisiana where slavery had been abolished by the Missouri Compromise of 1820 (*Scott v. Sanford*, 457). Eventually, Emerson returned to Missouri bringing Scott with him (*Scott v. Sanford*, 458). Scott sued for his freedom in the court in Missouri asserting that, having lived in a free state, he had acquired his freedom. A Missouri state court ruled that Scott was a free man, but the Missouri Supreme Court reversed that opinion in 1853 (*Scott v. Sanford*, 458). Emerson passed away and his widow sold Scott to Sanford. Scott's attorneys filed suit in federal court again asserting his freedom and ultimately the matter was heard by the US Supreme Court which upheld the federal district court's ruling in favor of Sanford and against Scott (*Scott v. Sanford*, 407).

Subsequent to the Supreme Court's ruling in *Scott v. Sanford*, the United States became embroiled in the Civil War with the issue of slavery central to that conflict. Behind the opinion of the Republicans and the Abolitionists was a view that Africans were human beings entitled to constitutional protections who could not be subjected to slavery. The Emancipation Proclamation was Abraham Lincoln's response to the Dred Scott case. The theme that had been expressed throughout Lincoln's presidency was stated in the opening phrase of his Gettysburg Address:

> Four score and seven years ago our fathers brought forth on this continent a new nation conceived in liberty and dedicated to the proposition that *all men are created equal* . . . [emphasis added].[25]

This statement by Lincoln was in direct conflict with the holding of the US Supreme Court in *Scott v. Sanford* and embodies what was lacking in the creation of US slavery laws, namely that Africans were human beings entitled to the benefits and rights of other human beings. This statement by Lincoln demonstrated empathy, which was lacking in the *Dred Scott* decision. Ultimately, the 13th Amendment to the US Constitution was adopted and ratified finally prohibiting slavery in America (US Const. amend. XIII).

HUMAN TRAFFICKING IN TWENTIETH-CENTURY EUROPE

Previously, we looked at specific causes and symptoms of human trafficking before we examined the history of slavery to identify factors that may have contributed to a change in society's attitude toward slavery. We hypothesized that the change in society's attitude toward slavery may have been triggered by the development of empathy as demonstrated in the conduct of two proponents of abolition, Lord Mansfield and President Abraham Lincoln. Now we are going to consider the rise of human rights abuse and slavery in Europe during the twentieth century to ascertain whether there was a lack of empathy and compassion toward victims of slavery, in society as a whole, which may have allowed slavery to flourish.

In the twentieth century in Europe, we again note a lack empathy resulting in slavery and genocide. Several years ago, I interviewed a Holocaust Survivor/Resistance Fighter named Casimir Biebers for a project on which I was working at the time. During the numerous interviews, Biebers made the statement that compassion was seen as weakness in the Nazi regime. Students were taught that showing compassion for victims of the Holocaust was not only a weakness but was disloyal to the Fuhrer. His comments reminded me of hearing the same words years earlier while working in Russia. I often heard that compassion in the Soviet Empire was undesirable and even punishable. These words caused me to ponder, is compassion and the lack of empathy another face of hatred? Is this the root cause of human rights abuses? At what point does lack of empathy assume the form of hate?

After WWII the international community began to accept the view that all nations have a responsibility to assure that certain minimum human rights are in place everywhere. In 1948 the General Assembly of the United Nations adopted the Universal Declaration of Human Rights.[26] Article 2 provides that the Declaration of Human Rights applies to all persons regardless of race, color, creed, religion, political affiliation, national origin, property, birth or other status (UN 1948). Article 3 provides that every person is entitled to life, liberty and security of person (UN 1948). Article 4 prohibits slavery in any form (UN 1948). The Universal Declaration of Human Rights is technically not a treaty and, thus, is not binding on nations. Nonetheless, it is often cited as authority in war crimes tribunals and other hearings involving human rights including human trafficking. It has been translated into five hundred different languages.[27]

In recent years there have been numerous provisions at the international, national and state levels designed specifically to address modern human trafficking. For example, in 2000 the United Nations General Assembly adopted the Protocol to Prevent, Suppress and Punish Trafficking in Persons Especially Women and Children.[28] This Protocol requires State members to enact laws to protect victims of human trafficking and to punish persons who engage in human trafficking (United Nations 2000). So, while it does not itself provide for punishment, it requires member nations to do so (United Nations 2000). A majority of countries have signed and ratified this Protocol.[29] Were these laws a direct result of overcoming racism and stereotypes on a global scale, which allowed society to become empathetic toward those who were victims of human rights violations and trafficking?

HUMAN TRAFFICKING IN THE MODERN WORLD

Despite extensive global efforts to eliminate human trafficking, this evil remains at an all-time high in every region of the world with sex trafficking among the highest categories. One reason for this is the high demand for sex-related activities. The internet is saturated with sexually explicit communications which creates an increased demand for sex. In his book, *Sex and the Internet: A Guide Book for Clinicians*, Al Cooper (Cooper 2002) identifies three broad categories of commercial aspects, positive connections and negative patterns of sex on the internet (Cooper 2002, 7–9). The commercial aspects present the most easily recognized cause of proliferation of sexually explicit material (Cooper 2002, 7–8). In reality, less than 1 percent of the people who visit sexually explicit sites actually spend money on them (Cooper 2002, 1). Nonetheless, the internet has become a pathway to marketing romance, sexual relationships and sex products (Cooper 2002, 8). Cooper identifies a positive impact this has in the form of social networking on various sex-related topics such as pregnancy, abortion, sexually transmitted illnesses, rape and other topics that many would be embarrassed to discuss without the anonymity of the internet (Cooper 2002, 8–9). Nevertheless, Cooper also recognizes the negative potential of the internet in fostering sexual dysfunction, relationship disharmony, sex addition and compulsive sexual aggression. Without question the full impact of the internet on sexual and social behavior is yet to be understood but it clearly fosters an appetite for sex which can translate into sexually deviant behavior (Cooper 2002, 9).

The impact of the internet on human trafficking has been explored at length by Opal Singleton, CEO of Million Kids, and author of *Seduced, The Grooming of American Teenagers* (Singleton 2015). Million Kids is a non-profit organization devoted to fighting human trafficking by educating professionals, parents and teenagers about the dangers that lead to trafficking situations. Under Opal Singleton's direction they have provided education to over 250,000 professionals ranging from law enforcement, judges, attorneys, medical personnel, social workers and others in situations where human trafficking may be encountered.[30] Singleton opines that sex on the internet serves as a gateway to human trafficking.[31] She identifies the "dark web" as an obscure place where traffickers identify and solicit their victims often through feigned romantic interest or a promise of money and fame.[32] In the feigned romantic relationship, the trafficker pretends to have a romantic connection to his victim, frequently a minor. He then arranges a meeting and eventually persuades her to engage in acts of prostitution or other forms of trafficking. So subtle are their efforts that often the victim is unaware she is being trafficked until she attempts to leave the relationship (Singleton 2015, 139–162). Having taught over 250,000 educators, law enforcement officers, judges and others, Singleton has identified the common methodology of traffickers who utilize the internet. She also identifies clues to parents that their child may be delving into the "dark web" where they can fall prey to the abuses of traffickers.[33]

Human trafficking remains one the worst forms of human abuse today. With rampant and massive worldwide exploitation, efforts to eliminate this condition require education, legislation and enforcement. Education is required to inform potential victims of the risk they face and to inform parents and others of signs for which to watch as their loved ones and acquaintances meander into this arena. Education is also important to teach society that victims of trafficking are real people with emotions who suffer and feel pain like the rest of us. This is the key to developing empathy for the victim of slavery. Legislation prohibiting any form of slavery, with teeth for effective prosecution, is required to provide the tools law enforcement needs to fight this epidemic. The willingness of law enforcement officers and judges to prosecute slave traffickers is paramount to discouraging the industry. This requires cooperation between nations and between agencies within nations. With willingness and effort, trafficking can be eradicated. Perhaps in time, we will see a world truly free of slavery.

CONCLUSION

This chapter has explored human trafficking as an etiology of ethnocentrism that allows victims to be viewed as monsters, immoral subhuman beings deserving of their fate. The chapter discussed the manner in which victims are perceived not only by a society that often refuses to offer asylum but also by traffickers who exhibit no empathy. The chapter attempted to place trafficking in a historical context to demonstrate that it is a new form of age-old slavery. The goal was to show that society and the slave traders once justified their actions on the premise that black persons were subhuman beings who deserved the fate they were receiving. We saw that this premise has been disproven historically. In the same fashion, the stereotypes about modern victims of slavery as immoral people who "deserve their fate" should be seen as a monster image based on a subconscious ethnocentrism that views a world of "us versus them." To the monster trapped in this jaded prism, the situation seems hopeless which increases their vulnerability to victimhood.

Overcoming stereotypes and prejudices about people who are today trapped in human trafficking is paramount to overcoming human trafficking. One of the single most important ways to overcome the monster image is to teach society to be empathetic toward human trafficking victims. This education begins in school with programs that discuss the experiences of trafficking victims. Perhaps a required high school course should be on the topic of human trafficking with accounts of the lives of the victims. This program would serve a multi-tiered purpose. First, it would teach high school students about the perils and the horrors of human trafficking. Second, it would teach high school students that the victims of human trafficking are real people who suffer real pain and emotions just like the rest of society. Third, this program would teach students how to avoid falling victim to human traffickers and what to do if one finds herself in a situation of being solicited for trafficking purposes.

As second important aspect of education is to teach adults, ranging from parents to law enforcement officials, medical care providers, educators and social workers about the perils of human trafficking. Again, this education would need to be coupled with information to help the recipient to become empathetic to victims of human trafficking. The importance would be to demonstrate that the trafficking victim is a human being with the ability to feel pain and emotions. This is critical to allowing the student to become empathetic to the plight of the victim which is critical to eradicating trafficking.

Lastly, one of the most effective ways of disseminating information about any social problem is the entertainment media. The entertainment industry has led the fight in many areas of social injustice such as racial and ethnic discrimination to toxic pollution. For example, the movie *Erin Brockovich* (*Erin Brockovich*, 2000) brought the public's attention to toxic dumping which was allegedly contributing to cancer upon the local citizens. The entertainment media is a powerful tool for shaping public opinion. Human trafficking is another area where the entertainment industry could use its resources to educate the public about the perils and evils of this industry. Perhaps, even more importantly, this medium can be used to teach empathy for victims of trafficking by telling the story of victims either in documentaries or in dramatizations.

Overcoming the monster moniker which perpetuates itself through increased discrimination and lack of empathy is critical to encouraging government officials to take measures with legislation and enforcement of anti-trafficking laws. In the same way that traditional slavery was technically abolished when society became empathetic to the victims of slavery, members of society can be encouraged to understand the suffering of victims of trafficking and thereby become empathetic to their plight, particularly against the insight that contemporary human trafficking is simply slavery for this age. This in turn could result in more legislation and more effective enforcement efforts, as well as the diminishment of incentive for customers of trafficked victims to hire victims for trafficked activities.

NOTES

1. See *Strauder v. West Virginia* 100 US 303 (1880)—held West Virginia prohibiting blacks on juries unconstitutional; *Yick Wo v. Hopkins* 118 U.S. 356 (1886)—held law prohibiting Chinese from holding laundry license unconstitutional; see also, *Hernandez v. Texas* 347 U.S. 475 (1954)—prohibiting discrimination against Mexican Americans in jury service; *Civil Rights Act*, 42 USCS § 2000e (1964)—prohibited discrimination on the basis of race, color, religion, sex and national origin.

2. See Medina, Jennifer, "The Town where Immigrants hit a Human Wall," *The New York Times*, July 3, 2014, https://www.nytimes.com/2014/07/04/us/influx-of-central-american-migrants-roils-murrieta-calif.html; see also, Martinez, Michael, Yan, Holly, "Showdown: California Town Turns Away Buses of Detained Immigrants," CNN, July 3, 2014, https://www.cnn.com/2014/07/02/us/california-immigrant-transfers/index.html.

3. See ILO, *21 Million People Are now Victims of Forced Labour*, International Labour Organization, June 1, 2012, https://www.ilo.org/global/about-the-ilo/newsroom/news/WCMS_181961/lang--en/index.htm.

4. See Free the Slaves, "Slavery Is Everywhere," 2020, https://www.freetheslaves.net/our-model-for-freedom/slavery-today/.

5. See Boonchalaski, Wathinee and Philip Guest, *Prostitution in Thailand, A Report Prepared for the Research Project, The Sex Sector: Prostitution and Development in Southeast Asia*, Salaya, Thailand, Mohidol University, 2–5.

6. See ILO, 1996 Prevention and Suppression of Prostitution Act B.E. 2539, October 14, 1996.

7. See UNICRI, 2005. *Trafficking in Minors for Commercial Sexual Exploitation*, p. 22, http://www.unicri.it/topics/trafficking_exploitation/archive/minors/countries_partners/dr_thailand.pdf.

8. See O'Connor, Joseph and Son Nguyen 2018, "Record year for Thai tourism but not so good for Thailand's bar girls and luxury hotels as market has changed," *Thai Examiner.com*, December 29, 2018, https://www.thaiexaminer.com/thai-news-foreigners/2018/12/29/thailand-sex-industry-thai-tourism-new-tourist-prostitution/.

9. See Free the Slaves, "Slavery is Everywhere," 2020, https://www.freetheslaves.net/our-model-for-freedom/slavery-today/#section_top.

10. See Hume, Tim, et al., "The Women Who Sold their Daughters into Sex Slavery," CNN, 2013. See also, Backhaus, Anne, "Daughters for Sale: India's Child Slavery Scourge," *ABC News*, October 12, 2013, https://abcnews.go.com/International/daughters-sale-indias-child-slavery-scourge/story?id=20540368.

11. See Child Soldiers International, 2020. *Child Soldiers World Index*, childsoldiersworldindex.org.

12. See Bartlet, Michael, "Britain's Child Soldiers," *The Guardian*, March 11, 2011, https://www.theguardian.com/commentisfree/2011/mar/11/britain-child-soldiers-army.

13. See Leland, John, "For Adoptive Parents, Questions without Answers," *The New York Times*, September 16, 2011, https://www.nytimes.com/2011/09/18/nyregion/chinas-adoption-scandal-sends-chills-through-families-in-united-states.html.

14. See US Department of State, "Intercountry Adoptions," https://travel.state.gov/content/travel/en/Intercountry-Adoption/Adoption-Process/understanding-the-hague-convention.html. HCCH, *33: Convention of 29 May 1993 on Protection of Children and Co-operation in Respect of Intercountry Adoption,* May 29, 1993.

15. See ILO, *Global Estimates of Modern Slavery,* 2017, https://www.ilo.org/global/publications/books/WCMS_575479/lang--en/index.htm.

16. See Wolf, Kenneth B., 1994, The 'Moors' of West Africa and the beginnings of the Portuguese slave trade, *Journal of Medieval and Renaissance Studies* 24, no. 3: 457–59.

17. See National Archives, *Britain in the Slave Trade*, http://www.nationalarchives.gov.uk/slavery/pdf/britain-and-the-trade.pdf.

18. See National Geographic, 2019, *The Plantation System,* https://www.nationalgeographic.org/encyclopedia/plantation-system/.

19. See Hinks, Peter P., John R. McKivigan and R. Owen Williams, *Encyclopedia of Antislavery and Abolition*, Greenwood Publishing Group, 2007, 643.

20. See Walvin, James, *The Zong: A Massacre, the Law and the End of Slavery,* New Haven, CT, Yale University Press, 2011, 1–4.

21. See Sparticus Educational, *Society for the Abolition of the Slave Trade*, https://spartacus-educational.com/REantislavery.htm.

22. See Parliament.UK, "Parliament and the British Slave Trade, 1600–1833," https://www.parliament.uk/about/living-heritage/transformingsociety/tradeindustry/slavetrade/overview/parliament-abolishes-the-slave-trade/.

23. See The Abolition Project, "The 1897 Act and its Effects," 2009, http://abolition.e2bn.org/slavery_113.html.

24. See ISB, "Slavery Abolition Act of 1833," http://www.irishstatutebook.ie/eli/1833/act/73/enacted/en/html.

25. See Lincoln, Abraham, 1809–1865. *The Gettysburg Address and Other Speeches,* New York: Penguin Books, 1995, 1.

26. See United Nations, 1948, *Universal Declaration of Human Rights,* https://www.un.org/en/universal-declaration-human-rights/.

27. See United Nations (1948), *Universal Declaration of Human Rights*, https://www.un.org/en/universal-declaration-human-rights/.

28. See United Nations, *Protocol to Prevent, Suppress and Punish Trafficking in Persons Especially Women and Children*, November 15, 2000, https://www.ohchr.org/EN/ProfessionalInterest/Pages/ProtocolTraffickingInPersons.aspx.

29. See United Nations, *Signatories to the CTOC Trafficking Protocol*, Treaties.un.org.

30. See Million Kids, "Keeping Kids Safe from Predators," www.millionkids.org.

31. See Singleton, Opal, *Seduced*, Exulon Press, 2015, 47–74.

32. See Singleton, Opal, "Exploited, Crimes against Humanity," *Voice America*, https://www.voiceamerica.com/show/2560/exploited-crimes-against-humanity.

33. See Singleton, Opal, "Exploited, Crimes against Humanity," *Voice America*, https://www.voiceamerica.com/show/2560/exploited-crimes-against-humanity.

REFERENCES

Backhaus, Anne. 2013. "Daughters for Sale: India's Child Slavery Scourge." *ABC News*, October 12. Accessed January 11, 2020. https://abcnews.go.com/International/daughters-sale-indias-child-slavery-scourge/story?id=20540368.

Bartlet, Michael. 2011. "Britain's Child Soldiers." *The Guardian*, March 11. Accessed January 11, 2020. https://www.theguardian.com/commentisfree/2011/mar/11/britain-child-soldiers-army.

Boonchalaski, Wathinee, and Philip Guest. 1994. *Prostitution in Thailand, A Report Prepared for the Research Project, The Sex Sector: Prostitution and Development in Southeast Asia*, Salaya, Thailand, Mohidol University.

Byrne, Paula. 2001. *Belle: The True Story of Dido Belle, The Slave Daughter and the Lord Chief Justice*. New York, NY: Harper/Perennial.

Child Soldiers International. 2020. *Child Soldiers World Index*. Accessed January 11. childsoldiersworldindex.org.

Civil Rights Act, 42 USCS § 2000e (1964).

Cooper, Al. 2002. *Sex and the Internet: A Guide Book for Clinicians*. New York, NY: Brunner-Routledge.

Dred Scott v. Sanford, 60 US 393 (1857).

Erin Brockovich. 2000. Directed by Steven Soderbergh. March 17, Universal Pictures, Columbia Pictures, Jersey Pictures, film.

Free the Slaves. "Slavery Is Everywhere." Accessed January 13, 2020. https://www.freetheslaves.net/our-model-for-freedom/slavery-today/.

———. 2018. "Trafficking and Slavery Fact Sheet," April. Accessed December 4, 2019. https://www.freetheslaves.net/wp-content/uploads/2018/04/Trafficking-ans-Slavery-Fact-Sheet-April-2018.pdf.

Gregson v. Gilbert (1783) 3 Doug KB 232.

HCCH, 33: *Convention of 29 May 1993 on Protection of Children and Co-operation in Respect of Intercountry Adoption*, May 29, 1993.

Hinks, Peter P., John R. McKivigan and R. Owen Williams. 2007. *Encyclopedia of Antislavery and Abolition*. Westport, CT: Greenwood Publishing Group.

Hernandez v. Texas 347 U.S. 475 (1954).

Hume, Tim, Lisa Cohen and Mira Sorvino. 2013. "The Women Who Sold their Daughters into Sex Slavery." CNN. Accessed January 11, 2020. http://www.cnn.com/interactive/2013/12/world/cambodia-child-sex-trade/.

ILO. 2012. "21 Million People are now Victims of Forced Labour." *International Labour Organization*, June 1. Accessed January 8, 2020. https://www.ilo.org/global/about-the-ilo/newsroom/news/WCMS_181961/lang--en/index.htm.

———. 2017. *Global Estimates of Modern Slavery*. Accessed January 11, 2020: https://www.ilo.org/global/publications/books/WCMS_575479/lang--en/index.htm.

———. 1996. "Thailand: Prevention and Suppression of Prostitution Act, B.E. 2539 (Unofficial translation)." *NATLEX, UN International Labor Organization*, October 14. Accessed January 10, 2020. http://www.ilo.org/dyn/natlex/docs/WEBTEXT/46403/65063/E96THA01.htm.

ISB. "Slavery Abolition Act of 1833." *Irish Statute Book*. Accessed January 12, 2020. http://www.irishstatutebook.ie/eli/1833/act/73/enacted/en/html.

Kara, Siddharth. 2009. *Sex Trafficking: Inside the Business of Modern Slavery*. New York, NY: Columbia University Press.

Leland, John. 2011. "For Adoptive Parents, Questions without Answers." *The New York Times*, September 16. Accessed January 11, 2020. https://www.nytimes.com/2011/09/18/nyregion/chinas-adoption-scandal-sends-chills-through-families-in-united-states.html.

Lincoln, Abraham. 1995. *The Gettysburg Address and Other Speeches*. New York: Penguin Books.

Martinez, Michael, and Holly Yan. 2014. "Showdown: California Town Turns Away Buses of Detained Immigrants." CNN, July 3. Accessed January 5, 2020. https://www.cnn.com/2014/07/02/us/california-immigrant-transfers/index.html.

Medina, Jennifer. 2014. "The Town where Immigrants hit a Human Wall." *The New York Times*, July 3. Accessed January 5, 2020. https://www.nytimes.com/2014/07/04/us/influx-of-central-american-migrants-roils-murrieta-calif.html.

Million Kids. "Keeping Kids Safe from Predators." Millionkids.org. Accessed January 12, 2020. www.millionkids.org.

National Archives. n.d. *Britain in the Slave Trade*. Accessed January 11, 2020. http://www.nationalarchives.gov.uk/slavery/pdf/britain-and-the-trade.pdf.

National Geographic. 2019. "The Plantation System," June 20. Accessed January 11, 2020. https://www.nationalgeographic.org/encyclopedia/plantation-system/.

O'Connor, Joseph and Son Nguyen. 2018. "Record year for Thai tourism but not so good for Thailand's bar girls and luxury hotels as market has changed." *Thai Examiner*, December 29. Accessed January 11, 2020. https://www.thaiexaminer.com/thai-news-foreigners/2018/12/29/thailand-sex-industry-thai-tourism-new-tourist-prostitution/.

Parliament.UK. n.d. "Parliament and the British Slave Trade, 1600–1833." Accessed January 12, 2020. https://www.parliament.uk/about/living-heritage/transformingsociety/tradeindustry/slavetrade/overview/parliament-abolishes-the-slave-trade/.

Singleton, Opal. n.d. "Exploited, Crimes against Humanity." *Voice America*. Accessed January 12, 2020. https://www.voiceamerica.com/show/2560/exploited-crimes-against-humanity.

———. 2015. *Seduced, The Grooming of American Teenagers*: Xulon Press.

Somerset v. Stewart (1772) 98 ER 499.

Sparticus Educational. "Society for the Abolition of the Slave Trade." Accessed January 12, 2020. https://spartacus-educational.com/REantislavery.htm.

Strauder v. West Virginia 100 US 303 (1880).

Taken. 2008. Directed by Pierre Morel. Paris, France: 20th Century Fox, Film.

The Abolition Project. 2009. "The 1897 Act and its Effects." Accessed January 12, 2020. http://abolition.e2bn.org/slavery_113.html.

Trafficked. 2017. Directed by Will Wallace. Los Angeles, California: KK Ranch Productions, Film.

UNICRI. 2005. *Trafficking in Minors for Commercial Sexual Exploitation*, page 22. Accessed January 12, 2020. http://www.unicri.it/topics/trafficking_exploitation/archive/minors/countries_partners/dr_thailand.pdf.

United Nations. n.d. *Signatories to the CTOC Trafficking Protocol*. Accessed January 12, 2020. https://treaties.un.org/Pages/ViewDetails.aspx?src=TREATY&mtdsg_no=XVIII-12-a&chapter=18&lang=en.

———. 1948. *Universal Declaration of Human Rights*. Accessed January 12, 2020. https://www.un.org/en/universal-declaration-human-rights/.

———. 2000. *Protocol to Prevent, Suppress and Punish Trafficking in Persons Especially Women and Children*, November 15, 2000, https://www.ohchr .org/EN/ProfessionalInterest/Pages/ProtocolTraffickingInPersons.aspx.

US Constitution Amendment XIII.

US Department of State. n.d. "Intercountry Adoptions: Understanding the Hague Convention." Accessed January 11, 2020. https://travel.state.gov/content/travel/en/Intercountry-Adoption/Adoption-Process/understanding-the-hague-convention.html.

Walvin, James. 2011. *The Zong: A Massacre, the Law and the End of Slavery*. New Haven, CT: Yale University Press.

Wolf, Kenneth B. 1994. "The 'Moors' of West Africa and the beginnings of the Portuguese slave trade." *Journal of Medieval and Renaissance Studies* 24, no. 3: 457–59.

Yick Wo v. Hopkins 118 U.S. 356 (1886).

Chapter Eleven

Visualizing Monsters and Just Wars in Legal and Public Analyses of Eastwood's *American Sniper*

Marouf Hasian Jr.

Friedrich Nietzsche, who has influenced so many critical cultural critics and others, once observed: "He who fights with monsters might take care lest he [*sic*] thereby becomes a monster. And when you gaze long into an abyss the abyss also gazes into you."[1] Can counter-terrorists avoid becoming monsters?

For those who are interested in the nexus that exists between the movie *American Sniper* (2014) and traditional formalistic analysis, there a variety of topics that readers might be interested in. They could use the case of *Ventura v. Kyle* to study the elements of defamation cases,[2] or it could be used to study how gun rentals needed to be regulated.[3] Perhaps it would be used to amend the ways that we think about the jurisprudential application of death penalties in situations where veterans might be suffering from PTSD.[4] These are weighty issues, that will involve the parsing of the words that are circulated in many hearings and courts, but in this chapter I am more interested in how these topics are assembled together in ideological formations that use stories of snipers and their trials and tribulations in more "critical," ideological oriented ways. In other words, I am interested in investigating how viewers of *American Sniper* co-produce legal and public rhetorics that are strategically used to tell us something about the societal "monsters" (especially "fundamentalist" or "Islamic") that Western neoliberals fight during their "just wars."

Since the beginning of what many Anglo-Americans call the Global War on Terrorism (GWOT), there have been a growing number of scholars who have identified themselves as members of Critical Securities Studies (CSS) movements, where researchers are drawn to the ideas of Bruno Latour, Michel Foucault, Paul Virilio, and others who care about power, knowledge, discourse, and various securitized rhetorics. Bothered by the normalization of what they perceive to be excessively powerful national and international security states, CSS investigators study many of the taken-for-granted, quotidian activities that are used to maintain the hegemonic power of those who profit from war machines, militainment, and the artifice that is used to convince populations that they profit from fighting "perpetual wars." Antoine Bosquet, for example, extended the path-breaking work of Paul Virilio,[5] and in 2017 he wrote about tracking, aiming, and technological lasers that can be used to create "logics of perception" that guide both visual gazes and actual weaponry.[6]

This chapter extends the work of CSS scholars in order to study a different, but related logic of perception—one that involves the usage of both material and symbolic treatments of military sniping overseas as a way of commenting on broader issues. More specifically, as I explain in more detail below, stories told about the prowess of American snipers—especially during the Operation Iraqi Freedom (OIF) years (2003–2011)—have been used in the formation of particular monsters that have to be overcome during a lingering twenty-first century "clash of civilizations." Talking, reading, and writing about sniping allows ordinary US citizens to feel as though they have gained tacit knowledge about the perceptual issues raised by those who care about precision-warfare, counterterrorism, counterinsurgency, or "irregular" warfare. We will see that it is no coincidence that so many living in this age of (in)security express their desires that specially trained forces keep foreign monsters away from American shores.

While there are many heuristic avenues that might be taken in the decoding of some of sniping logics of perception, this chapter invites readers to review how various mediated conversations about Chris Kyle's book,[7] and debates about Clint Eastwood's movie, *American Sniper* (2014) are used in legal, military, and public conversations as entrée points for populist defenses of American exceptionalistic practices during the GWOT.

Eastwood's *American Sniper* is based on the life of an American, Chris Kyle, who lost his life in early 2013 when he was on a firing range in Texas. Newspapers across the country reported that Kyle had been killed by Eddie Routh, an Iraqi War veteran. At the time of his death Kyle had been trying to help Routh recover from post-traumatic stress syndrome.[8]

While Eastwood and some of the actors who played leading roles in *American Sniper* have insisted that theirs is an "anti-war" movie that tells little about Washington, D.C. politics or foreign policy affairs, critics oftentimes view this very denial as even more evidence of the entrenched nature of those logics of perception.[9] There are many complex reasons why the story of Chris Kyle, "the Legend," has resonated with so many neo-liberal Americans, but there is little doubt that those who engage in heated debates about the film added even more layers of sedimented meanings to what Michel Foucault and others have called *dispositifs*.[10] Regardless of the subject positions of those who defended Kyle's sniping activities during his tours in Iraq, the very fact that different generations still debate about the "meaning" of his life underscores the rhetorical point that many felt that they identified with this particular sniper. I argue that Kyle's articulated positions, as well as his actions, helped those who wanted to turn Kyle's sniper scope into an iconic image that put on display how trained Americans could fight monsters in more and legal ways.

In theory, the more kills that professional snipers amassed overseas, the fewer existential dangers could be posed by terrorists or insurgents who threated the American Homeland, diplomatic bases overseas, our allies, or our ideographic "way of life." Even a cursory review of many blog sites shows that while media coverage of Kyle's sniping seemed to peak in 2015–2016, his interpretations of the "rules of the engagement" (ROE) and how one fought efficacious "just wars" still resonates with many generations.[11] CSS scholars might view all of this lingering interest bordering as a form of neo-colonial amnesia, but keep in mind that contemporary campaigns against ISIS in Iraq, Boko Haram in Nigeria, or those whose chemical weapons in Syria remind us that when bin Laden was killed, or when the troops came home in 2011, these did not end the flow of morphing perceptual logics. Former soldiers, veterans, and many others who follow these current events suture Kyle's narratives into other sniping tales.

It is perhaps telling that even after the famous wrestler, and former Minnesota governor, Jesse Ventura seemed to have initially won a defamation case against Kyle's widow, Tara, he experienced firsthand what it meant to be the iconoclast who makes the mistake of thinking that dissident views on local bar violence will carry any weight in the court of public opinion. For several years Ventura talked incessantly about how Kyle, a former Navy SEAL was not a hero, and that he needed an apology from Chris Kyle's estate for some of the allegations that Kyle made about him in his 2012 book. Kyle's detractors were quick to join those who placed a spotlight on Ventura's efforts, but these critics had to watch as Ventura's attacks backfired. In the eyes of many of those who lionized Chris Kyle, the very filing of this lawsuit was problematic.

By June of 2017 Ventura was having to explain to reporters that he was now viewed as the pariah, the former underwater demolitions expert who was treated as an outcast for having betrayed his comrades. From a Foucauldian standpoint, Ventura's attempt to take advantage of heterotopic societal spaces had failed miserably when the perceptual logics of Ventura's supporters clashed with the aura of utopianism that swirled around Kyle's sniping and his valor. "I can't get a job in the U.S.," Ventura explained to Minneapolis journalists, and he elaborated by noting that after the filing of his highly publicized defamation lawsuit, even members of some actors' unions were throwing him "in the dirt."[12] An embarrassed ex-UDT operator had to watch as Russian President Vladimir Putin volunteered to help him.

When Ventura filed his defamation lawsuit he may have thought that a legal courtroom would become the venue that would allow enlightened liberal cosmopolitans to witness some epic, insightful debate about the truthfulness of passages in Chris Kyle's autobiography. However, Ventura apparently did not realize that this jurisprudential squabble was just a sideshow in a much larger dispute, where Ventura played the role of the post-Vietnam leftist, the person who must have been "high" when he sued Kyle's estate in the first place. Ventura's standards for heroism looked nothing like the dense, tangled Judeo-Christian, and capitalist positions of those who openly aligned themselves with Kyle's religion, family, Navy SEAL heritage, and patriotic values.

Ventura, and other public figures like Michael Moore, would become entangled in all of this wrangling, but it would be Kyle's prowess at sniping, and his scope, that would become a part of so many of these image events. Bruno Latour might argue that it would be the *dingpolitik*—the politics of objects that were related to human deliberation—of Kyle's sniper scope that was used by colleagues of Kyle to fight those who knew "the latest beheadings by fanatics in Falluja," that provided so many Anglo-Americans with the "*res*" of "*res publica.*"[13]

Here I want to explain just why Ventura misanalyzed this rhetorical situation, and I want to show in this chapter how the shooting of some projectile from as far away as a mile can become entangled in what Latour has called the "assembly of relevant parties," where an "object" can turn into an enthymematic device that depends on a "different set of passions, indignations, opinions," and other signs of ruptures that may be "spewing out."[14]

In this particular case Kyle's sniper scope would be one of the objects that would be tethered to the other half of Latour's suggested methodological topic for critical analyses—the *realpolitik* of those who deal in abstractions, sophistry, and rhetoric—the politicians. Kyle and Ventura became ciphers in webs of signification that formed assemblages that had everything to do with rationales for OIF, treatment of Iraqis or Jihadist enemies, and the rectitude of American or Coalition fighters. Between 2012 and 2017, many soldiers, milbloggers, and even mainstream newspaper writers seemed to be obsessed with the "American Sniper's" scope, Kyle's book,[15] and other revered objects, and all of these social agents co-produced the fragments and the condensation symbols that went into dense securitized *dispositifs*. This security apparatus, that contained the reservoir of many clichéd arguments about aggressive sniping, could be used by populists who wanted to express their views regarding the efficacy and legality of US long-distance killings of enemies during just wars.

I argue that by visualizing, and by comparing, the acts of particular terrorist or counterterrorist "monsters" (depending on one's ideological points of view, POV), diverse US communities could converse—using elite or vernacular rhetorics—about their preferred understanding of what military analysts call the "law of armed conflict" (LOAC) and what NGO communities call "international humanitarian law" (IHL). As I explain in more detail below, although there are passages in Kyle's book and portions of Clint Eastwood's movie that hint that he got in trouble with his superiors for not strictly following contentious rules of engagement, both the movie, and his defenders, have interpreted this reprimand as a failure of those who want to mollycoddle the enemy.

I argue that those who go see *American Sniper* are provided with colloquial ways of understanding *jus in bello* (justifications for going to war in the first place) and *jus ad bellum* (the methods that we use during war) principles. For some critics viewing Chris Kyle's acts through select ocular lenses put on display the undeserved demonizing of Iraqi enemies—that risked turning some counterterrorists into the very "monsters" they are supposed to be fighting—but this was not the way that many American citizens felt about Kyle's sniping.

With this in mind the rest of this chapter is divided into four major subsections. I begin by providing readers with a brief overview of some OIF rules of engagement and explain how views regarding American sniping are related to "just wars." Then I unpack some of the scopic features of Eastwood's *American Sniper* that attracted so much journalist and public commentary just before, and after, Chris Kyle's untimely death. The third section extends some of this analysis by commenting on the *realpolitik* and the *dingpolitik* associated with "Juba," the insurgent sniper. Juba would play the role of the barbarian "other," the realistic terrorist who was not constrained by the idealist principles of distinction, humanity, proportionality, or necessity. This third section also explains how the fusion of sacred and security commentaries about sheep, wolves, and sheepherders allowed Judeo-Christian audiences to see how Kyle behaved as he battled Islamic fundamentalist foes like Juba. Finally, the concluding section explains what Kyle's scope, and the hagiographic commentary that swirled around this famous sniper's memories, tells us about the opportunities and dangers that come from fighting military and societal monsters.

RULES OF ENGAGEMENT AND SNIPING DURING OPERATION IRAQI FREEDOM

As Kimberly Haley has argued at the "Humanity in War" blog, Chris Kyle's "story is a case study on how the fundamental principles of IHL (proportionality, distinction, humanity, and military necessity) are applied in modern warfare and the steps the US military takes to ensure those principles are followed even in the most dangerous scenarios.[16] According to many legal formalists, obeying these rules is supposed to help with the balancing of the "force protection" of the troops so that they can come home, with the need to differentiate between illegitimate civilian targets and legitimate enemy fighters. Hague Conventions and Geneva Conventions have tried to codify, and formalize, some of the common law principles that have been used to help global societies see the differences that exist between civilized combat and unregulated barbaric destruction. In theory, international law students, jurists, and those who go into battle have to learn about these guidelines before they pick up their rifles and travel to distant shores. For example, those who want to defend interventionism could argue that "defensive" measures after 9/11 triggered America's rights and duties based on *jus in bello* principles that dictate that states can defend themselves. As Leonard Campos explained, the usages of lethal force after the terrorist attacks of 9/11 were "justified in the service of self-defense" and fighting a "just war," and this triggered the "reinforcing" of an increasing defensive stance by the "United States against any potential attacks in the future."[17]

Coalition warriors are taught that their training and the flexible ROE that are provided by their commanders on the ground help ensure that they don't violate the LOAC. By following strict guidelines US forces can provide the rest of the world with proof that Americans and their allies are following *jus ad bellum* principles for how to behave while fighting twenty-first century battles. As Haley explained in 2016, ROE are not meant to prohibit all violence, but are used to help "define the circumstances and conditions in which the use of force may be authorized, the admissible degree of force that may be applied, and the manner in which such force may be applied."[18]

Lay persons and elites may differ about whether this is all legalese, or whether these international law principles are "paper tigers" or actually constraints on the dispensation of violence, but these *topoi* provide a powerful example of what Latour calls "*realpolitik*" abstractions that sometimes make little sense if they are detached from things and concrete situations. That is why seeing through the sniper's scope helps turn theory into praxis.

Those, like Chris Kyle, who go to one of several different types of sniper schools are taught about the need to keep track of confirmed or unconfirmed "kills," how rules help distinguish between legitimate and illegitimate targets, and how certain enemy activity signals what may be called hostile "intent" or "behavior." Military science and objective calibrations are supposed to help move the sniper's point of view away from ambiguous, subjective decision-making to more intersubjective or objectivist points of view that keep those who pull triggers stay out of jail or courtrooms. Gary Solis, a law professor at Georgetown Law School and a retired Marine, has explained that before someone can fire against particular targets they must "positively identify that individual as representing a threat to you or your fellow Marines or soldiers," and if you cannot positively identify that "individual representing a threat to you" or your fellow soldiers you are not supposed to "fire on him or her."[19]

Debates about Eastwood's *American Sniper* provided the opportunity for critiquing those vaunted ROE.

VISUALIZING ROE AND THE RESONANCE OF EASTWOOD'S CINEMATIC REPRESENTATION OF AMERICAN SNIPERS IN IRAQ

Chris Kyle—both the legend and the real individual—left textual materials, visual commentaries, and other representations of his sniping activities in Iraq that allowed Clint Eastwood's *American Sniper* to be turned into a proverbial Rorschach test for analyzing wartime behavior. This movie, that starred Bradley Cooper in the role of Chris Kyle, doesn't provide viewers with any overt, vocalized interpretations of the LOAC or IHL principles that I mentioned above, but that has not prevented soldiers, veterans, journalists, or others from recognizing that there might be preferred reading that can be picked up by paying attention to the operationalization of scopic ROE applications.

As readers might imagine, depending on how one felt about the shooting of civilians or wartime necessities, there were varied reactions to some of Cooper's and Eastwood's representations of Kyle's sniping decisions. For example, Kenneth Turan of the *Los Angeles Times* averred that this was an "impeccably crafted" film that went beyond the traditional war hero movie.[20] While Turan was willing to admit that parts of Eastwood's movie reminded viewers of Gary Cooper's role as Sergeant York or Audie Murphy in *To Hell and Back* there seemed to be something else in *American Sniper* that needed to be respected. Instead of viewing the film as some type of "revisionism," he explained, we needed to see how Kyle was indeed a "thorough-going patriot" who "never stopped believing completely in his mission."[21] This implied that neither Kyle's values, nor the mediated representation of those American ideals, had anything to do with artifice or revisionism. Turan remarked that just because a hero was on the "right side" did not mean that he "could solve all problems," and he elaborated by noting how the movie displayed Kyle's vulnerabilities and the costs of his sacrifices when both he and his wife had to deal with military duty's stresses.[22]

Latour might view this quest for realism as an expressed desire for unmediated objectivity,[23] but for many Anglo-American moviegoers *American*

Sniper was about more than Kyle's inner demons or familial difficulties. After all, Kyle, like Kurtz in Conrad's *Heart of Darkness*, was on an odyssey that was filled with challenges, perhaps even Sisyphean tasks, as he tried to kill as many of the enemy as he could while working within the assigned ROE. He, like Kurtz, began his journey by thinking about civilizing missions, and perhaps ended up "going native" when shocked observers wondered if he became as barbaric as his enemies.

Was it any surprise that defenders of less restrictive rules of engagement—that prioritized force protection over the preservation of Iraqi fundamentalist life—were some of his strongest supporters?

At the same time, frustrated critics of OIF, that had not succeeded in derailing the war with their discourse about the absence of WMDs, now tried their best to show that the perfidious nature of Chris Kyle's sniping put on display the systemic barbarism of the occupation itself. For example, some contemporary critics of the GWOT, and Kyle's sniping modalities, could recycle old anti-imperialists rhetorics as they tried to convince others that when you confront savages during heated foreign interventionism you can't help fighting "wars of savagery."[24]

Both supporters and detractors of Chris Kyle's actions and Clint Eastwood's filmic representations could not avoid talking about beasts, monsters, and other dark creatures as they tried to contextualize the sniper's quandaries. One journalist, writing for British audiences, remarked that during Kyle's four tours of duty, insurgents characterized him as the "Devil of Ramidi, a monster in the shadows to be hated and feared."[25] John Hogan, writing for *Scientific American*, concluded that *American Sniper* was simply war propaganda, that had more to say about America's collective maladies than it did about justified killings. During the time that Navy SEAL Chris Kyle was serving in Iraq, Hogan noted, the US coalition forces had killed at least 1,201 children between 2003 and 2011.[26] Extending Margaret Mead's classic 1940 work on how "War is Only an Invention-Not a Biological Necessity," Hogan could comment on the choices that were made by those who seemed to be engaged in creative destruction and violations of the laws of humanity.

Scholars also added even more layers to these thick ideological figurations when they commented on both Eastwood's film and popular reactions to the film. There were no shortages of excellent criticisms of *American Sniper* that alluded to the biopolitical or the thanatopolitical features of this 2014 production. For example, Florentina Andreescu was convinced that *American Sniper* was one of those cinematic representations of war that invited "viewers to experience a unique, exhilarating kind of enjoyment generated by representations of the military *dispositif*."[27] Deborah Cohler, during the spring of 2017, characterized *American Sniper* as an example of a biopolitical visual representation that promoted a particular ideological way of viewing a "necropolitical war."[28]

Some critics in the United Kingdom have echoed these sentiments. David Martin Jones and M.L.R. Smith, of the War Studies Department of King's College in London, have argued that since 2005 the American film industry has been involved in the production of visualized works about Afghanistan and Iraq that reflect, and shape, US capitalist and imperialist agendas. They argue that films like *American Sniper* represent the rise of what they call "dark Americana," where certain on-screen depictions of the GWOT allow us to see how audiences back home want to think about the US cultural mainstream, rendition, surveillance, and homeland security.[29]

Yet it could be argued that from a praxiological vantage point, *American Sniper* was a success because Kyle's decision-making on the screen—where vicarious witnesses can peer over his shoulder and see what he sees through his scope—refracted the decisions that most Americans would make if they had been put in the same subject position. An "object-oriented" approach (Latour) would ask us to study the fluid, but discernable, assemblages that were made up of all sorts of gestures, including Warner Brothers act of donating $1 million to the Wounded Warrior Project.

Is it too much to say that the firing of each and every shot—that did not put Kyle in the brig—put on display the morality and legality of US counterterrorist efforts that were as necessitous as they were controversial. One writer, for example, mentioned the scene where Kyle was being questioned about some of his sniping decision-making, and while this heroic sniper responded by disagreeing with more restrictive rulemaking, he "nevertheless" displayed for viewers how he was going to reluctantly obey his military's then-current "rules of engagement."[30] When Kyle killed, he did so without crossing the line into unjustified killing, or murder.

In a host of ways, the stories that were produced by Kyle and Eastwood, as well as the journalistic, military, or public defenses of Kyle's sniping, had everything to do with the fighting of "just wars." As Christopher Finlay explains, the efforts of organizations like the International Committee of the Red Cross (ICRC) to teach so many about how to protect both combatants and civilians through correct interpretations of the IHL is just one example of how the "importance of informing public opinion" motivates those who care about "writing on Just War Theory."[31] In 2016 Finlay argued that popular cinema has tried to encapsulate some of this interest in learning and debating about the laws of war so that post–Cold War audiences can go and watch what he calls "Just War Cinema." By suturing together characters, action, events, and normative judgments from several different wars—including the "Greatest Generation's" Second World War—those who act, produce, and watch just war cinema can feel as though they have a good understanding of arguments that used to be the exclusive domain of ethics experts and political philosophers like Michael Walzer.[32]

Some of the origins of just war theorizing have to do with the clerical and militarist arguments that were used by Catholic, Protestant, Islamic, Jewish, or other religious leaders who had to find ways of rationalizing why good human beings had to go to war or fight wars in Godly ways. Some of just war cinema implicitly or explicitly allows both producers and audiences to reflect on the contemporary relevance of some of these ancient just war creeds that can be traced back to Medieval times. For example, notice the conversation that takes place in one particular scene in *Saving Private Ryan*, where one of the US Rangers surveys some of the carnage on the battlefield and asks: "If God's on our side, who is the hell could be on theirs?" Corporal Upham—who is filled with his own contradictory feelings—in this instance corrects his comrade by citing the original Biblical quotation from St. Paul's Letter to the Romans 8.31, that says: "If God is with us, who can be against us?" Finlay makes the excellent point that regardless of version, these interpretations suggest that the "power of God is such that no enemy can withstand" the power of the Allies, in the same way that medieval Christian *bellum justum* arguments were once used to explain that the "righteous party" was acting to enforce God's law.[33]

Part of the rhetorical beauty of Eastwood's *American Sniper* is that it presents sniping scenes that are strategically framed in ways that appeal to audiences who come to the Cineplex with their knowledges and preconceptions, who care about discovering either sacred or secular rationales for fighting just wars. Beth Williams asked whether Chris Kyle "has to be seen as immoral," argued that fighting just wars was important because "of necessity" and that soldiers "don't have the luxury of sensitivity." Without some types of combat and sacrifices, she argued, "slavery would be legal in the Confederate States of America, and Auschwitz would still be in operation."[34]

While some might argue that populist sniping defenses brought moral clarity, other observers are not so sure. For example, Jared Taylor argued:

> The advent of the American sniper program in the middle of the Nineteenth Century confused American beliefs about "just" war, which historically have been linked to principles of self-defense, masculine honor, and moral self-restraint among soldiers. Such beliefs have also been mythologized in popular culture representations. . . . Once criticized for remaining too distant from bodily harm, snipers in an age of smart bombs and Predator drones are considered today to be held as morally suspect for being too close to the tragedies of war.[35]

These are key societal logics of perceptions.

In a host of ways, Clint Eastwood's *American Sniper* draws on the notion that some just wars have to be fought in dirty ways, and the "crusader nation image" is used to evidence how America's new way of fighting urban warfare is simply responding to the "elusive nature of the enemy."[36]

At the same time, don't just wars require unjust enemies for their legitimation?

JUBA THE WOLF, AND CHRIS KYLE, THE SHEEPHERDER

Long before the publication of Chris Kyle's book, or his appearance at various interviewing forums, television shows, and conferences, Anglo-American mass-mediated outlets were already filling mediascapes with tales of mobile terrorists. The coverage of the growing insurgency in Iraq also carried along stories of a mythic person named "Juba" who was sniping away at Americans and UK soldiers. During the fall of 2005 the *Guardian*'s Rory Carroll was writing about how Coalition commanders were weighing their options as they confronted an "elusive sniper" who was sapping US morale in the fighting in and around Baghdad:

> They have never seen Juba. They hear him, but by then it's too late: a shot rings out and another US soldier slumps dead or wounded. There is never a follow-up shot, never a chance for US forces to identify the origin, to make the hunter the hunted. He fires once and vanishes. Juba is the nickname given by American forces to an insurgent sniper operating in southern Baghdad. They do not know his appearance, nationality or real name, but they know and fear his skill.[37]

For many, Juba signified the irregular fighter who did not follow the rules of conventional warfare, the invisible and implacable foe who stood in the path of Iraqi reconstruction. The bullets that came out of Juba's sniping rifle provided the *dingpolitik* that complemented the *realpolitik* of those who could argue that perhaps greater latitude out to be given to those American snipers who might need to become as barbaric as their foes if they wished to win OIF.

By the fall of 2006, Juba's reputation was magnified to the point where he became a figurative device that put on display the cancerous growth of an insurgency that seemed to be spiraling out of control. More than three years after the initial successes of "shock and awe," American soldiers and politicians in Washington, D.C. started to think the unthinkable—was this another "quagmire" like Vietnam? Or could the Coalition move away from knocking down doors and toward the winning of "hearts and minds" so that adaptive US forces could fetch good from evil? These concerns impacted the ROE that appeared on cards handed out to troops.

Juba became entangled in the rhetorical fragments that were crafted by those who circulated military and security *dispositifs* that pitted defenders of traditional "force protection" oriented ROE against those who wanted stricter regulations of those who may have been killing too many civilians. For some in Washington, D.C. or Baghdad, it seemed as though the Coalition forces were having a difficult time calculating gains and losses in this "fourth generation," hybrid war, irregular conflict, or asymmetrical battlefield. Given the fog of the war, and the difficulty of gauging Iraqi populist support, what martial values needed to be published in order to help win the GWOT?

In the same way that Soviet tales about famous Russian snipers were used to boost the morale of those who had to fight Nazis at places like Stalingrad, now observers noted how neutralizing an IED (improvised explosive device) or sending through the air a strategically placed bullet could influence perceptions. Small victories or defeats in places like Falluja, Ramadi, Mosul, or Baghdad mattered.

The fighting that had moved from conventional warfare to urban warfare frustrated those who were now unsure what to do with some of their ROE, and they watched as overpowered insurgents on the battlefield could nevertheless feel that they were winning some telegenic warfare. Patrick Cockburn and Jerome Taylor reported that by November of 2006, it seemed as though enemy propagandists were using stories of Juba, the "insurgent marksman," as a persuasive way of convincing Iraqi fighters and foreign supporters that they were making headway in their battle for Iraq's major cities. Diary entries were prepared by enemies who celebrated by telling potential supporters about Juba's "personal log" that showed some 37 kills. Some 33,000 people visited this site, and one of the videos—reposted on YouTube—had some mysterious character saying: "I have nine bullets in this gun and I have a present for George Bush. I am going to kill nine people."[38] After this scene is presented viewers get to see Juba, the famed sniper, climbing into a vehicle. Viewers are then presented with a montage of a separate scene, showing nine individuals being shot.

The not-so-veiled message is clear: in spite of the overwhelming firepower of the Coalition forces, the infidels can be turned away—as long as true believers are willing to take Juba as a role model. As late as 2015 one *Washington Post* reporter argued that the Chris Kyle, the "titular marksman" in what was by a then a "wildly successful film," had a "clear foe: A mysterious insurgent dubbed, Mustafa, believed to be a former Syrian Olympian."[39] Kyle, in his co-authored book, only made passing reference to Mustafa, noting that he knew that someone was posting videos on the web, "boasting of his ability." Kyle also mentioned that other snipers thought that they had killed Mustafa, but Adam Taylor reported that insurgent tales of Mustafa—or Juba—were getting "deep under U.S. troops' skins."[40]

While some military officers treated Juba as the stuff of legend, a mysterious but fictional figure who had no clear and identifiable referent, others seemed to view this phantasmagorical enemy sniper as a very real threat, a soldier who had mercilessly killed hundreds of Coalition fighters. For countless soldiers, veterans, and milbloggers, the existential dangers posed by Juba—that pitted different monsters against each other—also signified the need for American exceptionalism and more flexible ways of thinking about counterterrorism.

Chris Kyle the individual quickly morphed into the American exceptionalist "punisher." Leonard Campos has explained just why Kyle's 2012 autobiography, *American Sniper* "exemplifies how cultural gender, religious, racial, and military scripting converged to interface with the individual life" script:

> His life story is open to the public and illustrates how an individual can enact cultural script values and feelings. . . . To live out this script, Kyle (2012) felt destined to join the military and its subculture. As a U.S. soldier in Iraq, he described how he viewed insurgents as ''evil'' savages (p. 4), and his purpose as a sniper was to kill ''the bad guys'' (p. 167). He candidly admitted how during his deployments he ''loved'' killing bad guys (p. 251) while doing his job as a ''duty to my country,'' and, as reflected in the subtitle of his book, he became the ''most lethal sniper in U.S. military history.'' He wore a Crusader's Cross on his arm and viewed insurgents as Islamic fanatics who hated Christian Americans because they practiced a different religion (p. 98). At the end of his story, he concluded that ''everyone I shot was evil. . . . They all deserved to die'' (p. 432).[41]

One observer called this a "heartfelt salute to U.S. muscle."[42] It was, for Xan Brooks, a Green Beret movie for the war in Iraq, so filled with "patriot fervor and bullish male bonding" that even those who resented the way the narrative was told could nevertheless relish the drama.[43]

Chris Kyle's tattooed "crusader cross" would become a potent signifier for milbloggers who were familiar with comic book renditions of the Punisher. This example of embodied rhetoric, that could draw from comic book figures as well, allowed many to be thankful that a righteous warrior was pulling the trigger.[44]

From a CSS vantage point, both Kyle's *American Sniper*, as well as many defenses of Eastwood's movie, were often interpreted as media devoid of politics or moralizing. Advocates could remark that all of Kyle's commentary in his book, and Cooper's reading of his lines in the movie, were accurate depictions of what war, and life in places like Iraq, was really like. In some of these textual and visual rhetorics, Iraq becomes simply a backdrop, a "shithole" place, where Kyle's 160 kills are used to protect "his comrades and his homeland."[45]

Over and over, in both his interviews and recirculated ideological fragments on his commentaries, we hear Chis Kyle mentioning how he considers Iraqi fighters to be "savages," and that one of the few regrets of "the Legend" is that he could not kill more of the enemy before returning home. When questioned by one psychologist about whether he had any moral qualms about all of this mayhem, he simply replied in a way that may have resonated with millions of viewers: "The only thing that haunts me is the guys I couldn't save." This type of response is why some intoned that, ultimately, "Iraq provides the background scene" for the celebration of the American values that allow heroic confrontations with unmitigated evil "in the shape of Al Qaeda in Iraq or Shi'ite militias in Sadr city on Kyle's fourth tour."[46]

No doubt part of Chris Kyle's charm had everything to do with his ability to come across as the average American patriot, who represented the coast-to-coast values of others who were willing to selflessly lay down their lives. He grew up in Odessa, Texas, and his memoirs and his chroniclers could write of a youth spent hunting, his competition in rodeos, and his seemingly destined journey as he joined the ranks of the Navy SEALs. Like many of those who arrived in Iraq during 2003, he too had to decide how to decipher Coalition ROE and standard operating procedures.

Given his insightful recognition that some might question his sniping ethics, it made sense that Kyle decided to open his own book with a story about his first kill in Nasaria, when he spotted a woman on a road who was pulling a grenade from under her clothes as she walked toward an advancing Marine patrol that Kyle could see through his sniper scope. Kyle explained in his book that he did not regret participating in the killing of that woman, because he was just trying to make "sure she didn't take any Marines with her."[47] The movie rendition only drove the point home.

Some of those who have been puzzled by the resonance of *American Sniper* have missed the ways that talk of ROE could be tethered to military science and professionalized, clinical ways of discussing the morality of distance sniping.

There are of course many ways of explaining how one keeps one's moral compass, and what differentiates between just and unjust wars, and for many neo-liberals one of these ways involves the inculcation that comes from hearing the parable of the wolf, the sheep, and the sheepdogs. In one of Lieutenant Colonel Dave Grossman's essays, he explains:

> If you have no capacity for violence then you are a healthy productive citizen: a sheep. If you have a capacity for violence and no empathy for your fellow citizens, then you have defined an aggressive sociopath-a wolf. But what if you have a capacity for violence, and a deep love for your fellow citizens? Then you are a sheepdog, a warrior, someone who is walking the hero's path.[48]

Make no mistake the use of these rhetorical figurations about the sheep, the wolves, and the sheepdog was not some novel invention created by Grossman, Kyle, or Eastwood. On November 24, 1997, William Bennett, in a lecture to the US Naval Academy, explained that "most of the people in our society are sheep," but you would be in denial if you did not admit that there were wolves out there who were trying to feed on the sheep without mercy. The moment you forget about the wolves, opined Bennett, you become a sheep. Bennett then told those cadets—some four years before September 11, 2001—that he was a sheepdog and that he lived to protect the flock and confront the wolf. As far as he was concerned, a "sheepdog, a warrior," was someone who was walking that "unsheltered path."[49]

For many Americans, who knew all about these Biblical allusions, Kyle was not just some secular warrior fighting demons like Juba—he was a sheepdog, part of a long line of identifiable historic characters.

CONCLUSION: POST-INVASION NOSTALGIA, MEMORIES OF CHRIS KYLE, AND THE JUSTNESS OF MANY FUTURE TWENTY-FIRST CENTURY GWOT CAMPAIGNS

This chapter supports Finlay's conclusion that oftentimes "Just War Cinema has "foreshadowed Just War Theory in the decades since the Second World War, sometimes anticipating and sometimes echoing, reinforcing, or challenging several of its central ethical arguments."[50] Looking through Kyle's scope allows American viewers to become performative supporters of lax rules of engagement so that sheepherders can protect us from the wolves.

With the passage of time many of those who fought, or observed, various facets of the US-led Coalition of the Willing will undoubtedly leave us with a host of both competitive and multi-directional memories of this violent conflict. I share Cohler's view that it very likely that *American Sniper* will become an important part of the "ideological constructions" of home and "ware waging" as viewers of all political stripes will place Chris Kyles' *ouvre* in the patriotic archives that will be used to shore up a "politics of redemption that venerates American exceptionalism."[51] Sniper books sell at a brisk pace.

As viewers watch some of Kyle's sniping, they get the sense that his just world is not filled with many greyish, ambivalent choices that test his resolve. His moral compass provides him with a perceptual faith that guides him throughout the movie. Unlike characters in other cinematic representations he is "methodical and imperturbable" when he is perched on rooftops in places like Ramadi or Sadr City.[52] In theory, his American training in urban warfare, and the situated awareness that he has gained from hundreds of kills, means that he—unlike idealists—understands where to draw those ROE lines. As Denby explains, in order to protect his country this is a sniper who is willing to shoot insurgents, members of Al Qaeda in Iraq, and "when he thinks it necessary, a woman and a child."[53] Killing, again, does not have to be viewed as the unlawful application of lethal force.

There will of course be those who will continue to argue that *American Sniper* has nothing to do with Washington politics, the legality of interventionism in Iraq, or the justness of sniping activities. Bradley Cooper, for example, has said that this movie was not about the Iraq War, but was instead a "character study" of a man.[54] This conveniently ignores the social agency of millions who saw something more in Kyle's scope.

One vocal critic of Kyle's just war imaging focused on how he seemed to sincerely believe that every single one of the people he killed in places like Fallujah or Ramadi was a "bad guy," who deserved what they got. For Laura Miller, Kyle's apparent certainty, and the visualized conveyance of his utter convictions, did not represent any clear moral vision but rather "bloodthirstiness and general indifference to Iraqis and their country." After all, he did not even try to make sure that those he had killed actually were Iraqi insurgents or foreign Islamic militants. "Kyle's patriotism is of the visceral kind," Miller argued, wherein his version of this Iraq conflict was one fought between "Americans, who are good by virtue of being Americans," and "fanatical Muslims whose 'despicable evil' led them to want to kill Americans simply because of they are Christians."[55]

Sadly, the recent conflicts in the Middle East, which involve battles over Syrian usage of chemical weaponry, or the horrors of ISIS, remind us that the world's military and security forces will have no shortage of real or invented monsters, and Nietzsche's admonition will continue to haunt those who view the next enemy through a sniper's scope.

NOTES

1. Friedrich Nietzsche, 1886, Aphorism 146 in *Jenseits von Gut und Böse. Zur Genealogie der Moral*, edited by Giorgio Colli and Mazzino Montinari (Munich: Deutscher Taschenbuch Verlag, reprint 2002).
2. *Jesse Venture v. Taya Kyle*, US Court of Appeals for the Eighth Circuit, No. 14-3876, see Defendant's Memorandum in Opposition to Plaintiff's Motion to Compel (Minneapolis: US District Court, 2013), https://docs.google.com/file/d/0BwVkb6p7OhGiSGVmTllrWDNfQkU/edit.
3. Ira P. Robbins, "Regulating Gun Rentals," *UCLA Law Review* 64 (2017): 1–64.
4. Julia Filip, "Should Veterans with PTSD Be Exempt from the Death Penalty," *The Atlantic*, January 30, 2015, https://www.theatlantic.com/national/archive/2015/01/should-veterans-with-ptsd-be-exempt-from-the-death-penalty/384940/.

5. Paul Virilio, *War and Cinema: The Logics of Perception*, translated by Patrick Camiller (New York: Verso, 1989).

6. Antoine Bosquet, "Lethal Visions: The Eye as Function of the Weapon," *Critical Studies on Security* (2017): 1–19, http://www.tandfonline.com/doi/abs/10.1080/21624887.2017.1329471.

7. Chris Kyle, Schott McEwen, Jim DeFelice, *American Sniper: The Autobiography of the Most Lethal Sniper In U.S. Military History* (New York: William Morrow, 2012).

8. Mile Spies, "Inside the Tortured Mind of Eddie Ray Routh, The Man Who Killed American Sniper Chris Kyle," *Newsweek*, November 23, 2015, http://www.newsweek.com/2016/01/08/inside-tortured-mind-man-who-killed-american-sniper-chris-kyle-397299.html.

9. See, for example, some of the comments following Ben Beaumont-Thomas, "Clint Eastwood: American Sniper and I are anti-War," *The Guardian*, last modified March 17, 2015, https://www.theguardian.com/film/2015/mar/17/clint-eastwood-american-sniper-anti-war.

10. For a helpful introductory overview to Foucault's notion of *dispositif*, see John Pløger, "Foucault's *Dispositif* and the City," *Planning Theory* 7, no. 1 (2008): 51–70.

11. See, for example, Marc LiVecche, "New Rules of Engagement Help the Battle," *Providence*, October 4, 2017, https://providencemag.com/2017/10/rules-engagement-jim-mattis/.

12. Associated Press Staff, "Putin Offers to Help Save Jesse Ventura's Career," *New York Post,* last modified June 9, 2017, paragraph 4, http://nypost.com/2017/06/09/jesse-ventura-finds-new-life-to-his-career-in-russia/.

13. Bruno Latour, "From *Realpolitik* to *Dingpolitik*, or How to Make Things Public," *Making Things Public-Atmospheres of Democracy*, edited by Bruno Latour and Peter Weibel (Cambridge, MA: MIT Press, 2005 4–5).

14. Ibid., 5.

15. Scott McEwen, the co-author of Chris Kyle's autobiographer, *American Sniper*, recently published *The Sniper and the Wolf: A Sniper Elite Novel* (New York: Touchstone, 2016). This is a part of a very popular series of books on sniping.

16. Kimberly Haley, "*American Sniper*: The Rules of Engagement, and the Principle of Distinction," *Humanity in War Blog*, January 14, 2015, paragraph 1, http://nypost.com/2017/06/09/jesse-ventura-finds-new-life-to-his-career-in-russia/.

17. Leonard P. Campos, "Cultural Scripting for Forever Wars," *Transactional Analysis Journal* 45, no. 4 (2015): 276–288, 279.

18. Haley, "*American Sniper*," paragraph 4.

19. Gary Solis, quoted in Haley, "*American Sniper*," paragraph 6.

20. Kenneth Turan, "Review: '*American Sniper*' Goes Above and Beyond War-Hero Tradition," *The Los Angeles Times*, last modified December 24, 2014. http://www.latimes.com/entertainment/movies/la-et-mn-american-sniper-review-20141225-column.html.

21. Ibid., paragraph 4.

22. Ibid., paragraph 14.

23. Latour, "From *Realpolitik*," 5–6.

24. This discourse regarding savage wars has been around since colonial and imperial times. See, for example, Elbridge Colby, "How to Fight Savage Tribes," *The American Journal of International Law* 21, no. 2 (April 1927): 279–288. For a key essay on the rhetorical nature of some of the representations, see Robert L. Ivie, "Images of Savagery in American Justifications for War," *Communication Monographs* 47, no. 4 (June 1980): 279–294, http://dx.doi.org/10.1080/03637758009376037.

25. Xan Brooks, "*American Sniper* Review," paragraph 1.

26. John Hogan, "What War Propaganda Like '*American Sniper*' Reveals About Us," *Scientific American*, February 2, 2015, https://blogs.scientificamerican.com/cross-check/what-war-propaganda-like-8220-american-sniper-8221-reveals-about-us/.

27. Florentina C. Andreescu, "War, Trauma and the Militarized Body," *Subjectivity* 9 (2016): 205–223, 205. doi:10.1057/sub.2016.2.

28. Deborah Cohler, "*American Sniper* and *American Wife*: Domestic Biopolitics at Necropolitical War," *Feminist Formations* 29, no. 1 (Spring 2017): 71–96.

29. David Martin Jones and M.L.R. Smith, "The Rise of Dark Americana: Depicting the 'War on Terror' On Screen," *Studies in Conflict and Terrorism*, 39, no. 1 (2016): 1–21. doi: 10.1080/1057610X.2015.1084802.

30. Andrew O'Hehir, "'*American Sniper*' and the Cultural Wars: Why the Movie's Not What You Think It Is," *Salon*, January 20, 2015, paragraph 4, http://www.salon.com/2015/01/21/american_sniper_and_the_culture_wars_why_the_movies_not_what_you_think_it_is/.

31. Christopher J. Finlay, "Bastards, Brothers, and Unjust Warriors: Enmity and Ethics in Just War Cinema," *Review of International Studies* 43, no. 1 (2016): 73–94, 74.

32. Michael Walzer, *Just and Unjust Wars: A Moral Argument with Historical Illustrations* (New York: Basic Books, 2001 [orig. pub. 1977]. See also Jeff McMahan, *Killing in War* (Oxford University Press, 2009); Jeff McMahan, "Rethinking Just War," *New York Times*, last modified November 12, 2012, https://opinionator.blogs.nytimes.com/2012/11/12/rethinking-the-just-war-part-2/.

33. Finlay, "Bastards, Brothers, and Unjust Warriors," 87.

34. Beth Williams, "Must 'American Sniper' Chris Kyle Be Seen as Immoral," *Patheos.com*, last modified January 24, 2015, paragraphs 4–5, http://www.patheos.com/blogs/unfundamentalistchristians/2015/01/its-b-s-to-say-american-sniper-chris-kyle-must-be-immoral/.

35. Jared Taylor, Abstract. "The Cultural Impact of the American Sniper Program," *Historia: The Alpha Rho Papers*, 2011, epubs.utah.edu/index.php/historia/article/download/577/439.

36. Jones and Smith, "The Rise of Dark Americana," 9.

37. Rory Carroll, "Elusive Sniper Saps U.S. Moral in Baghdad," *The Guardian*, last modified August 4, 2005, paragraph 1, https://www.theguardian.com/world/2005/aug/05/iraq.usa.

38. Patrick Cockburn and Jerome Taylor, "Conflict in Iraq: The Sniper Who Shoots on Video," *The Independent*, last modified November 9, 2006, paragraphs 3–4, http://www.independent.co.uk/news/world/middle-east/conflict-in-iraq-the-sniper-who-shoots-on-video-423530.html.

39. Adam Taylor, "Iraq Sniper: The Legendary Insurgent Who Claimed To Have Killed Scores of American Troops," *The Washington Post*, last modified January 22, 2015, paragraph 1, https://www.washingtonpost.com/news/worldviews/wp/2015/01/22/iraqi-sniper-the-legendary-insurgent-who-claimed-to-have-killed-scores-of-american-soldiers/?utm_term=.1c80fa3cfeb3.

40. Ibid, paragraph 3.

41. Leonard P. Campos, "Cultural Scripting for Forever Wars," *Transactional Analysis Journal* 45, no. 4 (2015): 276–288, 282–283. The pagination that Campos uses in this paragraph comes from Chris Kyle, *American Sniper: The Autobiography of the Most Lethal Sniper in U.S. Military History* (New York, NY: HarperCollins, 2012).

42. Xan Brooks, "*American Sniper* Review: Clint Eastwood's Heartfelt Salute to U.S. Muscle in Iraq," *The Guardian*, November 21, 2014, https://www.theguardian.com/film/2014/nov/21/clint-eastwood-heartfelt-tribute-us-muscle-iraq.

43. Ibid, paragraph 3.

44. Laura Miller, "Death of an American Sniper," *Salon*, February 7, 2013, paragraph 6, http://www.salon.com/2013/02/07/death_of_an_american_sniper/.

45. Jones and Smith, "The Rise of Dark Americana," 11.

46. Ibid, 11.

47. Chris Kyle, quoted in Miller, "Death of an American Sniper," paragraph 4.

48. Grossman, quoted in Michael Cummings and Eric Cummings, "The Surprising History of *American Sniper's* 'Wolves, Sheep, and Sheepdogs' Speech," *Slate*, January 21, 2015, paragraph 4, http://www.slate.com/blogs/browbeat/2015/01/21/american_sniper_s_wolves_sheep_and_sheepdogs_speech_has_a_surprising_history.html. For just one of Grossman's examples, see "Preface: Hunting Wolves," *Global Crime* 7, no. 3/4 (2006): 291–298. For a much longer discussion of the relationships that exist between killing, avoidance, innate resistance, and post-traumatic stress disorder for some veterans, see David Grossman, *On Killing: The Psychological Cost of Learning to Kill in War and Society* (New York: Back Bay Books, 1995).

49. William Bennett, "To Jill Edwards, Student, University of Washington; Subject; Sheep, Wolves and Sheepdogs," quoted by The Honorable Mahlon F. Hanson and Honorable Elisabeth A. Hacker, *Immigration Reform Law Institute*, April 17, 2015, http://www.irli.org/single-post/2016/03/23/Sheep-Wolves-and-Sheepdogs

50. Finlay, "Bastards, Brothers, and Unjust Warriors," 75.

51. Cohler, "American Sniper," 71.

52. David Denby, "Living History," *The New Yorker*, December 22 and 29, 2014, paragraph 7, http://www.newyorker.com/magazine/2014/12/22/living-hist.

53. Ibid, paragraph 7.

54. Bradley Cooper, quoted in Alex Needham, "Bradley Cooper Denies *American Sniper* is a 'Political Movie,' *The Guardian*, last modified December 16, 2014, https://www.theguardian.com/film/2014/dec/16/bradley-cooper-american-sniper-not-political.

55. Miller, "Death of an American Sniper," paragraph 6.

REFERENCES

Andreescu, Florentina C. 2016. "War, Trauma and the Militarized Body." *Subjectivity* 9: 205–223, 205.

Associated Press Staff. 2017. "Putin Offers to Help Save Jesse Ventura's Career." *New York Post,* June 9. http://nypost.com/2017/06/09/jesse-ventura-finds-new-life-to-his-career-in-russia/.

Beaumont-Thomas, Ben. 2015. "Clint Eastwood: American Sniper and I are anti-War." *The Guardian*, March 17. https://www.theguardian.com/film/2015/mar/17/clint-eastwood-american-sniper-anti-war.

Bennett, William. 2015. "To Jill Edwards, Student, University of Washington; Subject; Sheep, Wolves and Sheepdogs." *Immigration Reform Law Institute*, April 17. http://www.irli.org/single-post/2016/03/23/Sheep-Wolves-and-Sheepdogs.

Bosquet, Antoine. 2017. "Lethal Visions: The Eye as Function of the Weapon," *Critical Studies on Security* 5, issue 1: 1–19, http://www.tandfonline.com/doi/abs/10.1080/21624887.2017.1329471.

Brooks, Xan. 2014. "*American Sniper* Review: Clint Eastwood's heartfelt salute to US muscle in Iraq." *The Guardian*, November 21. https://www.theguardian.com/film/2014/nov/21/clint-eastwood-heartfelt-tribute-us-muscle-iraq.

Campos, Leonard P. 2015. "Cultural Scripting for Forever Wars." *Transactional Analysis Journal* 45, no. 4: 276–288, 279.

Carroll, Rory. 2005. "Elusive Sniper Saps U.S. Moral in Baghdad." *The Guardian,* August. https://www.theguardian.com/world/2005/aug/05/iraq.usa.

Cockburn, Patrick and Jerome Taylor. 2006. "Conflict in Iraq: The Sniper Who Shoots on Video." *The Independent*, November 9. http://www.independent.co.uk/news/world/middle-east/conflict-in-iraq-the-sniper-who-shoots-on-video-423530.html.

Cohler, Deborah. 2017. "*American Sniper* and *American Wife*: Domestic Biopolitics at Necropolitical War." *Feminist Formations* 29, no. 1, Spring: 71–96.

Colby, Elbridge. 1927. "How to Fight the Savage Tribes." *The American Journal of International Law* 21, no. 2 (April): 279–288.

Cummings Michael and Eric Cummings. 2015. "The Surprising History of *American Sniper's* 'Wolves, Sheep, and Sheepdogs' Speech." *Slate,* January 21. http://www.slate.com/blogs/browbeat/2015/01/21/american_sniper_s_wolves_sheep_and_sheepdogs_speech_has_a_surprising_history.html.

Denby, David. 2014. "Living History," *The New Yorker*, December 22. http://www.newyorker.com/magazine/2014/12/22/living-hist

Filip, Julia. 2015. "Should Veterans with PTSD Be Exempt from the Death Penalty." *The Atlantic*, January 30. https://www.theatlantic.com/national/archive/2015/01/should-veterans-with-ptsd-be-exempt-from-the-death-penalty/384940/.

Finlay, Christopher J. 2016. "Bastards, Brothers, and Unjust Warriors: Enmity and Ethics in Just War Cinema." *Review of International Studies* 43, no. 1: 73–94, 74.

Grossman, David. 2006. "Preface: Hunting Wolves." *Global Crime* 7, no. 3/4: 291-298.

Grossman, David. 1995. *On Killing: The Psychological Cost of Learning to Kill in War and Society*. New York: Back Bay Books.

Haley, Kimberly. 2015. "*American Sniper*: The Rules of Engagement, and the Principle of Distinction." *Humanity in War Blog*, January 14. http://nypost.com/2017/06/09/jesse-ventura-finds-new-life-to-his-career-in-russia/.

Hogan, John. 2015. "What War Propaganda Like '*American Sniper'* Reveals About Us." *Scientific American*, February 2. https://blogs.scientificamerican.com/cross-check/what-war-propaganda-like-8220-american-sniper-8221-reveals-about-us/.

Ivie, Robert L. 1980. "Images of Savagery in American Justifications for War." *Communication Monographs* 47, no. 4 (June): 279-294. http://dx.doi.org/10.1080/03637758009376037.

Jesse Venture v. Taya Kyle, US Court of Appeals for the Eighth Circuit, No. 14-3876, see Defendant's Memorandum in Opposition to Plaintiff's Motion to Compel (Minneapolis: US District Court, 2013), https://docs.google.com/file/d/0BwVkb6p7OhGiSGVmTllrWDNfQkU/edit.

Jones, David Martin and M.L.R. Smith. 2016. "The Rise of Dark Americana: Depicting the 'War on Terror' On Screen." *Studies in Conflict and Terrorism* 39, no. 1: 1–21.

Kyle, Chris, Schott McEwen, and Jim DeFelice. 2012. *American Sniper: The Autobiography of the Most Lethal Sniper in U.S. Military History*. New York: William Morrow.

Latour, Bruno. 2005. "From *Realpolitik* to *Dingpolitik*, or How to Make Things Public." *Making Things Public-Atmospheres of Democracy*, edited by Bruno Latour and Peter Weibel. Cambridge, MA: MIT Press.

LiVecche, Marc. 2017. "New Rules of Engagement Help the Battle." *Providence*, October 4. https://providencemag.com/2017/10/rules-engagement-jim-mattis/.

McEwen, Scott. 2016. *The Sniper and the Wolf: A Sniper Elite Novel*. New York: Touchstone.

McMahan, Jeff. 2009. *Killing in War*. Oxford, UK: Oxford University Press.

———. 2012. "Rethinking Just War." *New York Times*, November 12. https://opinionator.blogs.nytimes.com/2012/11/12/rethinking-the-just-war-part-2/

Miller, Laura. 2013. "Death of an American Sniper." *Salon*, February 7. http://www.salon.com/2013/02/07/death_of_an_american_sniper/.

Needham, Alex. 2014. "Bradley Cooper Denies *American Sniper* is a 'Political Movie.'" *The Guardian*, December 16. https://www.theguardian.com/film/2014/dec/16/bradley-cooper-american-sniper-not-political.

Nietzsche, Friedrich. 2002. "Aphorism 146." *Jenseits von Gut und Böse. Zur Genealogie der Moral*, edited by Giorgio Colli and Mazzino Montinari. Munich: Deutscher Taschenbuch Verlag.

O'Hehir, Andrew. 2015. "'*American Sniper*' and the Cultural Wars: Why the Movie's Not What You Think It Is." *Salon*, January 20. http://www.salon.com/2015/01/21/american_sniper_and_the_culture_wars_why_the_movies_not_what_you_think_it_is/.

Pløger, John. 2008. "Foucault's *Dispositif* and the City." *Planning Theory* 7, no. 1: 51–70.

Robbins, Ira P. 2107. "Regulating Gun Rentals." *UCLA Law Review* 64: 1–64.

Spies, Mile. 2015. "Inside the Tortured Mind of Eddie Ray Routh, The Man Who Killed American Sniper Chris Kyle." *Newsweek*, November 23. http://www.newsweek.com/2016/01/08/inside-tortured-mind-man-who-killed-american-sniper-chris-kyle-397299.html.

Taylor, Adam. 2015. "Iraq Sniper: The Legendary Insurgent Who Claimed To Have Killed Scores of American Troops." *The Washington Post*, January 22. https://www.washingtonpost.com/news/worldviews/wp/2015/01/22/iraqi-sniper-the-legendary-insurgent-who-claimed-to-have-killed-scores-of-american-soldiers/?utm_term=.1c80fa3cfeb3.

Taylor, Jared. 2011. Abstract. "The Cultural Impact of the American Sniper Program." *Historia: The Alpha Rho Papers*. epubs.utah.edu/index.php/historia/article/download/577/439.

Turan, Kenneth. 2014. "Review: '*American Sniper*' Goes Above and Beyond War-Hero Tradition." *The Los Angeles Times*, December 24. http://www.latimes.com/entertainment/movies/la-et-mn-american-sniper-review-20141225-column.html.

Virilio, Paul. 1989. *War and Cinema: The Logics of Perception*, translated by Patrick Camiller. New York: Verso.

Walzer, Michael. 2001. *Just and Unjust Wars: A Moral Argument with Historical Illustrations*. New York: Basic Books.

Williams, Beth. 2015. "Must 'American Sniper' Chris Kyle Be Seen as Immoral." *Patheos.com*, January 24. http://www.patheos.com/blogs/unfundamentalistchristians/2015/01/its-b-s-to-say-american-sniper-chris-kyle-must-be-immoral/.

Chapter Twelve

Monstrous Discourses, Jihadi Cool, and Emergent Counter-Terrorist Narratives

The Case of Ahmad Khan Rahami (a.k.a. Ahmad Rahimi) and the 2016 New York/New Jersey Bombings

Caroline Joan "Kay" S. Picart

INTRODUCTION

This chapter furthers the trajectory of a research project focused on the proliferation of discourses and images linking the monstrous with terrorism in law and media (Picart and Greek 2007, 256–88), and on the analysis of the evolution of self-radicalizing terrorists as linked to principally emotional (or at least non-rational) catalyzing (though non-determinative) factors (Picart 2019, 43–59). Both of these are often magnified by imagined relations facilitated by virtual relations enabled by the Internet (Picart 2015a, 354–83; Picart 2015c, 58–74).[1] Nevertheless, this chapter develops these lines of inquiry further by analyzing how the concept of the monstrous functions in counter-terrorist rhetorical mechanisms that are placed in relief against the allure of *jihadi cool* culture. While recognizing that combatting real-world global terrorism inevitably and pragmatically entails sustained and collaborative international and national military efforts,[2] policy adaptations,[3] and, within the United States, a review of relevant law such as the *Patriot Act* and *Freedom Act*,[4] among others,[5] this analysis applies available theoretical perspectives of the phenomenon of "jihadi cool" to case studies of domestic self-radicalizing individuals in the United States, in particular, that of Ahmad Khan Rahami (a.k.a. Ahmad Rahimi). Rahami is the individual who was arrested and charged (and eventually found guilty) with three bombings, as well as other planted bombs that had either failed to detonate or had not yet been detonated, in the New York metropolitan area (inclusive of Seaside Park, New Jersey; Manhattan, New York City; and Elizabeth, New Jersey) on September 17–18, 2016, injuring twenty-nine people (*Rahami* 2016; *Rahami* 2017). The chapter then proceeds on to an analysis of the counter-terrorist rhetorical tactics that were deployed, both in various media and in the courtroom[6] to reframe Rahami's self-proclaimed attempt to declare himself a "Soldier of the Caliphate."

Rahami's case is instructive because it gives us the opportunity to assess whether or to what extent a culture of jihadi cool (Picart 2017, 41–62)[7] was a significant factor in his self-radicalization, despite the reported death of Abu Muhammad al-Adnani, the chief architect of this rhetorical strategy, during an August 2016 military "precision strike" near Al Bab, Syria. In addition, the case is also useful, in terms of assessing whether and to what extent counterterrorism measures have been effective in adapting to the unpredictability of self-radicalizing terrorists, and in educating the American public about the reality of self-radicalizing terrorists, and perhaps inoculating, to some extent, against the lure of jihadi cool. Even more strikingly, the case illustrates how US criminal law or jurisprudence, in relation to self-radicalizing individuals, may be evolving into a more effective weapon. Posner (2007, 185) lamented in his critique of criminal law as a means to counteract terrorism:

> Criminal law enforcement is no more likely to win the "war on terrorism" than it is to win the "war on drugs." It is maladapted to both struggles. We should be deemphasizing the effort to prevent terrorism by means of criminal prosecutions, especially but not only in the regular courts, which are not designed for the trial of people who pose a serious threat to national security. Our counterterrorism efforts would be more effective, and at the same time, the dilemma of defeating terrorism while respecting essential civil liberties minimized, if we downplayed the judicial role in counterterrorism.

As this study preliminarily illustrates, criminal law may not be as ineffective as Posner feared, though, of course, criminal law is probably not a panacea to cure terrorism's multi-nodal and viral infections.

This analysis begins with a characterization of jihadi cool, as it appears relevant to the self-radicalization of Rahami. It also shares the non-deterministic position adopted by Clarke McCauley and Sophia Moskalenko in their identification of twelve pathways to radicalization (McCauley and Moskalenko. 2011), and like McCauley and Moskalenko, this chapter cautions that there are numerous and non-exhaustive factors that come into play in the generation of self-radicalizing lone wolves. My analysis adopts, where applicable, their framework in the examination of Rahami's transmogrification from an avid consumer of radical jihadi propaganda to an active terrorist bomber, albeit one without any clear connections to radical jihadi groups, save imaginatively. From there, the chapter proceeds on to a review of the multitude of counter-terrorist rhetorical mechanisms brought into play in the search for, capture of, and trial and sentencing of Rahami, which collectively served as functional counter-narratives to the narrative of jihadi cool.

THE RHETORICS OF "JIHADI COOL"

In order to understand the power and allure of jihadi cool, an analysis of its genesis and evolution, and its rhetorical force as targeted at specific audiences using particular techniques of storytelling, is necessary (Nacos 2016; Picart 2017, 17–26).[8]

The Genesis and Evolution of "Jihadi Cool"

Salman Rushdie defined "jihadi-cool" as "the deformed medievalist language of fanaticism, backed up by modern weaponry" and opined that "it's hard not to conclude that this hate-filled religious rhetoric, pouring from the mouths of ruthless fanatics into the ears of angry young men, has become the most dangerous new weapon in the world today" (Coyne 2014). The term "jihadi cool" was originally coined by psychiatrist and former CIA operations officer, Marc Sageman, to describe al-Qaeda's growing influence on the Internet (Jones 2013). Despite the prevalence of monstrous metaphors pointing to an utterly foreign menace infecting or seducing American or British men, ironically, the concept of "jihadi cool" probably began with Adam Yahiye Gadahn, an American who was raised in a goat farm in Riverside County, California, and who spent some of his teenage years with his Jewish grandfather in Santa Ana (Walker 2014). Gadahn left for Pakistan in the 1990s, and emerged around 2004 on propaganda videos as an English-speaking spokesman for al-Qaeda (Walker 2014). Although Gadahn's early videos as "Azzam the American" were viewed as more "laughable" than "scary," these rough productions were nevertheless noted as among the first English-language radical jihadist propaganda efforts attempting to reach out to Western audiences (Walker 2014).

Additionally, the slick website of Revolution Muslim became a precursor of what has evolved into the look of "jihadi cool." Over an eighteenth-month period, this small New York-based organization peaked, until government officials arrested one of its leaders and shut down the website (Walker 2014). Revolution Muslim was created by three American converts to radical Islam, all of whom are serving prison sentences (Walker 2014). At the height of its popularity, the website was used by authorities to monitor the communication, recruitment, and activities of aspiring radical jihadis (Walker 2014).[9]

With the shutdown of the Revolution Muslim website, *Inspire* magazine, an online publication run by the group al-Qaeda in the Arabian Peninsula targeting English language speakers, moved in to fill the gap (IPT News 2013). Described as akin to "the *Sports Illustrated* of jihad," this magazine has published articles such as that giving instructions on creating explosive devices, a copy of which was found in the backpack of one of the Tsarnaev brothers (Walker 2014).

Yet even *Inspire*'s glossy and sophisticated manipulation of the media has been eclipsed by ISIS's deft deployment of social media, such as Twitter and Facebook, which feature items as diverse as graphic videos to T-shirts (Brittany 2014) featuring the ISIS's logo, which is a black flag (Walker 2014). Former Director of the National Counterterrorism Center Michael Leiter acknowledged that ISIS "is using more social media than al[-]Qaeda ever did" (Arter 2014). Furthermore, ISIS has taken "jihadi cool" to new merchandising extremes: it now features its own online clothing line run by a company, Zirah Moslem, which specializes in ISIS-themed T-shirts and hoodies, sold via websites in Indonesia, where it is legal to sell jihadi-themed products ("The Jihad Shopping Network, Courtesy of ISIS" 2014).

Explaining the Seductive Appeal of "Jihadi Cool"

How does one explain the prevalence of "jihadi cool" popularity? One factor appears to be the seductive appeal of being a "badass." As UCLA sociologist Jack Katz noted: "In many youthful circles, to be 'bad,' to be a 'badass' or otherwise overtly embrace symbols of deviance is regarded as a good thing" (Katz 1988, 80). Katz identifies three stages of aggression that a badass aspirant must undergo and become, in order to be initiated into the ranks of the truly "badass." First, he must be tough and morally impermeable—not someone who can easily be influenced by others. Second, he must appear alien—uncompromisingly "hostile to any form of civilization" and irreducible to anything comprehensible to "native sensibilities," resulting in his presence or acts as "unnerving" (Katz 1988, 80). Third, and ultimately, to be a "badass" requires a genuine meanness, or spontaneous ability to engage in acts of violence, devoid of considerations of either utility or self-preservation; "badasses manifest the transcendent superiority of their being, specifically by insisting on the dominance of their will" (Katz 1988, 81).

Perhaps the seduction of "jihadi cool" is simply the paradigmatic appeal of the "badass" given a jihadi mask (Cottee 2014). However, a second—and, to some extent, contrary explanation—is the success of promoting a romanticized notion of making one's mark on the world through adventure, linked with a promise of earthly pleasure—to which allure the badass is theoretically immune, with his imperviousness, toughness, and meanness. This notion, the idea of a "five star jihad," appears to have two components: (1) the allure of celebrity, and (2) the attractions of living in luxury while being "virtuous." There are numerous accounts of young jihadi warriors posting "selfies" of themselves glamorously atop tanks and brandishing guns, or showing some heartwarmingly human aspect. One such Internet celebrity was a Dutch national of Turkish descent, who engaged in the armed struggle against the Syrian regime, called Israfil Yilmaz (Leigh and Crumley 2014). Some of Yilmaz's popular photos included one of himself tenderly cradling a Syrian toddler swathed in pink, and another of himself, immortalized in the quintessential warrior pose, dressed in a black jacket and camouflage, with one leg propped up and his rifle by his side (Leigh and Crumley 2014). Yilmaz's self-promotion paid off: not only did he develop a following among Syria watchers, but he also achieved a presence in international news when the *New York Times* blogged about him (Leigh and Crumley 2014). Hardly surprising, his success spawned imitators—"Other jihadis emulated him, posting photos of themselves on Facebook, Twitter, and other platforms looking happy and relaxed, pointing fingers in the air and casually slinging guns or other weapons" (Leigh and Crumley 2014). The ripple effects are clear, pointing to the power of jihadi cool.

Analyzing the Rhetorical Mechanics of "Jihadi Cool"

Part of the reason that the "jihadi cool" message is so popular among particularly young men is its careful tailoring and understanding of its targeted audiences, using emotional and imaginative rhetorical tools. Historically, both the look and the content of "jihadi cool" were crafted principally by American radical jihadi converts: Anwar al-Aulaqi, a New Mexico-born Muslim cleric based in Yemen; Omar Hammami, an Alabama native who rose to become a senior commander in Somali and starred in a rap recruiting video, which became an Internet sensation, in which Hammami led an armed group of fighters to a catchy musical beat; Adam Gadahn, a native Californian who became an al-Qaeda spokesman and was charged with treason in 2006; and others (Hsu 2010). Both the ability to communicate in the American vernacular in a manner that appeals to the youth and a command of what it takes to create an MTV aesthetic are crucial components of jihadi cool's rhetorical persuasiveness. Videos created specifically for Western audiences try to depict jihad as a "Hollywood-like video game" (Behn 2014).

Yet despite this imagined appeal to the virtual worlds of Hollywood video and MTV aesthetics, these "jihadi cool" videos attempt a connection to "reality" by humanizing the radical jihadi warriors. Hence, radical jihadi warriors are shown with cats and dogs (Mauro 2014), and with American products that would appeal to their young audiences, such as Nutella, a chocolate spread, and Skittles, a rainbow-like colorful candy (Behn 2014). The irony of jihadi cool is that it deploys Western rhetorical tools to destroy the very culture that created these derivative rhetorical forms and culture, and continues to buttress jihadi cool with powerful persuasive appeal.

As Elizabeth Pearson observed regarding what she termed "Grand Theft Auto Culture": "Being a 'Jihadi' is not just about ideology; it's about status, as a man. Increasingly, a nexus is being recognized between the macho masculinity of British street culture and criminal gangs, and the behaviours associated with pathways to violent extremism" (Pearson 2013). Interestingly, many of the radical jihadi converts were initially neither overtly religious, nor openly political; many of them seemed *normal* to the point of being banal. But the rhetorical elements of jihadi cool seemed an irresistible siren's song. "Rap videos, romanticized notions of revolution and adventure; and first-hand accounts of the 'fun' of guerilla war—are the latest tactics used by militant recruiters as part of what experts have identified as an 'intensification or radicalization,' both in the United States and elsewhere" (Porter 2014).

Having analyzed the mechanics of jihadi cool, the chapter now proceeds to sketching McCauley and Moskalenko's analysis of non-exhaustive pathways to radicalization, prior to applying these two frameworks to Rahami's case.

MCCAULEY AND MOSKALENKO'S TWELVE PATHWAYS TO RADICALIZATION

McCauley and Moskalenko are social psychologists who are acknowledged radicalization experts and consultants to the Department of Homeland Security (Picart 2017, 8-9). McCauley and Moskalenko (2011) sketch twelve diverse pathways to radicalization into terrorist activity, echoing contemporary academic findings that there is no single monolithic pathway toward radicalization. Of particular significance to this chapter are a number of pathways that may lead to violent radical action, and may be characterized as "a-rational" (and even principally emotional) because they are responses neither to ideology nor to political exigencies. Instead, these pathways are responses to combinations of sometimes subtle social factors such as group dynamics, boundary hardening, and even love.

Because Rahami was a "lone wolf" or self-radicalizing individual, this analysis builds principally from McCauley and Moskalenko's (2011) descriptions of six individual level mechanisms of radicalization, and uncovers the relevant pathways operative in this case. Briefly summarized, these six individual pathways are: (1) personal grievance, in which one seeks revenge for harm done to the self, or to loved ones; (2) group grievance, in which one seeks revenge for harm done to a group or cause about which the individual cares; (3) slippery slope, in which an individual is radicalized through increasing political involvement; (4) love, in which one becomes radicalized through attraction to someone already radicalized; (5) risk and status, which can move individuals (especially young men) toward violence regardless of ideology; and (6) unfreezing, in which an individual becomes open to new ideas and identity after losing long-standing reference points (McCauley and Moskalenko 2011, passim).

As this chapter posits, although there is some cross-pollination or interaction across the different pathways, there appear to be primary mechanisms at work. Here, occasional comparisons are made to other recent male US self-radicalizing terrorists, such as the Tsarnaev brothers (the "Boston Marathon Bombers") and Omar Mir Mateen (the "Orlando Night Club Shooter"), only to highlight significant similarities and differences, so as to both point out commonalities (which are non-deterministic), but also to parse out individual differences that make the Rahami case unique.

For example, as a quick overview, deploying McCauley and Moskalenko's (2011) framework, in the case of Tamerlan Anzorovich Tsarnaev, it was likely pathway (1) personal grievance, conflated with pathway (2) group grievance, as well as pathway (5) risk and status, all of which were the prime moving elements. Correlatively, in the case of Dzhokhar Anzorovich "Jahar" Tsarnaev, it was probably pathway (5) risk and status, along with pathway six (6) unfreezing, which were of crucial import. In Mateen's case, probably pathways (1) personal grievance, and (6) risk and status, were crucial to his movement from radical thought into radical action. In the case of Rahami, as the next section of the chapter shows, pathway (1) personal grievance; pathway (2) group grievance; and pathway (6) unfreezing, in which an individual becomes open to new ideas and identity after losing long-standing reference points (such as family affiliations), appear to be the crucial factors in his becoming inspired to self-radicalize.

Thus, this chapter next, as applied to Rahami, traces the powerful emotional and imaginative appeal of jihadi cool, while refusing a linear and reductive model of how self-radicalization occurs. Hence, the analysis illustrates how emotional factors (interacting with imagined relationships fortified by a fantasy propagated by jihadi cool) help catalyze the movement from radical thought to radical action, while also recognizing that each "conversion" always occurs within a unique interplay of various factors. This analysis is essential as a foregrounding to the scrutiny of counter-terrorist narratives in the courtroom and media that emerge in Rahami's eventual capture, trial, and sentencing.

This chapter's findings are very much in line with current research with regard to how individuals evolve into terrorists. For example, former CIA officer and psychologist Marc Sageman analyzed over 500 cases, to arrive at the insight that although one could describe distinct stages of radicalization (Sageman 2008, 71–88),[10] Sageman cautioned against the illusion that "one can simply draw a line, put markers on it and gauge where people are along this path to see whether they are close to committing atrocities" (Sageman 2008, 72). Similarly, the RAND Corporation, based on a fourteen-year study of the process of radicalization, concluded that "no single pathway towards terrorism exists" (US Congress, House 2009), and that the attempt to predict who, among a group of similarly situated individuals, would likely adopt radical views, much less turn violent, is fraught with difficulty, as much seems to be due to "happenstance" (US Congress, House 2009; see also Jenkins 2010). Finally, in a Department of Homeland Security-supported study, McCauley and Moskalenko (2010) concluded that although they had outlined twelve possible pathways to radicalization (while leaving room for the possible discovery of more), that "radicalization progression cannot be understood as an invariable set of steps or 'stages' from sympathy to radicalism" (McCauley and Moskalenko 2010, 82–91).

Having outlined the essentials of McCauley and Moskalenko's (2011) framework, the chapter now proceeds to analyzing how the allure of jihadi cool, and other mechanisms, factored into Rahami's self-radicalization.

AHMAD KHAN RAHAMI: FROM ASPIRING CRIMINAL JUSTICE STUDENT TO DISGRUNTLED OUTSIDER

Unlike other well-known self-radicalizing individuals, such as Tamerlan and Jahar Tsarnaev (the "Boston Marathon Bombers"), little is known about the "Chelsea Bomber." Born in Afghanistan in 1988, Ahmad Khan Rahami emigrated to the United States in 1995, following his father, who had arrived a few years earlier, seeking asylum. Like Jahar Tsarnaev Rahami's naturalization appeared to have occurred without incident in 2011. In a striking set of similarities, Rahami, like Tamerlan Tsarnaev, and Omar Mateen (the "Orlando Night Club Shooter"), seemed initially focused on becoming a law enforcement officer, and majored in Criminal Justice. Although Tsarnaev and Mateen did graduate with degrees, Rahami attended Middlesex County College in Edison, New Jersey, from 2010–2012, but failed to graduate (Shoichet 2016). Like Jahar at roughly the time of the Boston Marathon Bombing (whose once-promising academic future became derailed by his marijuana dealings, thrill-seeking activities, and plummeting grades), upward mobility via an education was now out of reach for Rahami. There is much that is obscure about how and why Rahami self-radicalized, but below are a few reported facts that appear to be crucial to his conversion from radical thought or expression to radical action.

In 2011, the Rahami family filed a lawsuit against the city and its police department, alleging discrimination and harassment, "selective enforcement," and conspiracy (Buncombe 2016), in issuing citations against them for allegedly violating a city ordinance with regard to the hours of operation of its family-run restaurant, First American Fried Chicken, in Elizabeth, New Jersey. The Rahami family had a history of conflicts with the city and the community with regard to the restaurant, which used to be open twenty-four hours per day (Shoichet 2016). According to Mayor Chris Bollwage, a 2012 ruling on the case was decided in favor of the city, with the court noting that the family's restaurant was "disruptive in the city for many, many years" (Shoichet 2016). Thus, using McCauley and Moskalenko's framework, pathway (1) personal grievance, with regard to the perceived "selective enforcement" and (religiously-based) discrimination of the local police and government against the family's attempt to attain the iconic American Dream through its running a restaurant open around the clock was probably a crucial factor.

In 2011, Rahami married a Pakistani woman (Asia Bibi Rahami) at Quetta (known to be a stronghold of Islamic extremists and home to Afghan refugees) (Buncombe 2016), while he was visiting the country (Shoichet 2016); upon his return, Rahami, in response to questions raised by immigration officials, stated that he had been visiting family and attending an uncle's wedding. Rahami and his family traveled several times to Pakistan, and on one trip, Rahami, together with his brother, Mohammad, stayed for a year (Santora et al. 2016). In 2011, Rahami reportedly received three weeks of "lectures and religious education" at the school in Kuchlack, which is approximately 20 kilometers north of Quetta, in Pakistan. Kuchlack is a well-known hub for the Taliban (the militant Islamic movement that has waged more than fifteen years of insurgency against the local government and NATO forces in the geographically proximate Afghanistan) and their *madrasas* (religious centers or seminaries linked with the Taliban) (Boone 2016b). Abdul Samad, the reported owner of the Kuchlack *madrasa*, has been identified by Western experts on the Taliban as an important figure in maintaining an area where both Taliban and ISI (Inter-Services Intelligence Directorate, an army-run spy agency) can mingle; although Samad is an adherent of a mystical, Sufi strain of Islam, which is despised by the more militant factions, he appears to enjoy both protection and prestige, running a school of over 200 students (Boone 2016b). Samad's role in facilitating an area where both government spies and the Taliban can mingle appears to embody Pakistan's double-edged game, appearing to support both counterinsurgency efforts in Afghanistan while also enabling the Taliban by allowing use of its territory as a base (allegedly effectively functioning as a command center) (Boone 2016b). A Pakistani government official, who spoke on condition of anonymity, also revealed that Rahami had also visited other sensitive areas in the country, inclusive of Surkhab and Nushki (Boone

2016b), where former Taliban leader Mullah Akhtar Mansoor was killed by a US drone in May 2016 (Boone 2016a).

Rahami also traveled to Afghanistan multiple times, including to the city of Kandahar. Although Rahami was questioned every time he returned from his overseas trips, in keeping with standard procedure, there appeared to be nothing sufficiently out of the ordinary to raise governmental suspicion that he had been radicalized (Buncombe 2016). Even if real-world contact, arguably, had occurred between Rahami and the Taliban during his overseas trips, there is no evidence his radicalization was the result of that contact, especially as the Taliban is known for its position of focusing purely on foreign troops out of Afghanistan, rather than espousing international jihad, as Al-Qaeda has (Boone 2016b). Nevertheless, using McCauley and Moskalenko's (2011) framework, pathway (2) group grievance, was also a likely factor.

While Rahami was in Islamabad in 2014, there is record that Rahami contacted the office of US Representative Albio Sires, requesting assistance for his wife's passport and visa, as her Pakistani passport had expired. However, once it was renewed, it was discovered that Mrs. Rahami was pregnant, and she was informed that it was necessary to acquire a visa for the unborn child as well; there is no record of what happened to the child (Shoichet 2016). Although Mrs. Rahami legally entered the country at an unspecified date, she left the country before the bombing attacks. Again, deploying McCauley and Moskalenko's framework, Rahami may have internalized the difficulties in acquiring a visa for his Pakistani-born wife, and his unborn child, indicative of further religiously-based "selective" targeting and discrimination, further magnifying his personal grievance (pathway [1]).

Also in 2014, after a violent domestic dispute, in which Rahami stabbed his brother and hit his mother (Dearden 2016a), Rahami's father sent a tip to the FBI, alleging that his son had been converted to terrorism, leading to an interview of the father. Mohammad Rahami, the father, reported that his son had become increasingly drawn to radical Islamist movements, watching Taliban and Al-Qaeda videos, and listening to their poetry; a former employer of the younger Rahami also spoke of how Rahami (the son) had shown sympathy for the Taliban cause (Boone 2016b). However, the FBI, at that time, believed that the matter was purely a domestic dispute, and chose not to interview Rahami; Rahami was never included in the FBI database of potential terrorists (Shoichet 2016). A spokesperson for the FBI stated that "the FBI conducted internal database reviews, interagency checks and multiple checks, none of which revealed ties to terrorism" (Dearden 2016a). After a roughly two-month inquiry into what was labeled a "domestic incident," a grand jury chose not to indict him, and no prosecution followed (Dearden 2016a).

The domestic violence incident was a crucial one, as it indicates a severe rupture with the family unit, a traditional tie, along with Rahami's reportedly increasing gravitation towards virtual representations espousing a culture of jihadi cool. Thus, McCauley and Moskalenko's (2011) pathway (6), unfreezing, in which an individual becomes open to new ideas and identity after losing long-standing reference points (such as family affiliations), appeared to have been an additional crucial factor. This factor, combined with the allure of an imagined heroic brotherhood, magnified by virtual and technological means (in virtual fantasy form), characteristic of a culture of jihadi cool, supplanted Rahami's failed real-life family relations with a more idealized or mythicized global "family." A retrospective look at a YouTube account, yaaghankid786, believed to be linked to Rahami, revealed viewings of the more warlike *nasheeds*, or Islamic chants, which glorify jihad, and in specific, "jihad nasheed ya shahid," a martyr's anthem, and "best jihad nasheed," a montage of battle imagery against the romantic backdrop of the desert, with a running commentary, glorifying violence, and martyrdom (Crilly 2016). One section quintessentially exemplified jihadi cool as it proclaimed: "The filthiest of bandits have attacked us. . . . So where are the swords? They have forgotten we are defiant ones who defend like lions. We are those who built our forts out of skulls" (Crilly 2016). Perhaps in an unconscious miming of the self-styled manner in which jihadi cool youths are portrayed as not only mythic, fearsome warriors but also as human beings capable of tenderness, romantic feeling, and a range of human emotions, Rahami's other viewings included an eclectic mix. Among these were: an instructional video on how to tie the full Windsor knot on a tie (the mark of a gentleman); a slideshow of sinister clowns (quintessential outsiders who dare to bear the mark of their outsider status in their grotesque and Gothic masks); several Bollywood romantic songs, including one from a 2006 Hindi thriller (miming jihadi cool's mythic warriors' passionate love for their women, though with a dark twist, with regard to the thriller); an instructional video on how to change a front bumper replacement (revealing Rahami's passion for not only custom-making cars, but also racing them, and thus the propensity for risk-taking and thrill-seeking—McCauley and Moskalenko's [2011] pathway [5] risk and status); and a viral cat video (correlating with how jihadi cool warriors constantly posed with cats, dogs, or infants, in their self-promotional videos) (Crilly 2016).

Hip-hop artist Flee Jones, who had known Rahami since they were teenagers, alleged that he had noticed that Rahami had changed in demeanor and dress, becoming more overtly "religious," outwardly growing a beard and wearing traditional Muslim garments, after a trip to Afghanistan in 2014 (Buncombe 2016). Nevertheless, Mr. Jones was quick to add that in his view,

Rahami was simply "more quiet and more mature," although he stated that he knew that Rahami was lying when he said he had been away on vacation because Rahami's younger brother had told him that they had traveled to Afghanistan (Buncombe 2016). The general consensus, outside of the Rahami family, was that Rahami was simply religious, but not radicalized. Ryan McCann, a regular at the family-run restaurant reported that Rahami had a passion for "soup[ing] up and rac[ing]" Honda civics (Buncombe 2016). Salaal Ismial, a community worker at the Al-Hadi mosque in New Jersey, reported that Rahami appeared to be a regular attendee of various religious festivals, and was a familiar face at the restaurant, but that there was nothing extraordinary or suspicious about these (Buncombe 2016).

Although clues to Rahami's motives in self-radicalizing are sparse, what is clear is that a journal (blood-stained in photos due to Rahami's wounds during the confrontation with the police that led to his capture) recovered from him reveal "inspiration" from Al-Qaeda propaganda. The journal praised Nidal Malik Hasan, who massacred thirteen individuals at Fort Hood in Texas, "brother Osama bin Laden," and Anwar al-Awlaki, the American-Yemeni al-Qaeda recruiter killed in a US drone strike in 2011, but whose writings appeared to outlive his mortal life (Dearden 2016a). Photos in the journal that were revealed to the press also made direct references to Al-Qaeda's chief propagandist and second-in-command, Abu Muhammad al-Adnani (Dearden 2016a). Even more telling was an excerpt from the journal, tracing crucial language from radical online recruiters' well-known for calls for action, that read: "I looked for guidance an Alhumdulilah [praise God], guidance came Sheikh Anwar [al-Awlaki], Brother Adnani/Dawla . . . Said it clearly attack the kuffar [disbelievers] in their backyard" (Dearden 2016a). Rahami's journal thus directly referenced Adnani's call to the "Soldiers of the Caliphate" who could not travel to the Caliphate to attack the enemy whenever or however they could. Adnani's exhortation has inspired a number of US self-radicalizing individuals to act, resulting, in among others, the Boston Marathon Bombing, the San Bernardino massacre, and the Orlando Night Club mass shooting. Like these other self-radicalizing individuals, Rahami's journal expressed a desire for martyrdom, and stated ominously: "Inshallah [God willing] the sounds of the bombs will be heard in your streets. Gunshots to your police. Death to your oppression" (Dearden 2016a). Even more directly, the journal referenced pipe bombs and pressure cookers—the very devices that failed to kill any of the victims at New York and New Jersey—by the telling phrase: "in the streets they plan to run a mile" (Dearden 2016a), which seems a miming of the havoc wreaked by the Boston Marathon Bombing.

On September 15, 2016, just two days before the Chelsea bombings, a family member shot a home video that showed footage of a partially buried device being lit and exploding, followed by billowing smoke and the sound of laughter, just before Rahami entered the frame to retrieve the debris (Dearden 2016a).

In summary, therefore, using McCauley and Moskalenko's (2011) framework, the pathways or factors that seem to have catalyzed Rahami's movement from extremist thought or speech into radical action were: pathways (1) personal grievance; (2) group grievance; and (6) unfreezing, in which an individual becomes open to new ideas and identity after losing long-standing reference points (such as family affiliations). As such, Rahami's conversion story seems a hybrid of Tamerlan Tsarnaev's conversion (in that both pathways [1] and [2] personal and group grievance, as well as pathway [5] risk and status, appeared to be crucial), and Jahar Tsarnaev's conversion (in that pathways [5] risk and status, and six [6] unfreezing, were the principal catalytic factors). Like Tamerlan, Rahami appears to have had real-world contact and at least religious instruction from radical jihadi groups, and returned, changed in demeanor and dress, after his overseas travels, especially in 2014. Like Jahar, Rahami gravitated towards jihadi cool propaganda and instructional materials espoused by Al-Qaeda, who incited global jihad based on a romanticized and binary vision of a righteous religious war against the Infidel. Nevertheless, overall, a crucial factor, in all three cases, was the powerful allure of an imagined heroic brotherhood, magnified by virtual and technological means, characteristic of a culture of jihadi cool.

COUNTERTERRORISM'S COUNTER-NARRATIVE AND FRAMES OF HORROR

The framework I use to analyze how recent counterterrorism efforts in the United States have sought to appropriate, and reverse, the narrative and persuasive power of "jihadi cool/chic" has deep roots in a critical analysis of how "monstrous" or "teratological" discourses work, against the normative terrain of the law. Etymologically tracked, "teras," is a Greek term that means "monster" (that is, something "pointed to" and against which one is warned), and "logia," another Greek term meaning "a speaking, discourse, treatise, doctrine, theory, science" (*Online Etymology Dictionary*, s.v. "tera"; "logia"). Conventional thinking, therefore, construes monstrous discourses as law's dark other; indeed, as I have shown, jihadi cool/chic's mastery of an extremely conservative gendered narrative of warriors versus the *kuffar* ("infidels"/"nonbelievers"),[11] and its deployment of sophisticated and state-of-the-art cinematic and virtual tools appears to be the penultimate embodiment of such a discourse. The question that has plagued counter-terrorist efforts, therefore, has been how does one create a competing narrative (and eventually, adaptive policy and a reinterpretation of laws that define the balance between national security and privacy, among others) that prevents the further spread of jihadi cool/chic's toxic allure?[12]

Thus, this chapter draws from analytic tools developed in the Law and Literature movement, which has since expanded to include analyses of film and of popular culture (see Greenfield et al. 2010; Mezey and Niles 2005, 91–186; Sarat 2011); the chapter applies these tools to the narratives deployed by the culture of jihadi cool, and their counter-narratives. Hence, this chapter builds from two basic assumptions that Orit Kamir (2005, 27–81) outlined in her detailed analysis of Roman Polanski's *Death and the Maiden*. On a superficial level, both law and film "reflect and refract fundamental values, images, notions of identity, lifestyles, and crises of their societies and cultures" (Kamir 2005, 27–28) and recur, like leitmotifs, in the historically and sociologically grounded construction of "subject, community, identity, memory, gender roles, justice and truth" (Kamir 2005, 28). Additionally, both law and film provide "major sociocultural arenas where collective hopes, dreams, beliefs, anxieties, and frustrations are publicly portrayed, evaluated and enacted" (Kamir 2005, 28). Thus, jihadi cool narratives and their counter-narratives, in a manner analogous to, for example, Holocaust films (Aristodemou 2000), whether documentary or fictional, evoke underlying fundamental values, cultural aspirations, and collective anxieties or traumas in their staging of events.

Also, as Kamir (2005) has argued, films that connect with depictions of the law engage in "large-scale 'legal indoctrination,'" which Kamir interprets as the training of audiences "in judgment while examining—and often reinforcing—legal norms, logic, and structures" (Kamir 2005, 28; see also White 1999). Transplanting Kamir's analysis of the hidden hermeneutic of Holocaust films on to the popularization of jihadi cool/chic and counter-jihadi narratives, in such virtual representations, "judgment . . . is not merely portrayed but . . . actively performed . . . , together with their . . . constructed and/or actual viewers . . . [thus rhetorically constituting] a community of viewers and cinematic engagement in the social constitution of primary values, institutions, and concepts" (Kamir 2005, 28–29). This insight is not new to trial practitioners, among others. Much as a litigator or a defense lawyer carefully selects how facts are arranged and highlighted as well as pays close attention to the tone or tenor of the storytelling and to the defendant's demeanor and dress (Sherwin 2000), a film director may inculcate a broad spectrum of tools to foster audience identification with a particular character or to elicit almost automatic emotional reactions to a particular scene or character. Examples of such tools include "choices regarding genre, editing, methods of narration, plots, points of view, rhythm and casting" (Kamir 2005, 29).

The choice of genre-related tools is crucial to the construction of a narrative, and to implicitly conditioning its intended audience's reception of the narrative. Communication scholars have pointed to the rhetorical power of "logics of perception" embedded in, for example, virtual depictions of the global war on terrorism (see Virilio 1989; Bousquet 2017, 69–80), as well as to the persuasive force of horror framing (with its construction of the "monstrous other") with regard to political events (Ivie and Giner 2015). Prior work I have done in this area has identified two different types of horror frames: the classic horror frame and the conflicted horror frame (Picart and Frank 2006). The classic horror frame (which draws elements from a Gothic mode of narration) (Carroll 1990, 4), as instantiated in the iconic Universal Studios' *Dracula* (1931) and *Frankenstein* (1931), depicts monsters as "shar[ing] nothing in common with the audience . . . inhabit[ing] a different space, which they leave to attack the innocent" (Picart and Frank 2006 7). Hence, not only are classic monsters ontologically different (Prince 2004, 118–30), but also they inhabit spatially demarcated spaces—for example, the dark castle where Dracula lurks and Frankenstein's hidden laboratory, fetid with the stench of decaying body parts. Even more radically, classic monsters "[breach] the ontology of normal time," enabling the bracketing of horror, and allowing the audience a detachment from the eventual destruction of the classic monsters the narrative demands, while allowing them a vicarious thrill in the catharsis of the violence that such destruction requires. It is with the death of the classic monster that normality and normal time re-emerge. In contrast, the conflicted horror frame imbricates "evil [with] normality, refusing to recognize an unassailable gap between the two spheres" (Picart and Frank 2006, 9). Thus, conflicted horror frame's location of the "monstrous" is within the mundane, everyday, and normal, such as in contemporary horror films, like Hannibal Lecter in *Silence of the Lambs* (1991), who seems, outwardly, human, and operates in the ordinary world; unlike the classic monster, there is no cathartic "staking" at the end of the film, as Lecter not only survives but also escapes, with the horrors he is capable of committing breaching ordinary space and time (Montgomery 2019, 281–321, citing Picart and Frank 2006).[13]

Jihadi cool's master narrative shares key characteristics of the classic frame. The classic monsters, the *kuffar*, are depicted as irredeemably other and inhuman, undeserving of sympathy, and their acts, as deserving of utter annihilation. Jihadi cool's romanticized construction of warrior-heroes (and their brides—a separate gendered construction, "jihadi chic," which is not relevant to this chapter), set against the relief of the *kuffar*'s culture of contamination and moral decay, is one of jihadi cool's most powerful recruitment tools. The promise of a *pure* (and yet glamorous) Brotherhood, forged in the glory of battlehood demarcates the spaces and times of violence and death to the monstrous realm of the *kuffar*, set apart from the spaces and times of camaraderie allegedly enjoyed within the mythical City of God.

Jihadi cool's emergent counter-narrative/s appropriate and mirror aspects of the jihadi cool master narrative; however, effective counter-narratives do more than simply appropriate and mirror. By cross-fertilizing the spectatorial safety and policing function of the classic horror frame with elements of the conflicted horror frame, terrorist counter-narratives, while taking account of the power of a-rational elements that buttress the master narrative of jihadi cool, enable a potentially critical space of engagement to occur.

Rahami's Capture

Rahami's capture has been hailed as one of the most rapid and effective strikes against self-radicalizing terrorists. It is thus instructive to map what developments were unique to this case. One distinctive feature of the case was the early use of an iPhone alert feature usually reserved for notifications of natural disasters and Amber (child abduction emergency) alerts; in a prior, parallel observation, Posner (2007, 199) recommended that "[t]o limit the scope of surveillance, 'threats to national security' should be narrowly defined as threats involving a potential for mass deaths or catastrophic property or other economic damage." This appears to be the first time that type of recommendation (though in the context of a manhunt, not a surveillance operation) was actually enacted. On September 19, 2016, on or about 8:00 a.m., EST, the New York police issued a cell phone alert, which read: "WANTED: Ahmad Khan Rahami, twenty-eight-year-old male. See media for pic. Call 9-1-1 if seen" (Griffin 2016). The police department simultaneously shared the wanted poster via its Twitter account (Counter Extremism Project 2019). The notices warned that Rahami, simply a suspect in connection to the Chelsea bombing at that stage, could be armed and dangerous, and the photograph, issued in black and white, showed a bearded and unsmiling Rahami. Of note was that the cell phone notices in particular were impossible to ignore, as Apple "has built in a system that allows government messages to cut through settings like do-not-disturb that ordinarily would stop notifications from showing on iPhones" (Griffin 2016).

One immediately sees the frame of classic monstrosity deployed at the very outset of the narrative. Rahami was the dark threat—the theoretical person of interest already configured as a more-than-likely terrorist. New York Mayor Bill de Blasio, in echoing the alert, stated: "I want to be very clear. This individual could be armed and dangerous, he should be considered armed and dangerous. Anyone seeing him should call 9-1-1" (Withnall 2016). More importantly, Rahami occupied the monstrous spaces of the child kidnapper and a natural disaster—two monstrous figures dangerous enough to "point to" and "warn against" using the elite iPhone alert. The iPhone alert is generally reserved for extreme situations—emergencies in progress that might yet be averted with the voluntary assistance of the larger populace (thus justifying the intrusion into "private" or "normal" civilian time and space), and the innovative use of this technology was key to Rahami's relatively quick and effective capture. Additionally, the use of this technology pointed to the nature of the threat: an imminent threat that could not be reasoned with, and against which one had to react defensively. Nevertheless, the government balanced its warning of the imminent threat with a reassurance that the threat/monster, no matter how dangerous, could be contained, and that eventually, as in the classic horror frame, it would be vanquished. Mayor de Blasio, in his media interviews, declared: "We need to get this guy right away. . . . My experience is [that] on[c]e the FBI zeroes in on someone, they will get them" (Withnall 2016). The use of the metaphoric scope of a sniper "zeroing in" on not simply a singular monster, but on a plurality of them, as an endorsement of the track record of the FBI, magnified the optics of confidence embedded in the narrative.

Then-President Obama as well gave media interviews about the manhunt for Rahami just hours before the shoot-out and capture of the suspect. In the wake of the havoc wrought by the detonation of a pipe bomb beside a five kilometer run in New Jersey, and another bomb in Chelsea, which injured twenty-nine people, on September 17 and 18, 2016, Obama stressed that that the American way of life would not be undermined by fear and hate—potentially beginning a break away from the classic horror frame's emphasis on staking the monstrous with its fearful mob. Obama's rhetoric was more carefully measured, in terms of rhetorical registers of monstrosity, in terms of its call to action, stating: "If you see something suspicious, then you need to say something" (Revesz 2016). He also stated that the bombings were being investigated as *potential* acts of "terrorism," although general media coverage had suggested that the suspect was not on any terrorism watchdog list. Unlike de Blasio, who focused principally on the FBI's sniper-like strategy, Obama generally hailed the "outstanding first responders" inclusive of "federal, state and local" authorities who were "working together around the clock to prevent attacks and keep us safe" (Revesz 2016). The metaphor of a well-organized militia, selflessly and anonymously engaged in endless, unspecified, and invisible labors to defend normal time and space to demarcate and police the space of the monstrous, which lurks within the subterranean spaces underneath the surface of the normal, hinted at a conflicted, rather than classic frame. Continuing with his encomium, Obama stated: "They are the best of the best. Over the years they have [stopped] many plots and saved many lives and we are incredibly grateful for their service today and every day" (Revesz 2016). Obama also emphasized the need to continue to "go after" ISIS/ISIL, taking out their leaders, infrastructure, and territory in order to undermine their ideology, thus moving into an active appropriation and overturning of the pillars of a culture of jihadi cool. Obama justified this reverse-conquest, configured as a defensive measure, principally as an inoculation against the contaminative allure of jihadi cool, stating: "Over time that will make it harder to recruit people and inspire people to violence" (Revesz 2016). Obama's responses to the media, compared with de Blasio's, cross-fertilized elements of the conflicted horror narrative in that it acknowledged the embedding of monstrous space and time within normal space and time, as evidenced in the generation and "inspiration" of self-radicalizing individuals.

With the manhunt in progress, Harinder Bains, a naturalized Indian-born Sikh, who owned a bar in Linden, New Jersey, was watching news coverage of the recent New York bombing and the attempted New Jersey bombing, when he noticed a man asleep outside his business. He initially dismissed the sleeping man as simply another drunk, but then recognized him as Rahami, and alerted the police. Harinder Bains was lionized as a hero by the press, but his response resisted the rhetoric of heroism and simply chose the language of the good citizen: "I did what I think every American would have done. . . . My neighbor would have done the same thing. Any Jewish, Christian, Sikh, Muslim. Anybody would have done the same thing" (Dearden 2016b). Bains's statements were noteworthy, particularly against the backdrop of recent reports of a Sikh man wearing a turban (mistakenly identified as Muslim by a fear-ridden crowd) run over and beaten in California after the San Bernardino shooting (Dearden 2016b). Bains's remarks thus highlighted the Good Citizen's role as the counterpoint to the monster (as in the case of Rahami, himself a naturalized American) and to the equally monstrous monster-hunting mob. Invisibility or humility and groundedness in a common sense of justice and community thus appear key attributes of the Good Citizen as these inoculate themselves from the glamour-seeking aspirations disguised as a romanticized desire for purity embedded in the allure of jihadi cool.

Barely four hours after the unprecedented iPhone alert was sent out, after a brief firefight little described by the press, Rahami was subdued and lay wounded in the rainy streets of Linden, New Jersey (Santora et al. 2016). There was, however, much coverage of Rahami's blood-stained journal, which praised Nidal Hasan, who had massacred thirteen people at Fort Hood, Texas; "brother Osama bin Laden"; and Anwar al-Awlaki, the American-Yemeni al-Qaeda recruiter assassinated in a US drone strike in 2011 (Dearden 2016a). The journal reputedly ended with: "Inshallah [God willing] the sounds of the bombs will be heard in your streets. Gunshots to your police.

Death to your oppression" (Dearden 2016a). The journal was reported to also contain mentions of pipe bombs and pressure cooker bombs—the very devices that failed to kill any victims in New York and New Jersey on Saturday—as well as the sentence "in the streets they plan to run a mile" (Dearden 2016a). The journal's ramblings accused the US government of "slaughter against the mujahideen be it Afghanistan, Iraq, Sham [Syria], Palestine" and memorialized Rahami's plea "for shahadat [martyrdom]." Echoing the now infamous call to action of radical online recruiters, Rahami's journal revealed his intent that because he was unable to travel to wage jihad in Syria, he would follow al-Awlaki's to "attack the kuffar [infidels] in their backyard" (Dearden 2016a). "The FBI & Homeland Security [unintelligible . . . are] looking for me," the journal went on. "I pray to the beautiful wise Allah. Not to take jihad away from [me]" (Dearden 2016a). Although the widely circulated shot of the bloodied journal was mostly white space stained or blotted by either blood or rain, one could clearly make out the phrases: "I looked for guidance and . . . Alhumdulilah . . . Guidance come . . . Sheikh Anwar . . . Brother Adnani . . . Dawla. Said it . . . Clearly Attack the Kuffar in their back Yard" (Dearden 2016a). The journal, as framed by the press, effectively served as Rahami's most effective witness against him, and harked back to Jahar Tsarnaev's bloodstained manifesto, scribbled in pencil in the interior of a dry-docked boat, punctuated by bullet stains and streaked with blood, created during the eighteen-hour manhunt in search of the younger Tsarnaev brother (CNNWire 2015).

Rahami's Trial and Sentencing

Unlike Jahar Tsarnaev's much-covered trial, given the dubious title of being "America's Most Watched Trial," there was comparatively little coverage of the phases leading up to Rahami's trial, save for some coverage that like the younger Tsarnaev, Rahami was charged while he was in the hospital, recovering from gunshot wounds; and that he pleaded "not-guilty." Rahami was not charged with terrorism; this is important to note as the government had a history of unsuccessfully struggling with attempting prosecutions via military commissions (Bravin 2006, A1) or using terrorism as a charge. A study by the New York University Center for Law and Security (2006) detailed a dismal picture; in excerpted form, the study included the following summary (although the focus then was on organized sleeper cells rather than self-radicalizing lone wolves):

- Only four individuals have been convicted of federal crimes of terrorism, per se;

- Nobody affiliated with a radical Islamic group has been convicted of crimes related to chemical, biological, radiological, or nuclear weapons;
- No sleeper cell with logistical or tactical links to al[-]Qaeda has been convicted;
- *The vast majority of cases turn out to include no link to terrorism once the case goes to court* [emphasis added];
- The Department of Justice's [DOJ] pattern of pursuit is focused on early detection rather than conviction on federal terrorism charges;
- The DOJ often announces potential terrorism cases as such before the evidence is in place that will enable prosecution for a federal crime of terrorism.

Here, Rahami (like Jahar Tsarnaev) was indicted using criminal law. As depicted in the media, charges in Rahami's case included the use of weapons of mass destruction (Counts I and II in *Rahami* 2017, fn 2–3), bombing of a place of public use (Count III in *Rahami* 2017, fn 2), attempted murder of police officers, destruction of property by means of fire or explosive (Counts IV and V in *Rahami* 2017, fn 2–3), and "use of a destructive device" (Garcia 2016). The court documentation regarding the charges filed also indicated charges on the possession and transportation of bombs (Counts VII and VIII in *Rahami* 2017, 3–5), independent of their detonation, on which the Defense filed a Motion to Dismiss; the court denied the motion, citing precedent for maintaining those charges (*Rahami* 2017, 2, citing *Dye* 2013; *Garcia* 2011; *Smith* 2007; *Khalil* 2000; *Salameh* 2001).

Leading up to the trial, the Defense, in the media, was depicted as successful in getting Rahami's responses to police questioning while he was at the hospital suppressed due to improper interrogation; the Defense emphasized the vulnerability of Rahami's position, wounded, with a breathing tube inserted into his throat, reduced to answering only "yes" or "no" to the government's questions. However, a look at the actual case law presents a different picture. In a reframing of the arguments presented, the court denied the Defense motion to suppress statements on the ground that they were involuntary as "moot" because the State had stated that it had no intention of using these statements taken on September 27 and 29, 2016 (*Rahimi*, 2017, 1). Interestingly, the Defense's parallel strategy of attempting to suppress statements Rahimi had made when hair samples were collected from him, and of the hair samples seized, was not covered in the press, probably because the image of Rahami's hair being plucked was not as graphic as the image of an air tube being lodged in his throat while being compelled to answer "yes" or "no" questions without a lawyer present, as he lay wounded in a hospital bed. Again, this Defense motion was similarly denied as moot because the government stated that it would not introduce these into evidence *(Rahami*, 2017, 1–2). Ultimately, those hair samples would have been cumulative anyway, as the government had Rahami's fingerprints on the bomb fragments and the bombs that failed to detonate, as the chapter later shows.

As covered in the media, the Defense also argued vehemently against what they thought to be the government's intent to use the now-much defamed "radicalization theory" (Dubal 2012, 35; Patel 2011, 3; Huq 2010, 39–69), in its case against Rahami, in order "to make its case more 'compelling, dramatic and seductive'"—a classic case of the mirroring effect of the classic horror narrative, wherein the Defense's narrative posited that it was the government who was wrongly hyperbolizing Rahami's connection to terrorist groups (Associated Press 2017). Prior to that, in a case not covered by the media, the Defense had written a letter, which the New Jersey court treated as a motion, requesting the court to schedule an initial appearance and appoint counsel for Rahami, citing Federal Rule of Criminal Procedure 5(a)(1), which directs a person who "makes an arrest" to bring the person before the court "without unnecessary delay" (*Rahami*, 2016, 1). The court denied the motion principally on the basis that Rahami was then in state custody based on charges filed by the State of New Jersey, and that no federal charges at that time had yet been filed; thus, Federal Rule 5 was not triggered yet, as there was no federal arrest, and similarly, it was premature to assign counsel as appointments are appropriate at the "initial appearance before the United States magistrate judge or the [district] court" (*Rahami*, 2016, 1–2, citing *Alvarez-Sanchez*, 511 U.S. 350, 358 (1994) and 18 U.S.C. §3006A(c)). The court's refusal to exercise discretion essentially followed prior criminal law practice of detaining terrorist subjects on the ground that they posed a danger to national security by locking them up indefinitely, subject to periodic judicial review (Posner 2006).

Again in contrast to Jahar Tsarnaev's trial, which took three months (Andrews 2014), after only two weeks, Rahami was convicted of all charges, and the evidence presented at the trial was reframed retrospectively. In his closing arguments, Assistant US Attorney Emil Bove summarized the key pieces of evidence that connected Rahami to the pipe bombs (Crimesider Staff 2016). First, both his fingerprints and DNA were found on bombs in the September 17, 2016, attacks. Second, there was ample video footage that tracked Rahami's movements as he bore the bombs, concealed in suitcases through Manhattan streets, and footage of the explosion that rocked 23rd Street in the Chelsea neighborhood that injured thirty individuals. Third, although the second bomb failed to detonate, that was rhetorically counter-acted by testimony by a bomb squad investigator, who authenticated evidence of a severely mangled trash bin (weighing approximately one-hundred pounds) that was sent hurtling about 120 feet across the busy street by the bomb that did detonate, scattering ball bearings meant to function as shrapnel; that no one was hurt was framed as "miraculous" by the government but it was unambiguous what the inference was—regardless of the fortuitousness of that event, Rahami's murderous intent was clear. Fourth, the most damning of the evidence, Rahami's diary, took "credit" for the events.

The Defense's strategy, as expressed in Assistant Public Defender Sabrina Shroff's closing arguments, was simple: she did not question the government's fingerprint, DNA, and video footage, but urged the jury to acquit Rahami of three charges based on the lack of evidence with regard to Rahami's intent in relation to the bombs that failed to detonate. This was in reference to a bomb at 27th Street that was discovered and deactivated before it could explode; additionally, a homeless man and his friend alerted the government to a backpack with smaller bombs in a trash can in close proximity to a train station in Elizabeth, New Jersey (Crimesider Staff 2016).

Rounding off the government's final closing arguments, to rebut the Defense, Assistant US Attorney Andrew DeFilippis used a strategy that was effective at Jahar Tsarnaev's trial: he reminded the jury of how the video recounted "step after step after step" Rahami took, as he planted the bombs, with "cold and calculating" resolve (Crimesider Staff 2016); the implication, as in the younger Tsarnaev's trial, was that with each step, he could have turned back, but chose not to do so. He concluded with rebutting the Defense's argument about the lack of motive and the failure of the bombs to detonate by arguing that the government's burden lay in simply establishing that the accused had taken "substantial steps" to achieve his objective. Finally, again appropriating a rhetorical tactic from the younger Tsarnaev's trial, the government reminded the jury of footage that showed the accused hurrying off, in the aftermath of the bomb exploding "so he wouldn't get hurt while others bled" (Crimesider Staff 2016).

At sentencing, the government argued that Rahami had not only failed to show remorse[14] but also remained scornful of the American justice system (an argument iconized in the infamous photo of Jahar Tsarnaev irreverently pointing his middle finger at the camera), and had actually sought to radicalize his fellow inmates by allowing them access to the very materials that had inspired him to self-radicalize, such as speeches and lectures by Osama bin Laden, founder of al-Qaida, and Anwar al-Awlaki, the American-born cleric; and other radical propaganda materials, such as The Book of Jihad and bomb-making instructions (Associated Press 2018). There was a striking convergence between the incriminating materials found in Jahar's laptop, and these materials, to which Rahami presumably had access in preparation for the trial.

Rahami, given a chance to speak, denied harboring hate for anyone but neither admitted nor denied setting the bomb that exploded stating: "I didn't grow up hating anyone . . . I grew up in an environment where we're mixed with everyone . . . [Nevertheless, he stated that he eventually understood] why there is such a big frustration between the Muslims overseas and the American people" (Wilson 2018). The Defense brought up the fact that Rahami had once aspired to be a police officer and had worked as a security guard after studying criminal justice at a community college (Wilson 2018) in an effort to mitigate punishment by showing that Rahami did not espouse extremist views at the outset. Ironically, the Defense's attempt to mitigate punishment only underlined Rahami's similarities with Omar Mateen, the Orlando Night Club Shooter, who had also aspired to become a police officer and studied criminal justice but had to settle for being a security guard, and who was also a naturalized American citizen who had self-radicalized.

Judge Richard M. Berman, who sentenced Rahami to two life terms for the Manhattan attack, expressed surprise at the "puzzling" discordance between Rahami's "reasonable" statements and the hatred and violence the journal espoused and his actions (Wilson 2018). "You sound like most people and yet your actions are totally at odds with your voice," the judge stated. The judge also returned to the numerous video clips tracking Rahami's steps as he dragged the bombs in two suitcases and a backpack through Manhattan streets, stating: "It's really hard to square the way you appear in court to that other behavior" (Neumeister 2018).

Retrospectively analyzing how the counter-narratives were framed, it is important to note how the government used predominantly a classic horror frame in order to stress Rahami's dangerousness. During the two-day manhunt, by taking the step of inaugurating the use of the iPhone alert, the government underlined the exigency of capturing Rahami, effectively equating the urgency of the matter to that of attempting to circumvent a child kidnapping in progress, or evading or mitigating the destructive and indiscriminate effects of a natural disaster; what was of extreme importance was simply to hunt down the monster and deprive it of its power. At the trial, the government used numerous strategies to demonstrate the monstrousness of Rahami's intent and actions. It is important to note that the counter-narrative strategy was similar to that used in the Nuremberg International Military Tribunal on the Holocaust in which documentary footage of the death camps, gas chambers, and mounds of corpses or shoes played an important role in "attesting" to the Nazi crimes against humanity.[15] Here, the most effective "witnesses" against Rahami were not so much individual testimonies (although these played a vital role in the collective impact) but rather artifacts, such as the bomb fragments and his DNA and fingerprints; the video footage of Rahami literally and metaphorically taking numerous steps to effect his malign intentions; and most eloquently, the blood-stained journal claiming allegiance to Osama bin Laden and Anwar al-Awlaki and pridefully claiming ownership of these acts of violence, both actual and intended. At sentencing, the government sought to stress the unmitigated monstrousness of the acts of which Rahami had been convicted, and even more horrifyingly, his unrepentant lack of remorse over his actions and brazen attempts to spread the infection of self-radicalization to his fellow inmates, thus reiterating the point that Rahami's radicalization was so thorough and immune to reason that it resisted even incarceration. Although there were some traces of a conflicted horror narrative during the manhunt stage (evidenced specifically through then-President Obama's press remarks that implicitly recognized Rahami's status as a naturalized American citizen and of the persistent threat from within of self-radicalizing individuals), only the classic horror frame persisted in the government's arguments at trial and sentencing.

In contrast, the Defense's arguments attempted to appropriate, where possible, the rhetorics of classic horror framing when addressing the government's violation of Rahami's due process rights by interrogating him while he was wounded in the hospital, emphasizing the graphic image of an air tube lodged in his throat. The Defense, particularly at sentencing, attempted to use a conflicted horror frame to show that Rahami, in being a naturalized citizen who formerly aspired to become one of the country's defenders as a police officer, had been an ordinary citizen until the infection of radical propaganda effectively turned him into what he became. Although the Defense promised that appeals would follow, the effectiveness of the government's counter-terrorist narrative, deployed both on the media front and in the courtroom, using a principally classic horror frame, probably makes it highly unlikely that Rahami's sentences will be overturned.

In closing, in a parallel study, Naomi Mezey and Mark C. Niles (2005, 91–186), drawing from Jessica Silbey (2001, 97–116), make an effective argument for a complex and critical approach to the analysis of law as depicted in popular culture. In comparing how American popular film and television visualize narratives about law and crime, Mezey and Niles distinguish between a potential for radical critique in film versus a more domesticated narrative, characteristic of television. Nevertheless, they conclude that despite that difference, both media generally tend to reinforce dominant and pro-status quo perspectives on law. Analogously, this analysis has shown that although the use of a conflicted horror frame in constructing narratives of counter-terrorism, allows for a more nuanced critique, ultimately, counter-terrorist narratives, both in the courtroom and media, tend to fall back on a classic horror frame, which not only mirrors, but also appropriates rhetorical tools that the culture of jihadi cool uses. Ultimately, this turn to a classic horror mode, with its appeal to an implicit underlying communal understanding of justice upon which instruments of the law rely for their legitimacy, is not surprising because it is precisely the community of Good Citizens that is the Monster's counterpart. As Mezey and Niles (2016) conclude: "there is a mythic, shared and hegemonic sense of justice to which we can turn, and upon which we can rely. And it is this simple faith in justice that is the primary ideological product of our popular images of law" (Mezey and Niles 2016, 305). Nevertheless, to close, gesturing towards another project that attempts to pierce through, or negotiate, a revolving door of mirroring narratives, it is important to note, as Maan (2015) points out, that perhaps an effective counter-narrative to the (religious and nationalist) fundamentalism inherent in jihadi cool narratives, is to return to an American tradition of pluralist narratives, which allow for co-existence without requiring utter harmonization and the silencing of dissent.

CONCLUSION

After analyzing the mechanics of jihadi cool culture in order to understand the genesis of male self-radicalizing terrorists in the United States, my focus in this chapter has been an analysis of the capture, trial, and sentencing of Rahami. Rahami's case is instructive for its relatively swift resolution, and is useful as a marker in taking stock of the evolution of counterterrorism measures, inclusive of the attempt to educate the American public about the reality of self-radicalizing terrorists, and perhaps metaphorically immunizing, to some extent, against the lure of jihadi cool/chic. The chapter began with a characterization of jihadi cool, as a framework relevant to the understanding how Rahami self-radicalized. Then it adopted as a heuristic, where applicable, McCauley and Moskalenko's 2011 analysis of pathways to radicalization in the study of Rahami's transformation from consumer of radical jihadi propaganda to inspired terrorist bomber, with his conversion catalyzed by concrete connections to radical jihadi groups, and enhanced by a "Brotherhood" imaginatively constructed. Further, this chapter has analyzed a number of counter-terrorist rhetorical mechanisms deployed in the manhunt and capture, and trial and sentencing of Rahami, which collectively served as functional counter-narratives to the narrative of jihadi cool. Drawing from analytic tools derived from law and literature as applied to film and popular culture (and extended into the courtroom and media), this chapter notes the predominance of a narrative similar to the classic horror frame, which locates monstrous action within a frame different from the normal. This classic frame requires the utter containment of the monstrous, with some hints of a conflicted horror frame, which acknowledges that the threat of the monstrous lies within normal time and space. Crucial to the emerging counter-terrorist narrative/s and jurisprudence, enacted in mediated discourses and in the courtroom, are references back to the now-iconic capture, trial, and sentencing of Jahar Tsarnaev (*Tsarnaev* 2013a, 2013b, 2013c, 2013d, 2014a, 2014b, 2014c, 2014d, 2015a, 2015b, 2015c[1], 2015c[2], 2015d, 2015e, 2016a[1], 2016a[2]),[16] which appear to serve as emergent templates for evolving counter-terrorist policy and criminal courtroom procedure and argument.[17]

*Acknowledgments. The author wishes to thank Margaret Baker for her excellent and detail-oriented assistance; Sam Brawand for her patient and time-efficient help; and Harry Keyishian and Jerry Rivera for their conscientious reading and insightful commentary on prior drafts. The author also thanks Ashleigh Cooke and Kris Patenaude for their expert and efficient help at production.

NOTES

1. Lauren Newell analyzes how the Digital Generation shows a strong preference for online interaction via email, text messages, social networks, and instant messaging, rather than real-world interaction through face-to-face or telephonic conversations, resulting in poor real-world communication skills, underdeveloped social skills, and a less developed empathy, compared with earlier generations—which is a significant factor buttressing the allure of a culture of jihadi cool/chic. See Newell 2019.
2. For an evaluation of United States intelligence reform in response to terrorism, both in terms of its gains and failures, see Posner 2007. See also Yin 2019.
3. For a review of three activist approaches to applied political and legal philosophy, which may be useful as a jurisprudential heuristic to developing policy on countering terrorism, see Dempsey and Lister 2017, 313–327.
4. For a comparative review of US post-9/11 counter-terrorist strategies and European laws, institutions and practices, particularly in relation to pre-emption, see Schmitt 2010. See also Jordan and Philpott 2010.
5. For an analysis of how international law increasingly protects privacy over national security, ironically undermining privacy by throwing off the symbiotic balance between the two, see Cunningham 2012, 643–702 .
6. For a parallel analysis of how the romanticization of the power of science and the virtues of the legal system (and the correlative demonization of inept forensic scientists, plaintiff's experts, or social science, and judges untrained in science, lawyers as overly zealous advocates, or jurors as emotional, uncritical, and confused) requires an analysis that takes stock of the pragmatic aspects of science and law, associated with their local, social, rhetorical, and institutional features; see Caudill and LaRue 2004, 1–45.

7. There is a clear binary (heterosexual) gendering to jihadi cool culture, with jihadi chic being its counterpart and is specifically targeted for disenfranchised young women; however, as the subject of analysis in this case is male, that dimension is not relevant to the analysis in this chapter. For a fuller discussion, as applied, for example to Colleen LaRose, see Picart 2017, 41–62. See also Davis 2017.

8. On the "Rhetorics of 'Jihadi Cool,'" a more detailed analysis is available at Picart, *American Self-Radicalizing* (2017), 17–26. The adapted material here is published with permission from Cambridge Scholars Publishing. A preliminary version of the analysis of "Jihadi Cool/Chic" was published in Picart, *Societies* 5, no. 2 (April): 354–83 (2015a); the author has retained copyright for this material.

9. For a contrasting but parallel case study on how "[t]he Internet of Things, diversifying search engines, and the Dark and Deep Web undermine laws that seek to control Internet content" as applied to the European "right to be forgotten," see Cunningham 2017, 495–534.

10. Marc Sageman's (2008) four stages are: (1) moral outrage about the suffering of fellow Muslims; (2) the fit between this outrage and an individual's worldview; (3) the resonance of the jihadist interpretation with an individual's personal everyday experiences; and (4) mobilization by already existing networks (71–88).

11. For an overview of crucial concepts extremists use in order to justify the use of violence and acts of terrorism, see Gurski 2015, 51–74.

12. Using a Law and Philosophy approach, Kamir (2019) argues that the power and allure of a jihadi cool culture may be traced to the rejection of a humanitarian, universalistic culture that presumes our inherent human dignity and celebrates it as the basis of every individual's equal human rights in favor of an older, honor-based cultural structure that assumes new forms (such as social network shaming and some aspects of "victimhood culture"), and argues for a return to "dignity."

13. For an application of the classic and conflicted horror frames to the 2016 media campaign advertisements of Donald Trump and Hillary Clinton, and their underlying political import about popular cultural perceptions, see Montgomery 2019, 281–321.

14. Interestingly, at the State level, lack of remorse is an impermissible factor to consider at sentencing at criminal trials. See, for example, *Gage* 2014; *Lawton* 2016; *Jones* 1990.

15. For a comparative analysis of the functions of American and Russian documentaries entered into evidence as "witnesses" at the Nuremberg International Military Tribunal, see Picart 2015b, 1–20.

16. For a detailed examination of Jahar Tsarnaev's trial and sentencing, see Picart 2017, 82–136.

17. On July 31, 2020, the US Court of Appeal for the First Circuit affirmed in part, but also reversed in part, the lower court's decisions; crucially, it vacated Tsarnaev's death sentence and remanded the case down for resentencing. Generally described, the federal appeals court found that the lower court reversibly erred on the change of venue question because it not only failed to pose voir dire questions sufficient to identify prejudice, but also qualified jurors who had already formed an opinion that defendant was guilty based on media coverage. By failing to have the jurors identify what it was they already thought they knew about the high profile

case, the court made it too difficult to determine both the nature of any taint and the possible remedies for the taint (*Tsarnaev*, 2020). The evolution of jurisprudence in relation to Tsarnaev remains of crucial importance to emerging counter-terrorist narratives, both in the courtroom and in wider popular culture. For relevant news report summaries, see, for example, Dwyer, 2020; Gessen, 2020; and Wagtendonk, 2020.

REFERENCES

18 U.S.C. §3006A(c) (2016).

Andrews, Shelly. 2014. "Dzhokhar Tsarnaev: If Convicted, Will He Get Death Sentence?" *WTVR*, April 20. Accessed August 30, 2019. https://wtvr.com/2014/04/20/dzhokhar-tsarnaev-if-convicted-will-he-get-death-sentence/.

Aristodemou, Maria. 2000. *Law and Literature: Journeys From Her to Eternity*. New York: Oxford University Press.

Arter, Melanie. 2014. "Former Counterterror Official: 'We Don't Have Enough Muslim FBI Agents.'" *CNS News*, October 27. Accessed September 10, 2016. http://www.cnsnews.com/news/article/melanie-hunter/former-counterterror-official-we-dont-have-enough-muslim-fbi-agents.

Associated Press. 2017. "Accused Bomber Ahmad Khan Rahami Thrown Out of Court during Trial." *NJ.com*, October 2. Accessed August 30, 2019. https://www.nj.com/news/2017/10/accused_bomber_rahimi_tossed_from_courtroom.html

———. 2018. "Chelsea Bomber: Man Behind New York Attack Gets Multiple Life Sentences." *Guardian*, February 13. Accessed September 2, 2019. https://www.theguardian.com/us-news/2018/feb/13/ahmad-khan-rahami-jail-chelsea-bombings-new-york-life-sentences.

Behn, Sharon. 2014. "ISIS Militants Use 'Jihadi Cool' to Recruit Globally." *Voice Of America News*, September 5. Accessed September 9, 2019. https://www.voanews.com/world-news/middle-east-dont-use/isis-militants-use-jihadi-cool-recruit-globally.

Boone, Jon. 2016a. "US Drone Strike in Pakistan Kills Taliban Leader Mullah Mansoor." *Guardian*, May 22. Accessed January 21, 2019. https://www.theguardian.com/world/2016/may/21/us-airstrike-taliban-leader-mullah-akhtar-mansoor.

———. 2016b. "Ahmad Khan Rahami Spent Time at Pakistan Seminary Tied to Taliban." *Guardian*, September 23. Accessed January 21, 2019. https://www.theguardian.com/us-news/2016/sep/23/ahmad-khan-rahami-pakistan-taliban-new-york-bombing-terrorism.

Bousquet, Antoine. 2017. "Lethal Visions: The Eye as Function of the Weapon." *Critical Studies on Security* 5, no. 1: 62–80. Available online 1–19. Accessed September 20, 2019. http://www.tandfonline.com/doi/abs/10.1080/21624887.2017.1329471.

Bravin, Jess. 2006. "At Guantanamo, Even 'Easy' Cases Have Lingered: Balky Intelligence Agencies, War-Torn Crime Scene Hinder Legal Process," *Wall Street Journal*, December 18, 2006, A1.

Brittany, Morgan. 2014. "'Jihad Cool'—Recruiting Terrorists from America." *WND*, September 26. Accessed September 10, 2016. http://www.wnd.com/2014/08/jihad-cool-recruiting-terrorists-from-america/.

Buncombe, Andrew. 2016. "Ahmad Khan Rahami: Bombing Suspect's 'Personality Changed After Visits to Pakistan and Afghanistan.'" *Independent UK*, September 20. Accessed January 21, 2019. https://www.independent.co.uk/news/world/americas/ahmad-khan-rahami-bombing-suspect-visits-to-pakistan-and-afghanistan-a7317546.html.

Carroll, Noël. 1990. *Philosophy of Horror: Or, Paradoxes of the Heart*. New York: Routledge.

Caudill, David S. and Lewis H. LaRue. 2004. "A Non-Romantic View of Expert Testimony." *Seton Hall Law Review* 35, no. 1: 1–45.

CNNWire. 2015. "Boston Bomber Dzhokhar Tsarnaev Admits Guilt, Apologizes Before Being Sentenced to Death." *KTLA 5*, June 24. Accessed August 30, 2019. https://ktla.com/2015/06/24/boston-bomber-dzhokhar-tsarnaev-sentencing-hearing-underway/.

Cottee, Simon. 2014. "Islamic State's Badass Path to Paradise." *Los Angeles Times*, September 6. Accessed September 11, 2016. http://www.latimes.com/opinion/op-ed/la-oe-0907-cottee-badass-jihadi-cool-20140907-story.html#page=1.

Counter Extremism Project. 2019. "Ahmad Khan Rahami," *Counter Extremism Project*, n.d. Accessed August 26, 2019. https://www.counterextremism.com/extremists/ahmad-khan-rahami.

Coyne, Jerry. 2014. "Salman Rushdie Condemns 'Jihadi Cool.'" *Why Evolution Is True* (blog), October 12. Accessed September 10, 2016. http://whyevolutionistrue.wordpress.com/2014/10/12/salman-rushdie-condemns-jihadi-cool/.

Cragin, Kim. 2007. "Understanding Terrorist Motivations." Testimony presented before the US Senate, Select Committee on Intelligence, 110th Cong., 1st sess., June 12, 2007. Santa Monica, CA: RAND. Accessed September 9, 2019. http://www.rand.org/pubs/testimonies/CT338.html.

Crilly, Rob. 2016. "Ahmad Khan Rahami: New York Bombing Suspect's YouTube Account Offers Glimpse Inside His Mind." *Independent UK*, September 21. Accessed January 21, 2019. https://www.independent.co.uk/news/world/americas/ahmad-khan-rahami-ny-bombing-suspect-youtube-account-yaafghankid786-a7321556.html.

Crimesider Staff. 2016. "Chelsea Bomber Trial Verdict: Ahmad Khan Rahimi [*sic*] Convicted in New York Blast That Injured 30." *CBS News*, October 16. Accessed September 2, 2019. https://www.cbsnews.com/news/chelsea-bomber-verdict-ahmad-khan-rahimi-guilty-new-york-bombing-injured-30/.

Cunningham, McKay. 2012. "Privacy in the Age of the Hacker: Balancing Global Privacy and Data Security Law." *George Washington International Law Review* 44: 643–702.

———. 2017. "Privacy Law That Does Not Protect Privacy, Forgetting the Right to Be Forgotten." *Buffalo Law Review* 65: 495–534.

Davis, Jessica. 2017. *Women in Modern Terrorism: From Liberation Wars to Global Jihad and the Islamic State*. Lanham Maryland: Rowman and Littlefield.

Dearden, Lizzie. 2016a. "Ahmad Rahami: New York Bomber's Journal Vowed 'Death to Your Oppression' and Outlined Plans for New Jersey Attack." *Independent UK*, September 21. Accessed January 21, 2019. https://www.independent.co.uk/news/world/americas/ahmad-rahami-new-york-new-jersey-elizabeth-chelsea-bomber-journal-death-oppression-attack-al-qaeda-a7319861.html.

———. 2016b. "Sikh Man Who Led US Police to New York Bombing Suspect Says He Did 'What Any American Would Have Done.'" *Independent US*, September 21. Accessed August 30, 2019. https://www.independent.co.uk/news/world/americas/ahmad-khan-rahami-new-york-new-jersey-bomb-terror-attack-sikh-man-police-linden-harinder-bains-a7320011.html.

Dempsey, Michelle Madden and Matthew Lister. 2017. "Applied Political and Legal Philosophy." *The Blackwell Companion to Applied Philosophy*, edited by Kimberley Brownlee, David Coady, and Kasper Lippert-Rasmussen, 313–327. Malden, MA: Wiley-Blackwell Press.

Dubal, Venna. 2012. "The Demise of Community Policing? The Impact of Post-9/11 Federal Surveillance Programs on Local Law Enforcement." *Asian American Law Journal at Berkeley Law* 19: 35. Accessed September 3, 2018. http://scholarship.law.berkeley.edu/aalj/vol19/iss1/3.

Dwyer, Dialynn. 2020. "What to know about the decision overturning the death penalty for Dzhokhar Tsarnaev." *www.boston.com*, August 3. Accessed August 14, 2020. https://www.boston.com/news/local-news/2020/08/03/why-tsarnaev-death-penalty-overturned.

Fed. R. Crim. P. 5(a)(1)(A) (2016).

Gage v. State, 147 So. 3d 1020 (Fla. 2d DCA 2014).

Garcia, Feliks. 2016. "Ahmad Khan Rahami: Federal Charges Filed against New York and New Jersey Bomb Suspect." *Independent US*, September 20. Accessed August 30, 2019. https://www.independent.co.uk/news/world/americas/ahmad-khan-rahami-federal-charges-new-york-new-jersey-bombing-latest-a7319777.html.

Gessen, Masha. 2020. "Why a Court Overturned the Death Sentence for Dzhokhar Tsarnaev, the Boston Marathon Bomber." *The New Yorker*, August 5. Accessed August 14, 2020. https://www.newyorker.com/news/our-columnists/why-a-court-overturned-the-death-sentence-for-dzhokhar-tsarnaev-the-boston-marathon-bomber.

Greenfield, Steve, Guy Osborn, and Peter Robson. 2010. *Film and Law*. 2nd ed. London: Hart Publishing.

Griffin, Andrew. 2016. "Ahmad Khan Rahami: New York Police Issue Alert to iPhones Telling People 'See Media for Pic.'" *Independent US*, September 19. Accessed August 26, 2019. https://www.independent.co.uk/news/world/americas/ahmad-khan-rahami-new-york-authorities-issue-unprecedented-emergency-alert-to-all-iphones-telling-a7316431.html.

Gurski, Phil. 2015. *The Threat from Within: Recognizing Al-Qaeda-Inspired Radicalization and Terrorism in the West*. Lanham, Maryland: Rowan and Littlefield Press.

Hsu, Spencer S. 2010. "Arrest of Va. Man Spotlights al-Qaeda's New American Recruiters." *Washington Post*, August 1. Accessed September 9, 2019. http://www.washingtonpost.com/wp-dyn/content/article/2010/07/31/AR2010073102680.html.

Huq, Aziz Z. 2010. "Modeling Terrorist Radicalization." *Duke Forum for Law and Social Change* 2: 39-69. Accessed September 3, 2018. http://dflsc.law.duke.edu/article/modeling-terrorist-radicalization/.

IPT News. 2013. "Jihad is Cool: Jihadist Magazines Recruit Young Terrorists." *Investigative Project on Terrorism*, April 11. Accessed September 10, 2016. http://www.investigativeproject.org/3969/jihad-is-cool-jihadist-magazines-recruit-young#.

Ivie, Robert L. and Oscar Giner. 2015. *Hunt the Devil: A Demonology of US War Culture*. Tuscaloosa: University of Alabama Press.

Jenkins, Brian Michael. 2010. "Would-Be Warriors: Incidents of Jihadist Terrorist Radicalization in the United States Since September 11, 2001." Santa Monica, CA: RAND. Accessed September 5, 2016. http://www.rand.org/pubs/occasional_papers/OP292.html.

"The Jihad Shopping Network, Courtesy of ISIS." 2014. *Warrior*. June 24. Accessed September 11, 2016. http://warrior.scout.com/story/1414293-the-jihad-shopping-network-courtesy-of-isis.

Jones v. State, 569 So. 2d 1234 (Fla. 1990).

Jones, Allen Benjamin. 2013. "Jihadi Cool." *Not Theology: A Religious Studies Blog on Religion, Conflict and the Middle East*, July 24. Accessed September 10, 2016. http://nottheology.com/2013/07/24/jihadi-cool-2/.

Jordan, Robert T. and Don Philpott. 2010. *Is America Safe?: Terrorism, Homeland Security and Emergency Preparedness.* Lanham, Maryland: Government Institutes.

Kamir, Orit. 2019. *Betraying Dignity: The Toxic Seduction of Social Media, Shaming and Radicalization.* Vancouver, British Columbia, Canada: The Fairleigh Dickinson University Press.

———. 2005. "Cinematic Judgment and Jurisprudence: A Woman's Memory, Recovery and Justice in a Post-Traumatic Society (A Study of Roman Polanski's *Death and the Maiden*)." In *Law on the Screen*, edited by Austin Sarat, Lawrence Douglas, and Martha Merrill Humphrey, 27-81. Stanford, CA: Stanford University Press.

Katz, Jack, 1988. *Seductions of Crime: Moral and Sensual Attractions in Doing Evil.* New York: Basic Books.

Lawton v. State, 207 So. 3d 359 (Fla. 3d DCA 2016).

Leigh, Karen, and Bruce Crumley. 2014. "New Jihadi Recruitment Tool: Militants' Instagram Accounts." *Christian Science Monitor*, June 10. Accessed September 11, 2016. https://www.csmonitor.com/World/Middle-East/2014/0610/New-jihadi-recruitment-tool-militants-Instagram-accounts.

Maan, Ajit. (2015). *Counter-Terrorism: Narrative Strategies*. Lanham, Maryland: University Press of America.

Mauro, Ryan. 2014. "ISIS: 'Cool' Image Winning Over Next Generation of Jihadis." *Clarion Project*. August 31. Accessed September 11, 2016. http://www.clarionproject.org/analysis/islamic-state-winning-over-next-generation-jihadis.

McCauley, Clark and Sophia Moskalenko. 2010. "Individual and Group Mechanisms of Radicalization." *Topical Strategic Multi-Layer Assessment (SMA) Multi-Agency and Air Force Research Laboratory, Multi-Disciplinary White Papers in Support of Counter-Terrorism and Counter-WMD*, edited by Laurie Fenstermacher et al. (white paper, January 2010): 82–91. Accessed September 5, 2016. http://www.start.umd.edu/sites/default/files/files/publications/U_Counter_Terrorism_White_Paper_Final_January_2010.pdf.

———. 2011. *Friction: How Radicalization Happens to Them and Us*. New York: Oxford University Press.

Mezey, Naomi and Mark C. Niles. 2005. "Screening the Law: Ideology and Law in American Popular Culture." *Columbia Journal of Law and Arts* 28: 91–186.

———. 2016. "Screening the Law: Ideology and Law in American Popular Culture." In *Framing Law and Crime: An Interdisciplinary Anthology*, ed. Caroline Joan "Kay" S. Picart, Michael David Jacobsen, and Cecil Greek, 267–313. Madison and Teaneck, NJ: Fairleigh Dickinson University Press/Rowman & Littlefield.

Montgomery, Fielding. 2019. "The Monstrous Election: Horror Framing in Televised Campaign Advertisements during the 2016 Presidential Election." *Rhetoric and Public Affairs* 22, no. 2 (Summer): 281–321.

Nacos, Brigitte L. 2016. *Mass-Mediated Terrorism: Mainstream and Digital Media in Terrorism and Counterterrorism*, Third ed. Lanham, Maryland: Rowman and Littlefield, 2016.

Neumeister, Larry. 2018. "Chelsea Bomber Ahmad Rahami Sentenced to Life in Prison." *Independent*, February 14. Accessed September 2, 2019. https://www.independent.co.uk/news/world/americas/chelsea-bomber-ahmad-rahami-sentenced-life-in-prison-a8209406.html.

New York University Center for Law and Security. 2006. "Terrorist Trial Report Card: U.S. Edition: Executive Summary." New York University School of Law.

Newell, Lauren A. 2019. "Rebooting Empathy for the Digital Generation Lawyer." *Ohio State Journal on Dispute Resolution* 34 (2019): 1–97.

Online Etymology Dictionary. 2019. Accessed August 28, 2019. https://www.etymonline.com.

Patel, Faiza. 2011. "Rethinking Radicalization." Paper, Brennan Center for Justice New York University School of Law. New York (March 8): 1–55. Accessed September 9, 2019. https://www.brennancenter.org/publication/rethinking-radicalization.

Pearson, Elizabeth. 2013. "Macho Cool: The Appeal of Violent Jihad." *Connect Justice: Justice in Conflict* (blog), September 30. Accessed September 9, 2019. https://www.academia.edu/7100893/Macho_Cool_The_appeal_of_violent_Jihad_September_2013.

Picart, Caroline Joan S. 2015a. "'Jihad Cool/Jihad Chic': The Roles of the Internet and Imagined Relations in the Self-Radicalization of Colleen LaRose (Jihad Jane)." *Societies* 5, no. 2 (April): 354–83. doi: 10.3390/soc5020354.

———. 2015b. "Nationalities, Histories, Rhetorics: Real/Reel Representations of the Holocaust and Holocaust Trials and a Poethics of Film and Law," 29 *Dapim: Studies on the Holocaust*, no. 2 (May): 1–20. doi: 10.1080/23256249.2015.1034980.

———. 2015c. "The Radicalization of American Lone Wolves in Real/Reel Worlds: Strategically Mapping the Role of the Internet, and Beyond, in the Cases of Colleen LaRose (Jihad Jane) and the Tsarnaev Brothers (the Boston Marathon Bombers)." In *Lone Actors—An Emerging Security Threat*, edited by Aaron Richman and Yair Sharan, 58–74. NATO Science for Peace and Security Studies. Amsterdam, Netherlands: IOS Press.

Picart, Caroline Joan "Kay" S. 2017. *American Self-Radicalizing Terrorists and the Allure of "Jihadi Cool/Chic."* Newcastle Upon Tyne: Cambridge Scholars Publishing.

Picart, Caroline Joan "Kay" S. 2019. "American Self-Radicalizing Terrorists and Conversions to Radical Action: Emotional Factors and the Allure of 'Jihadi Cool/ Chic.'" In *Emotions and Crime: Towards a Criminology of Emotions*, edited by Michael Hviid Jacobsen and Sandra Walklate, 43–59. London: Routledge.

Picart, Caroline Joan "Kay" S. and David A. Frank. 2006. *Frames of Evil: The Holocaust as Horror in American Film*. Carbondale: Southern Illinois University Press, 2006.

Picart, Caroline Joan "Kay" S. and Cecil Greek. 2007. "Profiling the Terrorist as a Mass Murderer." In *Monsters In and Among Us: Toward a Gothic Criminology*, edited by Caroline Joan "Kay" S. Picart and Cecil Greek, 256–88. Madison, NJ: Fairleigh Dickinson University Press/Associated University Presses.

Porter, R. C. 2014. "'Jihad Cool'—Young Americans Lured to Fight for ISIS Militants; Seeds of Next 9/11?" *Fortuna's Corner*. June 28. Accessed September 11, 2016. http://fortunascorner.com/2014/06/28/jihad-cool-young-americans-lured-to-fight-for-isis-militants-seeds-of-next-911.

Posner, Richard A. 2006. *Not a Suicide Pact: The Constitution in a Time of National Emergency (Inalienable Rights)*. Oxford, UK: Oxford University Press.

———. 2007. *Countering Terrorism: Blurred Focus, Halting Steps*. Lanham, Maryland: Rowman and Littlefield Publishers.

Prince, Stephen. 2004. "Dread, Taboo and *The Thing*: Toward a Social Theory of the Horror Film." In *The Horror Film*, edited by Stephen Prince, 118–30. New Brunswick, NJ: Rutgers University Press.

Revesz, Rachael. 2016. "New York-Area Bombings: Terrorists Want to Inspire Fear in Us but We Will Not Succumb, President Obama Declares." *Independent US*, September 19. Accessed August 29, 2019. https://www.independent.co.uk/news/world/americas/ahmad-khan-rahami-new-york-new-jersey-bombings-president-obama-isis-terrorism-linden-elizabeth-a7317101.html.

Sageman, Marc. 2008. *Leaderless Jihad: Terror Networks in the Twenty-First Century*. Philadelphia: University of Pennsylvania Press.

Santora, Marc, William K. Rashbaum, Al Baker, and Adam Goldman. 2016. "Ahmad Khan Rahami Is Arrested in Manhattan and New Jersey Bombings." *New York Times*, September 20, A1. Available online September 19, 2016, last updated September 21, 2016. Accessed January 18, 2019. https://www.nytimes.com/2016/09/20/nyregion/nyc-nj-explosions-ahmad-khan-rahami.html.

Sarat, Austin, ed. 2011. *Imagining Legality: Where Law Meets Popular Culture*. Tuscaloosa: University of Alabama Press.

Schmitt, Gary J. Ed. 2010. *Safety, Liberty and Islamist Terrorism: American and European Approaches to Domestic Counterterrorism*. Washington DC: American Enterprise for Public Policy Research.

Sherwin, Richard K. 2000. *When Law Goes Pop: The Vanishing Line Between Law and Popular Culture*. Chicago: University of Chicago Press.

Shoichet, Catherine E. 2016. "Ahmad Khan Rahami: What We Know About the Bombing Suspect." CNN, September 20. Accessed January 17, 2018. https://www.cnn.com/2016/09/19/us/ahmad-khan-rahami/index.html.

Silbey, Jessica M. 2001. "Patterns of Courtroom Justice." *Journal of Law and Society* 28, no. 1: 97–116.

United States v. Alvarez-Sanchez, 511 U.S. 350, 358, 114 S. Ct. 1599, 128 L. Ed. 2d 319 (1994).

United States v. Dye, 538 F. App'x 654 (6th Cir. 2013).

United States v. Garcia, 2011 U.S. Dist. LEXIS 113748, 2011 WL 4634153 (E.D.Cal. Oct. 3, 2011).

United States v. Khalil, 214 F.3d 111 (2d Cir. 2000).

United States v. Rahami, 2016 U.S. Dist. LEXIS 130147 (D.N.J. September 23, 2016).

United States v. Rahami, U.S. Dist. LEXIS 96686 (S.D.N.Y. June 22, 2017).

United States v. Salameh, 261 F.3d 271, 279 (2d Cir. 2001).

United States v. Smith, 502 F.3d 680 (7th Cir. 2007).

United States v. Tsarnaev, 945 F. Supp. 2d 230 (D. Mass May 17, 2013a).

United States v. Tsarnaev, 951 F. Supp. 2d 209 (D. Mass. Apr. 29, 2013b).

United States v. Tsarnaev, Criminal Action No. 13-10200-GAO, 2013 U.S. Dist. LEXIS 152703, 2013 WL 5701582 (D. Mass. Oct. 18, 2013c).

United States v. Tsarnaev, Criminal Action No. 13-10200-GAO, 2013 U.S. Dist. LEXIS 168847 (D. Mass. Nov. 27, 2013d).

United States v. Tsarnaev, Criminal No. 13-10200-GAO, 2014 U.S. Dist. LEXIS 134596 (D. Mass. Sept. 24, 2014a).

United States v. Tsarnaev, 53 F. Supp. 3d 443 (D. Mass. Oct. 17, 2014b).

United States v. Tsarnaev, 53 F. Supp. 3d 450 (D. Mass. Oct. 17, 2014c).

United States v. Tsarnaev, Criminal No. 13-10200-GAO, 2014 U.S. Dist. LEXIS 176730 (D. Mass. Dec. 23, 2014d).

United States v. Tsarnaev, Criminal No. 13-10200-GAO, 2015 U.S. Dist. LEXIS 24 (D. Mass. Jan. 2, 2015a).

United States v. Tsarnaev, Criminal No. 13-10200-GAO, 2015 U.S. Dist. LEXIS 14562 (D. Mass. Feb. 6, 2015b).

United States v. Tsarnaev, Civil Action No. 13-10200-GAO, 2015 U.S. Dist. LEXIS 18089 (D. Mass. Feb. 13, 2015c(1)).

United States v. Tsarnaev, Criminal No. 13-10200-GAO, 2015 U.S. Dist. LEXIS 53758 (D. Mass. Feb. 13, 2015c(2)).

United States v. Tsarnaev, Criminal No. 13-10200-GAO, 2015 U.S. Dist. LEXIS 31159 (D. Mass. Mar. 13, 2015d).

United States v. Tsarnaev, Criminal No. 13-10200-GAO, 2015 U.S. Dist. LEXIS 167206 (D. Mass. Aug. 24, 2015e).

United States v. Tsarnaev, Criminal No. 13-10200-GAO, 2016 U.S. Dist. LEXIS 5428 (D. Mass. Jan. 15, 2016a(1)).

United States v. Tsarnaev, 2016 U.S. Dist. LEXIS 5428 (D. Mass., January 15, 2016a(2)).

United States v. Tsarnaev, 2020 U.S. App. LEXIS 24226 (1st Cir. 2020).

US Congress. House Committee on Homeland Security. 2009. *Violent Extremism: How Are People Moved from Constitutionally-Protected Thought to Acts of Terrorism?* Hearing Before Subcommittee on Intelligence, Information Sharing and Terror Risk Assessment of 111th Cong., 1st sess., December 15, 2009, Y 4.H 75:111–48. Testimony of Kim Cragin, RAND Corporation. Accessed September 9, 2019. https://www.govinfo.gov/content/pkg/CHRG-111hhrg56445/pdf/CHRG-111hhrg56445.pdf.

Virilio, Paul. 1989. *War and Cinema: The Logics of Perception*. Translated by Patrick Camiller. New York: Verso.

Wagtendonk, Anya van. 2020. "The Boston Marathon Bomber's death sentence has been overturned." Vox, August 1. Accessed August 14, 2020. https://www.vox.com/2020/8/1/21350736/boston-marathon-bomber-dzhokhar-tsarnaev-death-sentence-overturned

Walker, Theresa. 2014. "Has ISIS Reached O.C.? Arrest Here Intensifies Questions." *Orange County Register*, August 30. Accessed September 10, 2016. http://www.ocregister.com/articles/dandach-633351-isis-orange.html.

White, James Boyd. 1999. *From Expectation to Experience: Essays on Law and Legal Education*. Ann Arbor: University of Michigan Press.

Wilson, Michael. 2018. "Bomber Sentenced to 2 Life Terms for Manhattan Attack." *New York Times*, February 13. Accessed September 2, 2019. https://www.nytimes.com/2018/02/13/nyregion/bomber-chelsea-manhattan.html.

Withnall, Adam. 2016. "Ahmad Khan Rahami: New York Bombing Suspect Could be 'Armed and Dangerous.'" *Independent US*, September 19. Accessed August 29, 2019. https://www.independent.co.uk/news/world/americas/ahmad-khan-rahami-new-york-bombing-suspect-latest-news-armed-dangerous-police-image-identity-a7316421.html.

Yin, Tung. 2019. "An Information Operations Theory of Domestic Counterterrorism Efforts." *South Carolina Law Review* 71: 523–603.

Postscript

Gothic Criminology's Evolving Frontiers

Cecil Greek

Building upon the chapters in this edited collection, the reader is quite impressed by the breadth of topics and perspectives that have been incorporated in the less than two decades since Gothic criminology first made its appearance. What started out as a collaboration between criminology and literature and film studies has grown to include anthropology, sociology, law, gender studies, and communications (Caroline Joan "Kay" S. Picart and Cecil Greek 2008). Given recent events since the emergence of the Trump era in global politics, it will not be surprising that essays related to political science, public health, and environmental studies will undoubtedly be on the horizon.

In this short chapter, I would like to focus on three trends demonstrated in this edited collection that build upon the core of Gothic criminology studies. All of these are encouraging signs for the future of this theoretical model. First, the chapters here clearly recognize that several major theorists not discussed extensively in previous Gothic criminology pieces include elements in their models that can be interpreted as Gothic. The reintroduction of discussions of evil and monstrosity into the social sciences and related disciplines is now fully underway. Second, this edited collection adds to the panoply of Gothic character types and figures from history that can be used to analyze contemporary persons, events, and processes. We may soon have as many monstrous characters as the Marvel Universe has Avengers! Third, these studies build upon the Gothic fixation with place: some environments and situations are inherently imbued with the Gothic; while other mundane everyday spaces can be transformed quite dramatically into places where the monstrously evil appear. Finally, I would like to offer some suggestions for how we might start to analyze America under the Trump presidency, building upon an earlier essay on behemoth and dystopia (Cecil Greek 2016). Perhaps by discussing through a Gothic lens how we got here, we can suggest ways to work towards a brighter future, while recognizing the diligence required to avoid giving in to the evil and monstrous, and the ensuing chaos they can bring.

THE INCLUSION OF ADDITIONAL THEORISTS

Gothic criminology was originally built on combining ideas from literature and film studies with the works of sociologists and criminologists primarily from the period before the social sciences adopted their value free approach as a rejection of the transvalued religious approaches which had initiated much of the discussion of modernity (Cecil Greek 1992). Works such as E. A. Ross's *Sin and Society* (1907) and Robert Park (Stanford Lyman 1990) and Max Weber's discussion of "vampiric capitalism" (Donald Nielsen 1993) provided a social context, while the writings of Lonnie Athens (1989) and Jack Katz (1988) focused on the creation of more contemporary monsters and their behaviors.

Among the significant theorists employed in this volume are Cesare Lombroso, Sigmund Freud, and Michel Foucault. Frauley's revival of Lombroso to the discussion of the monstrous reopens the debate about biological aspects of deviant behavior, particularly focusing on deformity and/or biological inferiority. Criminology and the criminal justice system largely rejected biology when it became overly linked to the Eugenics Movement, both in America and during the Nazi era in Germany (Mark Haller 1963). However, the relationship between our behavior and our biology is linked in ways that cannot be thoroughly overcome by socialization, as nature and nurture are always intertwined. The recent return of biology to the study of criminology has been spearheaded by Kevin Beaver (2019) and the neuro-criminologists, and these efforts are likely to continue. In addition, the continuing fascination with true crime monsters in books, podcasts, and social media asks us to rethink the biology of criminal behavior. For example, the recent capture of the Golden State Killer, presaged by Michelle McNamara (2018) in *I'll Be Gone in The Dark*, was made into a major HBO documentary series.

The work of Sigmund Freud, particularly *Totem and Taboo*, is employed by Morton in a comparison to the ethnographic literature produced by Australian aborigines. Like Emile Durkheim (1915) in *The Elementary Forms of the Religious Life*, Freud looked for the origins of society and religion by first identifying the most "primitive" contemporary groups that were currently available for study. While Freud's "totemic horde" focused on the vengeful father, Durkheim's conception of the totem worship as a way to connect self to the group seems to come closer to Morton's usage here. Depth anthropological study of the traditions, tales, and myths such as Dreamtime offers an excellent source for understanding Gothic origins.

Finally, a brief mention of the underlying use of Michel Foucault in these chapters, as his deconstructionist starting position is still quite predominant in the social sciences and humanities. Picart is prescient to point out the effort here to move beyond Foucault's focus on power, that is, biopower, in trying to explain the definition of reality in human societies, and the movement beyond a simple relativism.

ADDING MORE MONSTER TYPES TO THE GOTHIC

Several of the case studies employing the Gothic criminology approach have used classic monster tales as the basis for comparison to real-world criminal behavior. The original case study used the vampire tradition and the constant need for blood as a way to understand the compulsions of serial killers as they have been described in the true crime literature and in the films that have been made based upon his books (Caroline Joan "Kay" S. Picart and Cecil Greek 2003). Picart and I have also written about the female serial killer, Eileen Wuornos, as both similar and unique from the male vampiric stalker (Caroline Joan "Kay" S. Picart and Cecil Greek 2009). I have previously compared monstrously deviant aspects of social institutions to creatures from Jewish folklore: rogue police departments as real/reel world Golem (Cecil Greek 2007) and governmental overresponse to current international social problems to Behemoth (Cecil Greek 2016).

Among the most significant new monsters is one from Jewish folklore, Lilith, who according to commentators is depicted as a dangerous demon of the night, who is sexually wanton, and who steals babies in the darkness. Kamir does an excellent job here of demonstrating the modern variance of this tradition in both fake news stories and political commentary regarding female politicians. It will be significant to observe whether such narrative stereotyping of female leadership, particularly considering the 2018 United States midterm election of female candidates and the 2020 choice of a female vice presidential candidate, persists. Donald Trump uses the word "nasty" to describe female leaders who differ with his political views.

Greenfield's chapter on medical doctors who are also serial killers would seem suited for a comparison to the Dr. Jekyll and Mr. Hyde story. And perhaps there are real-life versions of such monsters. However, here Greenfield argues that medical killings in the accounts he discusses document the ordinariness of the murders and the perceived banality of the killers. Comparison to Dexter, a Miami police medical examiner serial killer featured in the long-running Showtime series, might be interesting, as in his case the executions are always justified by the overwhelming immorality of his victims.

A more modern media-created folk type further developed in this volume is the jihad cool. Picart has led in the discussion of this prototype in the traditional news media, film representations, and the growing body of social media fascination with homegrown terrorism. Picart has expanded the concept as primarily a subculture appellation applied to individuals in developed nations who are recruited to travel to conflict zones on Jihad, by looking at cases such as the Boston Marathon bombers.

Future explorations could lead to significant contributions. Currently, I, along with sociologists Jamie Sommer and Andrew Hargrove, am working on analysis of the predatory behavior of Wall Street by viewing it through the lens of the werewolf tradition in folktales, literature, and film. Films such as the two Oliver Stone *Wall Street* films, *American Psycho*, and *The Wolf of Wall Street* feature animal-like transformations that ultimately justify the carnage left in the wake of hostile takeovers, fraudulent stock manipulation, and repeated stock market collapses.

These studies could be further amplified by incorporating the work of Karl Marx and the leading contemporary interpreter of his work, Thomas Pikkety (2017), combined with analysis of Behemoth nature of systematic capitalist exploitation of the natural environment, a significant factor in global climate change (Jamie Sommer 2018).

GOTHIC CRIMINOLOGY AND GOTHIC SPACES

One of the central aspects of Gothic criminology has been its focus on spaces and places that either serve as harbingers of the monstrous or, under certain conditions can be transformed into monstrous environments. "The hallmarks of the early Gothic novel included the graveyard and the convent, moats and drawbridges, dungeons, towers, mysterious trap doors and corridors, rusty hinges, flickering candles, burial vaults, birthmarks, tolling bells, hidden manuscripts, twilight and ancestral curses" (Caroline Joan "Kay" S. Picart and Cecil Greek 2008). This edited collection further develops this focus of place with discussion of criminal insane asylums and chapters showing both wild spaces (e.g., the Australian outback) and contested urban spaces racked by graffiti wars.

Morton's analysis of the relationships between gods and monsters takes place in the central Australian outback, where among the "Arrente" people the Dreamtime relationship between the sacred landscape and human origins is singularly important. The spirits of ancestors shaped the land in the past and remain active in sacred spaces today. Belief in the monstrous great lizard ancestor persists in the folklore traditions linking waterholes and rock formations to the god's sojourns.

Compared to the largely empty space of wilderness, Landry focuses on urban spaces which have become contested battlefields pitting property owners, business owners, and government buildings against graffiti artists. The city of Ottawa attempted to placate all members of the community by setting aside special areas where graffiti, redefined as urban art murals, would be accepted while enforcing its anti-graffiti policies everywhere else in the city. In the United States, in the summer of 2020, city governments often ignored graffiti seen as an expression of social protests (and in some cases advocating repainting streets with Black Lives Matter murals), but the attacks on federal government buildings (and Confederate statutes) caught the attention of Donald Trump, who saw it as an opportunity to stoke a culture war by labeling the protesting graffiti artists as left-wing agitators and rioters. In cities such as Washington DC and Portland, federal troops in military gear were used to prevent graffiti writing and other defacing of public property. Combining place with time factors, commentators have noticed the differences between the day crowds and the night crowds in some of these urban locations, showing the continuing Gothic significance of nocturnal deviant activity and law enforcement responses.

A more traditionally associated Gothic space, a Victorian era asylum for the criminally insane, is featured in Williams, Walklate, and Godfrey's chapter. The contemporary media's demonization of the patients sent there is even more surprising given that a significant number of the first clients were women who had murdered their children in an era in which knowledge of postpartum depression was not common. In an era before lobotomies and chemical treatments, the regime was one of rest and vocational rehabilitation. Many of the clients did quite well. One is reminded of the rest cure described by Charlotte Perkins Gilman (1980) in *The Yellow Wallpaper*.

Another important contributor to the ongoing spatial development of this theory is British criminologist Michael Fiddler (2007). In particular, he has focused upon dark spaces, particularly prisons, as depicted in film. His discussions of *Shawshank Redemption* and other films build upon Gothic criminology further enriching his analysis with additional concepts such as Freud's notion of the uncanny. In a second case study, Fiddler (2013) analyzed recent British home invasion films from a Gothic perspective. Rather than being a protective haven in a heartless world, home invasion films show that evil easily penetrates the home space, bringing unreason and potentially fracturing identity.

THE GOTHIC WORLD OF DONALD TRUMP: BATMAN OR THANOS?

Social scientists and others are already hard at work trying to make sense of the dystopian politics of Donald Trump (Amy Atchison and Shauna Shames 2019). From a Gothic perspective we could question whether he is a Bizarro World (Wikipedia 2020) version of Batman or the ultimate real-world Thanos? If the former, perhaps he has just fooled us into thinking that only he can solve our economic and political problems. Like Batman, we called upon Donald Trump in our hour of need. If the latter, has he been attempting to accumulate all of the rings of power that will make him indestructibly omnipotent and able to kill hundreds of thousands of Americans with impunity, by refusing to take seriously a global pandemic and concluding that such death "is what it is"? Unfortunately, there are no real-world Avengers who can take us back in time to a pre-Trump world and restore all those who have perished.

Is Trump Batman (Kwame Opam 2015)? An interesting comparison can be made between Trump's view of America and the image of America that one sees in the Christopher Nolan Batman films: *Batman Begins* (2005), *The Dark Knight* (2008), and *The Dark Knight Rises* (2012). Nolan's existentialism-based films feature recurring discussion of perception, deception, and choice in postmodern situations (Kaylin Walker 2012). Particularly important to Trump's worldview is the image of contemporary urban society as a living nightmare populated by illegal criminal immigrants, Antifa and other left-wing radicals bent on destroying the country, and hordes of roaming Black Lives Matter rioters looting and destroying property, including Confederate statues that traditionally supported white supremacy. Likewise, "visiting Nolan's Gotham City is supposed to be a bleak affair. It is the embodiment of urban blight, a city where the sun never shines, no matter what time it is. It is the kind of city that would give birth to a hero like Batman—dark, twisted, born of murder and mayhem, possibly insane. It is also inherently cinematic, which helps explain why Christopher Nolan—a filmmaker steeped in noir sensibilities—was drawn to it (Marc Bernardin, 2016).

Like Batman's Bruce Wayne, Donald Trump has no superpowers. Also, like Batman, Trump mythically created himself from his own wealth, creating a financial and real estate organization that has global political and economic influence. As Bruce Wayne has now turned from his life of idle pleasure fueled by his great wealth to one of helping society in time of greatest crisis, Donald Trump promised to work without pay, avoid playing golf, put his own money into his political campaigns, and ultimately sacrifice his business interests for the good of the nation. Trump promised that his ultimate legacy would be his ability to make great deals for the American people while bringing the country toward consensus, making America indeed great again. Unfortunately, unlike the soteriological Batman, at the end of Trump's four-year presidency his mythical origins as a self-made capitalist have been exposed repeatedly, none of his social promises have come to fruition, and multiple forms of pestilence have infected the country (an uncontrolled viral pandemic, massive unemployment and social dislocation, and nationwide protests advocating mitigating racial and gender inequalities and ending biased police practices aimed at minorities). Trump continues to see himself as the sole person who can save America, hoping to be forever enshrined on Mount Rushmore, as one of the country's greatest leaders.

A darker portrait of Donald Trump can be made by comparing him to the Thanos character in the Marvel sci-fi adventure films, particularly *Avengers: Endgame* (Anthony Russo 2019). According to the back story, as a younger monster on his home planet of Titan, Thanos developed a Malthusian-inspired plan to kill half of the population of the planet to save the other half. When rebuffed by his own people as an insane lunatic, he left to travel the universe and kill half of the population on each planet during his sojourn. Once he learned of the six rings, and that he could kill half of the population in the entire universe simultaneously, acquiring the rings became his life quest.

Like Thanos, Donald Trump seems to suffer from both "malignant narcissism" coupled with a life orientation diagnosed as "present hedonism" (not caring about what came before, or what will come after, but only about what's happening now and how it affects him). This makes him thoroughly incapable of ever admitting that he was wrong, and once he has chosen a poor solution such as how to respond to the Covid-19 virus (first by claiming that it was a hoax dreamed up by the Democrats and then simply promising that it would disappear), he cannot change his position without suffering overwhelming personal embarrassment (Bandy Lee 2017). Potentially, hundreds of thousands of Americans will ultimately die needlessly.

Unfortunately, those of us forced to live within the time and space continuum, unlike the Marvel Comic Universe, have not developed time travel technology so that the country could go back and undo the missteps that led to Trump's election and the shift toward authoritarianism. Once Trump realized that it was easier than ever imagined to simply pretend that the separation of powers built into the US Constitution could not be successfully defended, his authoritarian tendencies became more and more observable. Anyone who opposed him, whether watchdogs embedded in government to ensure the rule of law (who could be fired by the president), Democrats controlling one of the houses of Congress after the midterms (whose subpoenas would simply be ignored), an impartial investigation into the relationship between Russian involvement in the 2016 election and the Trump campaign (which was effectively quashed by installing Bill Barr as the de facto Trump totem to head up the Justice Department), or impeachment (which the Senate never took seriously by not calling any additional witnesses) never deterred him in any way. Claiming that he kept finding additional imperial powers that he never knew he had before, policies that started as seemingly innocuous tweets became executive orders, leaving unwitting minions to try to figure out how to implement them. The core of the Republican Party cowered before him as if he were the ultimate vengeful deity, one who could behead you by giving you a nickname. America has unleashed a behemoth monster, a bringer of chaos, who then claims himself to be the ultimate arbiter of law and order. Although this will not be published before the 2020 election, the question of whether the United States can remain a constitutional democracy has been thrust upon us in a way never imagined by the founding fathers.

THE FUTURE OF GOTHIC CRIMINOLOGY

Given the growing overlap between mass media accounts of real-world examples of monstrous evil and their fictionalized counterparts in film and television, it would appear that there is a growing need for theoretical models that attempt to seriously analyze this phenomenon that go beyond the current fascination with "liquid fear" (Zygmunt Bauman 2006). Perhaps there are real reasons to be fearful, and the reel world is trying to warn us about them. Recognition of the continuing influence of the Gothic, and its overlapping use by Hollywood, the news media, and, increasingly, the plethora of social media outlets spawned by the Internet, including those spreading dark tales, can assist in the understanding of how primordial and monstrous evil has impacted human history, influences our present condition, and is predicted to be part of the future. Unfortunately, we are left with trying to sort out which are the important and real stories of the monstrous and which are merely fake news (Cecil Greek 2017).

The Gothic model seems already deeply embedded into Hollywood's overall take on the future, pictured as a dark, dystopian existence brought on by humankind's own unwillingness or inability to deal with contemporary global issues such as overpopulation, climate change, competition over scarce resources, and the propensity for solving problems through violent conflict. One of the unique aspects of the Gothic model is its ability to root both contemporary and future interpretations of evil as an ongoing phenomenon which was much more easily identified perhaps in the past and currently; nevertheless, human behavior seems to persistently demonstrate our inability to overcome our darker natures. While Gothic criminology may be interpreted as a bleak commentary on human society, the perspective is not without hope. Only by clearly identifying the historical and current sources of monstrosity and evil can one hope to hold back the forces which have resulted in our current dystopian situation.

REFERENCES

Atchison, Amy and Shauna Shames. 2019. *Survive and Resist: The Definitive Guide to Dystopian Politics*. NY: Columbia University Press.

Athens, Lonnie. 1989. *The Creation of Dangerous Violent Criminals*. NY: Routledge.

Bauman, Zygmunt. 2006. *Liquid Fear*. Boston: Polity Press.

Beaver, Kevin M. 2019. *Biosocial Criminology: A Primer* (4th ed.). Dubuque, IA: Kendall Hunt Publishing.

Bernardin, Marc. 2016. "In the Super Movie Hero Arms Race, Has Warner Bros. Created Too Bleak a World in *Batman Versus Superman*?" *Los Angeles Times*. March 28. Available at: http://www.latimes.com/entertainment/movies/la-et-mn-batman-v-superman-too-dark-20160328-story.html.

Durkheim, Émile. 1915. *The Elementary Forms of the Religious Life*. London: G. Allen & Unwin; Macmillan.

Fiddler, Michael. 2007. "Projecting the Prison: The Depiction of The Uncanny in *Shawshank Redemption*," *Crime Media Culture: An International Journal*, *2*(2): 192–208.

———. 2013. "Playing *Funny Games* in *The Last House on the Left*: The Uncanny and the "Home Invasion" Genre," *Crime Media Culture: An International Journal*, 9(3): 281–299.

Gilman, Charlotte Perkins. 1980. *The Charlotte Perkins Gilman Reader: The Yellow Wallpaper, and Other Fiction*. NY: Pantheon Books.

Greek, Cecil. 1992. *The Religious Roots of American Sociology*. NY: Garland Publishing.

———. 2007. "The Big City Rogue Cop as Monster," in Caroline Joan "Kay" S. Picart and Cecil Greek (eds.): *Monsters in and Among Us: Towards a Gothic Criminology*, 164–198. Madison, NJ: Fairleigh Dickinson University Press.

———. 2016. "Globalization and the Rise of the Behemoth: A Study in Gothic Criminology," in Caroline Joan "Kay" S. Picart, Michael Hviid Jacobsen and Cecil Greek (eds.): *Framing Law and Crime: An Anthology*, 343–370. Madison, NJ: Fairleigh Dickinson University Press.

———. 2017. "Is Fake News News?" Presentation at the ASA Media Sociology Preconference, August 11. Montreal, Canada.

Haller, Mark H. 1963. *Eugenics: Hereditarian Attitudes in American Thought*. New Brunswick, NJ: Rutgers University Press.

Katz, Jack. 1988. *Seductions of Crime: Moral and Sensual Attractions in Doing Evil*. NY: Basic Books.

Lee, Bandy. 2017. *The Dangerous Case of Donald Trump: 27 Psychiatrists and Mental Health Experts Assess a President*. NY: Thomas Dunne Books.

Lyman, Stanford. 1990. "Rereading Robert E. Park: Toward a Gothic Perspective on Capitalism and Imperialism," in M.W. duQuesnay (ed): *Explorations: The Age of Enlightenment* (Volume IV), 29–108. Lafayette, LA: University of Southwestern Louisiana Foundation.

McNamara, Michelle. 2018. *I'll Be Gone in The Dark: One Woman's Obsessive Search for the Golden State Killer*. NY: Harper.

Nielsen, Donald. 1993. "A Gothic Sociology of Modern Civilization," *International Journal of Politics Culture and Society*, 7: 109–120. Available at: https://doi.org/10.1007/BF02142350.

Opam, Kwane. 2015. "Donald Trump Says He's Batman. He's Really Bizarro Lex Luthor," *The Verge*, August 27. Available at: https://www.theverge.com/2015/8/17/9164469/donald-trump-batman-bruce-wayne-bizarro-lex-luthor.

Picart, Caroline Joan "Kay" S. and Cecil Greek. 2003. "The Compulsions of Serial Killers as Vampires: Toward a Gothic Criminology," *Journal of Criminal Justice and Popular Culture*, 10: 39–68. Available at: http://www.albany.edu/scj/jcjpc/vol10is1/picart.html.

———. 2008. "Introduction: Toward a Gothic Criminology," in Caroline Joan "Kay" S. Picart and Cecil Greek (eds.): *Monsters in and Among Us: Toward a Gothic Criminology*, 11–43. Madison, NJ: Fairleigh Dickinson University Press.

———. 2009. "When Women Become Serial Killers: Sexuality, Class and Gender in the Case of Eileen Wuornos," edited by J.E. Browning & Caroline Joan "Kay" S. Picart: *Draculas, Vampires and Other Undead Forms: Essays on Gender, Race and Culture*, 37–62. Lanham, MD: Scarecrow Press.

Pikkety, Thomas. 2017. *Capitalism in the 21st-Century*. Cambridge, MA: Harvard University Press.

Ross, E. A. 1907. *Sin and Society*. NY: Harcourt Brace.

Russo, Anthony (Director). 2019. *Avengers: Endgame* [Motion Pictures]. United States: Marvel Studio.

Sommer, Jamie M. 2018. "Corrupt Actions and Forest Loss: A Cross-National Analysis," *International Journal of Social Science Studies*, 6(1): 23–34. Available at: https://doi.org/10.11114/ijsss.v6i10.3534.

Walker, Kaylin. 2012. *The Existentialism Behind Nolan's Batman*. Unpublished honors thesis. Available at: http://dlib.bc.edu/islandora/object/bc-ir:102479.

Wikipedia. 2020. *Bizarro World*. Available at: https://en.wikipedia.org/wiki/Bizarro_World.

Index

About the Editor and Contributors

EDITOR BIOGRAPHY

Caroline Joan "Kay" S. Picart is an attorney at law practicing in criminal and family law and is an adjunct professor of law at Florida A & M University, Orlando, Florida; prior to becoming a lawyer, she was a tenured associate professor of English and humanities and had a courtesy appointment at a law school. She is the editor of the Fairleigh Dickinson University Press Series on Law, Culture & the Humanities, and built it from the ground up. She has published nineteen scholarly books and edited collections, and numerous scholarly articles and book chapters nationally and internationally, and is the recipient of the 2015 *Dapim* Best Essay Award for her essay "Nationalities, Histories, Rhetorics: Real/Reel Representations of the Holocaust and Holocaust Trials and a Poethics of Film and Law," 29 *Dapim: Studies on the Holocaust* 2, 1–20 (May, 2015); doi: 10.1080/23256249.2015.1034980.

Among her most recent relevant publications are: "American Self-Radicalising Terrorists and Conversions to Radical Action: Emotional Factors and the Allure of 'Jihadi Cool/Chic,'" in *Emotions and Crime: Towards a Criminology of Emotions*, eds. Michael Hviid Jacobsen and Sandra Walklate (2019); (with Michael Hviid Jacobsen), "An Invitation to 'Radical Interactionism': Towards a Reorientation of Interactionist Sociology," in Critical and Cultural Interactionism, eds. Michael Hviid Jacobsen and Sandra Walklate (2019); *American Self-Radicalizing Terrorists and the Allure of "Jihadi Cool/Chic"* (2017); (edited with Michael Hviid Jacobsen and Cecil Greek), *Framing Law and Crime: An Interdisciplinary Anthology* (2016). She was an invited speaker to a NATO-sponsored advanced research seminar in Jerusalem, Israel, in 2014, which resulted in a book chapter, "The Radicalization of American Lone Wolves in Real/Reel Worlds: Strategically Mapping the Role of the Internet, and Beyond, in the Cases of Colleen LaRose (Jihad Jane) and the Tsarnaev Brothers (the Boston Marathon Bombers)" in *Lone Actors—An Emerging Threat* (Aaron Richman and Yair Sharan, eds., NATO Science for Peace and Security Studies, IOS Press, 2015). Her research interests include: Law and Crime; Terrorism and Counterterrorism; Law, Culture & the Humanities; Critical (Intersectional) Race Theory; Qualitative Research Methodology and Ethnography; Criminology & Popular Culture; Sociology/Rhetoric of Science; & Intellectual Property and Property Law.

CONTRIBUTOR BIOGRAPHIES

John Edgar Browning is a professor of liberal arts at the Savannah College of Art and Design (SCAD). He has over a dozen contracted or published books and over seventy-five shorter works that cluster around Dracula, vampires, zombies, horror, monstrosity, Bram Stoker, and the Gothic. He has published in *Palgrave Communications*, *Gothic Studies*, *ELT: English Literature in Transition, 1880–1920*, *Victorian Literature and Culture*, *Horror Studies*, and *Film and History*, and some of his recent books include *The Forgotten Writings of Bram Stoker* (Palgrave Macmillan, 2012) and *Zombie Talk: Culture, History, Politics* (Palgrave, 2015) (with David Castillo, et al.), as well as the forthcoming volumes *Dracula-An Anthology: Critical Reviews and Reactions, 1897–1920* (Edinburgh University Press) and *New Queer Horror Film and TV (Horror Studies)* (University of Wales Press) (with Darren Elliott-Smith). He is also co-editing, with David J. Skal, the second Norton Critical Edition of *Dracula* (forthcoming).

DW Duke is a California attorney and writer whose practice focuses extensively on human rights. He is involved in numerous organizations dedicated to human rights and human trafficking issues and works extensively with the US Office of Refugee Resettlement to find accommodations and foster homes for victims of human trafficking.

Barry Godfrey is professor of Social Justice and associate pro-vice chancellor for research in the Faculty of Humanities and Social Sciences at the University of Liverpool. He has authored/co-authored fifteen books on the history of crime; and is currently the principal investigator on the AHRC funded "Digital Panopticon" project which examines the lives of 90,000 people sentenced to transportation or imprisonment at the Old Bailey between 1750 and 1925.

Cecil Greek is emeritus professor of sociology at the University of South Florida at Tampa. Greek has taught for forty-two years in sociology and criminology programs at eight universities and all four campuses of the University of South Florida. His specialty areas include the history of sociology and criminology, mass media depictions of crime and deviance, cyber deviance and cybercrime, and qualitative research methodologies, particularly those that involve the visual, such as photography and film. His first book, *The Religious Roots of American Sociology*, focused on the founding generation of American sociology and their eventual turn from qualitative to quantitative methods (republished, 2018, Routledge). His second book, co-edited with Caroline Joan "Kay" S. Picart, *Monsters In and Among Us: Towards a Gothic Criminology*, proposed how a Gothic Criminology was a fertile interdisciplinary framework that could be used to analyze film as a medium for discussions on "monstrosity" and "evil." His most recent book, *Framing Law and Crime: An Interdisciplinary Anthology,* co-edited with Caroline Joan "Kay" S. Picart and Michael Hviid Jacobsen, focused on cinematic and media depictions of law and crime.

Jon Frauley is associate professor of criminology at the University of Ottawa, Canada, where he teaches courses on social and criminological theory, epistemology and methodology, and creative analytics. Jon's work can be found in the *British Journal of Criminology*, *Social & Legal Studies*, *Critical Criminology*, among others. He is the author of *Criminology, Deviance, and the Silver Screen: Fictional Realities and the Criminological Imagination* (Palgrave, 2011), is editor of and contributor to *C. Wright Mills and the Criminological Imagination: Prospects for Creative Enquiry* (Routledge, 2015), and (with Frank Pearce), *Critical Realism and the Social Sciences: Heterodox Elaborations* (Univ. of Toronto Press, 2007). He is currently editing and contributing to the *Routledge International Handbook of C. Wright Mills Studies*.

Steve Greenfield is a professor at Westminster Law School where he teaches a course on cinematic justice incorporating European and Indian films. He has written widely on various aspects of the relationship between law and popular culture covering substantive areas of law as well as the portrayal of law and lawyers. He co-authored *Film and the Law* (2nd edition, Hart, 2010) with Guy Osborn and Peter Robson and is currently exploring the contrasting portrayals of victims through the lenses of vigilantism and restorative justice

Marouf Hasian Jr. is a full professor in the Department of Communication at the University of Utah. His areas of interest include law and rhetoric, critical memory studies, postcolonial criticism, genocide studies, and humanitarian discourses. He is the author of more than a dozen books and his publications have appeared in *The Quarterly Journal of Speech*, *Communication Monographs*, *Critical Studies in Media Communication*, and *Third World Quarterly*.

Michael Hviid Jacobsen is professor of sociology at Aalborg University, Denmark. He has published extensively on topics such as death and dying, palliative care, emotions, utopia, critique, deviance, interactionism, ethics, criminology, qualitative research, and social theory.

Orit Kamir is an Israeli professor of law and a feminist activist. She has drafted Israel's sexual harassment legislation (in 1998). Her scholarly work focuses on human dignity and rights, and on cultural aspects of law and society. Her most recent book is *Betraying Dignity: The Toxic Seduction of Social Media, Shaming, and Radicalization* (2019).

Deborah Landry, Ph.D., is an independent writer and researcher in Ottawa, Ontario (Canada).

John Morton has worked in anthropology and Aboriginal studies for forty years and is currently an honorary research associate at La Trobe University, Melbourne, where he held a lecturing position between 1990 and 2011. He has held teaching positions at a number of other Australian universities and has also been employed as a museum curator. He now works as an independent consultant anthropologist, mainly in relation to Aboriginal native title. He has published widely on central Australian Aboriginal religion, and has authored many reports relating to Aboriginal land rights, native title, and other matters. He has co-edited three books—Géza Róheim's *Children of the Desert II: Myths and Dreams of the Aborigines of Central Australia* (with Werner Muensterberger, 1988), *Scholar and Sceptic: Australian Aborigines and Contemporary Social Enquiry* (with Francesca Merlan and Alan Rumsey, 1997), and *The Photographs of Baldwin Spencer* (with Philip Batty and Lindy Allen, 2005).

Matthew Sorrento is co-editor of *Film International* (Intellect Publishers; filmint.nu), where he regularly contributes, and Editor-in-chief of *Retreats from Oblivion*, a journal of noir, crime, and mystery fiction/culture. He teaches film and media studies at Rutgers University in Camden, NJ, USA and is on the advisory board of the Law, Culture, and Humanities Series at Fairleigh Dickinson University Press. The author of *The New American Crime Film*

(McFarland, 2012), he is currently at work on a study of contemporary genre cinema. His forthcoming books include *David Fincher's* Zodiac: *Cinema of Investigation and (Mis)Interpretation* (co-edited with David Ryan) and *Outcasts: Film Noir and the Blacklist* (co-authored with Dean Goldberg; both with Fairleigh Dickinson University Press), along with several book chapters and contributions in *Film & History, Critical Studies in Television*, and *The Journal of the Fantastic in the Arts*. Sorrento has served as editor for *Identity Theory* and *Film Threat* (where the LA Times [dis]honored him as one of the crankiest critics of 2007, at the expense of Disney's *Enchanted*). He lives in New Jersey with his wife and two children.

Sandra Walklate is Eleanor Rathbone Chair of Sociology at the University of Liverpool conjoint Chair of Criminology at Monash University, Melbourne. She was awarded the British Society of Criminology's outstanding achievement award for contribution to the discipline in 2014 and is currently editor in chief of the *British Journal of Criminology*.

DJ Williams is the director of research for the Center for Positive Sexuality and a social and behavioral scientist at Idaho State University. He completed doctoral and postdoctoral studies at the University of Alberta (Canada), and his scholarship intersects leisure science, forensic behavioral science, criminology, and sexology. Williams is a leading international expert on deviance as leisure experience, and he has been a consultant and/or expert witness on several high-profile forensic cases involving sexuality and actual or potential violence. His research has been published in numerous academic books and journals, including *Journal of Sexual Medicine*, *Homicide Studies*, *Deviant Behavior*, *Journal of Forensic Sciences*, *Leisure Sciences*, and *Critical Criminology*.

Dr. **Lucy Williams** is a postdoctoral research associate on the AHRC Digital Panoptic project. She gained her doctorate in 2014, and has published on intergenerational offending, offending and the life-course, prisoner demography, and on the uses of digital crime data. In addition to the Digital Panopticon, her primary research interest is the history of women, crime, and deviance 1850–1950.

www.ingramcontent.com/pod-product-compliance
Lightning Source LLC
LaVergne TN
LVHW011808200926
848484LV00005B/1100